HT
123.5
M4
A44

Allen, David
    In English ways

82189

DATE DUE			
SEP 1 1983			
FEB 2 7 1987			

In English Ways

David Grayson Allen

In English Ways

The Movement of Societies
and the Transferal of English
Local Law and Custom to
Massachusetts Bay in the
Seventeenth Century

Published for the Institute of

Early American History and Culture

Williamsburg, Virginia

by The University of North Carolina Press

Chapel Hill

The Institute of Early American History and Culture
is sponsored jointly by The College of William and Mary
and The Colonial Williamsburg Foundation.

This book was the winner of the Jamestown Manuscript Prize for 1976.

© 1981 The University of North Carolina Press

Manufactured in the United States of America
ISBN 0-8078-1448-2

Library of Congress Catalog Card Number 80-13198

Library of Congress Cataloging in Publication Data

Allen, David Grayson, 1943–
    In English ways.

    Bibliography: p.
    Includes index.
    1. Cities and towns—Massachusetts—History.
    2. Cities and towns—England—History.   I. Title.
HT123.5.M4A44   974.4'02   80-13198
ISBN 0-8078-1448-2

For Julyann

Contents

PART II

APPENDIXES

Illustrations

Tables and Graphs

Preface

THIS book is about the fundamentally English form and style of New England local institutions in the early seventeenth century. It demonstrates the remarkable extent to which diversity in New England local institutions was directly imitative of regional differences in the mother country. The first Massachusetts colonists, in other words, simply attempted to sustain their Old World ways in the New World.

In the second and shorter part of this book, I have explored the causes of the migration of people from various English regions to New England. A brief concluding section examines the transformation of New England town life in the later seventeenth and early eighteenth centuries, when a variety of social, economic, political, and legal conditions made old English ways unsuitable and impractical.

In spite of the assumed continuities between English social, legal, and institutional customs and arrangements and the first settlements in Massachusetts, surprisingly few historians have undertaken to study the English past with specific reference to the local characteristics of the American colonies. Since the fruitful beginnings by Sumner Chilton Powell in the early 1960s, almost twenty years have elapsed without another major investigation of the colonists' English origins, even though the New England town was itself intensively investigated a decade ago. In some respects, researchers in other disciplines have been quicker to appreciate the influence of English regional variations on early New England life than historians have been. A notable instance is Robert Blair St. George's discussion of early New England craft traditions and their local English antecedents, which appeared in the 1979 volume of *Winterthur Portfolio*. I hope that *In English Ways* will stimulate further studies along these lines.

A major part of this work is devoted to discussion of agricultural practices, for agriculture held a dominant and ubiquitous place in the lives of seventeenth-century men and women on both sides of the Atlantic. The occupational structure in both England and America, especially the latter, was still fluid. Even residents of boroughs and market towns were never far removed from agriculture, and those in trades or in semiskilled work often combined their occupational pursuits with some agricultural activity. English borough officers spent a good part of their time enforcing agricultural regulations within their jurisdictions. In sum, caring for livestock and growing crops were the common concerns of most Englishmen and New Englanders at this time.

A few technical points should be mentioned here. Some readers may be somewhat concerned by my use of the term "West Country" to describe Hampshire, but because its various subregional agricultural systems paralleled those of neighboring West Country Wiltshire, I have grouped those two counties together under a single classification in order to contrast them with two other English regions, the Yorkshire North Country and East Anglia. Likewise, for purposes of comparative analysis, I have expanded the term "East Anglia" to include the counties of Norfolk, Suffolk, Essex, and Hertfordshire.

Quotations from manuscripts or printed primary documents appear as they were written or published except for certain contemporary conventions. The ampersand, the thorn, and the tailed "p" have been expanded, the use of "i" and "j" and of "u" and "v" has been modernized, and superscript letters have been brought down to the line. All dates are rendered in New Style, with the year beginning on January 1 rather than March 25.

Portions of chapters 3 and 8 originally appeared in H. C. Allen and Roger Thompson, eds., *Contrast and Connection: Bicentennial Essays in Anglo-American History* (London and Athens, Ohio, 1976), 1–35, and in the *William and Mary Quarterly*, 3d Ser., XXIX (1972), 443–460. I am grateful to G. Bell & Sons, Ltd., London, and to the *Quarterly* for allowing me to reprint some of that material here.

This book is an outgrowth of a dissertation begun at the University of Wisconsin more than a decade ago. The English research was supported by several institutions, including the American Bar Foundation, the University of Wisconsin, and Linacre College, Oxford, where I held a studentship during the 1971–1972 academic year. Without their combined and generous help, plans to carry on extensive and detailed work in England would have been impossible.

Debts to others accrued over the years are too numerous to mention, but some individuals were especially helpful and encouraging along the way. Stanley I. Kutler of the University of Wisconsin was a tolerant and forbearing shepherd of this work in its early stages. Stanley N. Katz, now at Princeton University, originally sparked my interest in early American history and the possibilities of a comparative Anglo-American study. He has been a most sensitive and understanding critic at every turn. My year in England was greatly enhanced by my association with Mrs. Joan Thirsk, Reader in Economic History at Oxford, who served as my research supervisor while I was at Linacre College. For someone unfamiliar with local English records and beset by endless questions about them, she was a reservoir of information, help, guidance, and encouragement. Librarians and archivists in England were particularly helpful, though even to begin to list them would be impossible. Because of his unfailing courtesy and dauntless good humor on my first exploration of English records in the East Riding of Yorkshire as well as in response to numerous queries after my trip there, Mr. Norman Higson, then County Archivist and now Archivist at the Brynmor Jones Library at the University of Hull, made a strong impression on me. At various stages Kenneth A. Lockridge of the University of Michigan, Margaret Spufford of the University of Keele, and Mark Overton of the Department of Geography, Cambridge University, helped shape my ideas or provided useful information from their own research. I owe a lasting debt to Maurice W. Beresford of the University of Leeds and to Stephen Foster of Northern Illinois University, both of whom read the entire manuscript and supplied me with many useful suggestions for which I am most grateful. I also wish to thank K. C. Newton, Archivist of the Essex County Record Office, for permission to use three plans taken from John Walker Senior's 1586 Survey of Rivers Hall in Boxted, and the Syndics of the Cambridge University Press for the use, in modified form, of Joan Thirsk's map of English farming regions, 1500–1640. Both Norman S. Fiering and Cynthia Austin Carter, Editor and Managing Editor of Publications for the Institute of Early American History and Culture, have given the manuscript close attention. I appreciate their sensitive and careful editing as well as their many thoughtful suggestions. I am also grateful to the Jamestown Prize Committee and their sponsors, the Jamestown-Yorktown Foundation, the University of North Carolina Press, The College of William and Mary, and The Colonial Williamsburg Foundation, for selecting my manuscript in 1976 for publication. Lastly, the biggest debt of all goes to Julyann for all the reasons that only I know so well.

Short Titles

Allen, "In English Ways"	David Grayson Allen, "In English Ways: The Movement of Societies and the Transferal of English Local Law and Custom to Massachusetts Bay, 1600–1690" (Ph.D. diss., University of Wisconsin, 1974).
Banks, *Top. Dict.*	Charles Edward Banks, *Topographical Dictionary of 2885 English Emigrants to New England 1620–1650*, ed. Elijah Ellsworth Brownell (Philadelphia, 1937).
Bond, *Watertown Genealogies*	Henry Bond, *Family Memorials: Genealogies of the Families and Descendants of the Early Settlers of Watertown, Massachusetts, Including Waltham and Weston; To Which Is Appended the Early History of the Town*, 2 vols. (Boston, 1855).
Borthwick Inst. Hist. Res.	Borthwick Institute of Historical Research, St. Anthony's Hall, Peaseholme Green, York, Yorkshire.
Essex Co. Court Recs.	George Francis Dow, ed., *Records and Files of the Quarterly Courts of Essex County, Massachusetts*, 8 vols. (Salem, Mass., 1911–1921).
Essex Co. Probate Recs.	George Francis Dow, ed., *The Probate Records of Essex County, Massachusetts, 1635–1681*, 3 vols. (Salem, Mass., 1916–1920).
Hampshire R.O.	Hampshire County Record Office, Winchester, Hampshire.
Hingham Mass. Town Recs.	Hingham Town Records, 2 MS vols., 1635–1720, Town Clerk's Office, Hingham, Mass.
Humberside R.O.	Humberside County Record Office, Beverley, North Humberside (formerly Yorkshire).
Ipswich and East Suffolk R.O.	Ipswich and East Suffolk Record Office, County Hall, Ipswich, Suffolk.

Ipswich Town Recs.	Ipswich Town Grants, Town Meeting, 1634, and Town Records, 1634–1757, 2 MS vols., Town Clerk's Office, Ipswich, Mass.
Mass. Acts and Resolves	*The Acts and Resolves, Public and Private, of the Province of the Massachusetts Bay . . .* , 21 vols. (Boston, 1869–1922).
Newbury Town Recs.	Newbury Town Records, 1637–1695, 1 MS vol., Town Clerk's Office, Newbury, Mass.
NEHGR	*New England Historical and Genealogical Register*, vol. I to date (Boston, 1847–).
Norfolk and Norwich R.O.	Norfolk and Norwich Record Office, Central Library, Norwich, Norfolk.
Pope, *Pioneers of Mass.*	Charles Henry Pope, *The Pioneers of Massachusetts: A Descriptive List, Drawn from Records of the Colonies, Towns and Churches, and Other Contemporaneous Documents* (Boston, 1900).
Recs. of Mass. Bay	Nathaniel B. Shurtleff, ed., *Records of the Governor and Company of the Massachusetts Bay in New England*, 6 vols. in 5 (Boston, 1853–1854).
Recs. of Rowley	Benjamin P. Mighill and George B. Blodgette, eds., *The Early Records of the Town of Rowley, Massachusetts*, I, *1639–1672* (Rowley, Mass., 1894).
Savage, *Gen. Dict.*	James Savage, *A Genealogical Dictionary of the First Settlers of New England, Showing Three Generations of Those Who Came before May, 1692, on the Basis of Farmer's Register*, 4 vols. (Boston, 1860–1862).
Thirsk, "Farming Regions of England"	Joan Thirsk, "The Farming Regions of England," in Thirsk, ed., *The Agrarian History of England and Wales*, IV, *1500–1640* (Cambridge, 1967), 1–112.
Univ. of Hull	Brynmor Jones Library, University of Hull, Hull, North Humberside (formerly Yorkshire) (documents formerly in the East Riding Record Office, Beverley, North Humberside).

Watertown Recs. *Watertown Records* . . . [title varies], 6 vols. in 5 (Watertown, Mass., 1894–1928).

West Suffolk R.O. Bury St. Edmunds and West Suffolk Record Office, Angel Hill, Bury St. Edmunds, Suffolk.

Wiltshire R.O. Wiltshire County Record Office, County Hall, Trowbridge, Wiltshire.

Winthrop, *History of New England* James Kendall Hosmer, ed., *Winthrop's Journal, "History of New England," 1630–1649*, 2 vols., Original Narratives of Early American History (New York, 1908).

Part I

1 Introduction: People, Land, and Custom

N November 3, 1635, the Massachusetts Court of Assistants called John Pratt of Newtown to appear before it to answer for a letter he had written to friends in England. The court was particularly disturbed by the negative attitude about the colony that Pratt had displayed in his correspondence. According to the court, he had "affirmed divers things, which were untrue and of ill report, for the state of the country, as that here was nothing but rocks, and sands, and salt marshes." Pratt was prevailed upon by several ministers to write an apology, but even John Winthrop realized that it was at best only a halfway acknowledgment of error, one in which Pratt put "his own interpretation" on the disputed passages in the letter rather than the court's. What could not be denied, however, was that Pratt found this part of eastern Massachusetts an unsatisfactory place to practice the kind of husbandry he knew, and in less than a year he was off to Connecticut, leaving behind what was for him a region of undesirable land.

Given Pratt's background, his complaint was understandable. Having come from Wood Ditton, Cambridgeshire, an arable land largely of chalky loams where common-field farming was complemented by sheep raising, he found the soil around Newtown, Massachusetts (later called Cambridge) unacceptable. That was not true of emigrants from the parts of Essex and Suffolk where wood-pasture lands predominated. If not completely at home with rocks, sand, and marshes, they were nevertheless able to manage their dairying, weaving, and grain-growing economy in that setting. But in Pratt's eyes the idea of farming there was altogether futile: "I thought I could not subsist myselfe, nor the plantacion, nor posteritie," he said in his defense to the court. "The barrenes of the sandy grounds, etc." might be improved if "manured and husbanded," he suggested, but in the final analysis he was convinced that the community would have to resort to other activities such as fishing and trading if it hoped to survive.[1]

1. James Kendall Hosmer, ed., *Winthrop's Journal, "History of New England," 1630–1649*, 2 vols., Original Narratives of Early American History (New York, 1908), I, 165; Nathaniel B.

Pratt's discontent points up one of the major findings of this study: that English puritans who came to settle in New England gave up as little of their former ways of doing things as possible. Like Pratt, the people in the five Massachusetts communities studied here—Rowley, Hingham, Newbury, Ipswich, and Watertown—continued to practice the kind of agriculture with which they had been familiar in England. They also elected to local office men who they believed possessed the same qualities and characteristics of leadership that were common in their former English localities. And they expected and demanded of local government the same level of activity and kind of supervision (or lack of it) that was common in the Yorkshire marshland, East Anglian villages, or West Country forests from which they came.

The conclusion that New England communities continued the laws and customs of old England would hardly seem arresting had not American historians argued to the contrary for the past eighty years. Frederick Jackson Turner and others, reacting to the so-called Teutonic school, contended that the mere act of leaving the feudal and early modern institutions of England and settling in the hostile and primitive environment of North America brought forth a new man, the American. Even a work as sound as Sumner Chilton Powell's *Puritan Village* reflects this whiggish bias. "To emigrate from accustomed social institutions and relationships to a set of unfamiliar communities . . . meant a startling transformation," Powell argued. "The townsmen had to change or abandon almost every formal institution which they had taken for granted. . . . Life in Sudbury [Massachusetts] was indeed a 'new' England."[2]

But how much did these immigrants really have to change? Society was so much simpler in America that the early settlers could do without much of the excess cultural baggage of the Old World. The significant question is whether the New Englanders drastically altered their institutions, or whether they merely channeled the old, familiar ways of doing things into

Shurtleff, ed., *Records of the Governor and Company of the Massachusetts Bay in New England*, 6 vols. in 5 (Boston, 1853–1854), I, 358–360, hereafter cited as Winthrop, *History of New England*, and *Recs. of Mass. Bay*, respectively.

2. "The Significance of the Frontier in American History," in *The Frontier in American History* (New York, 1921), 3–4; Sumner Chilton Powell, *Puritan Village: The Formation of a New England Town* (Middletown, Conn., 1963), 142–143. In contrast, compare Henry Sumner Maine, *Lectures on the Early History of Institutions* (New York, 1875), 94, whose earlier yet more modern view stresses continuity, and the recent study of Josef J. Barton, *Peasants and Strangers: Italians, Rumanians, and Slovaks in an American City, 1890–1950* (Cambridge, Mass., 1975), especially p. 6; both of them emphasize the role of older forms of social organization and retention of traditional ties after migration.

simplified forms that roughly duplicated English ways. If the courts baron, courts leet, vestries, out-hundred courts, and countless other English institutions were discarded by those who moved to the New World, what did the absence of such institutions mean? Day-to-day decisions on routine matters, ranging from the regulation of agricultural affairs to the subtle qualifications for election to town office, were made in the town and selectmen's meetings. Was there a noticeable change in the way these groups conducted business?

The experience of people in the five Massachusetts towns suggests that in their most vital functions New England local institutions were adapted from the English backgrounds of each town's inhabitants. Sometimes it was simply a matter of local institutions not interfering with practices familiar to emigrants from particular English communities. But whatever the case, New England settlers were able to perpetuate old English practices and usually did so without interference from such extracommunity authorities as the General Court.

During the past decade a number of book-length studies and journal articles have explored the daily workings and mechanisms of New England town government in the seventeenth and eighteenth centuries.[3] Attention has been given both to the aggregate analysis of groups of communities and to single towns. Yet towns were not so much alike as some of these studies might indicate. The word "fields," for instance, in one town's records might not have the same meaning in another's; selectmen in one community responded differently to community problems than they did in another. These distinctions and others are typical of the variations in institutional and everyday life found among preindustrial, agricultural communities. To uncover these variations we must go beyond the structure and superficial workings of town governmental machinery to the detailed differences of town life.

This study is less concerned with the general workings of the system of local government in seventeenth-century Massachusetts than it is with the application of that system by particular towns. The five Massachusetts towns under consideration often differed strikingly from one another. In order to distinguish variations in the lives and activities of common ordinary people living in these small preindustrial towns, it has be

3. Several notable studies are: Kenneth A. Lockridge, *A New England Town* dred Years: Dedham, Massachusetts, 1636–1736 (New York, 1970); Michael *able Kingdoms: New England Towns in the Eighteenth Century* (New York, 1 Cook, Jr., *The Fathers of the Towns: Leadership and Community Struc* New England (Baltimore, 1976), but others are mentioned in the

essary to look carefully at dozens of personal inventories, at the words used in land grants and town-meeting records, and even at the meanings of common expressions.

Part I treats the English backgrounds and American experiences of settlers in each of the five Massachusetts towns (chapters 1–5). Since we are dealing with primarily agricultural societies, I have emphasized the differences in farming and land systems. How groups of men managed the large tracts of land in their New England townships provides one of the best historical indicators of the social and economic order they established in America. As we will see, that order corresponds well to the character of societies in the various parts of England they left behind. Agricultural practices remained remarkably intact in the transatlantic crossing, revealing, with other factors, that the transition from one continent to another was extremely conservative. Massachusetts was more a new "England" than a "new" England.

The surprising thing about this transatlantic transfer of agricultural practices is that the settlers in our five towns were more capable than many Englishmen of changing in a new environment. Most of them came originally from English areas of subsistence agriculture, which unlike regions of large-scale capitalistic, commercial farming were particularly vulnerable in times of bad harvests and industrial depression. Consequently they became versatile, adept in various sidelines ranging from part-time dairying to clothmaking. But despite this ability to adjust to difficulties in the English environment and to adapt to hard times or a changing economy, in Massachusetts they pursued what they had always known, rather than entering upon what might have been new and profitable ventures.

A major portion of this study focuses on the English experience of these settlers, in part because there are at present too few studies available upon which American historians can rely for an understanding of the lives of ordinary people before, during, and after migration. With the exception of Powell's monograph, Wallace Notestein's general treatment, and some exceptionally fine English studies like those of Sidney and Beatrice Webb on local government and Joan Thirsk on agricultural economy, there is almost no comprehensive literature on local English life during the early Stuart period and even less on the localities from which a sizable number of pu-ān emigrants came.[4] Even some of these works are seriously deficient.

ūallace Notestein, *The English People on the Eve of Colonization* (New York and Evans-
ʾ54); Sidney Webb and Beatrice Webb, *English Local Government from the Revolution
ʾl Corporations Act*, 9 vols. (London, 1906–1929), I, *The Parish and the County*

Powell studied individuals from scattered areas in England, although many emigrants to Massachusetts settled in groups from the same locality or region and thus shared a common set of institutional, social, and economic experiences. Notestein studied the general English background without pointing out the distinguishing differences in institutions from locality to locality that made some more important in people's lives in one area and less important in others. All English experiences were not equally influential when it came to founding colonies and new local governments. The Webbs' magnificent study of English local institutions is highly useful, but it focuses on the period from the late seventeenth to the early nineteenth century, and has little to offer on the years before and during the Great Migration of the 1630s.

Part II explores in detail some particular dimensions of early New England life. Chapter 6 contrasts the contexts and motives behind the emigration from different English regions and subregions. Chapter 7 examines the "contrapuntal life" of these early immigrants and of the two generations that followed. Even though these men and women were able to reproduce the order of life they knew and thereby to perpetuate the diversity of local England in the New England wilderness, they also developed an unmistakably new society in spite of themselves. Just as there were few restraints inhibiting the continuance of the practices of their English pasts, so there was also little to keep them from developing in new ways when conditions changed in New England. By the closing decades of the century, town life in the Bay Colony had been ineluctably altered by the growth of population, the scarcity of land, the development of non-agricultural pursuits, the increasingly rigid stratification of local society, and the emergence of a permanent class of poor people. As society became more complex and as problems arose that traversed town boundaries, there was a need for colony-wide superintendence, regulation, and direction. A hierarchy of authority developed, culminating at the level of provincial government, to deal with problems common in old England and now common to New England. This process of centralization is the topic of the final chapter. As English-style practices at the town level declined,

(London, 1906), II–III, *The Manor and the Borough* (London, 1908), *inter alia*; and Joan Thirsk, "The Farming Regions of England," in Thirsk, ed., *The Agrarian History of England and Wales*, IV, *1500–1640* (Cambridge, 1967), 1–112, hereafter cited as Thirsk, "Farming Regions of England." This statement is in no way meant to detract from the vast and profound outpouring of English regional studies during the past 20 to 30 years, excellent examples of which are too numerous to mention. Even here, however, nearly all of them concentrate on regions other than the emigration centers of the puritan migration, often detail county rather than local developments, or are too gentry oriented.

they were replaced by a system, equally English, of superintendence and direction of affairs by a local gentry, by the county courts, and by other institutions reminiscent of many aspects of English provincial life.

Diversity in Old and New England

Stereotypic views of seventeenth- and eighteenth-century New England have been remarkably persistent. These incorporated scenes that portrayed the archetypal town meetinghouse with its gleaming white spire, the town common or green, and wooden frame or Georgian brick houses, inhabited by the God-fearing, tyranny-hating puritans or Yankees who thrived in town meeting democracy. Some of these views have been fostered by the filiopietism of local historians and genealogists, but other stereotypes have been created from a more subtle perspective. Noting seventeenth- and eighteenth-century population and immigration trends, one historian has claimed, for instance, that the lack of economic enticements and the towns' distrust and dislike of strangers discouraged all but a trickle of immigration into the colony after the original Great Migration. In turn, according to this theory, such insularity only made the New England towns peculiar in their sameness, for the white Anglo-Saxon Protestants who inhabited the region never had to grapple with the cultural and ethnic challenges that European and African immigration brought to other colonies.[5]

This perspective, however, does not give adequate consideration to differences *within* the group of original English settlers. The degree of change or challenge arising from economic and social differentiation is not necessarily diminished by the absence of cultural or ethnic diversity. Our presentist concern with ethnic groups as political and social forces in nineteenth- and twentieth-century American history has perhaps obscured the existence of subcultures within groups such as the English.[6] Yet subcultural patterns of behavior, often manifested in regional and local differences, were a persistent phenomenon through the greater part of the seventeenth century in Massachusetts, and English regional distinctions in religion were a particularly prominent source of diversity in the Bay Colony.

5. Compare Zuckerman, *Peaceable Kingdoms*, 107–108.

6. Until recently, only two genealogists have discussed the composition of New England settlement in terms of English regional origins. George A. Moriarty was the first to assign different motives to West Country and East Anglian emigrants, and to define their points of geographical concentration in New England. See "The English Background of New England

Religious Diversity and Regional Influences

Emery Battis was one of the first to discuss regional religious variations among the early New England puritans, although his primary interest was in the social, economic, and psychological factors contributing to religious dissidence. Battis found that the followers of Anne Hutchinson were to a significant degree emigrants from an enclave in Lincolnshire.[7] Puritanism itself, of course, can be traced to certain regions in the eastern counties of England almost a century before Anne Hutchinson's banishment from the Bay Colony. Illustrative of this concentration in the east are figures showing the geographical distribution of puritan ministers during the reign of Elizabeth. Patrick Collinson has found that almost half of the ministers were from the East Anglian counties of Essex, Suffolk, and Norfolk, and if one adds nearby Lincoln, Northampton, and Rutland, then three-quarters were from this area. Although Collinson's figures exclude such important puritan strongholds in East Anglia and the southeast as Norwich, Bury St. Edmunds, London, Cambridge, and parts of east Suffolk, a pattern is clearly evident (see table 1).

Settlements," *Genealogists' Magazine* [London], I (1925), 98–105. Later he attempted to identify the English origins of the settlers in each early New England town in "Social and Geographic Origins of the Founders of Massachusetts," in Albert Bushnell Hart, ed., *Commonwealth History of Massachusetts: Colony, Province and State*, 5 vols. (New York, 1927–1930), I, *Colony of Massachusetts Bay, 1605–1689*, 49–65, especially 57–61. I have attempted to provide a revised estimate for all Massachusetts towns founded before 1650 in Appendix I of David Grayson Allen, "In English Ways: The Movement of Societies and the Transferal of English Local Law and Custom to Massachusetts Bay, 1600–1690" (Ph.D. diss., University of Wisconsin, 1974), 415–417; the geographical origins of settlers in the five Massachusetts towns studied here appear in Appendixes 1–5 of this volume. The other genealogist is Charles Edward Banks; see his *Planters of the Commonwealth: A Study of the Emigrants and Emigration in Colonial Times: To Which Are Added Lists of Passengers to Boston and to the Bay Colony; the Ships Which Brought Them; Their English Homes, and the Places of Their Settlement in Massachusetts, 1620–1640* (Boston, 1930), and also his *Topographical Dictionary of 2885 English Emigrants to New England, 1620–1650*, ed. Elijah Ellsworth Brownell (Philadelphia, 1937), hereafter cited as Banks, *Top. Dict.* See also Banks's "English Sources of Emigration to the New England Colonies in the Seventeenth Century," Massachusetts Historical Society, *Proceedings*, LX (1927), 366–373. Some recent studies have commented on regional differences. For the distinctive "West Country," nonpuritan character of northern New England, see Charles E. Clark, *The Eastern Frontier: The Settlement of Northern New England, 1610–1763* (New York, 1970), vii–viii, and 3–89 *passim*, and suggestions by Robert E. Moody, book review, *American Historical Review*, LXXVI (1971), 1586–1587; Timothy H. Breen, "Who Governs: The Town Franchise in Seventeenth-Century Massachusetts," *William and Mary Quarterly*, 3d Ser., XXVII (1970), 473–474, 473n–474n; and Bernard Bailyn, *The New England Merchants in the Seventeenth Century* (Cambridge, Mass., 1955), 124.

7. Emery Battis, *Saints and Sectaries: Anne Hutchinson and the Antinomian Controversy in the Massachusetts Bay Colony* (Chapel Hill, N.C., 1962), especially chap. 17, "'Vile Sectaries': The Social Pattern of Religious Protest," 249–285, and also 242–243 and 293–294.

TABLE I. *Distribution of Puritan Ministers in English Counties, 1580–1590*

	No. of Locations	No. of Ministers
Essex	78	88
Suffolk	58	77
Norfolk	47	51[a]
Northampton and Rutland	42	49
Lincoln	33	33
Lancaster	38	32
Kent	27	30
Sussex	24	27
Warwick	22	25
Leicester, Stafford, and Derby	17[b]	21[b]
Cambridge	14	13
Hertford	12	20
Oxford	11[c]	14[c]
Bedford and Huntingdon	9	11
Buckingham	5	5
Surrey	4	6
Total	441	502

Notes:

[a] Excludes ministers from centers of prophesying.

[b] Collinson believes this may be an overestimate of puritan strength in these counties.

[c] Excludes the town of Oxford.

Sources:

Patrick Collinson, "The Puritan Classical Movement in the Reign of Elizabeth I" (Ph.D. thesis, University of London, 1957). Data have been obtained from Appendix B, "Keys to Maps Illustrating the Distribution of Elizabethan Puritanism," *ibid.*, II, 1252–1281, and also I, 122–127. Figures for Devon and Cornwall have been excluded because they include ministers and locations from 1580 to 1660, rather than the restrictive 10-year period Collinson has proscribed for his other data. On the concentration of puritanism in the eastern counties before 1660, see Collinson, *The Elizabethan Puritan Movement* (London, 1967), 202–203, 253, 254, 168, 127–128, 129, 222–224. A somewhat smaller group of 281 puritan ministers was identified by Ronald G. Usher in *The Reconstruction of the English Church*, 2 vols. (New York, 1910), I, 248–256, for the 1600–1610 period. Although his identification of the geographical locations of the ministers is similar to Collinson's, Usher suggested that after 1600 "the brains and energy of the party" had shifted from East Anglia and Northamptonshire to London, Essex, Lincolnshire, and Hertfordshire.

East Anglian predominance in the puritan movement, in both the six-teenth and seventeenth centuries, appears to have rested largely on the re-gion's proximity to the Continent, on a strong strain of Lollardism from the early sixteenth century, on the considerable industrial and mercantile activity in the area, and on the important role that Cambridge University played under the guidance of Thomas Cartwright and Laurence Chader-ton, and others.[8]

Later religious movements also appear to have had regional centers. Quakerism, for instance, which developed and began to flourish in the 1650s, was "more a movement into untouched territory" than a reaction to puritanism. As George Fox's *Journal* carefully details, the great Quaker "convincements" occurred in the North in Cumberland, Durham, North-umberland, Westmorland, Lancashire, and Yorkshire and spread through-out the West Country, especially to Cornwall, Devon, Dorset, Gloucester, and Somerset.[9] As the barriers to communication between the different parts of England fell in the 1640s and 1650s, preachers like Fox were able to broadcast religious views, often more radical than puritanism, that had been isolated in pastoral and forest area pockets of the North and West for decades.[10] Quaker dissent in the Bay Colony mirrored the geographical dispersion of the movement in England. Of forty-five Quakers indicted in Essex County court through 1661, perhaps 90 percent had emigrated from the North and particularly the West of England, that is, from English counties that contributed less than one-third of the colony's total popu-lation.[11] To a significant extent, deviant religious and political behavior

8. Patrick Collinson, *The Elizabethan Puritan Movement* (London, 1967), 129; compare Mark H. Curtis, *Oxford and Cambridge in Transition, 1558–1642: An Essay on Changing Relations between the English Universities and English Society* (Oxford, 1959), 191–194.

9. Hugh Barbour, *The Quakers in Puritan England* (New Haven, Conn., 1964), 42–43, 83–86, 257; *Journal of George Fox; Being an Historical Account of the Life, Travels, Sufferings, Christian Experiences, and Labour of Love, in the Work of the Ministry, of That Eminent and Faithful Servant of Jesus Christ, Who Departed This Life, in Great Peace with the Lord, the 13th of the 11th Month, 1690*, 7th ed. with notes by Wilson Armistead, 2 vols. (London, 1852), I, especially 166–168, 249, and 101–102, 122, 132–133, 172–173, 269–270, 313, 360. Compare Mildred Campbell, "So-cial Origins of Some Early Americans," in James Morton Smith, ed., *Seventeenth-Century America: Essays in Colonial History* (Chapel Hill, N.C., 1959), 87, 88. Other historians have argued that the strength of Quakerism was not seriously deficient in formerly puritanized areas. See Richard T. Vann, *The Social Development of English Quakerism, 1655–1755* (Cambridge, Mass., 1968), 16n.

10. Thirsk, "Farming Regions of England," 2–15, 112.

11. Quakers convicted in Essex County court came from 9 English counties, *all* located in the North and West: Staffordshire, Cornwall, Somerset, Gloucester, Devon, Dorset, Wilt-shire, Hampshire, and Yorkshire. The greatest number came from Staffordshire and Somer-set, counties that contributed less than 6% to the Bay Colony's population (based upon the Banks-Brownell map and data in Banks, *Top. Dict.*, xi–xiii).

in early Massachusetts can be linked to the diverse origins of English emigrants.[12]

Recent evidence suggests that these regional religious differences continued well into the eighteenth century. Ministers who came to Massachusetts Bay from the North and West of England during the Great Migration were generally more committed to education and more missionary minded. North and West Country ministers and their clerical descendants also "insisted on the more pietistic form . . . of personal conversion for church membership." In Dorchester, Massachusetts, which was originally inhabited by West Country emigrants and later by many North Countrymen as well, the keeper of church records affirmed a typical pietistic view when he commented, after recording a church admission, that there was "a Corruption Creepinge in as an harbenger to old england practice vis. to make all members: (which god prevent in mercye)."[13] Ministers from the North and West, with only an occasional exception, opposed the 1662 compromise on church membership, the so-called Half-Way Covenant, which gave church membership to the children of members without requiring a religious conversion experience. Several generations later, the ministerial offspring of the opposition to the Half-Way Covenant became carriers of "New Light" theology during the Great Awakening.[14]

12. George Francis Dow, ed., *Records and Files of the Quarterly Courts of Essex County, Massachusetts*, 8 vols. (Salem, Mass., 1911–1921), II, 103–105, 107, 110, 118, 163, 202, 219, 262, 265, 315, III, 66, 66n–67n, IV, 74, V, 298, 355, VI, 101, VII, 110, 115, 242, 285, 348, 407, hereafter cited as *Essex Co. Court Recs.* See also Matt Bushnell Jones, "Thomas Maule, the Salem Quaker, and Free Speech in Massachusetts Bay, with Bibliographical Notes," Essex Institute, *Historical Collections*, LXXII (1936), 1–42, especially 1, 8; "Letter to Joshua Buffum at Shelter Island, Written Nov. 4, 1660, from the House of Correction in Boston, by John Smith, Now in the Possession of Mrs. Mary Cassandra Hodges of New York City," with notes by Sidney Perley, *ibid.*, L (1914), 245–252; and map of "Part of Salem in 1700" in James Duncan Phillips, *Salem in the Seventeenth Century* (Boston, 1933). West Country people were particularly conspicuous in indictments and convictions for a variety of related crimes in Essex County, such as being absent from meetings, denying infant baptism, abusing the ministry, disturbing the congregation, and slandering the church and ministry. For examples, see *Essex Co. Court Recs.*, I, 48, 52, 70, 81, 92, 98n, 99n, 101, 178, 245, II, 105, 225, 315n, 61, 100, 103, 109.

13. P.M.G. Harris, "The Recurring Reformation in New England, 1630–1750" (paper read at the convention of the American Historical Association, Dec. 29, 1970, Boston, Mass.), 6–11, 16–20, 25; C. H. Pope, transcriber, *Records of the First Church at Dorchester, in New England, 1636–1734* (Boston, 1891), 168 (Sept. 27, 1657).

14. Harris, "Recurring Reformation," 16–17. Communities selected for study in the chapters to follow give evidence of North and West Country opposition to the Half-Way Covenant and greater East Anglian acceptance of it. Rowley, a "North Country" village, finally succumbed to the practice later in the 17th century only after nearly all of the original covenanters had died. On the other hand, "East Anglian" Ipswich was probably the first New England town to adopt it (although the loss of church records makes that inconclusive)

Regional differentiation is also apparent in the motivations that led some people to come to the Bay Colony. Nathaniel Ward probably spoke for many of his fellow East Anglians when he stated that "Divers make it an Article of our *American* Creed, which a celebrate Divine of *England* observed upon *Heb*. 11.9. That no man ought to forsake his own Country, but upon extraordinary cause, and when that cause ceaseth, he is bound in Conscience to return if he can: We are looking to him who hath our hopes and seasons in his only wise hand." [15] This attitude may even have influenced the names East Anglians gave to the land they inhabited. Why would the Norfolk settlers of Hingham have called a small island in Hingham harbor "World's End" if they did not see themselves as living at that outpost described in Psalms 23:27? Why would the Essex, Suffolk, and Hertfordshire settlers of Ipswich have named a small brook on the outskirts of the town the "Egypt River" if they had not been reminded of the New Testament exile in Matthew 2:13–15? [16]

In character with his remarks, Nathaniel Ward returned to England in 1646. Of the 129 ministers who came to New England prior to the end of the Great Migration in 1640, East Anglian puritan clergy were a third to half again as likely to return to England by 1660 as were West and North Country puritan ministers. The East Anglians also tended to return earlier in the two decades between 1640 and 1660, whereas their counterparts from the opposite ends of England tended to trickle back much later, most

---

in the early 1660s after almost 15 years of campaigning by Nathaniel Rogers and John Norton, and their successor in the pulpit, Thomas Cobbett. Both Newbury and Hingham were shepherded by broadly presbyterian ministers, Thomas Parker and Peter Hobart, who both had adopted a policy of less restricted baptism, like that of most English parishes, since their arrival in their respective towns. Neither church seems to have adopted the Covenant during the lifetimes of their influential ministers.

In addition, highly "East Anglian" Roxbury adopted the formula of the Synod at an early date, as did Edmund Browne's Sudbury congregation. See Robert G. Pope, *The Half-Way Covenant: Church Membership in Puritan New England* (Princeton, N.J., 1969), 16, 23–24, 141–142, 193. Predominantly "East Anglian" Dedham probably approved the Covenant in 1672. See Kenneth A. Lockridge, "The History of a Puritan Church, 1637–1736," *New England Quarterly*, XL (1967), 412–414, and also, Letter to the Editor, *WMQ*, 3d Ser., XXV (1968), 331.

15. [Nathaniel Ward], "The Simple Cobler of Aggawam in America . . . ," in Peter Force, comp., *Tracts and Other Papers, Relating Principally to the Origin, Settlement, and Progress of the Colonies in North America, from the Discovery of the Country to the Year 1776*, 4 vols. (Washington, D.C., 1836–1846), III, 8, 19.

16. West and North Country towns were never so imaginative in the naming of their physical surroundings. Newbury seemed particularly inadequate to the task in labeling areas such as "artichoake river," "rasberry river," "the nine lots," or "field of exchange." Rowley gave descriptive names to most of its fields, such as "Bradford Street Field," or "Rye Field," but neither town used names with the subtle connotations East Anglians did.

often in the 1650s. Once back, East Anglians were more likely to stay. When their livings were taken away in 1662 with the restoration of the monarchy, no identifiable East Anglians remigrated. In contrast, men from the North and West such as Henry Sewell, John Woodbridge, Joseph Hull, and William Fletcher dealt with their ill fortune by going back to New England. In fact, unlike the case of the eastern counties, ministers from the North and West never ceased emigrating even after 1640, and their numbers increased substantially after 1660. This intense interest of the North and West in New England might be explained partially by their involvement in Indian missions. With the notable exception of John Eliot of Nazing, Essex, nearly all puritan missionaries to the Indians were men like Richard Bourne and William Walton of Devon, Thomas Mayhew of Wiltshire, and William Leverich who came originally from Warwickshire. In addition, North and West Country ministers were more mobile in New England, leading their congregations or lending their services broadly throughout the northeastern area, and even settling beyond the Bay Colony in New Jersey, Long Island, New York, New Hampshire, and Maine.[17]

Other English Regional Factors

Religious particularities were only one of a number of other regional factors that separated Englishmen. Climate and geography determined two broadly defined areas of agriculture in England, the pastoral highland (principally in the North and West) and the arable lowland zones. Each had its own agricultural practices, social structure, and local customs. The recent work of Joan Thirsk and Alan Everitt, among others, has shown that regional specialization in agriculture and certain distinctive features of community life were increasing in the sixteenth and seventeenth centuries, which accentuated many subregional differences within the two broadly defined zones (see figure 1). Of course, there were many countervailing tendencies, such as the growth of trade between parts of the country. But with more than seven hundred urban communities, nine thou-

17. Frederick Lewis Weis, *The Colonial Clergy and Colonial Churches of New England* (Lancaster, Mass., 1936), *passim*. There was also considerable remigration by other men with the financial means to do so, but most immigrants, of course, were probably economically unable to return to where they had so recently departed, even if they had wanted to. See William L. Sachse, "The Migration of New Englanders to England, 1640–1660," *AHR*, LIII (1947–1948), 259, 260; and Harry S. Stout, "The Morphology of Remigration: New England University Men and Their Return to England, 1640–1660," *Journal of American Studies*, X (1976), 151–172.

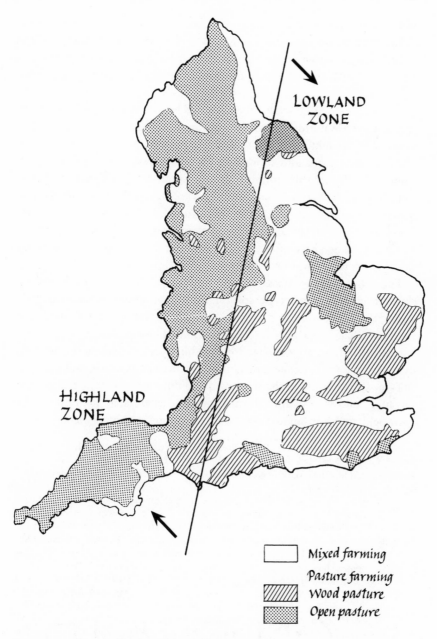

FIGURE 1. *Farming Regions in England, 1500–1640.*
Adapted from map in Joan Thirsk, "The Farming Regions of England," in Joan Thirsk, ed., The Agrarian History of England and Wales, *IV, 1500–1640 (Cambridge, 1967), 4. (Drawn by Richard J. Stinely.)*

sand rural parishes, and the "remarkable expansion of market towns between 1570 and 1640," along with the rise of county capitals, England remained, during the decades before the Civil War, a nation of regions and subregions with accompanying differences in farming practices and social structure.[18]

The settlers in each of the five towns of Rowley, Hingham, Newbury, Ipswich, and Watertown came as a group from a different locality in England and brought with them distinctive social and economic institutions.[19] The regions and subregions they had known in England ranged from the Yorkshire vales to the Wiltshire woodlands (see figure 2). Therefore, these early Massachusetts settlers were able at the same time to perpetuate a variety of local English ways and also to originate New World distinctions in local law and custom. Indeed, it is striking that the old local English ways persisted after the economic and social reasons for them had vanished on the American continent.

The belief that the Massachusetts colonists of the seventeenth century came from only three types of English communities—"the open-field manorial village; the incorporated borough; and the enclosed-farm East Anglian village"—is an oversimplification. The open-field manor predominated in both Yorkshire and Hampshire, yet an eighteen-day journey by foot separated these counties in the seventeenth century, and the agricultural institutions in them were quite different. Yorkshire was conservative, and its system retarded change, whereas in Hampshire the open-field manor promoted significant social and economic change. Such

18. See Alan Everitt, *Change in the Provinces: The Seventeenth Century*, Department of English Local History, *Occasional Papers*, 2d Ser., no. 1 (Leicester, 1969), especially 22–23, 36, 38–39, and his "The Marketing of Agricultural Produce," in Thirsk, ed., *Agrarian History*, IV, *1500–1640*, 467–477.

For an understanding of the increasing complexity that scholars are discovering in the regional variations of local English institutions and agriculture in Tudor and Stuart England, see: Joan Thirsk's new preface to C. S. Orwin and C. S. Orwin, *The Open Fields*, 3d ed. (Oxford, 1967), v–xv, and "Bibliography, 1954–1965," *ibid.*, 183–187; Thirsk, "Farming Regions of England," and "The Common Fields," *Past and Present*, no. 29 (1964), 3–25. This should be supplemented by annual bibliographies from *Agricultural History Review*, XIV to date (1966–). In addition, see: George C. Homans, "The Explanation of English Regional Differences," *Past and Present*, no. 42 (1969), 18–34; J. Z. Titow, "Medieval England and the Open-Field System," *ibid.*, no. 32 (1965), 86–102; Warren O. Ault, "Some Early Village By-Laws," *English Historical Review*, XLV (1930), 208–231; Ault, *The Self-Directing Activities of Village Communities in Medieval England* (Boston, 1952); Ault, "Village By-Laws by Common Consent," *Speculum*, XXIX (1954), 378–394; and Ault, "Open-Field Husbandry and the Village Community: A Study of Agrarian By-Laws in Medieval England," *American Philosophical Society, Transactions*, N.S., LV (1965), pt. vii.

19. For the English regional origins of immigrants to Bay Colony towns settled before 1650, see Appendix I in Allen, "In English Ways," 415–426.

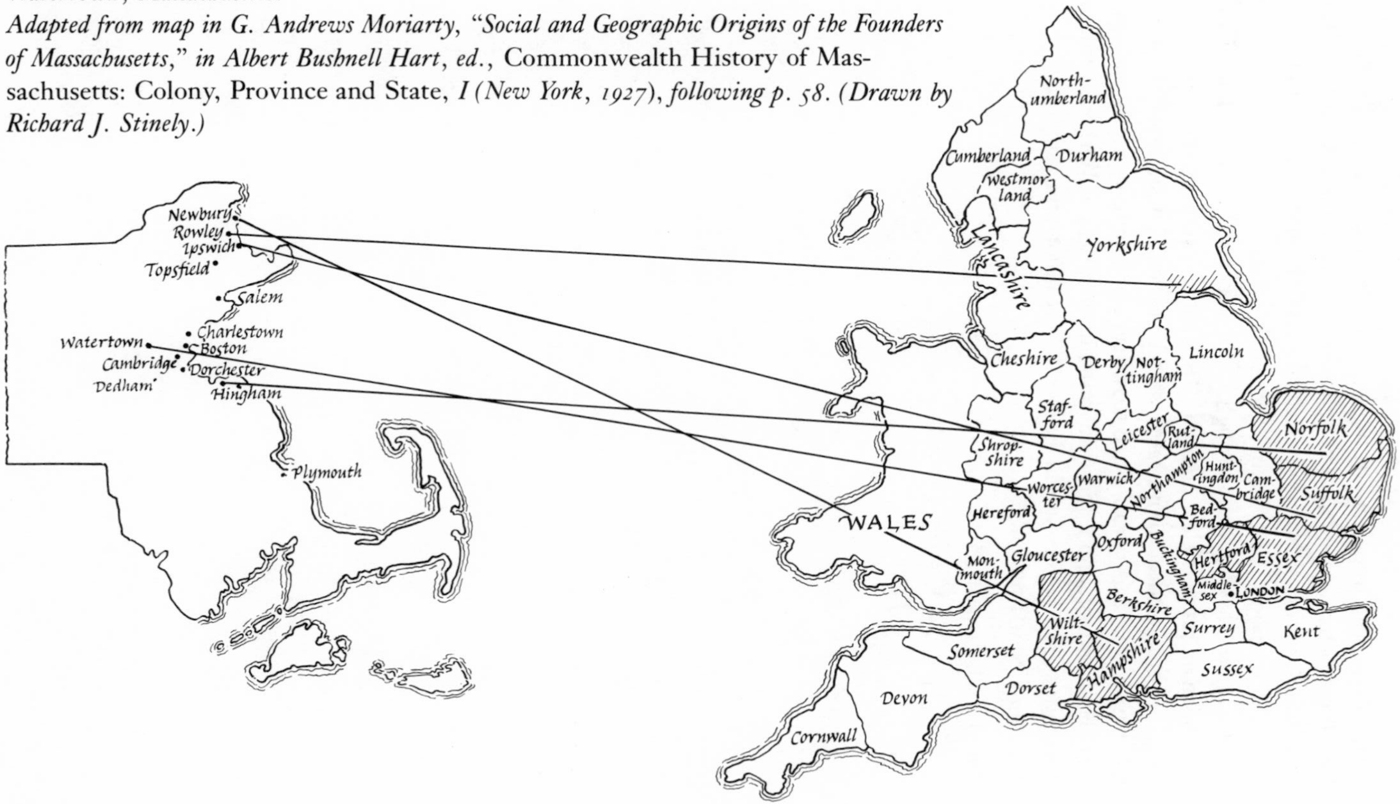

FIGURE 2. *English Origins of Immigrants to Rowley, Hingham, Newbury, Ipswich, and Watertown, Massachusetts.*

Adapted from map in G. Andrews Moriarty, "Social and Geographic Origins of the Founders of Massachusetts," in Albert Bushnell Hart, ed., Commonwealth History of Massachusetts: Colony, Province and State, I (New York, 1927), following p. 58. (Drawn by Richard J. Stinely.)

distinctions had important results in the development of Rowley and Newbury, Massachusetts. Though sharing a common boundary, they were hundreds of miles apart in their perceptions and attitudes toward society and economy. Similar diversity could be demonstrated with the examples of the incorporated borough and the enclosed East Anglian village, but the main point is clear enough. Regional and subregional variations in England produced a complicated social fabric. Manor, town, borough, and parish were inextricably tied to the type of economic life, social structure, landholding, and leadership found in each region. Without a full discussion of local factors in old England we cannot understand the varied society of New England.[20]

20. Powell, *Puritan Village*, xvii; *Essex Co. Court Recs.*, II, 13.

2 "Those Drowsy Corners of the North"

ENTLY rolling hills, wide and open fields, and small villages do not compose the usual picture of a remote frontier. Nevertheless, the wold and vale hamlets of the East Riding in Yorkshire were some of the last places in northern England to be ignited by the fire of puritan evangelicalism in the early decades of the seventeenth century. By 1640, however, puritanism there had reached its limits in both numbers and influence. Although religious evangelicalism would be rekindled in Yorkshire and other northern counties in the 1650s during the "great convincements" of George Fox and other radical religious proselytes, those who left to settle in Rowley, Massachusetts, in the 1630s and early 1640s probably knew little of such changes. Yet in departing from the land they had always known, they did not isolate themselves from their home country. Instead they recreated in New England the slow, stable "manorial" society of their immediate past, a society in which their social structure, agricultural pursuits, land system, and form of local government remained remarkably intact.

Not all the settlers of Rowley came from one specific locality, but a great number originated from three places in the East Riding: Holme-on-Spalding Moor, Cottingham, and Rowley, the New England town's namesake.[1] All of these parishes were located to the north and west of present-day Hull. Holme and Cottingham were situated on the western and eastern slopes, respectively, of the Wolds, a chain of low, rolling hills that stretch in a crescent from the Humber estuary west of Hull to Flamborough Head, where they reach the sea. Rowley parish was located between these villages in the Wolds.

Settlement in the North and West of England was relatively dispersed compared to East Anglia, and this geographic difference shaped and distinguished the backgrounds of settlers from the two regions. East Anglian Nathaniel Ward remarked in a letter that "some honest men of our town [Ipswich, Massachusetts] affirme that in their knowledge there are 68 townes in England, within as litle compasse as the bounds of Ipswich; I

1. For a listing of the English origins of the 59 landholders in the first division of land in Rowley, Massachusetts, see Appendix 1 of this book.

knowe neere 40—where I dwelt."[2] From such accounts one can gain an appreciation of the ease with which East Anglian puritans were able to mobilize relatives and friends from the same or nearby towns for the migration to New England. Rowley puritans from Yorkshire, however, were not so fortunate. The parish of Holme-on-Spalding Moor, for instance, covered 11,519 acres and was the largest in the East Riding. An Elizabethan rent roll summary shows at least four major settlement points within the parish—Water End, West End, Moor End, and Upper End— all fairly equally populated, plus five minor sites, one reputedly with its own chapel.[3]

Several miles away to the east in the Wolds was Rowley parish, which was also an area of large parishes and small, dispersed populations, "standing," as Cotton Mather described it a half-century later, "in the *centre*" of many dispersed hamlets, among them Bentley, Little Weeton, Riplingham, and Risby, from all of which the New England settlement of Rowley drew a number of immigrants.[4] Even in the West Riding, in Bradford, where the emigrant brothers William and Maximilan Jewett spent their earlier days, or in Batley, where Humphrey Reyner lived until his departure for New England, future Rowley settlers lived all around the fringes of their parishes.[5]

Scattered apart, often living considerable distances from their parish churches in small dispersed settlements, Yorkshire natives were likely to attend services only when extraordinarily induced. We have little specific proof of the locations of particular inhabitants in Holme-on-Spalding Moor in the early seventeenth century, but there is some evidence that people such as Thomas Elithorp, who later emigrated to Rowley, lived on

2. Nathaniel Ward to John Winthrop, ca. 1640, in Thomas Franklin Waters, *Ipswich in the Massachusetts Bay Colony*, 2 vols. (Ipswich, Mass., 1905–1917), I, Appendix C, 506–507.

3. Additional Manuscripts, 40132, fol. 20, British Library.

4. Cotton Mather, *Magnalia Christi Americana; or, the Ecclesiastical History of New-England, from Its First Planting, in the Year 1620, Unto the Year of Our Lord 1698*, 2 vols. (Hartford, Conn., 1853), I, 409 (italics his).

5. The Jewett brothers lived in the Barkerend district of Bradford, and Reyner came from Gildersome in Batley. T. T. Empsall, "Register of the Bradford Parish Church from 1596 to 1621," *Bradford Antiquary*, O.S., I (1886), 229; George Brainard Blodgette, comp., and Amos Everett Jewett, ed., *Early Settlers of Rowley, Massachusetts: A Genealogical Record of the Families Who Settled in Rowley before 1700 with Several Generations of Their Descendants* (Rowley, Mass., 1933), 168n, 321; Michael Sheard, *Records of the Parish of Batley in the County of York, Historical, Topographical, Ecclesiastical, Testamentary, and Genealogical* (Worksop, England, 1894), 153, 159; R. V. Taylor, "Yorkshire Churches: Batley Church," in William Smith, ed., *Old Yorkshire* (London, 1881–1882), 98n; and Horace Hird, *Bradford in History: Twenty-Four Essays on Life by the Broad Ford from the Celtic Age to the Present Day* (Bradford, England, 1968), 76.

the perimeter of the parish, probably at Bursea. Until the enclosure and the improved drainage of the depressed center of the parish in the late eighteenth century, much of it was moorland waste or bog that rendered travel from the outskirts to the parish center difficult and dangerous for a considerable portion of the year.[6] Indeed, local tradition describes the establishment in medieval times of a religious cell on the edge of the moor "for two monks, one of whome was employed in guiding travellers over the dreary wastes, and the other in imploring the protection of heaven."[7] The people in these Yorkshire parishes, if inclined toward religion at all, were particularly susceptible to the brand professed by itinerant puritan preachers. If their religious inclination was strong enough, they might be encouraged to travel to the nearest puritan parish. Because of their dispersed locations, these parishes became evangelical centers in the countryside. There, in addition to regular services, worshipers could attend separate devotional meetings like those conducted by Ezekiel Rogers of Rowley, who with his company of followers sailed from Hull in the summer of 1638, near the close of the puritan migration to New England.

Agricultural Structure

Although religion on the fringes of the Yorkshire parishes was novel, personal, and evangelical, other aspects of life had not changed since medieval times, nor was widespread social and agricultural change forthcoming until the mid-eighteenth century. The East Riding was a stable, static agrarian society, characterized by a population steady in size, a traditional open-field system of farming, specializing in grain and cattle, and a tightly defined social structure.[8] These were also the characteristics of the new society created at Rowley, Massachusetts.

While profound agricultural and social changes were taking place else-

---

6. In the sense used here, moor or moorland is not the high barren waste of the Brönte Pennine region, also in Yorkshire, but rather an ill-drained, low-level area that was reclaimed by means of numerous ditches and drains. The word was commonly used to describe similar areas in other parts of England.

7. *Bulmer's History, Topography, Directory of East Yorkshire (with Hull), etc.* (Preston, England, 1892), 643.

8. Tanner Manuscripts, vol. 150, fol. 37, Bodleian Library, Oxford; E.179/204/401, E.179/205/504, Public Record Office; and Cottingham Local History Society, *Journal*, I, 99, II, 129–130, all tend to indicate that there was no sharp change in population through much of the 17th century.

where in England at the time, such as the draining of the Fens in Lincolnshire in the 1630s, the introduction of new crops in southern England,
and the general enclosure movement in many areas, East Riding parishes
were not exposed to such sweeping alterations until after 1750. Drainage
had begun in the region around Holme-on-Spalding Moor, for instance, as
early as the Middle Ages, but the vast improvements that would help reclaim areas of the central and southern part of the parish did not come
about until the Market Weighton Canal was completed in the 1770s. Some
enclosure had also taken place before the seventeenth century, but little
occurred in the century and a half thereafter, so that by 1750 probably half
of the area of the East Riding remained unenclosed. In the Wolds alone
there was only one large enclosure, at Driffield, before 1740.[9]

Analyses of seventeenth-century East Riding glebe terriers (the listings
of church lands in parishes) indicate that most of the parishes from which
Rowley, New England, settlers came still farmed under the traditional
open-field system in which men possessed individual, noncontiguous
strips of land in large fields under common regulation rather than owning
enclosed, consolidated plots that they controlled by themselves.[10] There
was some enclosure in Rowley, Yorkshire, probably between 1645 and
1745, as there was in some of the claylands of Holme at about the same
time. As late as 1773, however, 7,847 acres out of 11,519 in Holme were
still unenclosed, and in 1800, Riplingham, a hamlet in Rowley parish, was
still unenclosed. Consolidation of holdings, especially in the wold villages,
began in earnest in the mid-eighteenth century, and within the next fifty
to seventy years many Rowley parish hamlets such as Risby, Hunsley,
Riplingham, and Rowley itself were depopulated, as fields and streets became trodden underfoot by sheep and the stone remains of structures became evidence to later historians of "lost villages."[11]

9. Compare Joan Thirsk, *English Peasant Farming: The Agrarian History of Lincolnshire from
Tudor to Recent Times* (London, 1957), 108–141; G. E. Fussell, "'Norfolk Improvers': Their
Farms and Methods," *Norfolk Archaeology*, XXXIII (1962–1965), 332–344; and June Alice
Sheppard, "The Draining of the Marshlands of East Yorkshire" (Ph.D. thesis [Geography],
University of London, 1956), 249–300.

10. Alan Harris, "The Agriculture of the East Riding of Yorkshire before the Parliamentary Enclosures," *Yorkshire Archaeological Journal*, XL (1959), 119; M. W. Beresford, "Glebe
Terriers and Open Field, Yorkshire," *ibid.*, XXXVII (1950), 356–357.

11. M. W. Barley, ed., *Parochial Documents of the Archdeaconry of the East Riding: An Inventory* (Yorkshire Archaeological Society, *Record Series*, XCIX [1939]), 120–122; "An Act for
Dividing and Inclosing the Several Open Fields, Carrs, Ings, or Meadow Grounds, and Commons or Waste Grounds, within the Township and Parish of Holme upon Spaulding Moor,
in the East Riding of the County of York," 1773, DDCC 48/1, Brynmor Jones Library, University of Hull, Hull, North Humberside (formerly Yorkshire) (documents formerly in the

All of this, of course, was in a future unknown to the Yorkshire emigrants, but it helps underscore, by contrast, the extremely slow pace of change there in the seventeenth century. Upon settling in their New England community, few of the inhabitants were attracted by the lure of more commercially oriented towns like neighboring Ipswich or ventured to start or join newer communities farther inland that might have offered greater opportunities for economic advancement. Among the 106 individuals who either held land granted by the new town or who had come before 1650 to settle in Rowley, 81 of them, or 76 percent, never emigrated from the community—a record of stability unmatched by any of the other four communities studied in this book. This lack of outmigration combined with little inmigration further helped to consolidate distinctive economic and social relationships.

The social structure of Rowley, Massachusetts, as measured by inventoried estates, was sharply defined like that of East Riding communities in the same period. From the 106 original or subsequent landholders and settlers of Rowley before 1650, 58 inventories survive. Although this number is only slightly more than half of the total that may once have existed, it appears to be a representative sample and not unduly overbalanced with wealthy testators. When compared to the original land grants, for example, the average landholding of the group whose inventories have survived was 25.9 acres, whereas the town average was 23.1 acres.[12] Between 1647

East Riding Record Office, Beverley, North Humberside), hereafter cited as Univ. of Hull; Notes on Holme upon Spaulding Moor Inclosure Award, 1773–1777, DDX 112/2, Humberside County Record Office, Beverley, North Humberside (formerly Yorkshire); Alan Harris, "Some Maps of Deserted Medieval Villages in the East Riding of Yorkshire," *Geographische Zeitschrift*, LVI (1968), 191; Harris, *The Open Fields of East Yorkshire* (East Yorkshire Local History Society, *East Yorkshire History Series*, no. 9 [1959]), 17–18; Harris, "The Lost Village and the Landscape of the Yorkshire Wolds," *Ag. Hist. Rev.*, VI (1958), 97, 97n, 100n; John Wacher, "Excavations at Riplingham East Yorkshire, 1956–7," *Yorkshire Arch. Jour.*, XLI (1964), 608–669; M. W. Beresford, "The Lost Villages of Yorkshire," *ibid.*, XXXVIII (1952), 67.

12. Over a decade ago Kenneth A. Lockridge, among others, raised the issue of bias in extant inventories when they were used to determine the social structure of New England communities. "A Communication," *WMQ*, 3d Ser., XXV (1968), 516–517. More recently, two historians have documented such biases for 18th-century Massachusetts inventories, finding them unduly overrepresentative of older and wealthier inhabitants. Gloria L. Main, "Probate Records as a Source for Early American History," and Daniel Scott Smith, "Underregistration and Bias in Probate Records: An Analysis of Data from Eighteenth-Century Hingham, Massachusetts," *ibid.*, XXXII (1975), 89–99, 100–110. See also, Jackson Turner Main, "The Distribution of Property in Colonial Connecticut," in James Kirby Martin, ed., *The Human Dimensions of Nation Making: Essays on Colonial and Revolutionary America* (Madison, Wis., 1976), 54–104.

While these doubts may be relevant for later generations of inhabitants of Rowley and

and 1697 the total wealth revealed in the 58 extant inventories shows that over one-third of this total was in the possession of only 6 individuals, or the wealthiest 10 percent (see table 2). The top quartile, some 15 testators, held 56 percent. Inventories ranged from that of Joseph Jewett (d. 1661) at £3,258 15s. 3d., to Henry Smith's (d. 1655) of £8 12s. Compared with the four other Massachusetts towns, Rowley had, with the exception of the commercialized-urbanized "East Anglian" town of Ipswich, Massachusetts, the highest concentration of wealth in its upper decile. On the other hand, it also had the highest proportion of wealth recorded among the

---

other towns, there is much less uncertainty about inventoried wealth delineating the social structure of the town for the first generation of settlers. This is borne out in the one surviving Rowley tax list of the period, made sometime between 1662 and 1664 (see table below). Of the 87 ratepayers listed, 34 were "new men," that is, men who had been entered in the town records after 1650. They were almost exclusively second-generation sons. Of the remaining 53 "pre-1650" or first-generation men, 6 out of every 7 had inventories. Unlike the figures for some 18th-century Massachusetts communities, Rowley inventories also show that the lowest rung of the local society was not underrepresented among extant inventories but that the second quartile of the tax list, where nearly half of the men without inventories were ranked, *might* be deficient. While this may exaggerate somewhat the discrepancy between the rich and the middle-to-poor inhabitants, other indicators such as the land grants demonstrate that such a disparity existed. For similar results in Ipswich, the only other town studied here for which a contemporary tax list exists, see chap. 5, p. 135.

Rowley Tax List, ca. 1662–1664

Ratepayers	No.	New Men	Pre-1650 Landowners and Settlers	Pre-1650 Men with Inventories[a]	Pre-1650 Men without Inventories	% of Pre-1650 Inventoried Men
Top 10%	9	1	8	7	1	88
Top 25%	22	1	21	19	2	91
Top 50%	44	6	38	32	6	84
Bottom 50%	43	28[b]	15	12	3	80
Total	87	34	53	44	9	83

Source:
Benjamin P. Mighill and George B. Blodgette, eds., *The Early Records of the Town of Rowley, Massachusetts*, I, *1639–1672* (Rowley, Mass., 1894), 132–133, hereafter cited as *Recs. of Rowley*, also printed as "Ancient Tax List of the Town of Rowley," *New England Historical and Genealogical Register*, XV (1861), 253–254.

[a] Includes several widows (and in one case a daughter) listed on the town rate whose recently deceased husbands (or parent) left inventories.

[b] Among the 28 in the bottom half was Thomas Remington, an original Rowley landholder, who had already moved from Rowley and whose later inventory reflected property in another town.

TABLE 2. *Wealth Distribution among 58 of the Original 106 Landowners and Settlers of Rowley, Massachusetts, 1647–1697*

	No. of Inventories	Cumulative Wealth in £	% of Total Inventoried Wealth
Top 10%	6	8,576/13/5	35.3
Top 25%	15	13,678/10/6	56.2
Top 50%	29	19,559/11/1	80.4
Bottom 50%	29	4,773/15/0	19.6
Total	58	24,333/06/1	100.0

Note:

The median wealth among the 58 settlers was £344/05/6; their average wealth was £419/10. In this table and in others below that show the distribution of inventoried wealth in different towns, the estate inventories used include all debts receivable; all debts payable have been subtracted.

Sources:

The group of first-generation Rowley men is somewhat broadened here to include not only Rowley grantees (compare table 4, below) but also almost a dozen others who settled (and remained) in Rowley before 1650, during the first decade of settlement. George Francis Dow, ed., *The Probate Records of Essex County, Massachusetts, 1635–1681*, 3 vols. (Salem, Mass., 1916–1920), I, 84–86, 93, 98–99, 109–116, 116–117, 129–130, 174–175, 202–203, 206–210, 232–233, 235–238, 244–245, 250–252, 253–254, 259–260, 294–300, 301–303, 320–322, 327–329, 334–335, 351–352, 371, 441, II, 5–8, 102–103, 110–114, 120–122, 147–151, 169–170, 214–216, 262–265, 387–389, 389–390, 413–416, III, 91–93, 162–164, 225–230, 246–250, 257–259; Dow, ed., *Records and Files of the Quarterly Courts of Essex County, Massachusetts*, 8 vols. (Salem, Mass., 1911–1921), V, 390n; Bound Wills and Inventories, vol. 302, pp. 99–100, 123, 174, vol. 304, pp. 4–6, 38–39, 73, 81, 145–146, 170–171, 254–255, 386–387, 408, vol. 305, pp. 57, 123, 265–266, and inventories on file, nos. 4009, 16706, 15429, Essex County Probate Office; Essex County Court Papers, Dec. 1636–Sept. 1694, 57 vols., XLV (Sept. 1685–Sept. 1686), 41, Office of the Clerk of Courts, Essex County Courthouse.

lower half of its population, 19.6 percent. In such a sharply defined society, the frequent, if incomplete, reevaluations of inhabitants' taxable wealth listed in the town records may have reflected, among other things, a Yorkshire consciousness of social place.[13]

In the stable, ordered community of Rowley, we should not be surprised to find much of the wealth in movable property rather than land. Land in Rowley had only slightly more value than its immediate produc-

13. *Recs. of Rowley*, 51–53, 58–60, 76–79, and *passim*. Compare also, "Freeholders of Rowley, 1677," *NEHGR*, XXVII (1873), 48–50.

tive worth. In two-thirds of the inventories before 1665, for example, landholdings made up less than half of the total worth of the estate, while in one-third of the inventories land was less than one-third of the value of the estate. Unlike the case in other communities, the inhabitants of Rowley do not appear to have invested or speculated in land, a tendency that was aided and abetted by the town's parsimonious land-granting policy.

We have no inventories from the period prior to 1688 for the East Riding villages and hamlets that are of interest to us. A study of the Lincolnshire wolds and claylands during the sixteenth and seventeenth centuries indicates, however, that on comparable terrain "the wold and heath villages were generally small, and the contrasts between rich and poor sharp," much as in Rowley, Massachusetts. A series of inventories for a short period of time from Holme-on-Spalding Moor in the late seventeenth century indicates accentuated extremes in degrees of wealth. Over one-half of the estates were below £20, and about one-quarter to one-third were above £80. In addition, a Holme manorial rental of the late 1610s shows that less than 15 percent of the householders in the parish were free tenants and that only about 20 percent held a customary tenancy.[14]

Whereas direct comparison of the size of estates in Rowley, Massachusetts, and Yorkshire is not possible, entries in the inventories themselves show how closely the economies of the two areas resembled each other. Rowley was similar to the lowland vale and marshland areas of Yorkshire, places such as Holme and Cottingham, the areas from which the greater number of settlers had come. In both old and New England areas, cattle and wheat were the main components of agriculture. Of certain inhabitants whose inventories survive, cattle accounted for about two-thirds of the value of all livestock on farms in Rowley and Holme, while horses constituted about 20 percent and sheep and swine ranged from about 11 to 12 percent (see table 3).

Of course, comparisons of inventories such as these at best give us only relative values. The absolute per farm average in New England is half again as large as in Yorkshire and probably reflects a scarcity of livestock in the New World. Nevertheless, the proportional figures reveal congru-

14. Thirsk, *English Peasant Farming*, 55–56, 83–84, 106–107, 171; Yorkshire Wills (and Inventories), 1688–1737, Probate Records, Exchequer Court, Diocese of York, Borthwick Institute of Historical Research, St. Anthony's Hall, Peaseholme Green, York, Yorkshire; Add. MSS 40137, fol. 5 (1617).

TABLE 3. *Comparative Analysis of Livestock Holdings in Rowley, Massachusetts, 1639–1681, and Holme-on-Spalding Moor, Yorkshire, 1688–1700*

	Average Value of Holding Per Farm in £		Value Per Farm in %	
	Rowley (1639–1681)	Holme (1688–1700)	Rowley	Holme
Cattle	47	32	65.3	70.3
Horses	17	8	23.6	17.6
Sheep	3	5	4.2	11.0
Swine	5	½	6.9	1.1
Total	72	45½	100.0	100.0

Sources:
  Based on inventories cited in table 2, and on the unindexed, unarranged, and un-cataloged wills and inventories of Holme, 1688–1700, Borthwick Institute of Historical Research, St. Anthony's Hall, Peaseholme Green, York, Yorkshire.

ences. Although the relationship of horses to cattle is greater in Rowley, these two animals constituted the chief forms of livestock holdings in both areas, representing in combined form for Rowley 89 percent and for Holme 88 percent of the total. Ownership of sheep and swine shows more variation between the two areas but, in either case, was only slightly above 10 percent of the total. If we look at Rowley between 1672 and 1681—only, that is, after a few decades of settlement in North America—the proportions are even more alike. During those years Rowley's livestock proportions were 74.1 percent for cattle, 14.9 for horses, 7.3 for swine, and 3.7 for sheep. Similar proportions have been found for the Plain of York, upon which Holme was situated, as a whole.[15]

It would appear that both Holme and Rowley, Massachusetts, specialized in fattening cattle and in raising horses. Rowley town records contain meticulous lists of calves, cows, and oxen, and the town meeting often elected several "searlher[s] of leyther." There was some dairying in both areas, for over half of the inventories from Rowley and from Holme mention pails, milk vessels, and, less often, butter and cheese. A comparison

15. See W. Harwood Long, "Regional Farming in Seventeenth-Century Yorkshire," *Ag. Hist. Rev.*, VIII (1960), 103–114.

of the number of foals with the number of mares suggests that horse raising was prominent in both regions. Surviving documents from Holme also
show that these two enterprises were actively encouraged. In enclosing 60
acres of land called Arglam in 1631, for instance, Sir William Constable,
the lord of the manor, stinted the enclosure to favor cattle and horses over
sheep.[16]

The various "Rakes upon Holme Comon" also provide a useful guide to
the direction of agriculture in early seventeenth-century Holme. That
community and neighboring Yorkshire villages were situated in an ill-
drained pasture area in the southern end of the Vale of York. For three-
quarters of the year much of Holme common was under water, as was a
great deal of Bishopsoil, Wallingfen, and the adjacent lands in Market
Weighton, Hotham, and Cave. During the summer, however, the area
provided tens of thousands of acres of pasture, and parishes like Holme
extended privileges (also called "intercommoning") for the use of its moor
to nearby towns. These privileges allowed oxen, "geld beasts," "shotts,
whys, and calves" on Holme land, but scrupulously excluded sheep from
the animals permitted there.[17]

Comparative analysis of cropping is difficult at best. Although inventories were compiled throughout the year, it was only during the months
from April to October or November that details about grains were carefully noted in them. Even then information about crops was often lumped
together under one entry in the inventories. Also, growing seasons were
different in the two regions. Finally, the comparison is complicated by
New England's use of Indian corn, a cheap and easily grown commodity
(undoubtedly only used on the farm) that is not found in Yorkshire inventories. Nevertheless, with the exception of Indian corn or maize and the
vegetable fibers hemp and flax, wheat and hay were the most common
crops found in Rowley inventories, followed by barley and rye. In both
the lowlands of East Yorkshire and in Rowley, Massachusetts, the marketable grains were wheat and barley. A 1666 order of Rowley recommended to townsmen that they could buy their supply of gunpowder
from the town "in good merchantable wheat or barley."[18]

Rowley, Massachusetts, was probably better known for its agriculturally related activity of clothmaking than for grain growing. When Samuel

<hr/>

16. *Recs. of Rowley*, 59–60, 60–61, 76–79, 83–84, 107, 118, 165, 201; Add. MSS 40132,
fol. 35. Compare also, *ibid.*, 40135, fol. 39.

17. Add. MSS 40135, fols. 36–37; compare also, fols. 33a–b.

18. See An Answer to the Georgical Enquiries from East and North Yorkshire, 1664,
Classified Papers, X (3), no. 23, Royal Society Library, London; *Recs. of Rowley*, 166.

Maverick visited the town sometime before 1660 he described the inhabitants as a "very laborious people" who "drive a pretty trade, makeing Cloath and Ruggs of Cotton Wool, and also Sheeps wool with which in few yeares the Contrey will abound not only to supply themselves but also to send abroad." Other contemporaries echoed Maverick's description. Governor John Winthrop mentioned that growing flax for linen and hemp for coarser fabric had become firmly established in Rowley, although nowhere else in the Bay Colony, and both Edward Johnson and John Josselyn marveled at the inhabitants' industry in clothmaking.[19]

Unlike the case in other Massachusetts towns where there might be incidental mention of hemp and flax in inventories, work with these fibers became a central preoccupation in Rowley. Not only were hemp and flax a constant feature in Rowley inventories, but these documents also refer to tablecloths, sheets, pillowbers (pillowcases), napkins, aprons, handkerchiefs, and "other small linen" in quantities too great for personal use. At least six looms appear in early inventories. William Law had "a cotton loum with furneture to it," while Michael Hopkinson left at his death "one payre of loomes, one shutel, one tenipel, 1 warping woof, one rings and one payre of [w]heels." Rowley was also distinguished by being the site of the first American fulling mill, which was operating as early as 1643. According to extant ledgers between 1672 and 1688, John Pearson's mill had accounts with 103 out of 104 Rowley families for dressing cloth.[20]

Even though the cloth industry never became as specialized in the East Riding as it did in the West around Leeds and Bradford, hemp and hemp yards and pits are mentioned in various sixteenth- and seventeenth-century documents there, particularly in wills and deeds, for Holme and nearby localities.[21] Reporting in the seventeenth century on the agricul-

19. Samuel Maverick, "A Briefe Diescription of New England and the Severall Townes Therein, Together with the Present Government Thereof," Mass. Hist. Soc., *Procs.*, 2d Ser., I (1884–1885), 235; Winthrop, *History of New England*, II, 120; J. Franklin Jameson, ed., [Edward] *Johnson's Wonder-Working Providence, 1628–1651*, Original Narratives of Early American History (New York, 1910), 183; John Josselyn, *An Account of Two Voyages to New-England, Made during the Years 1638, 1663* (Boston, 1865), 130.

20. George Francis Dow, ed., *The Probate Records of Essex County, Massachusetts, 1635–1681*, 3 vols. (Salem, Mass., 1916–1920), I, 236–237, 253–254, 372–373, II, 111–112, 170, III, 164, hereafter cited as *Essex Co. Probate Recs.*; Blodgette, comp., and Jewett, ed., *Early Settlers of Rowley, Massachusetts*, 272–273. Such activities seem relatively rare in early New England. Compare Percy Wells Bidwell and John I. Falconer, *History of Agriculture in the Northern United States, 1620–1860* (Washington, D.C., 1925), 15.

21. Compare, for instance, Bargains and Sales, Thomas and Matthew Barker, DDHA/4/48–49 (1621), Univ. of Hull; Glebe Terriers, Holme-on-Spaulding Moor, 1662, 1716, R.III.I, Borthwick Inst. Hist. Res.; William Sotheron, inventory, Oct. 1619, Probate Records, Exchequer Court, Diocese of York, *ibid.*; Add. MSS 40135, fol. 28.

tural practices of the area around Holme, a correspondent of the Royal Society devoted considerable detail to describing the methods of flax and hemp production, which he regarded as major farming pursuits in the area.[22] Hemp is mentioned in more than nine out of every ten inventories in Holme in the late seventeenth century, though it is often not listed in estates of the wealthy in the eighteenth. Some estates might contain, as did William Rumley's, "50 stone of hemp" valued at £7 10s., or "hemp pild and unpiled," as did Gilbert White's worth £21 5s., although in most inventories the fiber was assessed at closer to £4.[23]

Hemp is more commonly mentioned in Rowley inventories than flax. Hemp was easier to grow, demanded less attention during the growing stage, and depleted the soil less. A good supply of water was necessary to separate the plant fibers from the stem during the process of steeping—a need the men of Rowley probably took into consideration when they arranged house lots near or bordering on the town brook. Water regulations prohibiting the steeping of hemp and flax in springs and in running water were common in English villages growing these fibers. Similarly, in Rowley, Massachusetts, the inhabitants were warned that the town brook had to be "kept clear of all wood or any other incumbrances . . . that may hinder the passage of water" and could not "make stopage of the said brooke being thus done for the ratinge of hempe or flax under the penalty of five shillings." Fire regulations were also established in Yorkshire forbidding the drying of hemp in ovens or near an open fire, probably as much to curtail the offensive smell as to circumscribe the danger of fire. Unlike most other towns, the people of Rowley, New England, also legislated against the hazards of fire.[24]

The Land System

If the agricultural structure of Rowley was similar to that of Holme and other parts of the East Riding, its landholding system was also a replication of the Old World. The Yorkshire settlers came from a region of com-

22. Georgical Enquiries, and generally, Reginald Lennard, "English Agriculture under Charles II: The Evidence of the Royal Society's 'Enquiries,'" *Economic History Review*, IV (1932–1934), 23–45.

23. Inventories, Feb. 1693, June 1731, Probate Records, Exchequer Court, Diocese of York, Borthwick Inst. Hist. Res.

24. Bernard Jennings, ed., *A History of Nidderdale* [Yorkshire] (Huddersfield, England, 1967), 170; *Recs. of Rowley*, 91–92, 189–190.

mon fields and common regulation with strong manorial control. Not surprisingly, therefore, the first recorded divisions of land in Rowley, Massachusetts, between 1639 and 1643 show characteristically modest holdings, particularly in comparison with those of a community like Watertown, which was settled by East Anglians. Entirely different economic and social habits and customs were operating in these two communities. More than one-third of the 220 grants made in Watertown between 1630 and 1638, the years in which grants were made, were for parcels of land over 100 acres. In Rowley between 1639 and about 1642, when all of the early granting took place, only 2 percent of the total of 95 grants exceeded 100 acres. Two-thirds of the Rowley grants were under 20 acres, whereas only a little more than a quarter of the Watertown grants were that small (see table 4).

In 1642, several years after making its original grants, Watertown completed its first "inventory" of landholdings. Compared with the Rowley figures the difference is even more apparent. Watertown's inventory included 162 persons holding a total of 20,130 acres of land at an average of 124 acres per person. On the other hand, though Rowley's patent was large and extensive like Watertown's, the Yorkshire town granted a mere 2,196 acres of land to 95 individuals, with an average holding of 23 acres per person. Not only were the Rowley divisions small by the East Anglian/Watertown standard, they were also less equal. The top 10 percent in Rowley controlled 44.5 percent of the land in 1642, whereas only 31 percent was held by the same proportion of the population in Watertown.[25]

The widely varying size of the Rowley land divisions was one form of social stratification. Another was the actual location of those holdings. Each house lot and field division was carefully delineated in the town record book by location, and it is possible to reconstruct a map of house lots and field arrangements (see figure 3). Status was attached to settlers according to the street upon which their house lot was located. Most wealth in terms of land grants was concentrated on Wethersfield Street and on the nearby highway to Newbury. These house lots were larger than other Rowley grants, as were other parcels subsequently given to their owners. Most inhabitants of Bradford Street had holdings of about half to two-

25. *Watertown Records* . . . [title varies], 6 vols. in 5 (Watertown, Mass., 1894–1928), I, "Lands Grants Divisions Allotments Possessions and Proprietors' Book," 17–67. Bidwell and Falconer found that the "average" Essex County holding was 50 acres, about twice the Rowley average. *History of Agriculture in the Northern United States*, 37.

TABLE 4. *Land Distribution in the Original Grants for Rowley and Watertown, Massachusetts*

Acres	Rowley, 1639–ca. 1642[a] No. of Grants	Watertown, 1630–1638[b] No. of Grants
over 400		1
351–400		1
301–350		4
251–300		6
201–250	1	7
151–200	1	22
101–150		34
51–100	7	46
21–50	22	35
20 or less	63	54
no record	1	10
Total	95	220

Notes:
  [a] The terminal date for Rowley grants is estimated; it may have been later in the decade.
  [b] The Watertown grants were all made by 1638, but many granted that year were not fully determined until 1642.

Sources:
  Compiled from Benjamin P. Mighill and George B. Blodgette, eds., *The Early Records of the Town of Rowley, Massachusetts*, I, *1639–1672* (Rowley, Mass., 1894), 1–51; and *Watertown Records* . . . [title varies], 6 vols. in 5 (Watertown, Mass., 1894–1928), I, "Lands Grants Divisions Allotments Possessions and Proprietors' Book," 3–14.

thirds of the median, while those along Holme Street and nearby were equal to it.

The position of one's lot in the village apparently dictated the location and amount of land one held in nearby fields. For instance, Thomas Elithorp, who held a house lot on Bradford Street, was given property in the adjacent Bradford Street Field and in Batchelder Meadow and Batchelder Plain, both outward and to the west of his house lot. Richard Swan's house lot was on the north side of town on Holme Street, and he was granted land in Northeast Field, Marsh Field, and the Great Plains. Grants in the Great Plains and in Northeast Field were generally twice the size of those in Bradford Street Field.

In sum, those who were granted lots in Bradford Street Field usually received other holdings in Bradford Street Plain, Batchelder Plain, Marsh Field, and to a lesser extent in Pollipod and Rye fields, most of which were on the western side of the town. Grants in Northeast Field usually meant accompanying parcels in the Great Plains and in Marsh and Rye fields. These social distinctions, rooted in village and field patterns of ownership, were carried over into town business, and reference was often made to the various "parts" of this small community. For notifying the inhabitants of town meetings the town was divided into "circuits"; cattle herding was arranged by section of town; and overseers of "our end of town" or the "other end" were selected at the village assembly.[26]

The number of stinting rights, or what Yorkshire inhabitants called "gates," corresponded to the size of the landowner's house lot. Gates determined the number of animals each lot owner was allowed to put onto common pasturelands and were awarded on the basis of the landholder's initial grant. All acre and a half house lots received one and a half gates. Thereafter ratios between house lots and gates rose in greater than geometric proportions: two-acre lots received four and one-half gates; three-acre lots, thirteen and one-half; four-acre lots, twenty-two and one-half; and for the two six-acre house lots, forty-five gates were given.[27] An ambitious yeoman who lacked the prestige to get a well-located and sizable house lot in the village was also apparently blocked in several other ways as well; he was limited in the number of animals he could graze on the common lands and in the size of the fields he could farm.

Most men in Rowley, New England, held house lots that were only one and a half to two acres in size, and their major piece of arable land, in Bradford Street Field or in Northeast Field, was generally either four and one-half or eight acres. Marsh and meadow divisions were even smaller, averaging only one to two acres. In all, therefore, except for several large grants, most men in Rowley held between seven and ten different pieces or parcels of land in various arable, meadow, and marsh areas. Given such imposing obstacles in New England as the heavy forest, the unyielding terrain, and the long winter, it is surprising that the common-field system

---

26. *Recs. of Rowley*, 54, 57, 94, 106, 159, *passim*. See also Amos Everett Jewett and Emily Mabel Adams Jewett, *Rowley, Massachusetts: "Mr. Ezechi Rogers Plantation," 1639–1850* (Rowley, Mass., 1946), 147–155. Commenting on the relationship between field lands and house lots in another common-field village, W. G. Hoskins noted that "lands were always regarded as belonging to, or going with, a particular house in the village." *The Midland Peasant: The Economic and Social History of a Leicestershire Village* (London, 1957), 148.

27. *Recs. of Rowley*, 54.

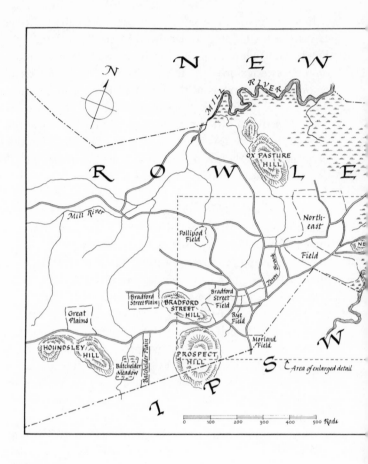

FIGURE 3. *Rowley, Massachusetts, ca. 1650.*
Based on frontispiece map in George Brainard Blodgette, comp., and Amos Ever-
ett Jewett, ed., Early Settlers of Rowley, Massachusetts: A Genealogical
Record of the Families Who Settled in Rowley before 1700 with Several
Generations of Their Descendants *(Rowley, Mass., 1933); Philander Ander-*

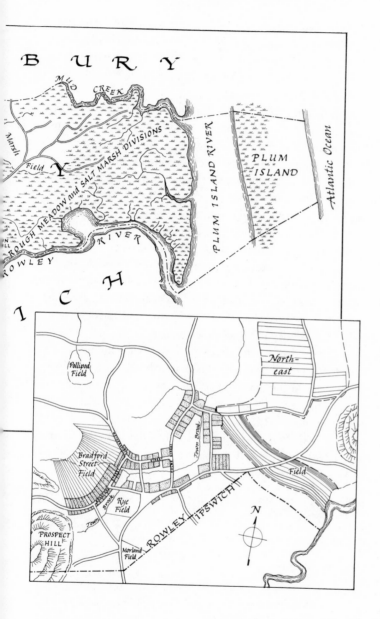

son's *1830 map of Rowley, Massachusetts Archives, State House, Boston; and in-*
formation in Amos Everett Jewett and Emily Mabel Adams Jewett, Rowley,
Massachusetts: "Mr. Ezechi Rogers Plantation," 1639–1850 (*Rowley,*
Mass., 1946), passim. (*Drawn by Richard J. Stinely.*)

was as faithfully nurtured and developed from the Yorkshire prototype as was the case in Rowley. So consistently was the English model reproduced that the average land grant in Rowley was comparable in size to the average individual landholding in the Yorkshire vales, which was between twenty and thirty acres.[28]

This land pattern continued in Rowley for more than a generation and persisted to some extent, the authors of one local history maintain, until recent times. Characteristic of the lack of change in the common-field system was a slowness, even a reluctance, to consolidate holdings. Land transactions recorded in Essex County court show only ten such "bargains and sales" before 1660 involving Rowley men and Rowley land, whereas in the bordering East Anglian-derived community of Ipswich, there were ten times as many in the same period. With the exception of one 130-acre transaction, Rowley transfers amounted to only a total of 55 acres, or an exchange of approximately 6 acres per transaction. In Ipswich, on the other hand, in the sixty-two cases in which the amount of land is mentioned, 1,791 acres of land were exchanged for an average of 29 acres per transaction. In addition to the wide differential in land sales, a rough tabulation of the Ipswich town deeds shows much greater horizontal mobility than in Rowley. At least half of the deeds indicate that a house lot was sold, often with a house on the property, which clearly suggests the movement of individuals inside the community and not merely a transaction involving an extraneous piece of harder-to-reach meadow or marsh, as was usually true in Rowley deeds.[29] Land transactions in Holme, as well as in Rowley and Cottingham, Yorkshire, probably occurred almost as infrequently during the decades prior to the exodus as those that were recorded in New England thereafter.[30]

28. Sheppard, "Draining of the Marshlands of East Yorkshire," 294–295; Add. MSS 40132, fols. 35–42; Harris, *Open Fields*, 9.

29. Jewett and Jewett, *Rowley, Massachusetts*, 147; Ipswich Deeds, I, 283–284, 292–293, 315–318, 320–321, 344–345, 360–365, 507–510, 554–556; 6–7, 20–21, 23–24, 30–33, 68–79, 83–85, 92–94, 121–126, 134–138, 147–150, 155–157, 160–161, 190–196, 198–208, 210–211, 238–239, 248–250, 254–256, 263–270, 276–279, 321–322, 327–328, 333–341, 360, 365–366, 369–370, 377–381, 397–398, 419–422, 426–427, 435–450, 459–463, 467–468, 492–495, 499–500, 513–515, 546–550, 561–572, 589–599, 606–607, 610–613, 625–629, 632–639, 642–645, 659–664, 666–667, Office of the Clerk of Deeds, Essex County, Salem, Mass.

Comparing these intratown land sales and taking into account differences in town population figures for 1647 and 1666, as estimated by Robert Emmet Wall, Jr., "The Decline of the Massachusetts Franchise: 1647–1666," *Journal of American History*, LIX (1972–1973), 303–310, Ipswich transactions occurred over three times as often as they did in Rowley.

30. For some comparative evidence, see chap. 4, pp. 106–107, 107 n. 45.

Of course, the New England Rowley land system did not remain entirely static throughout its early years. The town records indicate infrequent private sales, sometimes due to death or removal. In 1662 and 1665 Rowley made some small divisions, amounting in most instances to no more acreage per individual than in the previous grants of meadow and marsh two decades earlier. There were also occasional adjustments of property in land due to the incorrect laying out of fields or to the quality of a parcel having been improved after it was granted. Large grants were made in the late 1660s and early 1670s in the areas that were to become the separate communities of Boxford, Bradford, and Georgetown. Even this activity, however, did little to change the holdings of most of the residents, and if larger land grants were given to the wealthier men, it only maintained the imbalance in landholdings between the many small holders and the few large ones that was typical in the town.[31]

More important than purchasing land in Rowley was the buying and selling of gates, which were exchanged with frequency and which by 1662 were being offered for sale at thirty shillings apiece. Not only did the number of gates limit the number of cattle and other livestock one might graze on pasture, but individual gates might also increase in value as new pastureland was laid out by the town.[32]

Despite these moderate changes, the town through its meeting remained the center of land policy. It reclaimed rights to land if legal ownership became obscured and could compel the forfeiture of a grant if certain conditions were not met. The town could even sell public land for the purpose of raising money to repurchase more desirable property elsewhere, as it did with some of Ezekiel Rogers's land. In addition to these practices, the Rowley government could restrict the sale or granting of land. It could also use town lands in order to lower the town rate, either by renting vast areas as "farms" or by selling hay from the town meadows.[33]

Yorkshire men who came to settle in Rowley, Massachusetts, brought with them patterns of life and ways of doing things characteristic of their North Country environment. In a region touched by puritanism only within their own lifetimes, often living on the fringes of large open parishes in the wolds or vales, the men who settled in Rowley were much younger on the average than puritan emigrants to other areas of New En-

31. *Recs. of Rowley*, 88, 97, 98, 100, 116; 135–144, 157–158, 107–108, 164; 101–102, 164, 190–198, 207–213.
32. *Ibid.*, 119–127, 128, 170–180.
33. *Ibid.*, 70, 98, compare 95; 108–110, 117, 145; 105, 129, 186–189.

gland. Despite their youth, or perhaps because of it, they built on New England soil the same type of society that characterized much of the North Country and the English Midlands until the middle of the eighteenth century.

Society in the East Riding of Yorkshire was based on common-field agriculture and was tied to the dominant presence of the manor. Traditional patterns of life there remained relatively unchanged until the eighteenth century, when large-scale sheep raising and the enclosure movement transformed the countryside. In the early seventeenth century, in the era of the New England immigration, the social structure was stable and sharply stratified. Inhabitants farmed in common, raised livestock, and made cloth from flax and hemp. Landholdings were small and closely regulated. Since these men engaged in little commercial activity in land, there was little effort to enlarge or consolidate holdings. When Yorkshire settlers came to Massachusetts, they recreated these and other familiar patterns of life.

Leadership Patterns

Having carried across the Atlantic certain regional assumptions about social organization and about agricultural and economic relationships, Yorkshire men also perpetuated complementary ideas about who should govern and about how their Massachusetts town should function. Open-field agricultural societies required almost all village inhabitants to take on large and small responsibilities, and this necessity gave men of various social rankings a degree of experience in a wide range of local affairs. In addition to widespread officeholding, open-field English communities carried on their day-to-day agricultural business through the court baron, one of two distinctive courts held in this manor-dominated region. The court baron enacted agrarian bylaws through the tenants in assembly under the direction of the steward or lord. Not only were local inhabitants constantly involved in executing duties as officers, but they also took an active part in formulating local regulations. The men of Rowley, New England, continued these attitudes and practices, which were in sharp contrast to the ways of East Anglian emigrants in such towns as Cambridge and Dedham, or Ipswich and Watertown, Massachusetts.

During the last two decades scholarly controversy has raged over the nature of political leadership in Massachusetts Bay. The debate has tended

to center on the nature of town leadership and on the related matter of
freemanship, with specific attention focused on two communities in particular, Dedham and Cambridge. Recent criticism has devastated arguments that town offices in these two localities were wide open to those below the wealthy class.[34] Selectmen as well as other town leaders were
drawn from a fairly well-to-do group of individuals who were regularly
returned to office. This new interpretation, however, has not been tested
for other Massachusetts towns.

Rowley would appear on the surface to have all the signs of an elite-
dominated community like Dedham or Cambridge. Wealth was concentrated within a narrow group, and landholdings were small except for
those of a few persons near the top of the social order. Nevertheless,
Rowley town leadership was probably as democratic—in the sense of of-
fering widespread participation—as that of any town in Massachusetts.

Part of the difficulty in recognizing differences among Massachusetts
towns in the seventeenth century has been the unquestioned assumption
that the General Court controlled local government. The Court may have
regulated town activities insofar as they impinged on provincial affairs,
but it allowed the towns considerable latitude in managing local problems.
The so-called Town Act of 1635 actually recognized the diversity of existing practices rather than attempting to dictate rights and privileges based
on higher authority. The Court was well aware that the communities
"have many things which concern onely themselves" and granted to them
powers that the towns had already been practicing. They were given the
power "to dispose of their owne land, and woods," to "make such orders as
may concerne the well ordering of their townes," to enforce these orders
with bylaws establishing penalties not exceeding twenty shillings, and "to
chuse their owne particulr officers, as constables, surveyors for the high-
wayes, and the like."[35]

To a great extent, the law perpetuated the relationship between central
and local government that had existed in England. Vital matters, such as
who should manage town affairs and what role the town should play in the
lives of individuals, were left to the communities themselves. It is signifi-

34. For a review of the literature, see B. Katherine Brown, "The Controversy over the
Franchise in Puritan Massachusetts, 1954 to 1974," *WMQ*, 3d Ser., XXXIII (1976), 212–241;
and in addition, Arlin I. Ginsburg, "The Franchise in Seventeenth-Century Massachusetts:
Ipswich," *ibid.*, XXXIV (1977), 446–452, and Robert E. Wall, "The Franchise in Seventeenth-Century Massachusetts: Dedham and Cambridge," *ibid.*, 453–458.

35. *Recs. of Mass. Bay*, I, 172.

cant, for instance, that the selectmen who became the chief administrators (and in some towns the chief controllers) of town affairs were not officially designated or recognized by the General Court until 1641, when freemen were acknowledged as having the right to choose them.[36] Thus, the latitude of the provincial government allowed the towns to blend their own particular views on governing, based on their past experience in England, with the broad outline of local affairs drawn up by the General Court.

Rowley's views toward the office of selectman, when compared with those held in communities like Dedham and Cambridge, reveal the range of differences that was fostered by local particularities and by lack of central control. Although the earliest records of Rowley are missing, fairly complete lists (except for two years) exist of selectmen chosen from 1649 to 1673.[37] In these twenty-two years of selectmen's elections, forty-one men were chosen for ninety positions. Only one man served as many as seven terms and another served six. Four men held the position for five years, but all others remained for three years or less. Two-thirds of all the men elected served only two years. The top 10 percent of officeholders held 25 percent of all positions and the top 25 percent only half of all the positions available. The appointment of Ezekiel Northend, nephew of Robert Northend, lord of the manor of Little Weeton, Rowley parish, to seven terms as selectman may have been a response to inherited title to leadership. But past distinction did not always account for much in Rowley. Thomas Crosby, one of the two wealthiest men in Holme in the 1640 assessment and a man who had served as a Holme bylawman in 1620, was never elected a selectman in the New England community.[38]

In addition to town land grants as an indicator of socioeconomic position in Rowley, a surviving tax list drawn up sometime between 1662 and 1664 presents a clearer picture of the economic status of these men during the same years they served as selectmen.[39] The list contains eighty-seven names, many of them second-generation sons or relative newcomers who presumably were not so well-off as long-term residents. The tax list reveals that men who ranked as low as thirty-fourth, forty-ninth, sixty-

36. William H. Whitmore, ed., *The Colonial Laws of Massachusetts, Reprinted from the Edition of 1660, with Supplements to 1672* (Boston, 1889), 49.

37. *Recs. of Rowley, passim*, also printed as "Early Rowley Officers," Essex Inst., *Hist. Colls.*, XIII (1877), 253–262. Since other towns that have their earlier records show much turnover in office during the first decade, there is every reason to believe that if these records were available for Rowley they would only enhance the figures.

38. E.179/205/462, 17 Charles I, P.R.O.; Add. MSS 40135, fol. 37b.

39. *Recs. of Rowley*, 132–133.

TABLE 5. *Tax Ranking of the Most Frequently Elected Selectmen in Rowley, Massachusetts, 1649–1673*

	Years Served	Ranking in ca. 1662– ca. 1664 Tax Assessment
Ezekiel Northend	7	13
Thomas Lever	6	34
Samuel Brocklebank	5	17
John Pickard	5	6
William Tenny	5	[a]
Leonard Harrington	5	49
Matthew Boyes	3	[b]
John Trumble	3	69
Thomas Dickinson	3	8[c]
Richard Swan	3	11
John Dresser	3	5
Samuel Platts	3	71

Notes:
[a] Strangely, his name is missing from the list; Tenny died in 1685 with an inventory of £283/16/8, below the median of £344/5/6.
[b] Returned to England before 1657.
[c] Died Mar. 29, 1662; his wife was rated for the assessment.

Source:
Compiled from Benjamin P. Mighill and George B. Blodgette, eds., *The Early Records of the Town of Rowley, Massachusetts*, I, *1639–1672* (Rowley, Mass., 1894), *passim*.

ninth, and seventy-first in assessed wealth were nevertheless also among the most frequent officeholders (see table 5).

If Rowley tended to choose for town office men who were generally undistinguished by either wealth or social class, they also favored men with relatively little prior experience in local government. If the numbers of years in office of Rowley and Ipswich selectmen are compared, the East Anglian town leaders usually had about twice the experience per individual. In addition, if the cumulative experience of the boards of selectmen is compared, Ipswich selectmen had from two to four times as much prior service (see table 6).

Rowley may have differed from some of the other towns in part because of the limited expectations that Rowley men placed in their town officers.

TABLE 6. *Comparison of Years in Office of Selectmen in Rowley and Ipswich, Massachusetts, 1649–1673*

	Men Elected		Cumulative Years in Office		Years in Office per Individual	
	Rowley	Ipswich	Rowley	Ipswich	Rowley	Ipswich
1649–1659	35	56	51	115	1.5	2.1
1660–1669	36	60	79	323	2.2	5.4
1670–1673	20	28	66	175	3.3	6.2

Note:

These figures include only the dates for which Rowley lists of selectmen are extant, and they have been calculated in the final column on a per person basis since the Ipswich boards of selectmen usually included seven men and the Rowley group only five.

Sources:

Compiled from Ipswich Town Grants, Town Meeting, 1634, and Town Records, 1634–1757, Town Clerk's Office, Ipswich, Massachusetts; and Benjamin P. Mighill and George B. Blodgette, eds., *The Early Records of the Town of Rowley, Massachusetts, I, 1639–1672* (Rowley, Mass., 1894), *passim.*

The selectmen appear to have been appointed to carry out the wishes of the town meeting and little else. Occasionally the selectmen were allowed to promulgate the more mundane details of bylaws, but they were usually on the periphery of town government in Rowley. We have no records of the selectmen meeting as a group, but the chances are that they met infrequently, if the small number of bylaws they made is an indication of their efforts as a body. The town, however, met regularly. In the period from 1649 to 1673, for instance, the town convened on 102 occasions, averaging five meetings a year. During a comparable time period, "East Anglian" Watertown assembled as a town only half as often, while "East Anglian" Dedham from 1636 to 1736 never met more than three or four times a year.[40] In 1648 the Rowley selectmen were given in town meeting "full power to order and transact all the Common affaires of the Town of Rowley as to make Orders impose Fines for the better manageing the affaires of the said Towne provided that they do nothing Contrary to the orders of the General Court."[41] But this in itself did not encourage the selectmen to govern actively. The initiative was still lodged in the town meeting. Throughout the 1650s and 1660s no more than a dozen specific bylaws were drawn up by the selectmen, fewer even than the number of separate decisions the town meeting arrived at in a single meeting.[42] More often than not, the selectmen's discretionary power amounted to little more than making decisions that, in caretaker fashion, had to be handled in between meetings of the town. In other cases the matters acted upon by the selectmen were simply those delegated to them because they were too troublesome and time-consuming to be considered by the town in meeting. It was common, for instance, for townsmen to secure permission from the selectmen to mow hay in any common meadow belonging to the town, or to "barke girdle loppe or fall any tree" on town streets. The town meeting would often order them to perform thankless tasks such as reporting on the laying out of Rowley Village (later called Boxford), warning individuals whose animals had become nuisances, or restricting (stinting) the number of hogs each landowner was allowed on the common lands.[43] When the town required a small committee of men to look into an important matter, as was the case in 1672 when the church was in need of repair,

---

40. Kenneth A. Lockridge and Alan Kreider, "The Evolution of Massachusetts Town Government, 1640 to 1740," *WMQ*, 3d Ser., XXIII (1966), 574.

41. *Recs. of Rowley*, 55–56. There were, incidentally, few such specific prohibitions enacted by the General Court.

42. *Ibid.*, 88, 91, 92–93, 95, 96, 145–146, 150.

43. *Ibid.*, 166, 199, 86, 87, 88.

it usually chose a group other than the selectmen to study the problem. Occasionally, however, when a more delicate issue was involved, they were asked to make a decision.[44]

The pattern of local leadership revealed by Rowley's town records suggests that if we are to understand the political order in early Massachusetts, we must go beyond the question of the franchise. If it is true that Rowley had the highest percentage of freemen among the five towns studied here, perhaps it was in part because open-field farming required widescale participation in officeholding. Indeed, the help of many people was required to carry on the tiresome but necessary tasks of sustaining the open-field community. The livelihood of each participant was dependent on the active assistance of all. Therefore the franchise would be as unnecessary as an oligarchy of officeholders would be purposeless. In 1669, for instance, Rowley required the services of at least twenty-one men to serve as constables, town marshals, selectmen, "Overseers for the east end of the Town," "Overseers for the West end of the Towne," "Pinder for the north east feilld on the east side of Satchwell Brooke," "for the west side of Satchwell Brooke," "for Clarke to Call Towne Meetings," "for Judges to here the case of deliquents not comeing to towne meetings" for the east and west ends of the town, and "for Seallers of Leather," among others.[45]

The manorial records from Holme-on-Spalding Moor and Rowley parish are not extant, but short terms of office were probably the rule if the officeholding customs in fenland and Midland common-field manors are representative. In Wrangle, Lincolnshire, for example, every yeoman, husbandman, or artisan was expected to serve as churchwarden, overseer of the poor, surveyor of highways, dikereeve, or constable, and if he lived long enough, in all of those positions as well as others. From 1596 to 1650, over 90 percent of the men serving as churchwarden held that office for only one or two years. They usually served in other positions before their appointment. In Ashby-de-la-Zouch, Leicestershire, surviving records indicate that in a five-year period at least seventy-one people played some part in the administration of the town, either as manorial officers or as jurymen. On the basis of this figure, one out of every three families in the town was actively involved in local government. If corresponding ecclesiastical records existed with information on the numbers who served as

44. *Ibid.*, 226, 225.

45. Robert Emmet Wall, Jr., "The Massachusetts Bay Colony Franchise in 1647," *WMQ*, 3d Ser., XXVII (1970), 138; Breen, "Town Franchise in Seventeenth-Century Massachusetts," *ibid.*, 473–474, 473n–474n; *Recs. of Rowley*, 200–201.

overseers of the poor or of highways, as churchwardens, or in other offices, we might learn that the level of participation was even higher. In those areas of England where the seventeenth-century manor was still a viable institution, as in the East Riding, a strong tradition probably remained of widespread officeholding that required men to fill many small manorial positions and to enforce a complicated and time-consuming system of local bylaws.[46]

Government

A great number of the people who settled in Rowley, Massachusetts, had come from marshland areas in Yorkshire. Marshlands dotted the coastline of England and Wales, including such widely separated areas as the Broadlands in Norfolk, the lower Thames in Essex, Romney Marsh and smaller areas in Kent, the Somerset Levels in the west, and parts of Wales, Lancashire, and at the Solway Firth. The largest of the marshlands were the fens of Lincolnshire, Cambridgeshire, Ely, and Peterborough. Next in importance and almost equal to this fenland in area were the marshlands of the Vale of York and its southern continuation as the Vale of Trent, and various other areas in Holderness along the Humber such as the area around Cottingham. Few came to New England from such areas in England, with the exception of the small group who settled at Rowley.[47]

Sheer effort and large-scale determination helped reclaim and improve some lands in these Yorkshire areas during the Middle Ages. Constant attention and firm regulation by the marshland manors were necessary to preserve these gains as well as to sustain cultivation under such unfavorable conditions. Lords of manors could come and go, as several did during the lifetimes of men at Holme who would later leave for New England, but that mattered little in the day-to-day activities and concerns of villagers. In the course of the early seventeenth century the Constable family was replaced by the Langdales in the Holme manor, and the advowson of the vicarage came into the hands of London businessmen; still it was the

46. Frederick West, "The Social and Economic History of the East Fen Village of Wrangle, 1603–1837" (Ph.D. thesis, University of Leicester, 1966), 29–30, 317–320; C.J.M. Moxon, "Ashby-de-la-Zouch—A Social and Economic Survey of a Market Town—1570–1720" (D. Phil. thesis, University of Oxford, 1971), 211–216.

47. The terms marshland and fenland are used interchangeably here, although technically speaking the former is land on a coast liable to flooding from the sea, while the latter is low-lying land subject to flooding by rivers.

direction the community followed in the manorial courts in the appointment of officers and the enforcement of bylaws that guided the affairs
of future Rowley, New England, families like the Crosbys, Lamberts,
Barkers, and Elithorps.[48]

In addition to reclamation and improvement, manors like the one at
Holme governed a common-field system much like the one that was developed later in Rowley, Massachusetts. In such open-field villages arable
lands were divided into fields, which were then divided into individual
strips for each cultivator. Every landholder had noncontiguous strips in
the fields. From a modern point of view, such a system of scattered holdings seems highly inefficient, if not impracticable, but in agrarian societies
like these it had several advantages. The strips were about the size of a
single day's plowing, which meant that each day the farmer went to a different spot. It therefore mattered little whether a farmer took his team of
horses to the same part of a field or to different parts. Between times he
devoted himself to caring for livestock. The intermixture of strips meant
intermixed types of soil, which ensured some equality in the distribution
of land. Other features characteristic of the common-field system were the
exercise of grazing rights over the arable fields during the winter months
and fallow years, and the common consent of strip holders to keep certain
fields fallow every second or third year. Orders for these activities were
made in a meeting of the cultivators or producers, often in a manor court,
but occasionally in a village meeting.[49]

The earliest surviving glebe terrier, or listing of church lands and tenements, in Holme dates from 1662.[50] It describes a system of open fields
and parcels of meadow and pasture not unlike that outlined in the Rowley,
New England, land grants discussed above. Some consolidation by enclosure had taken place in Holme by the 1660s, but the persistence of the
system of common fields is evidenced by the generally small holdings in
Holme's three fields—North, Middle, and South—in which the parish
held lands "dispersed in the Said Feilds." Later terriers show that the field
system remained largely intact into the eighteenth century. The manors of

48. Frederick Harold Sunderland, *Marmaduke Lord Langdale of Holme-on-Spalding Moor Yorkshire (Colonel-General) and Some Events of His Time (1598–1661)* (London, 1926), 35n–36n; DDHA/4/3, Humberside R.O.

49. Thirsk, "Common Fields," *Past and Present*, no. 29 (1964), 3.

50. Holme-on-Spalding Moor terrier, 1662, R.III.I xxxi.16.1, Borthwick Inst. Hist. Res. On the significance of glebe terriers as indicators of the extent of enclosure, see: Beresford, "Glebe Terriers," *Yorkshire Arch. Jour.*, XXXVII (1950), 356–357; Beresford, "Glebe Terriers in Open Field Leicestershire," Leicestershire Archaeological Society, *Transactions*, XXIV (1948), 77–127; and W. B. Stephens, "Sources for the History of Agriculture in the English Village and Their Treatment," *Agricultural History*, XLIII (1969), 232.

Rowley parish also had a system of open-field farming much like Holme's, though less documentary evidence of it is extant.[51]

Manors normally had a court leet and a court baron, and sometimes a court for copyhold tenants as well. The court leet was responsible for policing the manor. It was here that crimes such as assault, theft, and drunkenness would be heard by the lord or the steward and a jury selected from among the inhabitants. More serious matters were presented to the county court of quarter sessions. From nominees made by the jury, the steward appointed a host of local regulatory officers, including a constable, officers of the markets, aleconners, and others. The number of positions available depended in large measure on the size and needs of a particular manor.

The court baron was concerned with the agricultural life of the manor and with the bylaws enacted by the tenants in assembly under the direction of the steward or lord. The lord or his steward may have provided the initiative for holding the assembly, suggested the precise formulation of the "pains," or bylaws, and performed the actual recording of them, but the bylaws were a cooperative product, the result of the active involvement of those who were directly engaged in peasant agriculture. Codified bodies of such bylaws were usually prefaced with the statement, as were those of Holme, that they had been "Laid and agreed to at several tymes by and with the consent of the Inhabitants of Holme." Bylaws represented the "common consent" of all members of the community and their common interest. Although few manorial records survive for the areas from which Rowley's settlers came, the influence of these local legal codes upon the development of early Rowley, New England, can be seen by taking as exemplary the enactment of bylaws in Holme-on-Spalding Moor and several of the Cottingham manors.

Bylaws themselves were only a small part of the "customs" known and followed by the villagers. Most customary practices were probably never formally written down in the assemblies of the court baron. Such important matters as landholding practices, social status, and the powers of various social and political institutions were regulated by age-old custom more than by written laws. Nevertheless, bylaws reveal an important segment of customary practices in seventeenth-century villages, and may be used to show the continuity of life from old to New England.[52]

51. Holme-on-Spalding Moor terrier, 1716, R.III.I xxxi.16.1a, Borthwick Inst. Hist. Res.; Rental, Holme Rectory, 1678, Add. MSS 40132, fols. 87–88; Rowley terriers, 1685, 1716, 1743, R.III.I liii.1, Borthwick Inst. Hist. Res.

52. M. W. Barley, "East Yorkshire Manorial By-Laws," *Yorkshire Arch. Jour.*, XXV (1943), 37–38; Ault, "Village By-Laws by Common Consent," *Speculum*, XXIX (1954), 383–384, 391, 394; see also by Ault: *Self-Directing Activities of Village Communities in Medieval*

In its first thirty years of existence hundreds of decisions were made collectively by the inhabitants of Rowley, Massachusetts. Many of them, such as those affecting land distribution and the appointment of town officers, to mention only two, required frequent and lengthy meetings. Other communal decisions—those pertaining to personal quarrels, problems with neighboring towns, relations with the Indians, and affairs with the colony government—were made infrequently, if at all. The most careful deliberations of the town in meeting took place during the formulation of its bylaws, documents that were accorded considerable respect by the community, given high-sounding preambles, codified, and occasionally repealed by common-field village men. Unlike other town orders, these reflected deliberation and consent in opening phrases such as "It is Agreed and voated," "it was granted by the Town," or "it is ordered."

During Rowley's first four decades some eighty-one bylaws were "agreed upon by the town." Two extant records of bylaws exist for Holme during this period in addition to some for the Cottingham manors. The Holme bylaws were codified in 1650 and 1670, both containing seventy-one items with no noticeable revisions over the two decades. The chances are that no major alterations had been made in the bylaws since the departure of Holme families to New England in the late 1630s and early 1640s. Some differences existed between Holme's bylaws and those of Rowley, Massachusetts, but in the main they reflect communities faced with common problems and finding common solutions.

One-quarter of the bylaws passed in Holme dealt with water drainage, which is not surprising in a land of excessively high water tables and little natural drainage. Eight bylaws were listed that specifically concerned drainage in common-field areas, anticipating nearly every possible problem that could develop there in the course of a year. Cutting or stopping "any dike with an intension to turn the water out of its course" was prohibited; owners and occupants of grounds in Holme were obliged to "have any old water-sewers" belonging to them "sufficiently" cleaned and cleared before the end of June and to continue maintenance of them; and so on. Such regulations were occasionally restated and directed at particular areas of the manor, such as East Ings and Bursea, that were perhaps unusually lax or troublesome.

Most of the drainage bylaws, however, concerned several individuals

England, 11; "Some Early Village By-Laws," *Eng. Hist. Rev.*, XLV (1930), 231; and "Open-Field Husbandry and the Village Community," Am. Phil. Soc., *Trans.*, N.S., LV (1965), pt. vii, 40–42.

and their enclosures. These men could plant when and what they wanted on their own enclosed land, but their action or inaction might affect many others, and they had to be subject to manorial regulation. Thus, the "Occupiers of Atkins Hasholme son's close" were required to "cleanse or scour the Ditch Atkinson's betwixt the said corn and moor Croft-Hill Closes close, before midsummer-Day and so maintain the same, as often as need requires." Similarly phrased bylaws or "pains" occur almost a dozen times in the Holme codes. They should be viewed as rather firm injunctions upon the actions of individuals made by a manor in a period when the institution was in its declining days in many parts of the realm.[53]

While Rowley, Massachusetts, contained no vast ill-drained, low-level moor like Holme, it did have extensive marshland and it supervised its land in a similar manner. And like its manorial court counterpart, the town meeting rather than a group of private individuals held the locus of power in deciding the obligations and rights of all. The similarity between Holme and Rowley is particularly noticeable in the granting of land. Occasionally land grants needed the formal sanction of a town bylaw, as the "Merimak" division required in 1658. In another instance the town ordered that "no parcell of Land shall be sould or given by the towne, by way of grant to any person or persons, untill it bee twice published, at two legall town meeting[s], and granted the third towne meetinge if the towne doe see cause." Somewhat later the bylaws stated that no land would be laid out without "some express grant in writing both for place and quantyty." Rowley guarded the potential of its untapped land as much as Holme protected its cropped arable from nuisances caused by private enclosures and commoners alike.[54]

The care and installation of fencing played an important part in the bylaws of both villages, though it concerned Rowley men more often. Every conceivable harm imaginable was checked by Rowley's fencing regulations. The major culprit in unfenced fields was livestock. Therefore, fences were necessary for all house lots bordering "all Common Pastiers and Inclosures which are not laid out for house lotts," so that unauthorized animals could not stray into private crofts, or, in the other direction, into common pasture. In addition, cornfield fences had to be maintained from March to November. It even became necessary to construct a fence with neighboring Newbury along the common border of the towns. Ul-

53. Holme bylaws, Add. MSS 40137, fols. 34–40, bylaws 6, 8, 30, 47–49, 59–60; 11–18, 20, 54, 71.
54. *Recs. of Rowley*, 101, 105, 204.

timately, nearly every field in Rowley must have been fenced, which was likely to have been the case for Holme's arable fields too, where common fences were set up to keep beasts out of the corn.[55]

Livestock regulations were also plentiful in the bylaws of both Holme and Rowley, occurring with about equal frequency in each. Since raising cattle was a main livelihood in both regions, the greater part of livestock bylaws concerned this activity. The primary aim of the cattle regulations, as well as those for other livestock, was to prevent the animals from grazing in the arable fields during the planting and growing seasons. Both villages allowed cattle to graze on stubble after the completion of the harvest was officially declared. "No inhabitant . . . shall put any of goods" (that is, livestock), reads a Holme bylaw, "into the Cornefields untill such tyme as the Corne be gotten out of the same neither untill there be warning given by the Bylawmen." Rowley implicitly provided for the same grazing restrictions when it prohibited cattle from remaining in the fields after November 20, that is, the time of winter planting.[56]

The next most important series of cattle regulations concerned stinting rights, or "gates." Individuals in Rowley were allowed to graze only as many cattle as were proportionate to the number of gates or rights in common pasture they held. When "any mans Catle" were found on the Rowley commons "above his proportion at any time not haveing hiered gates of some other, he shall be liable to pay foure shillings six pence a beast." Pasture rights like these were just as common in Holme. Rowley regulations also mention common herding and the care of young cattle, while Holme bylaws are silent on these activities, although similar practices probably existed there. Horses, swine, and sheep were the subjects of numerous other regulations that were comparable to the cattle bylaws in scope and purpose. The unruly pig was a constant object of regulation in New England, and at least four bylaws were passed in the 1650s and 1660s admonishing owners to ring their animals.[57]

A remarkable similarity existed between Rowley and Holme in governmental matters. Rowley's insistence that townsmen attend meetings was foreshadowed in a Holme bylaw. The fine for nonattendance in Holme carried a penalty of 3s. 4d., whereas in Rowley the penalty was only 2s. 6d., but it may have been more strictly enforced in the latter by the judges

55. *Ibid.*, 54, 55, 61, 71–72, 99, 104–105, 130–131, 131, 146–147, 148; Holme bylaws, Add. MSS 40137, fols. 34–40, bylaws 3, 22, 45.

56. *Recs. of Rowley*, 74, 86–87, 147; Holme bylaws, 21, 23, 25–26, 33, 36, 41, 64, 68, 38.

57. *Recs. of Rowley*, 104; 55, 58, 99, 132, 148–149; 55, 87, 88, 148, *passim*; compare brief, depositions, writ, and other papers, *Sir William Constable* v. *Marmaduke Doleman*, 1619–1633, DDHA 4/19, Humberside R.O.; Holme bylaws, 41.

of "dellinquents," who were appointed yearly (as were other officers). Officers were to be respected and not hindered or interrupted while impounding goods or performing any other duty, according to a Holme bylaw. They, however, were also subject to fine for not performing their duties. Rowley had comparable statutes.[58]

Officers in both villages were given various police and regulatory powers, which were to be exercised on given occasions. The inflammability of flax and hemp and of thatched roofs was the source of several fire regulations, such as those prohibiting the drying of vegetable fibers in or near ovens and the carrying of uncovered fire, and also those governing the construction of house chimneys. "Common days work," that is, the annual, unpaid labor performed by villagers on behalf of their community, was required in both Rowley and Holme and was directed by their officers. Both communities were suspicious of strangers or outsiders and alarmed by the prospect of having to support such people if they came to settle within their respective bounds. Holme declared that "no Freeholder or any other person within the Lordship do receive any Tenant in his under-setts [that is, on a tenant's subleased land] to dwell under him, except he be known to be of an honest conversation and sufficient to live of himself with out being chargeable to the Township or Parish." Rowley prohibited any "Inhabitant or owner of any house or land in the Towne [to] bring in any Tenant to Dwell thering" without the town's consent, adopting phraseology almost identical to that used in Holme.[59]

New England settlers adapted bylaws to suit different conditions. Holme had at least five bylaws involving common of turbary, the right to gather turf or peat for fuel. Cutting turf was the exclusive privilege of those who held rights in Holme, and no turf was to be taken from the township or sold to outsiders. Rowley perpetuated this practice in its administration of wood, the community's most common source of fuel, rigorously guarding the supply even though the community was on the edge of a vast forest wilderness. No doubt a Yorkshire mind was behind the regulation prohibiting the sale of clapboard and shingle in 1660 "upon Consideration of the Decay of usefull timber." Other regulations prohibited the sale of wood outside the town and limited the cutting of timber inside the community.[60]

58. Holme bylaws, 10; 5, 32, 34, 37, 56; *Recs. of Rowley*, 57, 91; 57, 68, 94, 99, 105, 156, 204, 222.

59. Holme bylaws, 39–40; 29, 50; *Recs. of Rowley*, 91, 91–92, 58, 148.

60. Holme bylaws, 9, 19, 42, 62, 65; *Recs. of Rowley*, 104, 149, 165, 166, 199, 205. For other East Riding pains of particular interest, see Cottingham manor pains, DDBL 8/24–27, Humberside R.O., and DDKG/45, Univ. of Hull.

Infractions of the bylaws were strictly punished, judging from the court leet records of Holme for October 17, 1670, and September 12, 1671. The first court handed down sixty-four separate penalties, with total fines of £7 18s. 6d., conservatively about 5d. per family head. For the most part fines amounted to either 3s. 4d. or 6d. The first twenty cases involved men who had allowed their livestock to intrude upon the ox pasture, and they were subject to fines from 1 to 4s. Twelve men had neglected to clear out their ditches, and each man was fined 6s., except one individual who was penalized 2s. 6d. Failure to ring swine resulted in eleven fines of 6d. each. Misuse of the commons, apparently for "lodging" livestock, involved a much heavier penalty of 3s. 4d. per offense in nineteen out of twenty-two cases, and 10s. for the remaining three. One villager was fined 3s. 4d. for plowing in the cornfield after All Saints Day. Several penalties were even more severe: a "Common destroyer of the corne field" was charged 10s., and for trespassing on the common, presumably by breaking down a common-field fence, the fine was 6s. 8d.[61]

The second court, held a year later, occasioned a smaller amount of fines, only £3 12s., but a wider variety of infractions. Nine additional types of offenses were cited, indicating that the bylawmen of Holme had been diligent the previous six months in their enforcement of the body of manor ordinances. Several cases involved violent misdemeanors, including an assault and a "bloody and fray," in which the parties were fined £1 and 3s. 4d., respectively. The most frequently cited offense (seven times) was failure to have a draft horse for common days work. For leaving animals on the common, four individuals were fined 3s. 4d. each. Trespassing on cornfields was a common offense this year as was tethering animals in forbidden areas. Two people were fined for taking turves from the common, another for plowing away the common "backs," or balks, and two men were found guilty of making "afrount to the fore man and his fellows."[62] Courts in Holme were apparently held consistently twice a year and just as regularly upheld manorial bylaws. The court of February 24, 1671, accounted for fifty-five offenses and collected £4 3d. Six courts were held in 1644, 1645, and 1646, and awarded a total of £12 1s. 6d. in penalties.[63]

Such a meticulous and seemingly effective system of bylaw enforcement was not, however, limited to Holme. It was the case in all those East

61. Add. MSS 40137, fols. 41–42. The per capita cost of fines is derived, in part, from population figures in Tanner MSS, vol. 150, fol. 37.
62. Add. MSS 40137, fols. 48–49.
63. *Ibid.*, fol. 14, *passim.*

Riding manors for which records have been found. The manor of Cottingham Richmond, for instance, which was probably one of the smallest in the Riding, according to a 1608 survey contained only twenty-seven freeholders and four leaseholders, but no fee farmers or copyholders. The manor held courts twice a year at Easter and Michaelmas and exacted from its inhabitants an average of £1 6s. 8d. per session during the years 1652 to 1679. In the year 1651 it recorded £13 13s. 6d. in fines.[64]

The bylawmen of Cottingham and Holme had counterparts in Rowley, New England, known as overseers. They were probably the most effective and certainly the most active officers in Rowley, yet their position and duties do not seem to have existed in most other Massachusetts communities. Enforcement of bylaws in Rowley became so time-consuming that the town was forced to assign a number of overseers every year to the specific task of inspecting the various sections of the town and some of its major fields, in addition to the small settlements, or districts, outside the town of Rowley but within the township. Consequently a large number of men served in this position over a short period of time.[65]

Like the bylawmen, the overseers strictly enforced village orders, as several extant accounts reveal. The overseers collected £2 15s. 2d. in fines during 1660, most of which involved either "delinquent" or "defective" establishment of bounds by lot owners at New Plain. In 1665 the overseers brought fifty-six charges (and collected £4 18s. 7d. in penalties) for "want of gates," presumably, that is, against individuals having more livestock on the commons than they were entitled to. Defective fencing was, however, the chief concern in most of the records that have survived. In four separate years this type of infraction accounted for fines in excess of £2.[66]

One contrast between the two communities, however, was Holme's protection of the lord's manorial rights. The inhabitants warned "that none within This Lordshipp shall fish or fowl but such as [have] leave from the Lord." In two other instances the manorial court prohibited villagers from plowing the lord's wastes or common balks, and in another regulation they prohibited use of the lord's earmark or brand on their own cattle; still, these were not extraordinarily broad rights granted to the lord and might well have applied to a neighbor's property.[67] Even so, the

64. An Abreviate of the Survey of His Majesty's Manors in the East and North Ridings of the County of York, by Aaron Rathbone, A.D. 1608, Lansdown MSS, vol. 169, fol. O.S., 86, N.S., 109, British Library; DDBL/8/31, Univ. of Hull.

65. *Recs. of Rowley*, 90, 95, 107, 118, 146, 156, 159, 165, 200.

66. *Ibid.*, 106, 145, 163, 168–169.

67. Holme bylaws, 4, 27, 46.

significant difference in America was that no such special rights were leg-islated by the Rowley village assembly.

Seventeenth-century East Yorkshire villages like Holme typified pat-terns of community life and local law and custom in the open-field regions of England. The physical conditions of the countryside encouraged local villagers to act in common in their agricultural pursuits. Through the manorial court system men were able to enact regulations and supervise their enforcement with bylaws passed by common consent. Common-field agriculture required the assistance of nearly all village men, which led to widespread officeholding. Local government in these areas was still largely unaffected by the great changes in agriculture and population that were taking place in other parts of the realm. Some enclosure had oc-curred, but it was relatively small. Landholdings for the most part were intermixed, and movements toward land consolidation, or brisk sales in the land market, were still rare. The structure of agricultural production remained unchanged, reflecting the type of farming to which people in the Vale of York and the Wolds had been accustomed for several centuries. As long as these patterns remained, so did their complementary governmen-tal practices. As the Barkers, Crosbys, Elithorps, and Brighams recreated the society and economy of their Old World home in Massachusetts, they also continued the customs of local government with which they were fa-miliar. In coming to New England they never left their lands in Holme.

3 A Tale of Two Towns

 HE wold and vale areas of the East Riding, York-shire, contrast sharply with the countryside of central Norfolk. Lacking the austere beauty of the Wolds and the expanse of the ill-drained lowland moors, the middle Norfolk region contains gently rolling hills dotted with many small villages. Mellow red roof tiles, arresting Dutch-style step gables, and the indigenous cracked flint and limestone cement used in the construction of churches and other structures all serve to give the area a distinctive appearance. It is a region in which both architecture and religion were influenced by Continental sources.

Spreading in every direction from present-day Hingham, Norfolk, are small villages overshadowed by churches that are often great monuments in now shrunken or nonexistent communities. From the bounds of Hingham itself as many as a dozen churches are visible, although several are now isolated and deteriorating. Seventeenth-century sources indicate that the area encompassed by the Norwich and Norfolk dioceses contained a very large concentration of parishes, compared with most areas of the country of equivalent size. The conspicuousness of the village church seems to have been matched by an equally important role for the parish in the community, or so appears to have been the case in Hingham.[1] In the New World also, emigrants from Hingham set up a "town" government based on parish organization. Still dependent upon common agricultural regulations as in the Midlands, yet situated in a region in which the manor no longer functioned in activities essential to the local villager, the people of Hingham, Massachusetts, set up a network of relationships in law, government, economy, and society that duplicated their English background. In coming to America there was much less of a "revolution in the systems of social and economic status" than has been formerly thought and hardly "a staggering number of changes."[2]

1. Roland G. Usher, ed., *The Presbyterian Movement in the Reign of Queen Elizabeth as Illustrated by the Minute Book of the Dedham Classis, 1562–1589*, Camden Society, *Publications*, 3d Ser., VIII (London, 1905), xxv; Tanner MSS, vol. 178, fols. 45–50. On the conspicuousness of the parish in Norfolk, see Peter Laslett, *The World We Have Lost* (New York, 1965), 58.
2. Powell, *Puritan Village*, 140, 83.

Hingham was not a very prominent English parish, though it was considerably larger than average. It was the head town of a deanery containing forty-three parishes, but this fact was of waning importance by the seventeenth century. Located about eighteen miles west of Norwich, its population at the beginning of the seventeenth century numbered five hundred communicants, or about eight hundred inhabitants in all (see map on p. 118). Although major market towns were much larger, contemporary documents refer to Hingham as a marketing center for the surrounding countryside and occasionally even call it a "Borowe."[3]

In addition to people from old Hingham, the New England Hingham community was settled by others from the surrounding Norfolk towns of Wymondham, Attleborough, Bridgham, and Hapton Hall.[4] Although geography and soil varied widely throughout Norfolk, Henry Spelman, a contemporary, described only two regions: "the parte of it toward the Sea and mutch of the reste Westward is champian: the other parte toward Suffolk, woodland and pasture grounde." Hingham and surrounding communities were on the fringe of these two agricultural regions, "betwixt the grazing and the Corn parts," and shared characteristics of both. Like the wood-pasture region this area was "susteined cheifely by Grazinge, by Deyries, and by rearing of Cattell," while on the other hand it normally produced sufficient quantities of grain (though few sheep), as in the champion country to the north.[5]

Although Hingham usually grew enough grain for its needs, it was vulnerable to times of crop failure and other natural catastrophes associated with the "woody part of Norfolk." The dense population of the wood-pasture country only exacerbated hard times when they came. This region supported many more small husbandmen than did the champion country. Here the small subsistence farmer possessed a larger holding than his counterpart in the open fields of the north where large landowners and

3. Laslett, *World We Have Lost*, 54–55; Francis Blomefield, *An Essay Towards a Topographical History of the County of Norfolk, Containing a Description of the Towns, Villages, and Hamlets, with the Foundations of Monasteries, Churches, Chapels, Chantries, and Other Religious Buildings . . .*, 11 vols. (London, 1805–1810), II, 424; W. G. Hoskins, "The Population of an English Village, 1086–1801: A Study of Wigston Magna," in Hoskins, ed., *Provincial England: Essays in Social and Economic History* (London, 1963), 187.

4. The English places of origin for the 157 Hingham, Massachusetts, settlers who came prior to 1640 are listed in Appendix 2 of this volume.

5. Henry Spelman, "Reasons agst a General Sending of Corne to the Marketts in the Champion Parte of Norfolke," T. S. Cogswell, communicator, *Norfolk Archaeology: or Miscellaneous Tracts Relating to the Antiquities of the County of Norfolk*, XX (1921), 11. For a description of the champion region to the north of the Hingham district, see K. J. Allison, "The Sheep-Corn Husbandry of Norfolk in the Sixteenth and Seventeenth Centuries," *Ag. Hist. Rev.*, V (1957), 12–30.

large-scale capitalistic farming predominated. Favorable as the size of his holding might have been for the wood-pasture farmer, this region swelled in population, creating social instability and insecurity in times of scarcity. Forehoe hundred, for instance, where both Hingham and Wymondham were situated, was among the most populous rural areas in the county judging by the royal rates collected in the late 1620s.[6]

In addition to dairying, rearing, and grain-growing activities, Norfolk farmers augmented their small incomes by taking up home "industries." In some regions these would have included woodcraft or iron production, but in the Norfolk woods where most inhabitants were dairy and cattle-men, "a greate many" were also "hand crafte men . . . [who] lyve by dress-ing and combinge of woolle, carding, spinning, weaving etc."[7]

Agricultural Structure

The effects of a vulnerable subsistent life in old Hingham on religion and migration in the decades before 1640 merit further discussion else-where.[8] Yet despite all the uncertainties of this English economic system it was reproduced intact in new Hingham. In Hingham, Norfolk, the economy consisted primarily of dairying, which was supplemented by growing grain on the limited amount of arable land to feed livestock and for local consumption. Nearly all the homes for which we have invento-ries, regardless of size, had a dairy room or buttery, including churns, pails, and other such equipment. The lack of agricultural equipment in many inventories suggests that, as in common-field areas, extensive shar-ing of needed farm equipment was customary. Clothmaking filled the spare hours allowed by tending cattle and provided extra income. A great number of inventories refer to yarn, wool, and hemp. Some state that there were "29 pounds yarne" worth £20, or "34 grose of woolsy" for £25 10s., but many estates list more humble entries, such as Margaret Beale's £3 1s. in wool and yarn.[9]

6. Walter Rye, ed., *State Papers Relating to Musters, Beacons, Shipmoney, etc., in Norfolk, from 1626 Chiefly to the Beginning of the Civil War* (Norwich, England, 1907), 21, 131, 132, 205; Yearly Valuation of Every Town and Hundred, 1626, Tanner MSS, vol. 189, fol. 8b. Unfor-tunately no ecclesiastical census survives for the area such as the one for 1603 in the Harleian MSS, vol. 595, British Library, or the Compton census of parish communicants like that compiled in 1676.
7. Spelman, "Reasons agst a General Sending of Corne," *Norfolk Arch.*, XX (1921), 11.
8. For a discussion of these factors, see chap. 6, below.
9. Eric Kerridge, *The Agricultural Revolution* (London, 1967), 85–86; Inventory Boxes 50A/4 and 51/71, Norfolk and Norwich Record Office, Central Library, Norwich, Norfolk.

The modest estate of John James, a yeoman who died in 1662 with an inventory valued at only £45 16s., provides an outline of the agricultural structure of this Norfolk community. James's estate included 4 cows and 2 bullocks, 9 sheep, 1 mare, hay in the barn, a plow and cart, a cart harness, poultry, a chamber with grain valued at £3 10s., and cheeses worth £3. Estates valued at ten times as much, left by men not primarily engaged in agriculture, were similarly distributed. When Edmund Dey, clerk of the church, died in 1667, his goods included 80 cheeses, 1 horse and mare, 3 milch cows, 3 heifers, a calf, some swine, grain and hay worth £28, some wood in the yard, carts and a plow with implements, and some malt.[10]

A fairly distinct picture emerges, then, from seventeenth-century Hingham, Norfolk, inventories. Most farmers in the area devoted their attention to dairying and rearing cattle, though the largest herds in Hingham, as judged from extant records, were never over a dozen head. There was also some interest in breeding horses, as is evident from the inventory of John Cowper, Jr., who had raised ten before his death in 1617. A number of farmers owned sheep, but they were never raised to the same extent as in the sheep-corn region of northern Norfolk. Pig raising and poultry keeping were important sidelines in the area.[11]

Several different grains were grown. The Hingham "Town Book" of the late seventeenth century refers yearly to the prices of four crops, presumably the four grown there, but possibly the most commonly imported or a combination of the two. These included barley, wheat, rye, peas (both gray and white), and oats as well as vetches, roughly in that order of importance. All are mentioned in local inventories of individuals who died during or just after the growing season. Robert Constable had 1 coomb (approximately 4 bushels) of wheat, 5 bushels of barley, and 10 coombs of malt worth £5 in his corn chamber, and Edward Lincoln, linen weaver, left 14 coombs of barley, and 5 each of wheat, rye, and white peas, altogether worth £11 15s. Wealthy Francis Bubbin had in his corn chamber 4 coombs of wheat, 2 of "mistlyn," 7 of malt, and 6 bushels of gray peas. Hay was a constant item in estates as well, as it was used to supplement other winter feed for dairy herds.[12]

By far the most arresting items in the Hingham inventories are the listings of wood and timber. Even the lowliest of estates contained "wood in yard" or "timber in wood house." A great variety of wood was available in the region, including hazel and oak as well as highly sought after ash,

10. Inventories, 55A/122, 52B/74, Norfolk and Norwich R.O.
11. *Ibid.*, 28/119.
12. *Ibid.*, 36/119, 61A/76, 50A/4.

which was used by coopers to make herring barrels for the fishing industry along the Norfolk coast. The lumber was readily sold and easily transported to various points by river and coastal vessels. The river Yare, which flows through Norwich on its way to Yarmouth, has its headwaters near Cranworth, only a few miles northwest of Hingham. As we shall see, in the New England Hingham such commercial uses of wood became a central concern, one which led to more town ordinances and controversy than any other single issue in the early years.[13]

Inventories filed in Massachusetts reveal the essential continuity of the structure of Norfolk agriculture in the New World. Hingham, Massachusetts, remained basically a dairying town. Oxen replaced Suffolk Punches as draft animals, but this was due in large part to the unusual labor required to cultivate heavy virgin soils. Raising pigs and rearing cattle were important secondary interests in Hingham, Massachusetts, as they had been in Norfolk; weaving remained a vital part-time occupation; and the kinds of grain produced included all those used in old Hingham except for white and gray peas, which were usually replaced by Indian corn.[14]

The predominance of dairying and rearing activities is apparent in several town regulations in new Hingham. As early as 1640 the town ordered that "there shall be no *Tree* or *Trees* cut, or felled upon the *Clay*, upon the *Payne* of *twenty shillings*, to be *levied* to the use of the Town, because all those Trees are to be preserved for the shading of *Cattle* in the summer time." Several years earlier, when land at Nantascus was being prepared for division among the proprietors, the distribution was made "according to the number of names—having some respect to men's stock—*that is to say*—three acres to a person—and of all other stock of lesser cattle, or goods proportionable as it amounteth to a Cow—be it more or less, being a rule nearest the rule of the word of God, as far as we are empowered." Later on, cattle became a significant variable in the determination of town rates. In addition, land improved for "corn," or broken arable, was rated at only thirty shillings per acre, whereas improved salt or freshwater meadow used for livestock was valued twice as high.[15]

13. For a general description of Norfolk agriculture, see Thirsk, "Farming Regions of England," 46–49.

14. See generally, Suffolk County Probate Records, II, 117–119, IV, 29–31, 62–63, and VI, 227–278, Suffolk County Probate Office, First Floor, Old Suffolk County Courthouse, Boston, Mass.

15. Hingham, Massachusetts, Town Records (originals), in 2 MS vols. (I, 1635–1655, and II, 1657–1720), I, Feb. 20, 1641, Mar. 5, 1638, II, Oct. 16, 1677, Town Clerk's Office, Hingham, Mass. In Norfolk's central region, too, pastureland generally rented for a higher price than plowland. See J. Spratt, "Agrarian Conditions in Norfolk and Suffolk, 1600–1650" (M.A. thesis, University of London, 1935), 119.

Inventories from new Hingham show the importance of dairying in the local economy, though it was supplemented by other activities in much the same way as in Norfolk. John Farrow, whose estate was valued at only £78 14s., left 1 ox worth £3, 3 cows at £7, 2 swine at £1 4s., some "lynnen and wollen" cloth at £2 10s., and lumber worth £1 14s. Another smaller inventory, that of Margaret Johnson, a recent widow, contained 2 cows, 2 shoats, some flaxen yarn, and pork, butter, suet, wheat, and cheese as household provisions. Thomas Thaxter's larger inventory of £213 18s. 4d. included 2 oxen, 4 cows, 2 three-year-old steers, 1 two-year-old heifer, 4 calves, 8 "milch gootes," 2 fat hogs, 6 shoats, 20 bushels of wheat, "2 Remnants of woolen cloth," 3 bushels of rye, 7 bushels of peas, some Indian corn and meal, and some pork worth £3 10s. that was for household consumption or for sale.[16]

New Hingham may have included more "corn land" or arable fields than old Hingham, which made it easier for New World settlers to supply their needs, but with the exception of some open-field areas granted to settlers in the first divisions, new Hingham did not contain extensive arable areas. The early inhabitants were more interested in meadow land or in salt or freshwater marsh, as the descriptive names of these numerous early grants indicate. Later, from the 1650s through the 1670s, grants of land were almost exclusively for timber rights, and a concerted effort never seems to have been made among the proprietors to acquire additional acreage of arable land in the seventeenth century.

Stephen Lincoln, who came from Wymondham in Norfolk, left an estate characteristic of this dairying economy. He owned no arable land, neither did he have a plow or oxen, but he raised 4 cows and a yearling, 1 mare colt, 5 ewes, 1 ram and a lamb, 3 hogs, and 2 pigs, and when he died must have just purchased a supply of salt marsh hay valued at £4 10s. for the winter of 1658–1659. In addition, he left a quantity of woolen cloth valued at £8, some sheep's wool, cotton wool and yarn, some stored cheeses, and a valuable collection of carpenter's tools. Men like Lincoln, while dependent upon others for the products of the arable, found independence and flexibility in pursuits ranging from cheesemaking and clothmaking to carpentry.[17]

Lincoln was not alone in retaining the weaving habits of the Norfolk woods, where this occupation often supplemented the strong dairying and rearing economy. There was a rough parity between the Old and New

16. Suffolk Probate Recs., X, 83, III, 180, and II, 117–119.
17. Ibid., III, 131.

World communities in the numbers engaged in this part-time livelihood. At least three men in Hingham devoted most of their time to weaving and owned spinning wheels, pairs of cards, and supplies of wool, cotton, and sometimes flax in addition to finished cloth. Two out of three Hingham inventories mention more modest supplies or equipment, particularly "woolen and linnen yearne" as in Edward Wilder's, but some contain more ambitious lists, such as Nicholas Jacob's 14 pounds of wool or John Tucker's 4 yards of "searge" and 12½ yards of "holland." [18]

As in Hingham, Norfolk, a significant portion of the local economy was devoted to the sale of wood and lumber by inhabitants from their own lands. Samuel Maverick characterized Hingham as principally a supplier of Boston "with wood, timber, leather and board" as well as trees for masts. Edward Johnson also visited Hingham in the early years and stated that its "people have much profited themselves by transporting Timber,, Plank and Mast for Shipping to the Town of Boston, as also Ceder and Pine-board to supply the wants of other Townes, and also to remote parts, even as far as Barbadoes." Although inventories do not indicate the whole scope of this activity in Hingham, they do show some of its aspects. Thomas Andrews's estate included £12 in wages due him from the county for a load of cedar bolts, while Nicholas Jacob's inventory had an entry referring to "board wood and a boat of Barke" valued at £5 4s. In addition, the town records show, for instance, that in 1638 Thomas Nichols sold 3 acres of "planting land" to Ralph Smith "for *five hundred* of merchantable Cedar *boards*." The underlying significance of the timber and lumber trade in Hingham, as we shall see later, was more important than these scattered entries indicate. [19]

The Land System

The position of Hingham, Norfolk, halfway between two distinct forms of agricultural production, also affected its land system. In simplest terms the landholding pattern of central Norfolk contained elements of both the Midland open-field system, such as that found in Rowley and Yorkshire,

---

18. *Ibid.*, V, 272–273, VIII, 199, III, 83–84, IV, 29–31.

19. Maverick, "A Briefe Diescription of New England and the Severall Townes therein," Mass. Hist. Soc., *Procs.*, 2d Ser., I (1884–1885), 239; Jameson, ed., *Johnson's Wonder-Working Providence*, 116; Suffolk Probate Recs., VIII, 198, III, 83–84; Hingham Mass. Town Recs., I, Feb. 1, 1639.

and the enclosed consolidated farmsteads of the woodlands in Suffolk and Essex to the south. Village land surveys in many parts of central Norfolk reveal this characteristic blend. In Horstead and Lessingham, Norfolk, for example, the usual "strips" of open-field agriculture had become field blocks or "pieces," as they were called, varying in size from 5 acres to 1 rood. In the wood-pasture country of Forncett, as early as the fourteenth century "the rolls contain no clear indications that there were within the vill three great fields," as in the Midland system; "'campi' are mentioned, but they were numerous and small." Therefore, the central Norfolk pattern typically consisted of blocks of land, which were tiny and unconsolidated by the standards of farmsteads in Suffolk and Essex, yet small enough, and often roughly defined and scattered enough in "fields" to demand some sort of common regulation and supervision, though not necessarily in the Midland open-field manner.[20]

The 1633 Hingham glebe terrier highlights some important features of the central Norfolk land pattern of small holdings in "fields." The glebe contained twenty-three parcels of land, excluding the parsonage and its 6-acre lot, ranging in size from a plot of 3 roods to one of 3 acres. The average size of each lot was only about seven-eighths of an acre. Some lands did lie in "fields," such as Church Field where several were "newly inclosed," or in West Field, but as the enclosures in them suggest, the agricultural significance of the "field" as such was diminishing here, and undoubtedly it had been abandoned altogether in other parts of the town. In fact, the chief roads of the township appear to be the determining element in the location of much glebe land, rather than positions in "fields." In a great many instances, the small Hingham glebe plots were parcels, often "pightles," in various closes or crofts—both enclosed areas—in such places as Woodcock, White, and Shoemaker Close. In addition, there was some apparent consolidation as a small number of parcels abutted each other, and several others were "lyeing nyghe" one another in fields. Possibly land owned by individuals was more consolidated than the church glebe, since many of the closes were given the name of a contemporary rather than that of a predecessor on the land. Nevertheless, the lands of old Hingham residents were also dispersed. Peter Sharpe's lands adjoined the glebe parcels throughout the village—at the Sharp Close, Dumes

20. W. J. Corbett, "Elizabethan Village Surveys," Royal Historical Society, *Transactions*, N.S., XI (1897), 67–87; Howard Levi Gray, *English Field Systems* (Cambridge, Mass., 1915), 307–334; Kerridge, *Agricultural Revolution*, 84–85, 87–88; Frances Gardiner Davenport, *The Economic Development of a Norfolk Manor, 1086–1565* (Cambridge, 1906), 27.

Close, "Five Roodes," and three other unspecified locations—as did the lands of Robert Cooper, Henry and Richard Lincoln, and Robert Longe.[21]

In sum, in seventeenth-century Hingham, Norfolk, there were a large number of small scattered enclosures, each of which was probably further divided up into enclosed plots by a small group of men rather than an equitable distribution among most villagers, leaving most of the countryside, as contemporaries remarked, with a distinctly wooded appearance. Quite likely, men who owned land in each close got together from time to time to adopt regulatory orders for the land by private agreement. The manor or town could intervene in the activities of these men in their enclosures in a general way if it became necessary, and undoubtedly used its authority over individual farmers to regulate the use of the common grazing lands and wastes. Since commons and wastes were not uniformly enclosed until 1780, a century and a half after the Hingham emigrants left, there must still have been some common regulation of grazing areas and arable fields in the 1630s.[22] This reluctance to change was also reflected in the inactive state of land transactions in the town as judged by surviving feet of fines (conveyancing) records.[23] Land was being bought and sold at a slow rate, not dissimilar to that of contemporary Yorkshire. Consequently, Hingham's hybrid land system remained stable and unaffected throughout the seventeenth century.

From the first day of which we have record, June 18, 1635, land in Hingham, New England, was distributed in a haphazard pattern of small parcels. It was never divided into large open fields with strips where all the proprietors could receive their appointed share. Except for the house lots, the original "planting" lots, and the "Great Lots," which were soon expended, no sizable number of inhabitants received land from the same "fields." Even in these "lots" there was not an equitable division as in open fields like those of Rowley. Only eighteen men received grants in the

---

21. Hingham terriers, 1633, nos. 35 and 104, Norwich Diocesan Terriers—Hingham, Norfolk and Norwich R.O. Compare also the Hingham terrier for 1613, no. 105, which reveals a similar pattern.

22. "An Act for Dividing and Inclosing the Commons and Waste Lands within the Parish of Hingham, in the County of Norfolk," Private Acts, 21 George III, 1780–1781. There was some local enclosure in the 16th century. See I. S. Leadam, "The Inquisition of 1517. Inclosures and Evictions," Royal Hist. Soc., *Trans.*, N.S., VII (1893), 127–218. For examples of the interest shown in livestock by the "Town" or vestry meeting in Hingham, Norfolk, see the meetings of 1680–1682 in the Hingham Town Account Book, 1660–1752, MS 9935, Norfolk and Norwich R.O.

23. Rye Index to Norfolk Fines, Charles I to 1650, Colman and Rye Libraries, Central Library, Norwich, Norfolk.

"Great Lots," for instance, and not all of the original proprietors ever received land there or even in comparable arable fields elsewhere.

Instead, most parcels of land were segments of relatively small lots found widely distributed throughout the township. These lots were subdivided into anything from a few to as many as twenty pieces of property. The place names for these odd-sized enclosures convey some impression of how they were originally appropriated by the settlers. On June 12, 1637, several men received from the town the "fresh meadow as you go to Weymouth myll," while others on the same day were given portions of "a little meadow lying to the north west of the fresh meadow going to Weymouth Mill" or portions of "Salt marsh, at Lawford's Liking as you go up to the Strayts Pond, in the South side of the river, that run[s] east and west." It would appear from these and other examples that Hingham men were expected to petition the town for scattered areas of land wherever they might be found throughout the unclaimed portion of the township.

It is not surprising that the old Hingham patterns of land division were followed in Hingham, Massachusetts. Some of the initial land grants, such as the Nantascus division of March 5, 1638, were made under the direction of townsmen Anthony Eames, Edmund Hobart, Sr., Samuel Ward, Thomas Hammond, Edmund Hobart, Jr., and Joseph Andrews, all "*deputed* by the Town, and *body* of *Freemen.*" Two-thirds of these men were from old Hingham or other parts of East Anglia. By 1640, when the "Conyhasset" divisions were made, only two of the nine-man committee in charge of the task can be identified as having come from outside this eastern English region. The town, however, was never as careful in supervising the allotment of land to all settlers, like Rowley did, as it was for groups. Townsmen usually sought out small pockets of desirable land for themselves and petitioned the town for ownership. It was assumed that men entitled to land would receive it "in a place convenient, as soon as a place can be discovered." [24]

Unlike Rowley, Massachusetts, with its distinctive English Midland system of noncontiguous strips equally proportioned among the fields, Hingham land patterns showed no such evidence of rationalization. In Rowley, in addition to house lots, there was a total of twenty different sections of land in various parts of town—planting fields, meadow, pasture, and marsh—divided up among inhabitants. In Hingham there were probably three dozen or so ill-defined areas dispersed around the township, ranging from the relatively large "Great Lots" located near the house

24. Hingham Mass. Town Recs., I, July 6, 1640, Aug. 14, Oct. 8, 1637, Mar. 5, 1638.

lots, where each holding averaged over 10 acres, to such odd and tiny areas as "upland upon wear neck" containing five proprietors with parcels ranging from 2 to 5 acres, and to even smaller parcels such as "fresh meadows of Glad Tidings Rock," "Great Cove Salt Marsh," and "Turkey Meadows." In short, the landholding system in Hingham, New England, during the first decades of settlement had some of the characteristics of the open-field system, particularly in the size of holdings in various scattered divisions, but at the same time it showed signs of the pattern common to the neighboring English counties of Suffolk and Essex, where holdings were not distributed in orderly field arrangements and where parcels typically were irregularly shaped enclosures.

The size of landholdings in Hingham, New England, before 1670 varied widely. Some 146 individuals received lands in the original divisions and most grants were rather modest. The average holding in Hingham was 22½ acres, while the median figure was 15 acres. The average grant in Hingham was about half again as large as the usual holding in central Norfolk in the early seventeenth century, but new Hingham was never overcrowded with small freeholders as was the Norfolk countryside during this period. Nevertheless, the size of the holdings indicates that no "revolution of status" accompanied the crossing of the Atlantic by Hingham settlers. The top 10 percent of the landholders in new Hingham controlled about 36 percent of all the land granted, while the top 25 percent held 61 percent. The bottom half, by contrast, held little more than 13 percent of the total. Land was more evenly distributed here, however, than in sharply stratified Rowley, Massachusetts.[25] Furthermore, study of the land records reveals that these Massachusetts settlers, like their Norfolk counterparts, were not greatly inclined to value land for its commercial potential or as a speculative investment. In contrast to men in other Massachusetts towns, the Hingham settlers never made an absorbing ambition of consolidating their widely separated landholdings or of selling off unwanted or unused portions for more profitable parcels.[26]

25. Compiled from Hingham Mass. Town Recs., I and II, including all grants from the original house lots to the Dec. 1670 division. For the size of holdings in central Norfolk, see in the P.R.O.: Wymondham Survey, 6 James I (1610), Augmentation Office, Miscellaneous Books, no. 360, fols. 43–92; East Dereham Survey, 5 James I (1609), Land Revenue, Miscellaneous Books, vol. 201, fols. 186–271; Parliamentary Surveys, Norfolk: no. 10, East Dereham, no. 19, Wymondham alias Wyndham (Survey and Rental); and also Spratt, "Agrarian Conditions in Norfolk and Suffolk," 198.

26. Examples are few, and the size of acreage in Hingham land sales between Hingham men was small, but see for the years to 1662, Suffolk Deeds, Liber I (Boston, 1880), 70, 89, 103, 133, 221–222, Liber II (Boston, 1883), 103, 161–162, 255–256, Liber III (Boston, 1885), 63–64, 372–373, 376, 396, 400–401, 401–403, 403–405, 470–472.

The men who settled Hingham, Massachusetts, created an agricultural economy remarkably like that they had left behind in old Hingham. Both economies were devoted to dairying and to part-time clothmaking. There was a self-sufficient amount of grain growing in both towns and considerable interest in selling timber. Even though the geography of Massachusetts would have permitted the New World farmers to shift their agrarian activities toward the raising of more diversified livestock and crops, they clung to the practices of their former Norfolk home. Secondly, the Massachusetts community perpetuated with extraordinary fidelity the land system that characterized central Norfolk in the early seventeenth century. Along with this remarkably well-transplanted economic structure came institutions of government that were equally durable.

Leadership Patterns

The government of new Hingham, no less than its economy, differed sharply from that of new Rowley. The widespread officeholding of the Yorkshire-derived community contrasted with the oligarchy of leading families found in new Hingham and in its parent Norfolk community. In addition, the settlers from the East Anglian community did not hold the manor in as high regard as those from Holme and Rowley did. In the wood-pasture region of Norfolk manorial institutions never exercised the same influence over agriculturalists that they did in open-field country. East Anglia nurtured a different institution, the town or parish, which increasingly directed the activities of men in that area. When Hingham men established their community on Massachusetts Bay in the 1630s, they brought with them notions of "townsmanship" not known by the Yorkshire men. The lack of strong manorial control, the practice of farming techniques different from those followed in Yorkshire, and the consciousness of the market community as a "town" in the East Anglian sense were all factors that promoted differences in government.

One of the most apparent distinctions between the two English regions was the control of government by a smaller number of men in both Hinghams. For the period between 1660 and 1690 we have a fairly complete listing of Hingham, Norfolk, parish officers and good records of selectmen's elections in Hingham, Massachusetts. A comparison shows how closely men in the New World community carried over Old World assumptions of leadership.

Two churchwardens were annually chosen in Hingham, Norfolk, so that in the period from 1660 to 1690 (excluding 1681), there were 61 positions (including one created by a resignation) to be filled. A total of 47 men served, 35 for only one year, 10 for two, and 2 for three years. Thus, about 25 percent of the men controlled 40 percent of the positions.

During this same period there were 129 positions to be filled among the overseers of the poor, the other important English parish office. Normally, 4 were chosen each year, although the number was occasionally increased to 6. In all, 97 men served, 76 for only a year, 16 for two, 1 for three, 3 for four, and 1 for six years. Taken separately, the overseers, who managed the largest share of town finances each year, do not appear to have been dominated by a small group of townsmen. But when the names of overseers and churchwardens are matched, several patterns develop. The top 10 percent of the most frequently elected individuals to both offices filled 48 out of 190 positions, or 25 percent of the total. The top 25 percent controlled 93 positions, or 49 percent. If constableships and certain manorial positions were also included, even greater consolidation of officeholding would be apparent.[27]

There was also a strong correlation between the number of terms an individual served and his economic position. Unfortunately, few tax records for seventeenth-century Hingham, including the Hearth Tax returns of the 1660s and 1670s, have survived. However, one record for 1689 that lists 118 ratepayers does exist. Of course, the list does not include all those who held office between 1660 and 1690, but of the officeholders listed, nearly all of them were among the top 25 percent of the town in rated wealth (see table 7). The rankings of these men would have been even higher if some of those at the top of the rate list, such as the lord of a manor and the rector, plus gentlemen of property who did not reside in Hingham were excluded.

One other pattern emerges from a study of the leadership of Hingham, England. To men in this town and perhaps other towns of similar type and size in seventeenth-century England, a local office or position may have been almost as much a proprietary right as it was a vehicle to promote the common good. Fathers were replaced by their sons, and sons by their sons. Counting last names alone, some 51 men related by name held 88 positions as overseers or churchwardens from 1660 to 1690, filling about 45 percent of all positions available for those offices.

27. Compiled from the Hingham [Norfolk] Town Account Book, 1660–1752. Hingham manor records after 1690 are located at Payne, Hicks Beach and Co., Solicitors, 10 New Square, Lincoln's Inn, London, W.C. 2. A rough check of manor officers elected in the decade after 1690 suggests that they were the same names that appear as parish officers in the Town Account Book.

TABLE 7. *Tax Ranking of the Most Frequently Elected Churchwardens and Overseers in Hingham, Norfolk, 1660–1690*

	Years Served	Ranking[a] in the 1689 Tax Assessment
Samuel Pyke	6	14
Barnaby Parlet	5	17
Isaac Fison	4	11
Samuel Gilman	4	21
John Amyas, Gentleman	4	6
John Duffield	4	29
Henry Andrews	4	36

Note:
[a] The tax assessment listed a total of 118 ratepayers.

Source:
Compiled from the Hingham [Norfolk] Town Account Book, 1660–1752, Norfolk and Norwich Record Office, Central Library, Norwich, Norfolk.

This relation between family connections and leadership was one of the most clearly transmitted presumptions carried to new Hingham. In the years prior to 1686 there had been forty separate elections for selectmen in the new town, accounting for a total of 226 positions. Three families alone held more than a third (35 percent) of all the positions. These included the Hobarts (Edmund, Sr., Edmund, Jr., Joshua, Josiah, David, and Thomas), the Cushings (Matthew I, Matthew II, and Daniel), and the Beals (Joshua, Caleb, John, Sr., Nathaniel, and Jeremiah) who accounted for 78 positions. In all, 39 men of the total of 67 chosen as selectmen were related to each other as father, son, or grandson. These closely related kin groups accounted for over 58 percent of all the men chosen and 64 percent of all the positions available.[28]

In other Massachusetts towns, even those settled primarily by men from nearby Suffolk or Essex, there was never such a close relationship between family and officeholding. Ipswich and Watertown may have had fewer men holding more offices for longer periods of time, but no large percentage of these men was known to be directly related to each other or to share a common last name. In Watertown, for instance, only 28 of the 76 men chosen as selectmen before 1686, or 37 percent, were so related,

28. Compiled from Hingham Mass. Town Recs., I and II, *passim*.

while in Ipswich the number was even lower, 18 out of 65, or 28 percent, during the same period.[29]

"Proprietary" family claims on leadership certainly encouraged consolidation of officeholding in new Hingham and may help to explain it. The respect paid to these claims may tell us why men like Joshua Hobart, son of the town patriarch and brother of the town minister, began his seventeen terms as selectman (and his twenty-four terms as town representative to the General Court) in 1644 at age thirty and was able to hold on to these and other town positions through the consent of the inhabitants after older leaders died. Perhaps, too, Minister Peter Hobart's "tendency to Presbyterianism" in church government, so often commented upon by contemporaries, reinforced or complemented ideas about local leadership.[30]

Whatever the reasons, Hingham, Massachusetts, had a tightly knit group of town leaders. The top 10 percent of the most frequently elected of them, some 7 men, controlled 83 positions, or 37 percent of the total available. The top quartile, or 18 men, held 144 positions or 64 percent of the total. As in Hingham, Norfolk, their social position was high. Of these 18 men, 11 had inventories recorded before 1692, and nearly half of those 11 were in the highest 10 percent of inventoried town wealth, while 90 percent were in the top 25 percent.[31] Although there is no evidence that the leaders of new Hingham were from "the very families that had held positions of leadership in the old country," as John Waters has stated, it does seem certain that the Hingham settlers brought with them attitudes toward leadership that they perpetuated in the New World.[32]

29. Compiled from Town Grants, Town Meeting, 1634, and Town Records, Land Grants, 1634–1757, Town Clerk's Office, Ipswich, Mass.; *Watertown Recs.*, I and II, *passim*.

30. Jameson, ed., *Johnson's Wonder-Working Providence*, 116–117, 116n; William Hubbard, *A General History of New England from the Discovery to MDCLXXX* (Mass. Hist. Soc., *Collections*, 2d Ser., V–VI [Boston, 1815]), VI, 418–419, hereafter cited as Hubbard, *General History of New England*.

31. Regrettably, inventories do not exist for important selectmen who died after 1692. These include Daniel Cushing (d. 1700), Matthew Cushing II (d. 1701), Jeremiah Beal (d. 1716), Joshua Beal (d. 1718), and Nathaniel Beal (d. 1708). Two that have survived— those of John Smith (d. 1695) valued at £1,106 18s. and John Jacobs (d. 1693) at £1,298 5s.—suggest that these men may have been very wealthy as a group. Suffolk Probate Recs., XIII, 295–296, 611–612.

Robert Wall, Jr., has recently suggested that Dedham, Mass., was similarly dominated by several families—the Lushers, Fishers, and Alduses. Further research may reveal that *small* market towns such as Fressingfield, Suffolk, from where many Dedham settlers came, may have had a social and leadership structure similar to that in Hingham, Norfolk. See Wall, *Massachusetts Bay: The Crucial Decade, 1640–1650* (New Haven, Conn., 1972), 28–29.

32. John J. Waters, Jr., *The Otis Family in Provincial and Revolutionary Massachusetts* (Chapel Hill, N.C., 1968), 15.

Government

The structure of town government offers another example of how Norfolk settlers carried over institutions intact from their English setting. Hinghamites brought with them notions of "townsmanship" not common to all other settlers in Massachusetts. It has already been suggested how little the manor seemed to affect the life of these Norfolk villagers. There were some specific reasons for manorial "decay" here. In the first place, Hingham manor was not coterminous with Hingham parish. In all, there were at least three manors existing within Hingham bounds in the early seventeenth century—Hingham, Hingham Gurneys, and Hingham Rectory—and possibly a fourth, Ellingham Hall manor. Several centuries earlier there may have been twice as many in the township. In Norfolk as a whole there had been a general consolidation of manors, so that by 1600 only one village in three had more than one manor. Hingham was in sharp contrast to this development.[33]

In addition to the lack of effective territorial control over the expanse of the parish, the records of Hingham Rectory manor suggest that, for the most part, manorial government functioned only periodically there. During the reigns of James I and Charles I, for instance, the manor court met at most three times. The court may have governed more in the time of Philip and Mary, when the records began, and we know it met more regularly in the later Stuart and early Hanoverian periods, but its institutional presence must have been barely known to future Hingham emigrants in the early seventeenth century. Similarly, the Hingham manor records, which have survived from the 1690s, contain evidence of only basic manorial functions such as homage, jury selection, and other routine matters.[34]

Norfolk manors generally suffered from other weaknesses as well. Weak or "open" manors could not control rapid population growth where there was land to attract those who had none. Little effort seems to have been made to check the movement of the landless within the wood-pasture manors of central Norfolk. Also, the region was one in which there were few resident major gentry and hence little manorial supervision. Hingham was a variation on this theme. Though the Woodhouse family, lords of Hingham manor, lived in nearby Kimberly, their local presence never led

33. Blomefield, *Topographical History of Norfolk*, II, 422–445; Spratt, "Agrarian Conditions in Norfolk and Suffolk," 20.

34. Hingham Rectory Manor Court Book, 1553–1723, Parish Chest, St. Andrew's parish, Hingham, Norfolk; Hingham Manor Records; and compare Henry Gurnay's Common-Place Book, Containing an Account of Courts Held and Leases of Land at Ellingham, Hingham and Irstead, Tanner MSS, vol. 175, *passim*.

to much interest in the management of Hingham manor. The Woodhouses were large landowners and controlled several manors in the region, but their interests were directed away from the locality to the county level, where they served as justices of the peace and played a very active part in the county militia. One family member became deputy lieutenant of Norfolk during the early seventeenth century.[35]

In addition to the weakness of the manors, Hingham township had other special characteristics. For instance, it enjoyed unusual royal privileges of which the local inhabitants were probably keenly aware. Being an ancient demesne of the crown, Hingham inhabitants were exempted from jury service at the assizes or quarter sessions. In addition, tenants were excused from the payment of tolls while going into Norwich and traveling throughout the country. They were also exempt from contributing to the expenses of knights in Parliament. These privileges, most of which were granted in the fourteenth and fifteenth centuries, were repeatedly reconfirmed throughout the period, in 1564, 1610, and 1703. Special rights such as these probably gave a special sense of corporateness to Hingham inhabitants that many other Englishmen did not possess.[36]

Hingham residents must also have derived part of this sense of corporateness from the acts of selecting manor and parish officers and requiring duties of them. The villagers expected to choose men who represented them and provided service for their section of town. When in 1656 the manorial court leet appointed as constables four men who were all "remote from Market Stead or Town Street," a complaint was made to quarter sessions that "Hingham inhabitants" were "accustomed to choose one or two constables" for that section of town. To expedite their appeal, these townsmen submitted a "list of suitable names" to the Norfolk quarter sessions so that the justices might quickly fill the void.[37]

The meetings at which the parish officers were chosen were, in a strict sense, vestry meetings, though inhabitants at the time referred to them

---

35. B. A. Holderness, "'Open' and 'Close' Parishes in England in the Eighteenth and Nineteenth Centuries," *Ag. Hist. Rev.*, XX (1972), 126–139; Spratt, "Agrarian Conditions in Norfolk and Suffolk," map adjacent to p. 101; J. H. Gleason, *The Justices of the Peace in England, 1558 to 1640: A Later Eirenarcha* (Oxford, 1969), 145–163; A. Hassell Smith, "Justices at Work in Elizabethan Norfolk," *Norfolk Arch.*, XXXIV (1969), 93–110; and Rye, ed., *State Papers Relating to Musters*, 6, 31, 48, 78, 101, 102, 124, 125, 129, 130, 132, 140, 143, 156, 157, 165.

36. *History of Hingham, Norfolk, and Its Church of St. Andrew* (East Dereham, England, 1921), 5; Blomefield, *Topographical History of Norfolk*, II, 439–440; Patent Rolls, C.66/1000, membrane 27 (1564), P.R.O.

37. D. E. Howell James, *Norfolk Quarter Sessions Order Book, 1650–1657* (Norfolk Record Society, *Publications*, XXVI [1955]), 89.

simply as "town" meetings, as some of them would call their periodic assemblages in New England. In addition to the election of churchwardens and overseers of the poor, this annual meeting in Hingham assumed most of the responsibilities concerning the constables, except for their election by the court leet.

In superintending the constables, and in electing churchwardens, surveyors or way wardens, and overseers each year and supervising their actions, Hingham inhabitants were endorsing public officials who were levying rates on them that were abnormally high for English parishes of this size during the seventeenth century (see table 8, which lists each account separately, except for those years when several were combined). Based on the number of ratepayers on the list for 1689, the only one extant for the period, a total group of only 118 ratepayers were taxed from 12s. to £2 per individual each year. In many parishes, rates were levied only on special occasions, but in Hingham they were demanded with ceaseless regularity. Churchwardens' rates fluctuated according to the needs of the parish and were often related to the current state of repair of church property. Even though Hingham's rates varied from year to year, they were generally higher than towns and boroughs much larger in size.

North of London in Berkhamsted, Hertfordshire, for instance, the borough churchwardens over a period of twenty-five years levied rates irregularly, ranging in size from £5 5s. 1d. to £35. One rare £600 assessment in 1630 stated that the ratepayer was to "be rated as he has been up to £1," which was below Hingham's maximum rate. With few exceptions, however, the churchwardens of Berkhamsted seldom made assessments in excess of those of the small market town of Hingham. In Cottingham, Yorkshire, in a parish more comparable in size to Hingham, the rates varied in amount, but were generally much lower than in Hingham. In the decade of the 1660s, for instance, for three years no assessment was made, and for two years the rate was £56 and £34, respectively. Most other years it was nearer £10.[38]

The remarkable fact about the Hingham figures is the consistently high level of funds allocated to the overseers for disbursement among the poor. With the enactment of the Elizabethan poor laws the parish became the focal point of social change and policy at the expense of the manor. The consequences were most marked in places like central Norfolk where conditions were crowded, manors weak, and harvests uncertain. Whatever the

38. Powell, *Puritan Village*, 36–40; Cottingham Churchwardens' Accounts, 1660–1890, Cottingham Churchwardens' Book, PR 782, Humberside R.O.

TABLE 8. *Hingham, Norfolk, Town Accounts, 1661–1690*

	Constables' Accounts	Churchwardens' Accounts	Overseers' Accounts
1661	8/02/04	85/02/07	
1662	11/11/08	75/11/00	
1663	9/15/08	74/18/00	
1664	9/17/00	178/06/04	58/10/00
1665	10/18/04	99/14/02	52/01/05
1666	13/00/04	18/15/00	49/11/08
1667	13/00/00	25/19/00	43/17/04
1668	12/11/00	8/12/00	43/03/06
1669	8/08/08	9/15/00	38/12/00
1670	8/15/00	22/06/01	48/15/00
1671	6/10/06	23/07/00	55/10/06
1672	5/10/00	12/03/04	52/06/09
1673	6/10/00	8/12/00	53/12/06
1674	8/11/04	29/07/00	68/05/04
1675	19/08/07	20/10/05	68/04/10
1676	9/10/00	17/18/00	78/10/00
1677	9/08/06	41/11/00	67/12/02
1678	5/04/06	13/10/04	71/13/09
1679	8/07/04	28/16/06	71/03/06
1680	6/05/05	22/02/03	84/02/04
1681	12/13/02	12/03/00	78/00/00
1682	6/06/10	18/16/04	90/12/01
1683	9/09/05	113/16/07	
1684		18/08/00	82/10/06
1685	16/18/08	15/04/00	83/03/04
1686	10/04/10	8/17/03	91/15/09
1687	10/01/00	59/14/06	81/09/02
1688	9/05/07	20/03/00	76/00/09
1689	14/02/08	22/16/04	79/19/03
1690	8/01/05	17/15/02	82/04/01

Source:
Compiled from the Hingham [Norfolk] Town Account Book, 1660–1752, Norfolk and Norwich Record Office, Central Library, Norwich, Norfolk. Figures indicate the amount distributed or disbursed rather than revenue or income.

means by which such large sums were distributed by the overseers, the experience provided training in local government for those in charge and fostered a closer relationship between inhabitants and leaders through a "town" government.

The heavy responsibility and widespread power that local leaders had for levying taxes and disbursing funds did not ensure their immunity from challenge or protest. Whenever expenditures exceeded revenues, church-wardens would petition the town for reimbursement. In lieu of cash, the town "by the consent of the Inhabitants" would often allow the wardens the use of the "towne land" for a period of time. In 1667, for instance, Hingham's inhabitants granted the town land to Francis Stacy for one whole year, setting the rent of the land at £4, the amount of Stacy's bill. However, such additional expenses were not always so easily accepted by the town. In 1680 the churchwardens indicated that they had spent nearly £10 more in disbursements than their tax income covered. The deficit simply "was not accepted by the Inhabitants that day." Only after the church-wardens' constant "Importunity" was the town "prevailed upon" to allow them the following year's rent for the town land "in Full satisfaction of all their disbursements." They probably had to wait for some time before claiming the town land since the previous day the town had granted those lands to the overseers for half a year to compensate for their deficit of £3 16s. Because of the relationship between selectmen and town meeting, similar conflicts between leaders and townsmen were a constant theme in "town" government in Hingham, Massachusetts, during the seventeenth century.[39]

The men who came from old Hingham had definite ideas about towns-manship, and very early they incorporated them into their concepts and definitions of community life in Massachusetts. In some New England communities land proprietorship was the only definition of local citizen-ship, but in Hingham the relationship between the town and its inhabi-tants was established on a basis independent of and prior to land granting by the town. On September 18, 1635, the day on which the town records begin, "It was agreed upon that *everie man*, that is admyted to be Townes man, and have Lots *graunted* them shall beare charges both to Church and Commonwealth proportionable to their abilities." Town membership with its benefits and responsibilities was treated as a different category from

39. Hingham [Norfolk] Town Acct. Book, *passim*.

owning land, even though the latter usually followed the former. In 1638, Henry Chamberlain, the smith, was "recorded a Town's man—and is to have a House Lot" among other inhabitants. Three years later Edward Gould was "admitted a townsman, and is to stand to the Town's *Curtisie* in any question—and to require any thing of the Town, by vertue of his Township."[40]

In the first decade only "Freemen" could decide such questions as how the land was to be divided or could vote for officers such as selectmen. But this exclusive power did not last long in early Hingham. In January 1646 the town declared at a town meeting "that the 7, or 9 men chosen to order the prudential affayers of the Town, shall be chosen out of the body of the Town, as well non-Freemen as Freemen." Obviously if nonfreemen could serve as selectmen, they could vote for selectmen. This town enactment also made it implicitly clear that land divisions were a matter for town consideration.[41]

The variety of business in town and selectmen's meetings was typical of a Norfolk pastoral economy. The most important issues centered around the regulation of open fields, the granting of private rights to several landowners sharing small enclosures, and the enforcement of various timber laws. Several examples of the town's interest in and perpetuation of dairying have already been cited.[42]

Since new Hingham did possess some open fields, certain men were assigned field duties from time to time. Town orders concerning common-field fencing occurred irregularly, but when promulgated they were exacting and comprehensive. In 1656, for example, fences were established on three of the town's common-field arable and meadow lands: one including the smaller fields at Plain Neck, "Old Planter's Hill," and World's End; the second at Broad Cove Field; and the third at the Great Lots and Hockley Fields. The fence "orderers" were "to set up, or cause to be set up and mayntayned—the sayd fences from time to time—and to levy their charge upon every person according to their several acres of land and meadow within the sayd field." If persons refused to pay their share, it was "lawfull" for these men along with the constable to take "a distress upon the goods of such as shall refuse to pay." Fences in these "general fields" were maintained during the growing season so that, as one select-

40. Hingham Mass. Town Recs., I, Feb. 17, 1639, Feb. 10, 1642.
41. *Ibid.*, I, Jan. 30, 1646. See also the election of officers and granting of land at the May 24, 1652, town meeting.
42. See p. 59, above.

man's order stated, "no Cattle shall be kept in any *Common* Field from the first day of March, until Indian Harvest [corn or maize] be fully ended."[43]

Much of the land in the two Hinghams, however, was enclosed by small groups of proprietors. If some form of cooperation was required among the handfuls of men who occupied these pockets of land throughout the community, they managed it by private agreement rather than by general orders from the town or selectmen. Occasionally one of these agreements was included in the town records, such as the one involving Thomas Hammond, Stephen Gates, William Sprague, and Samuel Ward. All four men held parcels of arable and meadow at "Crooked meadow river." By joint agreement they fenced in the area according to the proportion of land each owned. The fences were "to be sufficient agaynst *great* cattle—and so to be mayntayned from year to year, by the owners and possessors of these aforesayd lands." They also did "*bind*" themselves to keep all livestock off the land from the first of March until the harvest of hay and corn; after that date "none [are] to put in any cattle, till there be notice given to either party." Thus, Hingham, Massachusetts, like its English namesake, incorporated a land system made up neither wholly of common fields with cultivators holding noncontiguous strips in them, nor entirely of enclosed land on which individual farmers decided how best to use their land.[44]

At the very first recorded assemblage in Hingham all those present must have been aware of the vast commercial potential of the cedar, pine, and oak trees within the township. It was ordered then "that all Cedar and Pine Swamps be in common and preserved for the Towne's use, although any should fall into any mans Lot." Between this session in 1635 and 1660, the town passed almost two dozen regulations concerning timber and lumber. Most of the orders restricted felling and the transportation of timber out of the town. A system of surveillance was devised to protect the timber. On September 4, 1641, at least seven men were fined for felling trees. The fine was eight pence per tree and the town warned others that unless "every Tree . . . is not now brought in and submitted to the fyne," the tree cutters would be charged a penalty of ten pence. Earlier in March the town had appointed three men to find and judge the "transgressors." Apparently, they were to hear the cases brought before them and then deal with the offenders "according to the nature of the offence." These town inspectors were "*to stand for one whole year*—and they have power to inquire into their [the transgressors'] offences which be *past*, as well as into

43. Hingham Mass. Town Recs., I, May 6, 1656; Selectmen's Records, Dec. 2, 1644, Town Clerk's Office, Hingham, Mass.
44. Hingham Mass. Town Recs., I, Mar. 10, 1651.

such as shall come within their year following." These offenses gradually became of greater concern to the town. By 1655 the town was penalizing the cutting or transporting of wood or timber for outside use with fines of twenty shillings, a thirtyfold increase since 1641.[45] As in Norfolk, the amount of time given to timber regulations and their enforcement reflected the importance of this local industry.

The role of the selectmen in new Hingham seems analogous to that of the parish officers in old Hingham. We find the selectmen taking firm control in agricultural matters, appointing subordinates, and enacting many, though often repetitious, agricultural bylaws. But unlike the selectmen in such Massachusetts towns as Watertown and Dedham, who ran most functions of local government with the tacit approval of the town meeting, the Hingham selectmen were given only limited jurisdiction in matters handed them by the town. Certain areas of local administration were clearly not within the selectmen's powers, such as making rates, though like parish officers in Norfolk they were allowed to collect and disburse them. Stinting the commons and giving away land were also considered too important to be left to the judgment of the selectmen.[46] So while the selectmen were allowed to handle some matters with more discretion than their counterparts in open-field villages like Rowley, the town meeting in new Hingham always protected its higher authority, just as in old Hingham where the "inhabitants" retained the upper hand in matters of difference with parish officers.

Movement from one side of the Atlantic to the other might have afforded Hingham townsmen the opportunity to change the structure of the society they knew, but seemingly without hesitation they continued their old communal relationships. The most arresting feature of the new community was the unexceptional origins of its leadership. The surviving lay subsidy tax lists for Hingham, Norfolk, provide some indication of the better-off inhabitants in the town. The one for 1625 lists four dozen heads of household, but only three of this number were among the many who left Hingham in the 1630s. These three—Adam Foulsham, Edward Gilman, and Joseph Peck—as it happened all left new Hingham several years after they settled in Massachusetts. Though no parish poor relief lists for the period have survived, it appears likely that those at the other end of the social spectrum were also not a part of the exodus from central Norfolk.

45. *Ibid.*, Sept. 18, 1635, Sept. 4, Mar. 10, 1641.

46. *Ibid.*, Mar. 12, 1647; compare Lockridge and Kreider, "Evolution of Massachusetts Town Government," *WMQ*, 3d Ser., XXIII (1966), 549–574.

Even servants who came with their employers from old Hingham seldom stayed for long.[47]

We can conclude that the emigrants who came to new Hingham did not include in significant numbers the social extremes of their native English village, yet despite this social change, they fashioned a society in the wilderness that strongly resembled the old order. A comparison of surviving inventories from both locations reveals a remarkable consistency, even though the New World immigrants did not bring with them either an established ruling class or a despised group of poor (see table 9).

Impressions drawn from the lives and backgrounds of the immigrants who settled in Hingham, Massachusetts, suggest that the remolding of old Hingham in the new community did not lead to a radical economic and social transformation. Edmund Hobart, for instance, was the patriarch of the Hobart family that eventually came to dominate the town in civil and church affairs through Edmund's sons Joshua and Peter. A 1637 land conveyance shows that the elder Hobart could not write his name and probably could not read. Men like Hobart made decisions concerning such matters as land grants, political offices, and law enforcement by drawing upon past knowledge of events in an oral culture where most transactions occurred through word of mouth. Illiteracy, in effect, was a conservative force, leading men to cling to what they remembered of past customs.[48]

William Ludkin, a locksmith from Norwich with early ties to old Hingham, never, it seems, engaged in agriculture while living in new Hingham, although it was primarily an agricultural community. The town granted him 22 acres of land, but none is mentioned in his inventory in 1652 nor is there any reference to the simplest of agricultural implements. Shortly before his death Ludkin moved his shop to Boston, probably in order to build up his business, which could only be accomplished in an urban setting, an American Norwich of sorts. Still, Ludkin typified his more agrarian new Hingham neighbors to this extent: even though people from the wood-pasture country were employed in various agricultural pursuits and some small industry, and were, therefore, likely to be more adaptable to the kinds of changes a new land might make them accept,

47. E.179/153/586, P.R.O., 1 Charles I (1625), Forehoe hundred, and compare E.179/153/556, 7 James I (1610), Mitford, Forehoe and Humbleyard hundreds. There seems to have been little correlation between wealth and emigration in neighboring Wymondham, Norfolk, either. Compare William Hudson, "Assessment of the Hundred of Forehoe, Norfolk, in 1621: A Sidelight on the Differences of National Taxation," *Norfolk Arch.*, XXI (1923), 285–309.

48. Record of land sale of Nicholas Jacob to Ralph Woodward, Nov. 6, 1637, Hingham Mass. Town Recs.

TABLE 9. *Comparative Analysis of Seventeenth-Century Inventoried Wealth in Hingham, Norfolk, and Hingham, Massachusetts*

	Hingham, Norfolk, 1642–1688	Hingham, Massachusetts, 1654–1692
	% of Total Wealth	% of Total Wealth
Top 10%	31.9	31.0
Top 25%	66.2	57.8
Top 50%	89.3	81.5
Bottom 50%	10.7	18.5

Note:
   The median inventory among Hingham, Norfolk, inventories was £55/02 and the average inventory among them was £112/06. Among Hingham, Massachusetts, inventories the median was £68/01/06 and the average was £112. (The Hingham, Massachusetts, figures are based on goods only [i.e., excluding land], as in English inventories.)

Sources:
   This table is based on Massachusetts inventories filed in the Suffolk County Probate Office, II–V, VII–X, XII–XIII, and N.S., I, II, New Suffolk County Courthouse, Boston; and for Hingham, Norfolk, on extant inventories in the Norwich Consistory Court records, Boxes 47A, 49A, 50A, 51B, 52A-B, 55A-B, 56, 60A, 61A, 63, 64. In addition, all wills filed for Hingham, Norfolk, testators from 1600 to 1688 have been reviewed. As in any other English community, testators who lived in this Norfolk town had their wills and inventories filed in one of three separate ecclesiastical courts, presumably depending on their personal wealth. For the wealthiest testators, the *bona notabilia*, that is, those who died at sea or overseas, or who held property in more than one diocese or peculiar, it was the Prerogative Court of the Archbishop of Canterbury, while the poorer members of the community used the Archdeaconry Court at Norwich (Anthony J. Camp, *Wills and Their Whereabouts: Being a Thorough Revision and Extension of the Previous Work of the Same Name by B. G. Bouwens* [Canterbury, 1963], 42, 51). Neither is used here since the archdeaconry court records have not survived and the few Hingham individuals who used the prerogative court might, in turn, bias the results if they were included (*Index of Wills Proved in the Prerogative Court of Canterbury and Now Preserved in the Principal Probate Registry, Somerset House, London*, V–IX [British Record Society, *Publications*, XLIII, XLIV, LIV, LXI, LXXVI (London, 1912–1942)], *passim*). Actually, if inventory wealth bears any relation to occupations listed, there seems to have been little difference between prerogative and consistory court testators; in addition, many consistory court testators were laborers, husbandmen, or widows, three groups that would seem more apt to file in the archdeaconry court. (For a different view on the social standing of testators in the consistory court records in Cambridgeshire, see H. Margaret Spufford, "The Significance of the Cambridgeshire Hearth Tax," Cambridge Antiquarian Society, *Proceedings*, LV [1962], 64; yet for an interpretation closer to the one presented here, see her "Peasant Inheritance Customs and the Land Distribution in Cambridgeshire from the Sixteenth to the Eighteenth Centuries," in Jack Goody, Joan Thirsk, and E. P. Thompson, eds., *Family and Inheritance: Rural Society in Western Europe, 1200–1800* [Cambridge, 1976], 170.)
   In any event, the Hingham, Norfolk, figures appear to represent the more general proportion of the population minus the extremes of wealth and poverty. Other evidence tends

to bear out this view. As the figures below suggest, the proportions of inventoried wealth in Hingham, Norfolk, show a close relationship to comparable proportions of the assessments for the town's ratepayers in the tax list for 1689, the earliest extant listing for the period covered in the inventories. The three top ratepayers—a member of the nobility, another of the gentry, and the minister—whose combined rates constituted 40% of the whole, have been "trimmed" from the list in order to study the general trends without such eccentric distortions. Once these men are removed, the figures show comparable proportions in the classifications: 65% for the top quarter; 86% for the top half; and 14% for the bottom half. The only exception is the upper decile, where 32% of the inventoried wealth contrasts with 40% of the community's wealth as measured by assessed value of property. This suggests that the consistory court inventories overrepresent the poorer segment of Hingham's population, but if so, not by much. It also suggests that without the few resident and nonresident men of wealth, who accounted for only 3% of the ratepayers, the two Hinghams were very much alike.

there is very little evidence that the new settlers substituted new livelihoods for those they had known in England.[49]

Others found economic opportunities in the town so reduced that their only hope of prospering was to assert that most significant element of seventeenth-century American freedom, the ability to move on. When Stephen Gates arrived in 1638 on the ship *Diligent* with many others from old Hingham, he did not receive a home lot or subsequent land grants. His inventory taken in 1662 shows that he was a farmer, so he probably rented land from some other settler during his years in Hingham. In 1650 he was a tenant on Samuel Ward's land. Gates's prospects did not improve in the decade after his arrival, and in 1646 he was excused from the payment of a fine imposed by the court because he was "so pore." He finally decided to leave town and in 1652 he settled in Cambridge. In the following year he became one of the original proprietors of Lancaster, Mas-

49. Percy Millican, ed., *The Register of the Freemen of Norwich, 1548–1713: A Transcript, with an Introduction, an Appendix to Those Freemen Whose Apprenticeship Indentures Are Enrolled in the City Records, and Indexes of Names and Places* (Norwich, England, 1934), 232; Suffolk Probate Recs., II, 51–54.

For a different assessment, see T. H. Breen and Stephen Foster, "Moving to the New World: The Character of Early Massachusetts Immigration," *WMQ*, 3d Ser., XXX (1973), 189–222. Taking their data on emigrants principally from urban areas, including a generous number from Norwich, the second largest city in the realm, Breen and Foster have postulated a migration of primarily urban artisans who upon arrival in the Bay Colony "gave up their English callings to become farmers in New England" (p. 220). It will be some time, if ever, before a figure for the actual number of urban emigrants can be made even from our incomplete data on the passenger lists of the Great Migration, and even longer before lifelong residents can be distinguished from less permanent men who arrived in London or Norwich and other provincial capitals from rural areas only years before embarkation to America. Still, it is more likely, as is shown in four of the five towns studied here, that a larger number of people came from small to medium-sized English market towns, or more remote localities, which made their adjustment from old to New England less difficult.

sachusetts, where he was made a freeman in 1656 and a constable in 1657. When he died in Cambridge five years later, Gates had a total wealth of at least £261 11s. 8d., and if his Cambridge home had been included in the inventory, that total might have exceeded £300, almost three times higher than the "average" Hingham estate. Had he remained in Hingham, he probably would have died as poor as he had been in the 1640s. Only by leaving Hingham with its conservative Norfolk assumptions of social order and opportunity could someone like Gates or the Hingham servants who emigrated ever hope to succeed in the New World.[50]

People from Hingham, Norfolk, straddled two different subcultures in seventeenth-century English local society. Their agricultural system contained elements of both the common-field and the enclosure systems. In addition, the region was characterized by a weak manorial order, which probably led to the prolonged continuation of some open-field agricultural practices. In place of the manor, a strong township operated by a small group of local families administered local poor relief and other social regulations during the seventeenth century. Ultimately, however, the "inhabitants" in the vestry or town meeting exercised control. Economic and social conditions improved for many who came to settle in Hingham, Massachusetts, but this development did not lead to the dissolution of the power of the town meeting.

50. Hingham Mass. Town Recs., I, Mar. 10, 1651; *Recs. of Mass. Bay*, II, 164; Bound Wills and Inventories, II, 53–57, Middlesex County Probate Office, First Floor, Deeds and Probate Building, East Cambridge, Mass.

4 "A Mixt Multitude"

NLIKE the settlers of Rowley and Hingham, the men who established the town of Newbury, such as Edward Woodman, Richard Kent, and John Pike, did not come from a single English locality. Most of their English homes, however, were not more than thirty or forty miles apart from each other, and many had only the distance of a village or two separating them. In spite of their proximity, these men came from a variety of subregions and derived their assumptions about law and social institutions, as well as about methods of agriculture, from very different sources. The fundamental character of this third New England town was shaped by people from the Wiltshire-Hampshire region, most of whom lived within a triangle of land bounded by Southampton and Andover, Hampshire, and the Malmesbury region of northwest Wiltshire.[1] Unlike peaceful Rowley or usually quiet Hingham, Newbury was born in contention and was easily aroused throughout the seventeenth century, flaring up once more in the 1740s fed by the fires of religious enthusiasm of the Great Awakening.

The famous antiquary John Aubrey, who came from north Wiltshire, remarked on the contrasts between the characters of his neighbors, especially the differences between those living in the dairy region and those living in the sheep and corn, or chalk, region. According to Aubrey, the various types of soil in England and throughout the world made "the *indigenae* respectively witty or dull, good or bad." In the "dirty clayey country" of northwestern Wiltshire the inhabitants were "phlegmatique, skins pale and livid, slow and dull, heavy of spirit." This region produced grain, but butter and cheese production were the most important activities, and in Aubrey's view, as a result little tillage or hard labor was required: "They only milk cows and make cheese: they feed chiefly on milk meats, which cool their brains too much and hurts their inventions." Soil and diet had

1. The English places of origin for the original 91 proprietors of Newbury, Massachusetts, are listed in Appendix 3 of this study.

further complications: "These circumstances make them melancholy, contemplative and malicious, by consequence thereof come more lawsuits out of North Wilts, at least double the number to the Southern parts. And by the same reason they are generally more apt to be fanatiques: . . . In Malmesbury Hundred etc (the wett clayey parts) there have even been reputed witches." To the south and east in the chalky sheep and corn champion country, on the other hand, "'tis all upon tillage, and . . . the shepherds labour hard, their flesh is hard, their bodies strong. Being weary after hard labour," Aubrey suggested, "they have no leisure to read or contemplate religion, but goe to bed to their rest, to rise betimes the next morning to their labour."[2]

Radiating from central Wiltshire's Salisbury Plain and extending far into the northern portion of Hampshire are the chalk downs. The chalk region was committed to large-scale capitalistic agriculture and dependent on sheep and corn. The general rise in population in late Tudor and early Stuart times and the accompanying rise in prices, the flight to the country by those who had made fortunes in trade and industry, and the increasing gravitation of the region into the orbit of the London food market awarded the land in the chalk country a market value far above what it had been in earlier times.[3] The region remained remarkably traditional in other ways, however. The form of society was deeply rooted in stable, stratified social classes, and the prevailing institutions were still the church and the manor house. Villages were nucleated, surrounded by common fields and open pastures and meadow. A steady amalgamation of holdings by gentlemen farmers was occurring, however, with a consequent general decline in the number of small landholders and an increase in wage laborers.

The manor was the key to the transfer of land in this region. In Yorkshire, where commercialization of the land was slow in coming, relatively strong manorial control inhibited change. But in the Wiltshire-Hampshire chalk country, rapid social and economic change in the early seventeenth century was encouraged by manorial direction. Manorial power could be

2. Anthony Powell, *John Aubrey and His Friends* (London, 1948), 38–39.
3. For some general conditions affecting land in southern and eastern England in the late Tudor and early Stuart period, see: E. A. Wrigley, "Family Limitation in Pre-Industrial England," *Econ. Hist. Rev.*, 2d Ser., XIX (1966), especially 84, 107–109; E. H. Phelps Brown and Sheila V. Hopkins, "Seven Centuries of the Prices of Consumables, Compared with Builders' Wage-Rates," *Economica*, N.S., XXIII (1956), 299, 305–306, and "Wage-Rates and Prices: Evidence for Population Pressure in the Sixteenth Century," *ibid.*, XXIV (1957), 289–306; Mildred Campbell, *The English Yeoman under Elizabeth and the Early Stuarts* (New Haven, Conn., 1942), 66–67; and Eric Kerridge, "The Movement of Rent, 1540–1640," *Econ. Hist. Rev.*, 2d Ser., VI (1953–1954), 16–34.

used in different ways in different places.[4] After the dissolution of the monasteries, the manor at Whitby in Yorkshire went through several changes of ownership and finally came into the possession of Sir John York. When he attempted to raise rents the tenants and inhabitants as a group brought Sir John into the Court of Requests, pleading that they "have holdyn and injoyed the premisses according to the olde auncient custome olde Rentes and Olde fynes, as herunder that may playnly apere, without enhansinge, or raysing without vexacon or trouble." They won judgment against "his interupcion." But the manorial structure could also be used to accommodate and facilitate change. In Crondal, Hampshire, a few years after the Whitby case, a manorial custumal (a written collection or codification of customary law) was drawn up to "put an end to all uncertainties" that had existed in that manor. The number of extant seventeenth-century manorial custumals from the Wiltshire-Hampshire chalk country testifies to the use of this device to redefine changing and increasingly complex relationships in times of rapid growth in order to avoid "confusion and uncertainty," while in other localities they helped to perpetuate older, more static relationships.[5]

The butter and cheese dairying region extended to the forests of Blackmore, Gillingham, Selwood, Chippenham, Melksham, and Braydon, which were clustered along the western border of Wiltshire, and over into the neighboring counties of Dorset, Somerset, and Gloucester, while the sheep and corn champion country covered central Wiltshire and much of northern and eastern Hampshire (see figure 4). Modern research has identified several additional subregions in Wiltshire-Hampshire from which Newbury settlers originated. Different types of societies characterized the Wiltshire Cotswolds, the lands in and abutting the New Forest along the two counties' common border in the south, and the wooded region primarily in Hampshire east of the New Forest, surrounding Southampton along the south seacoast. All of these subregions, it should be emphasized, were merely variants of the two major regions described by John Aubrey. While the Cotswolds were in transition from common to enclosed-field farming, the other two subregions resembled the wood-pasture dairying

4. Andrew Jones, "The Rise and Fall of the Manorial System: A Critical Comment," *Journal of Economic History*, XXXII (1972), 938–944; Eric Kerridge, ed., *Surveys of the Manors of Philip, First Earl of Pembroke and Montgomery, 1631–2*, Wiltshire Archaeological and Natural History Society, Records Branch, IX (1953), viii.

5. I. S. Leadam, ed., *Select Cases in the Court of Requests, A.D. 1497–1569* (Selden Society, Publications, XII [1898]), 199; Francis Joseph Baigent, *A Collection of Records and Documents Relating to the Hundred and Manor of Crondal in the County of Southampton* (London, 1891), 156.

regions but emphasized slightly different grain crops and livestock side-lines. A brief word about each may help to convey an even stronger impression of the diversity experienced by Newbury settlers in their native localities.

In the extreme northwest corner of Wiltshire lie the southern end of the Cotswolds, from where such men as Nathaniel Weare came prior to leaving for New England. The region was filled with nucleated villages, open fields, plentiful downland common, and, initially at least, only occasional signs of enclosure. As in Holme-on-Spalding Moor, Yorkshire, the parishes were often widely extended and settlement was dispersed into hamlets far removed from the main village. Brokenborough, where Weare lived, was a populated corner miles to the east of the village of Charlton and contained only a chapel. This remote edge of Wiltshire was being quickly overrun with enclosures by the time Weare left for New England. In a survey of Brokenborough in the 1660s, Aubrey commented that "this countrey was anciently a delicate campania, all ploughed fields as about Sherston: much have been enclosed since my tyme, and more and more will every day." Aubrey was witnessing not only a wave of land-hungry enclosure and consolidation, similar to that operating in the chalk country, but also the demise of strong notions of a traditional past, which along with the diversity in background and custom of other Newbury settlers would contribute to severe problems in the new community for several decades.[6]

The second distinctive subregion was the area of the New Forest. It was situated on sandy heath rather than on the heavy clay soils more common in the other forested areas of Wiltshire, and its inhabitants pursued a pastoral economy but tilled more arable than other forest farmers. Not only was grain more plentiful, but there also appear to have been few squatters on the land. Enclosures had been making headway in the villages along the New Forest edge, but people living there were undoubtedly familiar with New Forest law defining the rights of commoners, which continued to be published into the nineteenth century. Relying on the right of pannage, which allowed them to graze animals in the forests, and the extensive tracts of heathland common, New Forest farmers as well as farmers on its

6. E. J. Bodington, communicator, "The Church Survey in Wilts, 1649–1650; [Parliamentary (Lambeth) Vol. XIV, etc.]," *Wiltshire Archaeological and Natural History Magazine*, XLI (1919), 6; compare Harold Brakspear, "Corsham," *ibid.*, XLIII (1927), plate I, between 526–527, 532, and J. E. Jackson, ed., *Wiltshire. The Topographical Collections of John Aubrey, F.R.S., A.D. 1659–70, with Illustrations* (Devizes, England, 1862), 211, 83.

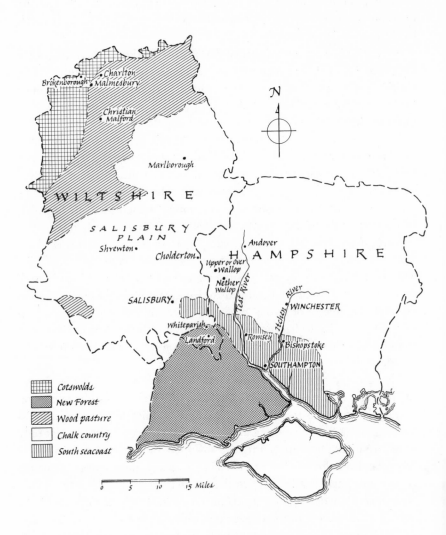

FIGURE 4. *Wiltshire-Hampshire Farming Regions, 1500–1700.*
Based on map in Eric Kerridge, "Agriculture, c.1500–c.1793," in Elizabeth Critall, ed., A History of Wiltshire, *IV,* The Victoria History of the Counties of England *(London, 1959), 43; and maps of Wiltshire and Hampshire in the atlas volume of Samuel Lewis,* A Topographical Dictionary of England, *5th ed., 4 vols. (London, 1842). (Drawn by Richard J. Stinely.)*

outskirts bred and raised cattle but specialized in raising pigs and breeding horses.[7]

The third center of emigration was the Hampshire woods region south of Winchester, which surrounded the important port of Southampton. Contemporaries noted the differences between chalk and wood regions within the county. In his ten-mile journey south from the chalk country encircling Winchester to Southampton, John Leland described the transition from champion to wood-pasture land, characterizing the latter's soil as "apter for brede of catelle than to bere corn."[8] Dairying was the primary concern here as in the other similarly wooded regions of Wiltshire, but in addition farmers developed some crop and livestock specialties for the nearby urban markets.

The butter and cheese dairying region and the other wood-pasture sub-regions produced a distinctive type of life, particularly in Wiltshire. Unlike the chalk country, scattered settlement, small farms, and old enclosures were often found in the wood-pasture areas. The family rather than the hamlet or village became the cooperative working unit for these independent farmers. Such family farmers in north Wiltshire produced cheese, and in the south, large quantities of butter. Arable land was meager, but common pasture was plentiful for grazing dairy herds, and little of it was enclosed. These wood-pasture regions as a whole lacked strong manorial control. Aubrey noted that as a result of manorial dismemberment, "the mean people live lawless, no body to govern them, they care for no body, having no dependence on any body." Not only were manorial regulations rarely enforced in this region where any remaining common cultivation was swiftly disappearing, but population tended to increase rapidly due to the lack of manorial control over the influx of people. As the population rose and the number of small, family dairy farmers increased steadily, few impediments stood in the way of a free market in land.[9]

The major wood-pasture region in western Wiltshire and the surrounding counties to the west did not escape the social tension of the early seventeenth century any more than the corresponding region in Norfolk did. Unlike the East Anglian county, however, conditions in Wiltshire led to

7. C. R. Tubbs, "The Development of the Smallholding and Cottage Stock-Keeping Economy of the New Forest," *Ag. Hist. Rev.*, XIII (1965), 23–39; *Abstract of Claims Preferred at a Justice Seat Held for the New Forest Hants . . . A.D. 1670* (London, 1858).

8. W. E. Tate, "Field Systems and Enclosures in Hampshire," Hampshire Field Club and Archaeological Society, *Papers and Proceedings*, XVI (1947), 258; F. Dorothy Escombe, ed., *Bygone Bishopstoke, with Personal Reminiscences* (Winchester, England, 1935).

9. For a general discussion, see Eric Kerridge, "Agriculture c. 1500– c. 1793," in *The Victoria History of the Counties of England, Wiltshire*, IV (London, 1959), 43–64.

open rebellion and bloodshed. Whenever hard times came to the region, as they did in the early decades of the century, people in the cloth trade experienced the repercussions first. Primarily affected were the small, part-time weavers and spinners who combined these activities with dairying, next struck were the clothiers, and finally the merchants. Since spinners and weavers had hardly enough money even in good times, this periodic economic misery led the numerous unemployed poor to engage in dangerous violent protests. In 1622, for instance, the justices of Wiltshire reported to the king's council that in the cloth trade "8,000 poor [are] out of work, some of them have attacked and seized corn, which was on its way to market, and several designing people having crept in amongst them, further outrages are feared." References to "pilfering vagabonds" and higher grain prices dot the justices' reports during the 1620s and 1630s. Even in moderately good times, as many of these years were, incomes in the cloth trade remained low, suggesting that social strain was never far below the surface.[10]

What distinguished the itinerant unemployed in this region, particularly in western Wiltshire, from those in such places as Worcester and Leicester was the scale and intensity of the disorder in the West Country that these people promoted and that has been described as "perhaps the largest single outbreak of popular discontent in the thirty-five years which preceded the start of the Civil War." New crises affected old, festering problems. In the late 1620s Charles I attempted to enclose the forest pasturelands in the royal forests of Gillingham in Dorset, Braydon in Wiltshire, and Dean in Gloucester. His actions were motivated by a fundamental need for revenue, but they galvanized certain long-standing resentments among the forest farmers who were threatened by the possible loss of their common grazing lands. Rallying under the standards of popular leaders such as the mysterious "Lady Skimmington," forest commoners tore down fences and hedges; they succeeded in their efforts at Braydon, where the crown was forced to give back most of the land it claimed. The discontent was fueled by other contemporaneous factors

10. For examples of contemporary conditions in Wiltshire, see *Calendar of State Papers, Domestic Series, of the Reign of James I [and] Charles I . . .* (London, 1858–1877), *1619–1623*, 579, 144, 343, 382 (quoted in text), 494, 584, 149; *1629–1631*, 474; *1631–1633*, 6, 183, 386, 352, 375, 387, 389, 434; *1633–1634*, 136, 231, 273, 274, 491, 534, 547, 550.

Conditions in Hampshire were never as distressing as in neighboring Wiltshire, but periodic adversity was felt in boroughs such as Basingstoke and Andover. New Forest and the wood-pasture regions in the southern part of the county acutely felt the scarcity of grain. See *ibid.*, *1619–1623*, 140, 488; *1628–1629*, 418; *1629–1631*, 519, 526, 481; *1631–1633*, 8, 9, 15, 18, 26, 35, 131, 318; *1633–1634*, 86, 261, 273, 280; *1637–1638*, 104.

such as the rise of extraparliamentary taxation and a downward swing in
the harvest cycle that, as in Norfolk, forced the forest and vale farmers of
Wiltshire to depend on supplies of grain from the champion country to the
east. Wiltshire was particularly sensitive to the short-term fluctuations of
the grain supply in the 1620s and 1630s, as Aubrey well understood. Spinners and weavers were especially hard hit by this recession, he observed,
and these wretched people "were trained up as nurseries of sedition and
rebellion." Aubrey also noted that the unstable woodland region was susceptible to religious dissent, describing the area as "a sour, woodsere country . . . [that] inclines people to contemplation" of religion induced by the
ease of living in an economy of dairying and clothmaking.[11]

Unlike the other towns studied here, Newbury was born in diversity,
even in contention. The Wiltshire-Hampshire inhabitants of Newbury,
despite their proximity within two English counties, represented a variety
of subregional characteristics and differed even in their ways of looking at
everyday relationships. They may have carried with them common western English traits, such as the propensity for rigid social structure found in
Newbury that was customary in both the chalk and wood-pasture villages
of Wiltshire and Hampshire, but they also manifested wide differences in
their views toward religion, ranging from mild episcopacy to radical per-
sonalized religion. Even their motives for leaving their English homes, as
we will see in chapter 6, varied from a desire to engage in profitable economic pursuits to the hope of perfecting a conservative puritan society in
the wilderness. By the end of the first thirty years of settlement such inherited differences helped produce an internal controversy of such dimen-
sion that it had to be carried to the General Court for resolution. The settlers of this town were aptly characterized by fellow West Countryman
John White as "a mixt multitude . . . of divers tempers."[12]

One of the clearest traditions that these people from Wiltshire-Hampshire brought with them was the propensity to establish a rigid, stratified
society. Extant inventories belonging to the town's proprietors and to a
few other early town inhabitants show a society more stratified economically than either Rowley or Hingham. One-third of the inventoried

11. D.G.C. Allan, "The Rising in the West, 1628–1631," *Econ. Hist. Rev.*, 2d Ser., V
(1952–1953), 76–85; Eric Kerridge, "The Revolts in Wiltshire against Charles I," *Wiltshire
Arch. Mag.*, LVII (1958), 64–75, especially 71; Jackson, ed., *Topographical Collections of John
Aubrey*, 4. See also *Cal. State Papers, Domestic, 1619–1623*, 336, 154; *1628–1629*, 11; *1631–
1633*, 67, 74, 87–88, 157, 168, 170, 190–191, 192, 192–193, 198, 257.

12. *The Planters Plea. Or The Grounds of Plantations Examined, and Usual Objections Answered*
(London, 1630), 81.

TABLE 10. *Distribution of Inventoried Wealth among 51 of the Original 102 Proprietors and Settlers of Newbury, Massachusetts, 1642–1701*

	No. of Inventories	Cumulative Wealth in £	% of Total Wealth
Top 10%	5	9,199/17/6	33.8
Top 25%	13	16,752/16/4	61.6
Top 50%	25	23,199/10/0	85.3
Bottom 50%	26	4,003/13/0	14.7
Total	51	27,203/03/0	100.0

Note:
The median among Newbury inventories was £377/12, and the average among them was £533/08.

Sources:
George Francis Dow, ed., *The Probate Records of Essex County, Massachusetts, 1635–1681*, 3 vols. (Salem, Mass., 1916–1920), I, 15–17, 21–22, 22–23, 67–72, 78–80, 82–84, 86–87, 186–188, 292–294, 308–311, 393–395, II, 30–31, 42–44, 52–56, 181–185, 190–192, 319–322, 323–324, 345–349, 378–379, III, 88–89, 133–135, 187–191, 210, 218–219, 287–289; Dow, ed., *Records and Files of the Quarterly Courts of Essex County, Massachusetts*, 8 vols. (Salem, Mass., 1911–1921), I, 271n–272n, 288n–289n, II, 7n–8n, 379n–381n, IV, 291, V, 161–162; Bound Wills and Inventories, vol. 302, pp. 29, 101–102, vol. 303, p. 251, vol. 304, pp. 22–23, 51, 112–113, 196, 207, 282, 302, vol. 305, p. 14, vol. 307, p. 236, vol. 312, p. 264, and inventories on file, nos. 5883, 14471, 14767, 25339, 25839, 27476, Essex County Probate Office. The list of 102 men includes all early settlers: those on the proprietors' list of 1642, and 11 others (nonproprietors) who settled in the town before 1640.

wealth was held by 10 percent of the settlers, while the top quarter owned a little more than three-fifths. In addition, mean and average inventory sizes were significantly larger than in the towns previously studied. In fact, with the exception of the distinctive urban-commercial form of economic differentiation found in Ipswich, Newbury had the greatest inequalities in wealth of the five New England towns studied here (see table 10).

Throughout Wiltshire-Hampshire the degree of economic stratification as found in the upper decile and quartile of extant inventories varied. The wood-pasture regions generally exhibited somewhat less differentiation in wealth than that found in champion or open-field areas.[13] In the wood-pasture subregions the degree of differentiation could vary widely, but on the whole it was higher than in an East Anglian town like Hingham. For

13. Thirsk, "Farming Regions of England," 64–71, especially 65, 69.

example, in the wood-pasture community of Christian Malford in western Wiltshire, from where Newbury leader Edward Woodman emigrated, economic stratification appears to have been similar to, though higher than, the Norfolk town. The top 10 percent in Christian Malford controlled 31 percent of the inventoried wealth, the top 25 percent, 66 percent, and the top half, 86 percent. But in other Wiltshire wood-pasture communities wealth was more concentrated. For instance, Whiteparish, near the New Forest, like Christian Malford has an excellent series of surviving inventories for the period. In this community the upper 10 percent controlled 56 percent of all inventoried wealth, while the top 25 percent had 68 percent, and the top half held 89 percent.

Such a high degree of economic stratification was evident in the chalk villages of eastern Wiltshire and Hampshire. In Upper Wallop, where the Kents lived before emigrating, the top 10 percent held 48 percent of the wealth while the upper 25 percent controlled 68 percent, and the top half nearly 89 percent. Since a number of Newbury settlers came from urban centers such as Marlborough, Romsey, Andover, and Devizes, where stratification was even more pronounced, the existence of a highly stratified society in Massachusetts must not have seemed unusual to them.[14]

A large number of the proprietors, men who had some stake in the town, left Newbury within several decades of settling there. At least thirty-three of the original ninety-one proprietors had moved by 1660, so that only about 64 percent of the original freeholders remained. This suggests that, among other reasons, opportunities for wealth and status were limited in such an economically stratified society. Considerably more people ultimately moved away from this "western English" village than did from either Rowley or Hingham.[15]

Limited economic opportunity was not the only factor that made people want to leave Newbury, however. Continued religious controversy between conservatives and evangelicals also took its toll. Unlike the situation

14. Wiltshire and Hampshire inventories referred to here and elsewhere include: Christian Malford, Wiltshire (Archdeaconry of Wiltshire, 1630–1640), Cholderton, Wiltshire (Archdeaconry Sarum, 1608–1639), and Whiteparish, Wiltshire (Consistory Sarum, 1635–1638; Archdeaconry Sarum, 1630–1640; and A. Sarum, Book 8, fols. 144, 145, 209, 305, 320, 326, Book 10, fols. 14, 43, 90 [1610–1635]), Wiltshire County Record Office, County Hall Annex, Trowbridge, Wiltshire; Bishopstoke, Hampshire (Winchester Peculiar Wills, 1623–1642; Winchester Consistory Court Wills, 1604–1605), Over or Upper Wallop, Hampshire (Winchester Archdeaconry Court Wills, 1600–1632; Winchester Consistory Court Wills, 1623–1635), and Nether Wallop, Hampshire (Winchester Archdeaconry Court Wills, 1600–1638; Winchester Consistory Court Wills, 1637–1638), Hampshire County Record Office, Winchester, Hampshire.

15. For the Hingham figures, see Waters, *Otis Family*, 21n.

in many Massachusetts communities, the town minister, Thomas Parker, played a major role in the development of the town in both religious and civil matters, just as many nonpuritan ministers in English parishes had actively participated in local affairs. Parker's puritanism was shaped in the conservative western English mode. In contrast to the East Anglian puritans, he and his cousin James Noyes, who served as teacher in the Newbury church, conceived of this church as hierarchical rather than congregational in organization and open to all but the most scandalous sinners. Brook described Noyes as opposed to the English church's ceremonialism, "yet he could have been satisfied with moderate episcopacy." In addition, "he held a profession of faith and repentence, and a subjection to the ordinance of Christ to be the rule for admission to church fellowship; but admitted to baptism the children of those who had been baptized, without requiring the parents to own any covenant or being in church fellowship." [16]

At the same time, as we earlier noted, the English West was more sensitive to evangelicalism during the 1650s and 1660s than the eastern counties were. Newbury and surrounding "western English" towns in Massachusetts manifested this sentiment by harboring Quakers, although the practice was roundly condemned by the conservative Parker. Activities like these underscored the deep religious divisions among people who came to New England from the West of England. At one point Parker wrote a letter, which was published in London in 1650, censuring his sister-in-law for her newfound Quaker beliefs. He condemned her views along lines

16. Joseph B. Felt, *The Ecclesiastical History of New England; Comprising Not Only Religious, But Also Moral, and Other Relations*, 2 vols. (Boston, 1855–1862), I, 431, 600, II, 150; and *The True Copy of a Letter, Written by Mr. Thomas Parker, A Learned and Godly Minister, in New-England, Unto a Member of the Assembly of Divines Now at Westminster, Declaring His Judgement Touching the Government Practiced in the Churches of New-England* (London, 1644). Even the less than orthodox puritan Thomas Lechford found Parker's view on church government untenable, citing Robert Parker's (Thomas's father) *De Politeia Ecclesiastica* (Frankfurt, 1616), as "that mis-learned and mistaken Book." *Plain Dealing: or, Newes from New-England* (Mass. Hist. Soc., *Colls.*, 3d Ser., III [Boston, 1833]), 92–94, hereafter cited as Lechford, *Plain Dealing*. On James Noyes's views on church organization, see his *The Temple Measured: Or, a Brief Survey of the Temple Mystical, Which Is the Instituted Church of Christ* (London, 1647), especially 63–66, and *Moses and Aaron: Or, The Rights of the Church and State; Containing Two Disputations* (London, 1661), *passim*, but note especially p. 4; Benjamin Brook, *The Lives of the Puritans: Containing a Biographical Account of Those Divines Who Distinguished Themselves in the Cause of Religious Liberty, from the Reformation under Queen Elizabeth, to the Act of Uniformity, in 1662*, 3 vols. (London, 1813), III, 261–262; and Rev. Leonard Withington, *A Sermon for the Two Hundredth Anniversary of the Standing of the First Church of Newbury, on Its Present Site, October 20, 1846* (Newburyport, Mass., 1846), 7. With regard to Parker's hierarchical views of church government, note the disposition of many in Newbury in the Pike controversy with the General Court. *Essex Co. Court Recs.*, I, 366n–368n.

that would have gained him favor with the national church clergy. She denied, Parker wrote, the necessity of institutions rising "above the glorious church of *New-Jerusalem*," which was "builded upon the Foundation of the Twelve Apostles, namely, upon their Doctrine, and in way of the holy Ordinances instituted by them." She claimed, he said, to be "above Ordinances, above the Word and Sacraments, yea above the Blood of Christ himself, living as a glorified Saint, and taught immediately by the Spirit." "Satan is loosed in these times," Parker concluded. Another Newbury figure, Benjamin Woodbridge, son of John Woodbridge and one who later contributed to the growing religious controversy in Newbury, confirmed Parker's views by stating that "I am unwilling to follow the Devils method in these days of Error."[17]

"Days of Error" in Newbury were not about to end. Religious difficulties had existed from the very beginning of the town. At the time the church was founded, nearly all of the original members were from the chalk country of eastern Wiltshire and Hampshire.[18] People from wood-pasture Wiltshire-Hampshire localities soon moved in, however, which may have precipitated an early controversy over church rates that non-church members refused to pay. In 1637 the General Court had to order the inhabitants of Newbury to pay a church rate of sixty pounds and to do so "by an equall and proportionall rate of every inhabitant there, haveing respect both to lands and other personall estate, as well of such as are absent as of those that are dwelling there." The Court granted the town power to levy a distress upon defaulters.

Uneasiness continued in the Newbury church for several decades. By the 1660s opposition to Parker's autocratic "presbyterian" ways centered around Edward Woodman, originally from the wood-pasture region of Christian Malford, Wiltshire. Eventually disaffection with Parker allowed Woodman and others to establish their own religious congregation. By the middle of the decade so much enmity had been engendered among the Newbury townspeople that a sizable number, who came originally from the chalk country of eastern Wiltshire and Hampshire, left to settle in New Jersey at Woodbridge. The town was no doubt named in honor of

17. *The Copy of a Letter Written by Mr. Thomas Parker, Pastor of the Church of Newbury in New-England, to His Sister, Mrs. Elizabeth Avery, Sometimes of Newbury in the County of Berks, Touching Sundry Opinions by Her Professed and Maintained Nov. 22, 1649* (London, 1650), 5–6, 13, and introduction; Norman Penny, "Quakerism in Wiltshire," *Wiltshire Notes and Queries*, II (1896), 125–129, 163–183.

18. The original 21 members of the Newbury church are listed in Eliza Adams Little and Lucretia Little Ilsley, eds., *The First Parish, Newbury, Massachusetts, 1635–1935* (Newburyport, Mass., 1935), 10–11. Only two of the men listed can be identified definitely as coming from outside the chalk region of Wiltshire-Hampshire.

Parker's handpicked successor, John Woodbridge, the stalwart protagonist in the last battles between the two groups, which raged for more than a decade. Only after a lengthy legal struggle and the arbitration of the General Court, in addition to changes in the town itself, were Newbury's internal differences settled.[19]

Discord in Newbury was not rooted solely in quarrels over church government and religious practices. Possibly a stronger tradition of manorial government like that in Rowley, or more experience in town government like that of "East Anglian" communities such as Hingham could have eased the tensions already described. But a great part of the difficulty townspeople had in getting along with one another undoubtedly originated with the removal of the town in 1642 to a new location approximately three miles to the north.

In Old Town, agricultural affairs had for the most part been operated on the open-field system by Thomas Parker's chalk-country settlers. Pastures, meadows, and arable were suitably fenced and regulated. In October 1637, the town fined fourteen men a total of £4 15s. for defective fencing, while other men appointed by the town were required to put up the town's "general fences" around the commons.[20] Removal to New Town was necessitated by the lack of sufficient agricultural land at the old site. But the decision to move was itself a divisive issue. A large number of inhabitants refused to move, and many of them attempted to keep the town church in Old Town, or at least petitioned for another. They continued their resistance for five years until the General Court stepped in on the side of "the major part," the men in New Town, "for peace sake." Undaunted, many Old Town inhabitants remained there, refusing to take part in church activities in New Town.

In addition to creating resentments, the removal dispersed inhabitants along the road from Old to New Town, making attendance at church even more difficult. Edward Johnson, who visited Newbury in 1650, described

19. *Recs. of Mass. Bay*, I, 216–217, III, 115, IV, 487, 549, 521–524; *Essex Co. Court Recs.*, IV, 122, 122n–124n, 143n, 232, 234, 232n–234n, 350, 350n–367n.

At least 15 men left in the summer of 1665 to settle Woodbridge, New Jersey. See Joshua Coffin, *A Sketch of the History of Newbury, Newburyport, and West Newbury, from 1635 to 1845* (Boston, 1845), 70. For details and a description of their settlement in New Jersey, see John E. Pomfret, *The Province of East New Jersey, 1609–1702: The Rebellious Proprietary* (Princeton, N.J., 1962), 34, 39–41, 148–149, 365–371, 395–396, and William A. Whitehead, *Contributions to the Early History of Perth Amboy and Adjoining County, and Sketches of Men and Events in New Jersey during the Provincial Era* (New York, 1856), 355–400.

20. Newbury Town Records, in one MS vol. (1637–1695), Oct. 16, 1637, Feb. 24, 1639, Mar. 12, 1642, Town Clerk's Office, Newbury, Mass.

the town as having "houses . . . built very scattering, which hath caused some contending about removall of their place for Sabbath-Assemblies." The appetite for land among these men from western England encouraged even the lowliest to bargain for a remote "farm." "Laborer" Thomas Coleman was so isolated on his farm that in 1645 he was excused by the town from laying out lots, and five years later John Poore was actually given some land at New Town by the town because he lived so far from the meetinghouse. Fragmentation of the community became so grave that by 1648 the town approved a fine for nonattendance at the town meeting and authorized the town moderator "to execute the order [so that] confusion be prevented."[21]

Nearly all the characteristics of English open-field life vanished with the removal to New Town. The offices associated with common agricultural practices remained mostly unfilled. The parcels of land regranted to New Town residents when they yielded up their former holdings contained no "field" names, and they rarely appear to have been held in common, with the exception of the small Plum Island divisions made in the early 1660s. A final symptom of geographic separation developed in 1653 when seventeen townsmen "desired to have their dissents recorded" against payment of a rate for maintaining a school during the coming year. All of the dissenters lived too far from the meetinghouse where the school was held for their children to attend it.[22]

Other forms of controversy periodically arose in seventeenth-century Newbury that were uncommon in other Massachusetts communities. Conflict over seating in the meetinghouse raged for several decades among a number of town inhabitants and became a hotly contested issue in both the town meeting and the county court. Quakers were entertained by more than one sympathetic Newbury resident, while other townspeople joined in the Quaker meetings. A controversy among townsmen arose over the oath of fidelity, and many in the community were involved in the alleged witchcraft of Elizabeth Morse in the early 1680s. Other residents became sympathetic to the Baptists and formed their own congregation in Newbury as early as 1682.[23]

21. *Ibid.*, Dec. 22, 1645, Nov. 12, 1650, Mar. 15, 1648; *Recs. of Mass. Bay*, III, 115; Coffin, *Sketch of the History of Newbury*, 44–46; Jameson, ed., *Johnson's Wonder-Working Providence*, 99.

22. Newbury Town Recs., May 14, 1653.

23. For several examples of church-seating disputes and the disorder they caused in the meetinghouse, see *ibid.*, Jan. 24, 1651, June 22, 1661, Feb. 25, 1669; and *Essex Co. Court Recs.*, IV, 136n–140n, 225, 225n–228n. Church seating had apparently been rigidly established according to rank and position in James Noyes's Wiltshire village of Cholderton. See Edwin P. Barrow, *Parish Notes* (Salisbury, England, 1889), 10–11. On the other town contro-

Agricultural Structure

The diversity of the people of Newbury was most specifically demonstrated in their attitudes and actions regarding individual agricultural pursuits, but, at the same time, their essential similarity is unmistakably clear
in their views toward landholding. Many continued to practice the type of
agriculture they were most familiar with in the regions or subregions of
Wiltshire-Hampshire from which they came. On the other hand, nearly
all were actively engaged in exchange and consolidation of holdings, a
common pursuit among the aggressive, land-hungry copyholders from all
these western English subregions.

Agriculture in the Wiltshire-Hampshire area varied among its distinctive regions and subregions, although in each of the wood-pasture areas
the variation was one of emphasis. In the wood-pasture region along the
seacoast of Hampshire, which extended northward toward Winchester
and westerly toward the New Forest, farmers engaged in raising cattle and
pigs, dairying, and cereal production, and supplied markets in nearby
Southampton and Winchester. Few farmers raised sheep, though wool
and hemp, which are often found in inventories, provided family members with part-time employment in spinning and weaving. Edmund Harfield of Bishopstoke, the same village where Richard and Stephen Dummer lived before emigrating to Newbury, left an inventory of £95 3s. 2d.
in 1628. Although it was higher in value than many, the estate delineates
the essential characteristics of south-seacoast agriculture as found in the
river valleys of Hampshire. Harfield's inventory included 2 mares, which
were probably used for draft purposes; 11 kine, his largest single asset; 3
steers and 3 heifers; 3 small bullocks; and 19 pigs. Besides raising cattle
and pigs for the nearby urban market and making cheese, Harfield produced a modest amount of grain, which at the time of his death amounted
to £13 in wheat and rye and £10 in oats. Harfield also may have planted
and harvested an orchard for the local market, since a large supply of fruit
was in his inventory. This region of Hampshire was enclosed, and like
most farmers in Bishopstoke, Harfield had his own husbandry tools: cart
and wheels, dung pot, harrow, plow, and yoke. Some hemp and wool
were also listed, suggesting that when his family had time left over from
their many activities, they also may have been weavers. As this and other

---

versies, see John J. Currier, *History of Newbury, Mass., 1635–1909*, 2 vols. (Boston, 1906–
1909), I, 149–155; *Essex Co. Court Recs.*, II, 107; "Newbury Troubles," *NEHGR*, VIII (1854),
274; and Coffin, *Sketch of the History of Newbury*, 127–134, 135–136.

estate entries indicate, Hampshire wood-pasture farmers do not seem to have been the indolent lot that John Aubrey described as characteristic of the north Wiltshire woods.[24]

A few miles to the north and west lay the chalk country, where conditions were very different. Unlike the south-seacoast region, dairying here never went beyond domestic or, at most, village needs. Richard Miller of Upper Wallop, Hampshire, had 10 cows, but they were greatly outnumbered in size and economic significance by his "180 sheep and 12 lambs at Grately £48," "114 sheep and 10 lambs at Wallop £31," "40 sheep at Andover £11," and "22 sheep at Ohotesten [Cholderton?] £5." Yet raising sheep was of secondary importance to him compared to the income he derived from cereal crops, especially wheat and barley. Miller's arable land was enriched by sheep dung, which was gathered in a "sheep-fold" system after the animals had fed on the grasses of the downs during the day. Richard Batt of Nether Wallop, Hampshire, where Newbury proprietors William Ilsley and Stephen Kent originated, died in 1607 leaving a medium-sized estate by the standards of the area. The inventory included 1 cow and calf valued at £2, 2 hogs at 13s. 4d., 1 horse at £3, and 48 sheep worth £11. In storage he had 20 quarters (about 160 bushels) of barley valued at £12, 2 quarters of wheat at 56s., and in addition, 15½ acres of wheat worth £12 and 5½ more in wheat worth £3. Batt had his own agricultural equipment, although it was more usual for open-field farmers to share their implements. The inventory contains no mention of wool, hemp, or flax; one finds only scattered instances of spinning wheels and looms in chalk-country estates. Wealthy farmers in this region often supplemented the basic economy, as Robert Hall of Middle Wallop did, by raising horses, pigs, and poultry.[25]

In the New Forest along the southern part of the Wiltshire-Hampshire border, the agricultural economy was similar to that found in the other wood-pasture regions, but with some variations. The soil in this area was poor, sandy heathland. Not surprisingly, the surviving inventories from the region reveal a relatively low standard of living, indicating that many of the farmers here were able to produce little more than what was needed

24. Winchester Peculiar Wills, 1628, Hampshire R.O.

25. Winchester Consistory Court Wills ('B" Wills), 1624, 1607, 1635, and Winchester Archdeaconry Court Wills ("A" Wills), 1630, Hampshire R.O. The chalk-country region usually had extensive arable. See G. W. Kitchin, ed., *The Manor of Manydown, Hampshire* (London, 1895), 178–195, for part of a typical manorial survey of the region during the Commonwealth period; Eric Kerridge, "The Note Book of a Wiltshire Farmer in the Early Seventeenth Century," *Wiltshire Arch. Mag.*, LIV (1952), 416–428; G. E. Fussell, "Four Centuries

for home consumption.[26] John Wilton's estate, proved in 1633, was richer than most filed in the Sarum Archdeaconry Court in the early seventeenth century, but it shows what small capacity men of average means living on poor lands had to extend themselves beyond household or local markets. Wilton's estate contained a milk house, cheesemaking forms valued at 4s., 2 cows, 2 bullocks, 2 sheep, half an acre of wheat mixed with a little hay valued at £8 10s., a small pig worth 4s., and some evidence that he or members of his family engaged in weaving. The largest single item in his estate was his lease for two lives (to remain in force during the lifetimes of Wilton and some other specified person) on the house and land belonging to it, valued at £30. The total value of his estate, including the lease, was only £42 13s. 4d.

For larger farmers, the New Forest region offered certain important advantages, such as the availability of more arable land to grow cereals. Robert Reade of Whiteparish, Wiltshire, grew 20 acres of wheat at Whelpley valued at £30, another 14 acres of barley valued at £21, 23 acres of oats and peas worth £23, 5 acres of peas in Hide Field worth £6, 6 acres of oats in Miloppet Park, and he had additional supplies of wheat in his barn. Farmers such as Reade raised cattle and pigs and bred horses, and as they were just outside the New Forest, Reade and other wealthy Whiteparish farmers were not restricted by the statute that prohibited raising sheep in the New Forest in order to allow grazing room for deer. Reade's livestock included 13 working horses and 7 colts valued at £74, 11 kine at £30 12s. 4d., 10 bullocks at £13 6s. 7d., 4 yearling bullocks at £5 13s. 4d., a yoke of oxen at £6 13s. 4d., 40 couples of ewes and lambs and 34 barren ewes at £29, 149 wethers at £32, and poultry worth 10s. His operation also included a milk house, a buttery, a "wool loft," and several outbuildings.

Reade's inventory was almost ten times larger than John Wilton's and was valued at £397 17s. 8d. However, once the assessors deducted £303 in debts owed by Reade, a high but not uncharacteristic figure for the region, the value of the estate plummeted to £94 17s. 8d., only twice that of Wilton's. Borrowing money appears to have been widespread in the Wiltshire-Hampshire region, affecting the whole social spectrum. It may well have been the rational response of aggressive yeoman farmers, both rich and poor, to new conditions in this wood-pasture subregion, where

---

of Farming Systems in Hampshire, 1500–1900," Hampshire Field Club and Arch. Soc., *Papers and Procs.*, XVII (1952), 264–270.

26. For some examples of poverty in the New Forest region, see *Cal. State Papers, Domestic, 1619–1623*, 393, and *1625–1626*, 506–507.

the effects of land speculation, rent and price rises, and growing urban markets were beginning to be felt.[27]

Dairying predominated in the wood-pasture region of western Wiltshire. Even the most modest listings included all the necessary implements for dairying and cheesemaking, and some were very detailed. Thomas Oven of Christian Malford had cheeses worth £6, "implements for making cheese" valued at 6s. 8d., 2 churns, 2 barrels, and other items valued at 8s., 1 cheese press at 6s. 8d., 15 milk pails and other items at 6s., 6 pails, 3 bowls and 12 other carrying vessels, 1 wooden tray at 15s., and 10 cheese vats and 2 butter "bathetes" worth 6s. Oven owned 4 swine valued at £5 and a couple of horses that were probably used for tilling the small amounts of arable in this region. Of primary importance were his 17 kine and bulls worth £62 5s. and his young calves valued at £6 10s. Acreages used for the production of cereals were very small, particularly when compared with the amount devoted to grass and hay. The inventory of John Box of Christian Malford, valued at £74 13s. 9d., listed £23 worth of hay and no cereal crops. The hay was stored up for the coming winter of 1634–1635 to feed his 2 calves, 1 mare, 4 unidentified young animals, and 5 cows. Larger farmers had supplies of grains, like John Geale, who owned wheat valued at £24, barley at £13, 20 bushels of malt at £3, and beans worth £13, but "grass around the corn grounds" or "hay upon the ground" was likely to be assessed at a high value as well.[28]

Few people in Christian Malford raised sheep, and those who did had only a small number. Phillip Boxe, for instance, had one ewe valued at 2s. 8d., and Humphrey Olyffe had 6 at £2. Weaving and spinning implements and materials were more in evidence. John Geale had over 10 pounds of wool, Humphrey Olyffe owned 2 spinning wheels, and Elizabeth Wisdome had an unspecified lot of "weaving apearel." Wood was also a valuable resource for many western Wiltshire farmers, as shown by inventories such as that made for John Dawmore, yeoman, which contained listings of wood and timber valued at £2 and "100 of boards and yards and planke" valued at £1. A "parcel of boards" or "wood about the house" were common estate entries. Finally, most of these wood-pasture farmers owned their own husbandry implements and used them on their own enclosed arable.[29]

27. Archdeaconry Sarum Wills, 1633, 1630, Wiltshire R.O.; Whiteparish terrier, n.d. [early 17th century], #8, Diocesan Record Office, Wren Hall, The Close, Salisbury, Wiltshire.

28. Archdeaconry of Wiltshire Wills, 1639, 1634, Wiltshire R.O.

29. *Ibid.*, 1632, 1634, 1636, 1640. For a discussion of the woolen industry in western Wiltshire and the surrounding wood-pasture region, see G. D. Ramsay, *The Wiltshire Woollen*

When settlers arrived in Newbury from their scattered forest and field Wiltshire and Hampshire homes, they developed an agricultural structure that reflected the significant differences in their origins. A town inventory of ratable property that includes a systematic assessment of Newbury agriculture for the seventeenth century has been preserved from the short, ill-fated Andros regime. The 274 inhabitants who were rated in the 1688 survey held a total of 1,309 acres of plowland, 1,523 acres of meadow, and 947 acres of pasture. On a general level, Newbury appears to have struck some sort of balance between predominantly arable production complemented by sheep raising as in the chalk country, and the strict preoccupation with "grassing and haying" of the wood-pasture regions.

Newbury's livestock inventory was even more suggestive of a blend of English agricultural regions. In all of Newbury there were 280 horses, 219 oxen, 1,205 cows and cattle, 2,300 sheep, and 387 hogs. It was typical in some areas of the Wiltshire dairy country for sheep to be 50 percent more numerous than cattle, but in late seventeenth-century Newbury sheep outnumbered cattle by 100 percent. In some parts of western Wiltshire, such as Christian Malford, few, if any, sheep were listed in inventories, so figures such as these represent a mixture of the two systems. The small number of one- or two-year-old horses, only 13 in all, indicates that horse breeding was not particularly important to the town's economy. Pig raising, however, was an important sideline.

In terms of individual Newbury inhabitants, the 1688 inventory also provides some evidence of the continuation of distinctive local English agricultural practices. Flocks of sheep were never very large in Newbury by chalk-country standards, though some were moderately so and certainly more numerous than in most other New England towns. The chalk-country settlers and their sons were principally responsible for carrying on the practice of raising sheep, though others were by no means excluded from the activity. Such chalk-country men as John Woodbridge, Deacon Noyes, Henry Short, Serjeant Moody, Serjeant Coker, John Bartlett, John Kent, Sr., George March, Stephen Jacques, and Captain Thomas Noyes are prominently listed as owners of large flocks. Unlike other townsmen with sizable flocks, most of these men devoted a considerable part of their interest in livestock to their sheep, which outnumbered three or fourfold their cows and cattle.[30]

Industry in the Sixteenth and Seventeenth Centuries (London, 1943); D. C. Coleman, "An Innovation and Its Diffusion: The 'New Draperies,'" *Econ. Hist. Rev.*, 2d Ser., XXII (1969), 428; P. J. Bowden, "The Wool Supply and the Woollen Industry," *ibid.*, IX (1956–1957), 57.

30. Walter Lloyd Jeffries, communicator, "Town Rate of Newbury, Mass., 1688," *NEHGR*, XXXII (1878), 156–164.

Newbury wills and inventories from other years in the seventeenth century usually show chalk-country men as the largest sheep owners. Such men as Henry Jacques with 67 head, William Ilsley with 40, Richard Kent, Jr., with 29, Anthony Morse with 38, William Titcomb with 30, and Nicholas Batt with 18 all came from this region in central Wiltshire-Hampshire. Of course others like Richard Dummer and Edward Woodman did own a number of sheep as part of a generally large holding in livestock, but nonchalk-country sheep owners such as John Cutting, Daniel Thurston, John Merrill, or Thomas Hale tended to come from outside the Wiltshire-Hampshire region rather than from the wood-pasture land of those counties.[31]

Although clothmaking was associated with pastoral farming in such areas of England as western Wiltshire and southern Norfolk, the economic connection between the two did not survive intact in Newbury, Massachusetts.[32] New World conditions doubtless lessened the need for the step-by-step specialization associated with an industry like clothmaking. Chalk-country men such as Henry Travers, Henry Lunt, William Ilsley, and Henry Jacques were involved in weaving and spinning activities. For the most part, however, these were aspiring men who had become engaged in all aspects of agricultural production, from dairying and raising cattle and sheep to growing cereal and making cloth, thus epitomizing the aggressive yeoman capitalism beginning to take hold in this part of England. William Ilsley, of Nether Wallop, Hampshire, who died in 1681, had the sixth wealthiest inventory among the early Newbury settlers and typified this pattern. Ilsley's livestock included 3 horses, 4 oxen, 6 cows, 1 steer, 3 heifers, and 3 two-year-old cattle all worth £72 10s., and 2 calves, 40 sheep, 5 swine, and 6 pigs, together valued at £23 5s. He also owned half interest in a boat, 10 loads of hay worth £5, 12 bushels of malt worth £2 8s., wool, flax, and yarn valued at £8, 80 yards of cloth at £20, and a loom and accessory equipment at £6.[33] Clothmaking in Newbury was also carried on by the professional weavers who had emigrated—Thomas Smith of Romsey, Hampshire, Nicholas Batt of Devizes, Wiltshire, Francis Plummer, and probably Giles Badger.[34]

31. *Essex Co. Probate Recs.*, I, 308–311, II, 30–31, 378–379, III, 88–89, 187–191, 218–219; Bound Wills and Inventories, vol. 303, p. 251, vol. 304, pp. 196, 207, 302, and inventories on file, 14471, 14767, Essex County Probate Office, Salem, Mass.

32. On clothmaking in rural areas, see generally Joan Thirsk, "Industries in the Countryside," in F. J. Fisher, ed., *Essays in the Economic and Social History of Tudor and Stuart England in Honour of R. H. Tawney* (Cambridge, 1961), 70–88.

33. *Essex Co. Probate Recs.*, I, 292–294, 393–395; *Essex Co. Court Recs.*, II, 7n–8n; Essex inventories on file, 14471, 14767.

34. *Essex Co. Probate Recs.*, I, 78–80, II, 42–44, 319–322, III, 187–191.

As the chalk-country men perpetuated the raising of sheep and cereals after moving to Newbury, so the men from the wood-pasture regions continued to breed cattle, graze cows, spin and weave wool, and make cheese and butter. Richard Dummer had large supplies of wool, flax, and hemp yarn, while John Poore's inventory contained 7½ yards of woolen cloth and 26 yards of linen. Henry Rolfe's estate also reflected Wiltshire wood-pasture agricultural life. His inventory contained 6 cows valued at £30, various other cattle worth over £40, hay valued at £4, butter and cheese as well as the barrels, churns, and other equipment used to make them, and some spinning wheels.[35]

At the same time that we find this continuity of English regional agricultural practices in Massachusetts, another pattern was also emerging. Newbury men showed a peculiar adaptability to agricultural change. Possibly this trait was encouraged by the lack of a common set of traditional agricultural practices in Newbury comparable to those brought over intact by the settlers of Rowley and Hingham. However that may be, we see in Newbury examples of a new type of agriculturalist that was emerging in seventeenth-century western England where the older ways of forest and field were being replaced by a commercially oriented system. William Ilsley is a good example. Although he originally came from Nether Wallop, Hampshire, in the heart of the chalk country, he diversified his farming after coming to Newbury. At his death in 1681 he was involved in raising cattle, sheep, and hogs, dairying, and clothmaking, and he had invested in a boat. While Ilsley's inventory ranked sixth among the early settlers, this pattern was equally in evidence lower down the social scale in the inventories of men such as Thomas Smith, who was rated twenty-second, and in those of others near the middle of the spectrum.

Smith, who died fifteen years earlier than Ilsley, was a weaver from Romsey, Hampshire, who came to Newbury in 1638. Although he continued to work in that occupation, as did most weavers who came to Newbury, he also actively engaged in raising livestock and grain. His inventory contained 2 oxen, 2 steers, 4 cows and 4 heifers, 2 two-year-old cattle and 2 yearlings, 4 calves, 2 sheep and 1 lamb, 5 swine, and a mare and colt worth £75. At the time of his death he also owned 17 acres of wheat, barley, and Indian corn worth £20. Smith must also have been involved in dairying, since the utensils needed for this work were listed in his estate. Both Ilsley and Smith, as well as numerous other Newbury men, exhibited what a fellow West Countryman, John White, described as "mens

35. *Ibid.*, I, 21–22; Essex Bound Wills and Inventories, vol. 304, pp. 112–113, 302.

itching humours," or a strong-willed ambition to develop, accumulate, and consolidate. These men were sensitive to the fundamental economic changes in their region, and when they came to America they immediately started to commercialize the New England countryside. This was most evident in their handling of the land.[36]

The Land System

Just as agricultural practices varied throughout the region, so did land-holding patterns. The two, of course, were entwined. In the sheep-corn lands of the chalk country, arable, pasture, and meadow were all part of a system of common-field husbandry. At Cholderton, Wiltshire, William Noyes, the father of James and Nicholas, held a church glebe containing "Comon and pasture for two Cows and one Bull in the Cowdoune and stubble field, as also Comon for our Boare and other hoggs and piggs in the stubble field," in addition to common and pasture for thirty sheep. The church was also entitled to 12 acres of land in the village's three open fields, which were almost equally divided among North, South, and Middle fields. Divisions within each field were very specific. North Field, for instance, contained 4 acres of glebe, "one Acre in the upper furlong not far from long hedge, halfe an Acre a little below not far from long hedge. one Acre in the same furlong comonly called Broad Acre. and one Acre and half in the middle furlong not far from long hedge." Although signs of enclosure were few in the chalk country at this time, some consolidation may have been taking place at Cholderton. In South Field "one Acre in the upper furlong, one Acre and half in the same furlong the lower end thereof" adjoined "the one Acre and half in the middle field."[37]

Farther north and west in the dairy country of Christian Malford, Wiltshire, the church possessed five "tenements" amounting to 60 acres in addition to four cottages. Each tenement contained an odd number of acres and was probably consolidated into blocks of land. David Button held 12 acres, an orchard, and a garden while Cudberds White possessed

36. *Essex Co. Probate Recs.*, I, 42–44; [White], *The Planters Plea*, 57.
37. Cholderton terrier, 1677, Salisbury Diocesan Record Office; "Grant of Queen Elizabeth to Edmund Froste, gent. and John Walker," Patent Roll, 24 Elizabeth, Part 10, No. 5 (1581–1582), *Wiltshire Notes and Queries*, II (1896), 74–75; rental lease, Sands Farm, Cholderton, Sept. 8, 1636, *ibid.*, 159. Enclosure was slow in this region, but steady throughout the period. Kerridge, "Agriculture 1500–1793," in *Victoria Hist. of Counties, Wiltshire*, IV (1959), 45, 47, and compare nearby West Tytherley in Norman Court Estate (West Tytherley, Hampshire), Daly MSS III, 5M50/2580, Hampshire R.O.

23 acres of land. Pasture, meadow, and arable are not specifically mentioned in the holdings, so it is quite likely that the holders of the tenements could do with the land as they wished. Probably the tenements were composed of small enclosed areas best suited to grazing herds, which were, in turn, probably leased to smaller farmers.[38]

In the northwestern corner of Wiltshire on the southern tip of the Cotswolds, landholdings contained both open-field strips and newly enclosed areas. The earliest surviving terrier from Brokenborough, dated 1671, indicates that enclosure had made some headway. Church lands contained a number of "closes," including 3-acre "Drylease" and two closes containing about 8 acres called the "Hay leases." Landholding in the three common fields was still more prevalent here than enclosure, however. Thirty-five separate strips in Home, Middle, and West fields contained 33½ acres of the church lands. This pattern of predominantly open fields did not differ much from the situation in the earlier seventeenth century.[39]

Like Brokenborough, the region near the New Forest in southeastern Wiltshire included both open and enclosed areas, but the process of enclosure had gone much further in the south. In Whiteparish, located along the New Forest edge and well known to Newbury men like John Musselwhite and the Pikes, John and John, Jr., enclosure was considerably advanced. It took place on both sides of the village, in the chalk downlands to the north and in the assarted land on the edge of the forest to the south. By 1350 about 30 percent of the land had been enclosed, and the process continued during the next three centuries, particularly in the open fields to the north. By the 1630s documents often refer to new closes such as "Sheppards close," "Pond close coppice [copse]," "the Ten Acres," and "the Twelve Acres." Just to the south of Whiteparish in the wooded village of Landford, arable, pasture, and copse lands were all in "closes," indicating that the process may have been more rapid there and in other nearby areas.

38. Christian Malford terrier, 1608, Salisbury Diocesan R.O.; Kerridge, "Agriculture 1500–1793," in *Victoria Hist. of Counties, Wiltshire,* IV (1959), 44, 45. Land in Bishopstoke, Hampshire, in the south-seacoast region was also well enclosed. See 30M65/20, Hampshire R.O.

39. Vicaria de Westport, cum Charlton, et Brokenborough juxta Malmsbury, 1671, Salisbury Diocesan R.O.; A Book of Rents and Other Monies Received by Henry Stevens for the Use of the Right Hon Thomas Earl of Berkshire Beginning July 1637 and Ending July 1641, 88/23/35, Wiltshire R.O.; Kerridge, "Agriculture 1500–1793," in *Victoria Hist. of Counties, Wiltshire,* IV (1959), 47; George S. Fry and Edward Alexander Fry, eds., *Abstracts of Wiltshire Inquisitiones Post Mortem, Returned into the Court of Chancery in the Reign of King Charles the First* (London, 1901), 107, 424.

Enclosure of land in Whiteparish was propelled by another factor characteristic of many areas of seventeenth-century Wiltshire-Hampshire.[40] Between 1560 and 1640 a new landholding class was established in Whiteparish. Men who had made their fortunes in commerce or industry outside the region came to Whiteparish to spend their wealth on new houses, estates, and farms, hoping to profit from grain cultivation and livestock production at a time of generally rising prices. During the first two decades of the century two new country houses were built by members of this new gentry. On the eastern and western ends of the parish eight new farms also appeared. One of them, Dry Farm, had remained open downland until the early part of the century when its 200 acres were enclosed. This farm was built up by the Stockton family of Downton, a parish several miles west of Whiteparish. The Stocktons also bought up several hundred acres of land in the surrounding area. Population increases as well as the breakdown of the manorial system hastened the process of enclosure and consolidation. In 1580 about 450 people lived in the village; by 1700 the population had risen to 700. As a consequence, new assarts and enclosures were made in the forests and on the downs (chalklands), many new houses were constructed on the common land, and some existing houses were divided into tenements. At the same time, if not earlier, much of the demesne land on the various manors was leased out to both large and small landowners.[41]

These three local factors—new landowners, population increases, and the growing availability of land—in addition to rising prices for agricultural goods contributed to a greater demand for land in Whiteparish and the surrounding countryside and to the creation of a market value far above that of former days. Another factor was the loosening of the ties that bound tenants to the manors, which resulted in the achievement of "free personal status" by numerous men in the late sixteenth and early sev-

40. For another indication of the extent of enclosure in the Whiteparish area, see the Landford terrier, n.d. [ca. 1588], Salisbury Diocesan R.O.

41. For the development of Whiteparish, see C. C. Taylor, "Whiteparish: A Study of the Development of a Forest-Edge Parish," *Wiltshire Arch. Mag.*, LXII (1967), 79–102, especially, 91, 94–97; "Manor of Alderston and Lands in Whiteparish, etc. Seinct Barbe v. Knight and others Chancery Decree, 37 Henry VIII–1545" [Chancery Decree Roll No. 3, entry nos. 120–137 Henry VIII, P.R.O.], *ibid.*, XXXIV (1905), 216–217; Will of John Rolfe, Archdeaconry Sarum, 1625, Wiltshire R.O. On the impact of new and rebuilt country houses for all classes of society during this period, see W. G. Hoskins, "The Rebuilding of Rural England, 1570–1640," in Hoskins, ed., *Provincial England*, 131–148. The study of population movements and changes, like that done for Whiteparish by Taylor (cited earlier in this note), deserves closer analysis at the local level and can only be explained in a very general way here.

enteenth centuries. For the first time these men had both the opportunity and the freedom to move from place to place in hopes of improving their condition. Ultimately, many former tenants were able to become yeomen, but at the same time a class of landless laborers was also created.

The emerging competitive economy was fueled, as inventories from the area show, by the rise in the marketing of agricultural goods, by the availability of money for the payment of services and rents, and, increasingly, by the practice among tenants of subletting and even mortgaging land. Inventories in or near Whiteparish made more frequent mention of leases. Emigrant Henry Rolfe's father, John, who died in Landford in 1625, left an estate of which over one-third was invested in three chattel leases, while another third was devoted to bonds and good debts. In John Wilton's inventory a lease for two lives of a house and land belonging to it was valued at £30, or three-quarters of his worth. William Ham held one chattel lease valued at £21 in an estate worth only £41 19s. 6d.[42]

The new economic conditions in Wiltshire-Hampshire affected men differently, but by and large the more prominent landowners and lessees benefited substantially, particularly in the chalk country where there was a steady increase in the landed resources of larger farmers at the expense of the small. Leases with tenants ran for a shorter time, owing to their profitability and increasing value to the lord. Fewer and fewer leases extended to three lives, while more lasted for only two or less. Those who possessed larger tracts of land might have a lease for just twenty-one years. Annual rents were low according to fixed custom, so it was through entry fines that lords made profits from their lands. Consequently, when a neighbor of future Newbury men Stephen Kent, Hugh March, and Anthony Sadler in West Tytherley, Hampshire, leased a small close of 2 acres, 2 rods, and 10 "luggs," or poles, in 1630, his rent was a nominal 2s. 6d., but his entry fine amounted to £25 12s. 6d.[43]

Entry fines clearly did not significantly deter land transactions in the two-county area, which contrasts sharply with another manor-dominated region, the East Riding.[44] In the quiet, stable, and traditional manors of

42. Wills and Inventories, Archdeaconry Sarum, 1625, 1633, 1638, Wiltshire R.O.
43. Compare "The Society's MSS. Grittleton Manor Deeds," *Wiltshire Arch. Mag.*, XLIV (1928), 216–217; R. B. Pugh, ed., *Calendar of Antrobus Deeds before 1625*, Wiltshire Arch. and Nat. Hist. Soc., *Recs. Branch*, III (1947), *passim*; Kitchin, ed., *The Manor of Manydown, Hampshire*, 181, 184, 187, 189; Wills and Inventories, Archdeaconry Sarum, 1638, A Sarum Book 10, fol. 90 (1635), Wiltshire R.O.; Norman Court Estate, 5M50/2590, 2591, Hampshire R.O.; Norman Scott Brien and Ethel Culbert Gras, *The Economic and Social History of an English Village* (Cambridge, Mass., 1930), 518–530.
44. Compare Arthur G. Ruston and Denis Witney, *Hooton Pagnell: The Agricultural Evolution of a Yorkshire Village* (London, 1934), 59, 77–84, 187–188.

that region of Yorkshire where Holme-on-Spalding Moor is situated, the annual number of land transactions recorded as entry fines averaged about two or four. In Brokenborough, Wiltshire, on the other hand, a total of thirteen were recorded in 1637, the one year for which the records have survived.[45] Other regions within the Wiltshire-Hampshire area were just as active as Brokenborough. Because of the tremendous traffic in land sales in this part of western England, land fines, which were normally entered in the manorial court rolls, were often listed separately in fine account books. One such example is the unusually long and fairly complete list of fines for Bishopstoke, Hampshire, the English home of Newbury settlers Richard and Stephen Dummer, derived from the pipe rolls of the bishop of Winchester. Over the course of the first four decades of the seventeenth century, the average number of fines entered each year was nearly a dozen.[46]

Following the manor lords came the wide-ranging group of tenants, from gentlemen lessees to poor copyholders. In contrast to the situation in East Anglia, in the Wiltshire-Hampshire region copyhold tenure dominated, but it no longer carried a social taint. In fact, men of all ranks held copyhold lands, from the manors on the western edge of Wiltshire to the chalk country of central Hampshire. In Hankerton near Brokenborough, Wiltshire, a manorial survey found only 9 acres held by lease from the lord, 137 by free tenure, and 523 by copyhold. Copyholders also predominated in Hampshire manors like Crawley and Manydown.[47]

45. Brokenborough fines, 1637, 88/2/35, Wiltshire R.O. One of relatively few attempts to measure land transactions in early modern England is that of John Kew in "The Disposal of Crown Lands and the Devon Land Market, 1536–58," *Ag. Hist. Rev.*, XVIII (1970), 93–105, but the total land market there appears to be much less turbulent than that experienced in the Wiltshire-Hampshire manors a century later. See especially p. 94.

Land transfers at this time, recorded as fines in the manorial court records, have not survived for Holme or many other nearby manors in the East Riding. One exception for this period (1612 to 1626) referred to above is Wighton cum Shipton (DDL/11/19, Univ. of Hull), a manor composed of Market Wighton and the chapel of Shipton. As one might expect, activity in land was not universally low in the East Riding since the lands in Market Wighton, an important market town on the road between Hull and York, recorded a level of transactions similar to Brokenborough or Bishopstoke, though neither of the Wiltshire-Hampshire manors contained important towns or was located on a major thoroughfare. Yet in Shipton, just a short distance away from Market Wighton and along the same principal road, the transferal of land was markedly slower, averaging a quarter or less of the Wighton figures. Presumably Holme, even more distant from a market town and not along as major a connecting route as Shipton, was even less active.

46. Winchester Pipe Rolls, Fines, Stoke, Twyford Bailiwick, Box 17, 155932, Box 18, 155941–155948, 155950–155951, and Winchester Fines, P.R.O. transcripts, 120/2, 5–7, 9, 121/1, 3, 5, 7, Hampshire R.O.

47. Hankerton Manorial Survey, 1616, 88/28, Wiltshire R.O.; Gras and Gras, *Economic and Social History of an English Village*, 112; Kitchin, ed., *Manor of Manydown, Hampshire*; Bro-

With the changing market for land and the increased freedom among tenants, many wealthier copyholders found that they could derive a profitable income from the land by leasing it out to others rather than by working it themselves. For less well-to-do copyholders and subtenants, however, the purchase of a copyhold lease in Wiltshire-Hampshire placed a great strain on a man's personal estate. As a result, many went without most of the new domestic comforts that had become available to small and middle-sized husbandmen of the late Elizabethan and Stuart periods. Throughout the two-county area, leases often accounted for over half of an entire estate, just as we saw in Whiteparish. In western Wiltshire at Christian Malford, a third of Humphrey Olyffe's inventory and half of Phillip Boxe's, for instance, were in the form of leases. In the champion country of Upper Wallop, Hampshire, David Pile held a lease of £30 value in an estate of £78 6s. 8d., while a quarter of William Bud's estate was invested in a leasehold.[48] The landlord's desire and need for a larger income from his land placed small landholders in a competition that either forced them out or "through the struggle" helped them to develop "sharpened powers and a new aggressiveness that affected both the[ir] character and fortunes." The acquisitive Wiltshire-Hampshire men who settled in Newbury shared this land hunger and a fundamental recognition of the commercial potential of land.[49]

In order to increase their profits and enlarge their holdings, men often went into considerable debt in order to take advantage of opportunities. A high incidence of debt, as well as a significant amount of "ready money," was common in Wiltshire-Hampshire inventories. Robert Reade of Whiteparish had a large and well-diversified farm worth almost £400 at the time of his death. He had 68 acres in wheat, barley, oats, and peas, over 260 sheep, 20 horses, 11 kine, 10 bullocks as well as other livestock, in addition to a milk house and some butter, and a wool supply in his wool loft. Reade had acquired a significant yeoman's estate in land, grain, livestock, and outbuildings, but by the time his will was proved it was little more than a paper empire. Reade's debts in notes, leases, and less formal arrangements amounted to £303, fully three-quarters of his estate. Enterprises like this, however, were not limited to the woods of southern

kenborough rents 1637–1639, 88/2/35, Wiltshire R.O.; R. H. Tawney, *The Agrarian Problem in the Sixteenth Century* (London, 1912), 25.

48. Hoskins, "The Rebuilding of Rural England," in Hoskins, ed., *Provincial England*, 139–141; Wills and Inventories, Archdeaconry of Wiltshire, 1636, 1632, 1630, 1629, Wiltshire R.O.

49. Campbell, *English Yeoman*, 65–72; H. J. Habakkuk, "English Landownership, 1680–1740," *Econ. Hist. Rev.*, X (1939–1940), 5.

Wiltshire. In common-field Upper Wallop, Hampshire, Robert Castle-
man's estate was inventoried at a total value of £175, but over £160 was
due at the time of his death in several bonds and "writings obligatory."
Richard Miller's heirs were obliged to pay out almost £240 from an estate
of £318. A certain amount of indebtedness was a healthy sign of expansion, development, and optimism among Wiltshire-Hampshire farmers and cottagers, but many people must often have found themselves
overextended.[50]

These individuals borrowed from one another, and debts "good" or
"desperate" due to or from estates were common throughout the two
counties. Margaret Whitier of Whiteparish had a total of £71 19s. 9d. in
ready money including debts due her in an inventory of only £85 14s. 5d.;
Cicily Cook of Christian Malford left a total estate worth £20 1s. 1d., but
£16 4s. 2d. of this total consisted of debts due her estate; and Richard
Scene of Nether Wallop owed £177 3s. from an estate valued at £332 7s.
10d. Many of the smaller estates in both forest and field regions lost one-
third to half of their value from debts payable. Economic stratification in
this area, it seems, induced people to take financial risks, but the price of
moving upward could produce liabilities leading to financial failure instead of advancement. Significantly, examples of indebtedness are prac-
tically nonexistent in Hingham, Norfolk, inventories and correspond-
ingly, new Hingham settlers were rarely in debt. In both Hingham,
Massachusetts, and Newbury, Old World attitudes were carried over into
the New World.[51]

Settlers of Newbury might disagree about how the land was to be used
for agricultural purposes, but they were in complete agreement concerning the commercial potential of land in their New England town.
Ownership of land, in fact, was the cornerstone of Newbury society. Unlike Hingham, for instance, a community in which men became towns-

50. Wills and Inventories, Archdeaconry Sarum, 1630, Wiltshire R.O.; Winchester Consistory Court Wills ("B" Wills), 1635, 1624, Hampshire R.O.

51. Wills and Inventories, Archdeaconry Sarum, 1630, Archdeaconry of Wiltshire, 1635,
Wiltshire R.O.; Winchester Archdeaconry Court ("A" Wills), 1630, Hampshire R.O. Con-
rad M. Arensberg, in The Irish Countryman: An Anthropological Study (New York, 1937), 172–
174, suggests that "to owe money is not merely to accept a convenience for either townsman
or country man. To owe money is to accept a social obligation." Accordingly, "if one's debt is
paid off one loses, not only a customer, but a friend quite literally." Such an explanation of
rural indebtedness, however, probably fits early 20th-century rural Ireland better than it
does the English West in the 17th century, which was clamorously commercial; moreover,
Arensberg's thesis does not explain the extent to which Wiltshire-Hampshire men allowed
themselves to fall into debt.

men first and landowners second, town rights in Newbury were vested in what was soon to become a small handful of men, the proprietors. In East Anglian towns, land was normally granted to many who came to live in the community, but in Newbury this procedure was severely restricted, as it was to some extent in "North Country" Rowley. The social order of Newbury was established on December 7, 1642, when ninety-one "proprietors" were listed in the town records and "acknowledged to be free-holders by the Town and to have proportionable Rights in all wast[e] lands, Common and Rivers undisposed and such as by from or under them or any of [the]m or theyr Heyrs, have Bought Granted and Purchased from them or any of them theyr Right and title there unto and none else." Occasionally the proprietors might grant small parcels of land to their own nonproprietary sons and to a few others, but as a body separate from the town meeting their control over town land lasted throughout the greater part of the seventeenth century. The proprietors also did not easily relinquish their control over undivided commons. Captain Paul White, for instance, was granted space for a wharf, a wharf house, and a dock in April 1655, but he received from the proprietors "no Liberty of freehold or commonage hereby." Similarly, when Richard Kent sold some land to John Bartlett in 1647, he stated in the deed that he did "not sell any part of my liberty right or interest in any of my common," and when three years later Richard Bartlett sold 4 acres to William Titcomb he did so "reserving the privilege of common." A Newbury proprietor, or a "freeholder" as they were known, eventually was defined as one who by grant, purchase, or inheritance became entitled to a share in all of the common and undivided lands.[52]

With such an exclusive proprietorship, it is not surprising that early grants in Newbury introduced a highly stratified division of land, with clearly more differential than is found in East Anglian agricultural communities such as Hingham and Watertown. The top 10 percent of the Newbury landowners controlled almost 60 percent of the land, about twice the amount held by the same group in Watertown, while the top quartile controlled over three-quarters of the grant acreage, half again as much as in Watertown. Compared with Hingham, Newbury's top decile and quartile both held half again as much land in each category (see table 11). Stinting rights in Newbury, which determined the number of animals a landowner was permitted to graze on the commons, followed the same

52. Newbury Proprietors' Book, fols. 144, 5, Town Clerk's Office, Newbury, Mass.; Newbury Town Recs., Jan. 10, 1653; Ipswich Deeds, I, 177–180, 222–223, Office of the Clerk of Deeds, Essex County, Salem, Mass.

TABLE II. *Distribution of Landholdings among the Original 99 Grantees in the Newbury, Massachusetts, Proprietors' Book*

	No. of Grantees	Cumulative Acreage	% of Total Landholdings
Top 10%	10	4,491	56.4
Top 25%	25	6,056	76.1
Top 50%	50	7,292	91.6
Bottom 50%	49	665	8.3
Total	99	7,957	99.9

Note:
    The median holding among the 99 grantees in Newbury was 33 acres; the average holding among them was 80 acres.

Sources:
    Compiled from Newbury Proprietors' Book, fols. 1–24, 26–41, Town Clerk's Office, Newbury, Massachusetts. Because Newbury, like Hingham and Rowley, contained a vast amount of common land, these early divisions left plenty to spare. Newbury proprietors parceled off three times the amount of land distributed at Rowley, yet there was still more left in the township. Within the limits of the township there were at least 30,000 acres of meadow, pasture, and upland, extending 13 miles in length and 6 miles in width at its most extreme points. See John J. Currier, *"Ould Newbury": Historical and Biographical Sketches* (Boston, 1896), 21.
    This distribution of landed property is an estimate, since no completely reliable contemporary listing exists of all grants given to the 91 proprietors and 8 other grantees in the years after settlement. The problem is further compounded by the removal of the town in 1642 from the Parker River on the southside of the township to the Merrimack on the north, and the ensuing resignations of land to the town by *some*, though not all, of the proprietors, the reassigning of comparable land by the town, and the continued claims of some proprietors thereafter. All of the early grants are recorded in the proprietors' book, which was still being used in 1672, though, of course, by that time some of the properties had been reassigned to new proprietors without reference to the original proprietors, and eight new proprietorships had been created, apparently out of the claims of older proprietors. While this is only an estimate, it corresponds with Joshua Coffin's partial list, as far as it goes, which includes all grants to proprietors who owned 80 or more acres. According to his figures, the concentrations of property were about 5% less in the upper decile and quartile. Coffin, *Sketch of the History of Newbury, Newburyport, and West Newbury, from 1635 to 1845* (Boston, 1845), 287.

pattern as land distribution, and like Rowley, with considerable concentration of rights in the hands of a few.[53] In both "North Country" Rowley and "West Country" Newbury, landholdings helped create and

53. The Stint of the Ox and Cow Common, Newbury Proprietors' Book, Mar. 12, 1642, fols. 2–3.

maintain the economically rigid and stratified societies that were founded in the New World.

If social and economic differences of a more extreme sort were apparent in Newbury, the potential for considerable upward mobility was still reflected in the market for land. In characteristic West Country fashion, men from all its subregions became active in the local land market in pursuit of profit. The Essex County court recorded some fifty-eight deeds prior to 1660 involving Newbury men and Newbury land. Forty-five of the recorded transactions contain information about the size of holdings. If we exclude four of the conveyances that involved exceptionally large parcels of land—411, two at 300 each, and 200 acres—the average size of the land traded was 17½ acres. This was three times as much land per transaction as was typical at Rowley, and the total number of transactions at Newbury was about six times greater than at Rowley.[54]

Differences in attitude toward land were demonstrated during the lifetimes of the inhabitants of these two towns as well as in each community. When the number of acres listed in inventories is compared with the original grants in the respective towns, among a sampling of six Newbury and nine Rowley men for the period from 1635 to 1664, the level of turnover of land in Newbury is shown to have been remarkably higher than in Rowley. The average turnover in Newbury was 51 acres and the median figure among the six men was 29 acres, while in Rowley the average among nine men was only 9 and the median was 4 acres. Even disregarding one large but not unusual transaction between the Newbury men, the average and median figures were still three and five times higher, respectively.[55] Many of the Newbury men in the sample came from open-field, manor-dominated villages similar to those with which Rowley men from

54. Ipswich Deeds, I, 5–6, 177–180, 184–190, 211–219, 222–223, 241–242, 245–248, 253–254, 262–263, 270–275, 279–283, 285–290, 301–307, 313–320, 322–327, 341–343, 358–360, 370–377, 405–409, 411–413, 463–476, 490–492, 500–501, 503–507, 510–511, 517–533, 573–576, 584–589, 605–606, 614–617.

Comparing these intratown land sales with town population figures for 1647 and 1666, as estimated by Robert Emmet Wall, Jr. ("Decline of the Massachusetts Franchise," *JAH*, LIX [1972–1973], 303–310). Newbury transactions occurred well over three times as often as in Rowley.

55. There are some dangers in using inventory figures for comparisons. Inheritances and special grants occasionally came to benefit the estates of townsmen, while on the other hand, incomplete recording of deeds might depreciate the size of those estates. Both factors have been taken into account. The inventories used here include *Essex Co. Probate Recs.*, I, 22–23, 67–72, 82–84, 286–288, 292–294, 308–311; 84–86, 208–209, 236–237, 250–252, 259–260, 301–303, 321–322, 351–352, 441. The figures include only one inheritance and no special grants made after the original divisions.

Yorkshire were familiar. Yet unlike their "North Country" neighbors, Newbury men acquired land at a rapid pace and consolidated their holdings whenever they could.

An interesting example of acquisition and consolidation is that of Richard Kent, Jr. Originally granted a 100-acre farm of meadow and upland, Kent increased his holdings through exchanges with the town, purchases from individuals, and exchanges with others until his farm was 250 acres in size. He then leased this large holding called "Kent's Island" for £46 per year.[56] Kent's origins in the open-field region of Upper Wallop, Hampshire, do not seem to have dulled his drive for real estate consolidation, although if he had remained in Hampshire he could not have expected to acquire more than additional field "strips" and very few enclosures. The only apparent tradition concerning the land that men from Wiltshire-Hampshire uniformly carried with them to Newbury was a compelling desire to possess, increase, and consolidate their holdings in New England.[57]

In addition to the buying and selling of land in Newbury, there was an active market in proprietors' "rights." Such "rights" in the beginning were restricted to the original ninety-one proprietors and only occasionally extended to newcomers. Unlike the "gates" in Rowley, for which a market had developed by the 1660s and early 1670s, proprietors' rights in Newbury were more extensive since they included "an interest in all Commons belonging to the Towne." Complete lists of proprietors were not kept after 1642, but an accounting to settle all claims arising from the sale or purchase of freehold or proprietors' rights in 1652 shows that at a minimum thirty-seven had changed hands. By the time of the small Plum Island division of 1661, records indicate that at least forty-six freehold rights (about half) had been exchanged and at least thirteen had been traded more than once during the previous two decades.[58]

While Newbury townsmen were in general agreement about the commercial use of land in their town, considerable rancor—much more than

---

56. Newbury Proprietors' Book, fols. 16–17; *Essex Co. Court Recs.*, I, 262n–263n; Russell Leigh Jackson, "Kent's Island," Essex Inst., *Hist. Colls.*, LXXX (1944), 197–207.

57. Although a great number of early Newbury land transactions were formalized by deed in Essex County court, the chief method of exchanging and consolidating land was through the town itself. Unlike East Anglian-derived Ipswich, Massachusetts, for instance, where the town merely recorded the sales and purchases of private individuals (if it did anything at all), the town of Newbury handled most transactions through the proprietors themselves. For examples of such exchanges and consolidations, see Newbury Town Recs., Dec. 16, 1646, May 18, 1647, Nov. 12, 1650, May 22, 1662, June 29, 1663; Newbury Proprietors' Book, fols. 21, 29, 15, 3, 22–23, 26.

58. Newbury Proprietors' Book, fols. 45, 67.

in other towns studied here—soon arose over specific grants to individuals and the land-hungry appetites of the proprietors. As early as July 1638, there had been "notice taken of much disorder in public town meeting by reason of divers speaking at one and the same time, some walking up and down some absent and divers other miscarriages," and "it was henceforth ordered that if any person shall offend against any order prescribed in this case [and in other cases involving land grants], there shall be exact notice taken of such offence in this respect [and] he shall be censored accordingly." When Henry Sewell complained that his farm was too small, the town replied that it was "sufficient and competant both in respect of the quality and quantity of the ground and farther that they see not for the present any ground or reason either to add any more land to his farm or else to alter any part or parcel thereof." A group of landholders was fined twenty shillings apiece in 1637 "for enclosing of ground not laid out nor granted by the town [and] contrary to town order." At another time the town formed a committee "to search out such lands that are common, belonging to the town, which particular men have inclosed in to their proprityes and to bring what they have found out to the town the next meeting."[59]

The lack of substantial new divisions of land after the first decade of settlement, coupled with a significant population increase, contributed to community strife and discord. In 1642 the original settlement was removed to a new location "for want of plough ground, remoteness of the common[,] scarcity of fencing stuff and the like," but only thirteen years later, in 1655, Joseph Swett was granted the right to Deer Island in the Merrimack River by the selectmen because the new town "had become so crowded and the accomodations so little." Consolidation of holdings encouraged a man to move from his house lot in town to an enclosed farm on the outskirts. While this was common in other communities by the eighteenth century, as early as 1650 Edward Johnson, as previously noted, observed the random settlement pattern existing in Newbury, which had caused contention over the location of the meetinghouse. Curiously, however, until the 1670s the Newbury town records show very little evidence of interest, compared to other towns, in dividing up more land. Even in 1670 the proprietors took steps to protect their "just liberties and privileges . . . for the prevention of utter ruin . . . for present and future generations." They were concerned about the number of cottages and dwell-

---

59. Newbury Town Recs., Apr. 14, July 6, 1638, Dec. 22, 1637, Apr. 16, 1673. For some other examples of disputes engendered by land controversies, see *ibid.*, Aug. 10, 1638, Dec. 16, 1646, Mar. 15, 1648, June 10, 1662, n.d., 1662, Mar. 27, 1662, and Nov. 10, 1663.

ing places erected by squatters on common land, the removal of firewood, fencing, and timber from the "rightful commoner," and the unlawful use of common meadow and pasture by trespassers for their livestock.[60]

Controversies concerning land in Newbury often went beyond the town's commissioners or the town meeting and had to be resolved, if at all, in the county court. The early Essex County court records reveal that the town of Newbury was involved in land controversies with townsmen more often than neighboring communities like Rowley and Ipswich were, and Newbury townsmen seem to have entered suits against fellow townsmen more frequently too. Individuals would sometimes refuse to grant possession of land after selling it, cut down wood on a neighbor's territory, use a townsman's land, fence in more land than they owned, deny passage on highways, or question leases, rents, or titles. In 1662, for instance, Francis Plummer and Richard Dole were unable to settle their differences through the arbitration of the Newbury commissioners in a case involving the "cutting and carrying away" of "hedging stuff" from Plummer's land. The debate centered around the size and shape of the lots, the physical appearance of the land, and its possession and use. Five years earlier John Pike had brought suit against Richard Kent "for cutting grass upon his lot at Plumb Island and carrying it away under pretense of trying the title."[61] Eventually, as more people in Newbury turned to nonagricultural occupations and as concepts of ownership were simplified with the extension of freehold rights, fewer such controversies erupted. But for the first and second generations, peaceful possession of land was repeatedly disturbed by such disputes.

Newbury was a town set apart from others. Unlike other communities studied here, it was founded by people who came from contrasting agricultural, social, and institutional environments. Differences were evident even in such day-to-day activities as farming, which often mirrored English regional and subregional agriculture. But differences also led to noticeable social, economic, and political contentiousness in the town and also may have perpetuated conflicting attitudes toward religion, ranging from mild episcopacy to radical evangelicalism.

Yet most men in Newbury shared at least one attitude: they all seemed

60. *Ibid.*, n.d., 1662, Oct. 12, 1670; Massachusetts Archives, XLV, 39 (May 25, 1655), State House, Boston; Jameson, ed., *Johnson's Wonder-Working Providence*, 99; Newbury Proprietors' Book, fols. 67–74.

61. Compare *Essex Co. Court Recs.*, I, 254, 262, 265n, 329, 417, 408, 232, 300, II, 30, 51, 52n, 347, 368, 109, 125, 248, 436, 436n–437n.

well aware of the commercial potential of their land. Whether they came from forest or field country, the manor in each region was the vehicle for adaptation to a market economy during the seventeenth century. Manorial custumals, or lists of local customs, from the Wiltshire-Hampshire area in this period suggest that in a time of rapid economic change, it was essential that the altering relationships between landlords and tenants be carefully redefined. Whether in open-field or wood-pasture regions, nearly all of the recorded customs were devoted strictly to copyhold tenancy relationships, the most typical form of landholding there, rather than, as in Holme-on-Spalding Moor, Yorkshire, to agricultural practices or manorial government.[62]

The only land policy acceptable to all in Newbury was that there would be no social or economic restrictions on a free market in the community. The town in its official capacity agreeably encouraged this practice by acting as the transfer agent between individuals. But land bartering and consolidation of holdings made people live farther apart both geographically and socially. Land also drove acquisitive and competitive Newbury inhabitants into controversies in town meeting and county court more often than in nearby towns. Such indigenous factors as soil and other natural conditions in Newbury were neither causes for dissatisfaction among proprietors nor reasons for contention. Similar factors were present in Rowley and Ipswich immediately to the south, but those communities never fared as poorly as Newbury.[63] Some towns, such as "East Anglian" Ipswich and Watertown, were able to combine a highly market-oriented society with a common, strong sense and tradition of local government. In Newbury only the former existed.

62. See, for examples, Canon F. H. Manley, transcriber, "Customs of the Manor Purton (*cir.* 1597)," *Wiltshire Arch. Mag.*, XL (1918), 111–113; G.A.H. White, communicator, "Certain Customs Belonging to the Manor of Christian Malford in the County of Wilts Taken Out [of] the Records, 1614," *ibid.*, XLI (1919), 174–177; Rev. C. V. Goddard, communicator, "Customs of the Manor of Winterbourne Stoke, 1574," *ibid.*, XXXIV (1905), 208–215; Rev. Chr. Wordsworth, ed., "Customs of Wishford and Barford in Grovely Forest with Further Notes on Wishford," *ibid.*, XXXV (1907), 283–316; "The Customs of the Manors of Calstone [1621] and Bremhill [1657]," *ibid.*, XLIII (1925), 192–206; Customs of Grovely Forest, 1597, 1603, 1618, 212A/36/9B, Brokenborough Custumal (1672), 88/31, Corsham Custumal 473/57 (1645), and Grittleton Customs, 415/33, Wiltshire R.O.

63. Edward Hitchcock, *Final Report on the Geology of Massachusetts* (Amherst and Northampton, Mass., 1841), 19, and "A Geological Map of Massachusetts," in pocket.

5 "Men of Good Ranke and Quality"

HE people who settled Ipswich and Watertown, Massachusetts, came primarily from the country-side and boroughs of the counties of Suffolk and Essex in the East Anglian region to the north and east of London.[1] Like the settlers from Wiltshire and Hampshire, they were familiar with the fast-paced transformations of land and society then un-derway in some parts of England, but for East Anglians these changes had become so well established by the 1630s that they no longer affected life with the same disquiet evident in parts of western England.

Though somewhat geographically isolated today, during the sixteenth and early seventeenth centuries East Anglia was a center of "industrial" (clothmaking) activity. Rivers in Suffolk and Essex fanned out like fingers, connecting inland towns by waterways and making local communities part of the international cloth trade (see figure 5). In the same way East Anglia became a source of agricultural produce for London as it was for industrial centers in this region. Agricultural lands were mostly enclosed in East Anglia, which meant that many small, family farms supplied these urban markets.

East Anglian parishes, or "towns" as they were called by contempo-raries, were also distinctly different from communities in the West or in the North Country. As we noted about Hingham, Norfolk, the East Anglian region as a whole, particularly in enclosed areas, showed evidence of manorial "decay" and the growth of the civil parish as the predominant local institution. During the early decades of the seventeenth century, concern in East Anglia over the cloth trade, poor harvests, and the large numbers of wandering poor was attended by Tudor legislation that placed more responsibility on local officials. The many lordships within most East Anglian parishes waned, and the care of the poor and other social

1. The English places of origin for the original 111 Ipswich, Massachusetts, commoners of 1642, and the English origins of the 120 grantees in the first division of land in Water-town, July 25, 1636, are listed in Appendix 4 and Appendix 5 of this study. Both of these listings represent a manageable sample of the East Anglian strength in the larger, permanent populations of these towns.

FIGURE 5. *The East Anglian Region.*
Based on maps of Norfolk, Suffolk, Essex, and Hertfordshire in the atlas volume of
Samuel Lewis, A Topographical Dictionary of England, *5th ed., 4 vols.*
(London, 1842). (Drawn by Richard J. Stinely.)

concerns became the chief preoccupation of the civil parish. East Anglian "towns" as well as boroughs also tended increasingly to select local officials from a small group of men, usually choosing individuals of substance rather than those sharing patrimonial ties or some other common bond.

Although the settlers of both Ipswich and Watertown came from the same general region in England, they created communities with a different emphasis. Contemporaries were quick to note the differences. Edward Johnson described Ipswich in 1650 in very respectful tones, stating that it was peopled by many men "having the yearly Revenue of large Lands in England before they came to this Wildernesse," while another contemporary—this time from Ipswich—described Watertown, only a few miles from Boston on the Charles River, as "a Plantation for Husbandmen Principally." Ipswich was, indeed, an agricultural community, as were all Massachusetts towns at this time, but it combined this activity with commercial trading. As early as 1633, John Winthrop noted that Ipswich was "the best place in the land for tillage and cattle," and soon it was marketing its large surplus of corn and cattle since the inhabitants had "many hundred quarters to spare yearly, and feed, at the latter end of Summer, the Towne of Boston with good Beefe." [2]

There was a marked difference between the types of people who settled in Watertown and those who settled in Ipswich. The one notable figure who came to Watertown during the early years, Richard Saltonstall, remained there only briefly, returning to England in 1631. In Ipswich, on the other hand, the leadership was peopled by such men as John Winthrop, Jr., son of the lord of Groton manor in Suffolk, Samuel Symonds, a manorial lord in Great Yeldham, Essex, and Samuel Appleton, a manorial lord in Little Waldingfield, Suffolk. A large number of men with urban backgrounds also came to Ipswich, such as George Giddings, John Tuttle, and William Fellows from St. Albans, Hertfordshire, and Robert Lord and Giles Firman from Sudbury, Suffolk, as well as a good supply of East Anglian merchants, such as William and Robert Payne. Many of these men played a conspicuous role in seventeenth-century Ipswich town government as well as at county and colony levels. In addition, town documents reveal a heightened awareness in Ipswich of the important role of merchants, tradesmen, artisans, and manufacturers in the workings of government in this New World society.

Strangely, however, most historians have hitherto regarded Ipswich as an Essex County backwater, significant only because John Winthrop, Jr., was one of its original founders. [3] Yet in terms of community wealth and population as reflected in the general assessments and levies by the General Court, Ipswich ranked second only to Boston in late 1637, which was only four years after its establishment, and it remained in that position into the eighteenth century, though by 1750 the town had declined as a major port. [4] The people of Ipswich, as we shall see, viewed town soci-

2. Jameson, ed., *Johnson's Wonder-Working Providence*, 96; Hubbard, *General History of New England*, 142; Winthrop, *History of New England*, I, 98.

3. One recent study presenting this view is Wall, *Massachusetts Bay*, 36–37.

4. See the town assessments exacted by the General Court from Sept. 1630 to Aug. 1645, in *Recs. of Mass. Bay*, I and II (conveniently summarized in a table in Henry Bond, *Family Memorials: Genealogies of the Families and Descendants of the Early Settlers of Watertown, Massachusetts, including Waltham and Weston; To Which is Appended the Early History of the Town*, 2 vols. [Boston, 1855], II, 983, hereafter cited as Bond, *Watertown Genealogies*), and those based

ety and the colony as a whole as people who lived in English boroughs might have. They somewhat consciously divided men into specific political gradations (leaders, freemen, commoners, and inhabitants, inspired in no little degree by comparable divisions in English boroughs such as St. Albans, Hertfordshire, Sudbury, Suffolk, or Colchester, Essex), forwarded the interests of their town in the colony, and vigorously developed their community to its greatest potential vitality. These facts make it easier to understand the contempt that even the minister of Ipswich had for deputies of smaller towns in the 1680s when he described them as "being most[ly] . . . of mean estate, and small understanding in matters of state."[5]

Watertown did not differ essentially from Ipswich in the type of men elected to office. Unlike the other towns we have looked at, the same men (though not the same families) were repeatedly elected in both towns, and they were usually very wealthy and often economically remote from the common townsmen who lived in the community. The economic and political separation of selectmen from other inhabitants in Watertown produced a system of town government not unlike the select vestries of cloth towns and country parishes in East Anglia. This system was becoming more prevalent as a type of local government and administration in East Anglia in the decades just prior to the 1630s. In any case these East Anglians produced local governments run by either the "principal" men of Ipswich or simply by the "few" in Watertown; both societies were in this sense led by "men of good ranke and quality."

Despite the differences in tone and emphasis between Watertown and Ipswich, these East Anglian communities shared important characteristics. Both perpetuated an agricultural economy similar to those regions of East Anglia familiar to the inhabitants, and both continued the distinctive landholding practices characteristic of eastern England.[6] As in Wiltshire-Hampshire and many parts of southern England at this time, the East Anglian land market was brisk. The same general causes, such as lack of manorial restraint and rising populations, that were operating in the West affected Essex, Suffolk, and Hertfordshire, and all encouraged the buying

---

on the provincial tax assessments in *The Acts and Resolves, Public and Private, of the Province of the Massachusetts Bay*, 21 vols. (Boston, 1869–1922), I, 177–180 (for 1695) and 743–748 (for 1714). By the 1765 Massachusetts census, however, Ipswich had declined in size to the ninth largest town in the colony and had diminished rapidly as a port town. Whatever the outcome for Ipswich in the half-century after 1750, prior to that time it was second to Boston in terms of wealth, population, and commerce within the colony.

5. Hubbard, *General History of New England*, 392.

6. East Anglian agriculture is discussed in Allen, "In English Ways," 239–242, 313–324.

and selling of land. In East Anglia, holdings were invariably enclosures of land rather than strips in fields, and such enclosures were often purchased for the purpose of consolidating land into individual farmsteads. These attitudes toward the land were carried over by the settlers of Ipswich and Watertown, Massachusetts. There, huge quantities of land were granted to settlers within a short time after settlement, an active and thriving market in land was soon created, and men sought to consolidate their lands into separate farmsteads.

The Land System

The East Anglian land system was shaped both by historical circumstances and contemporary events. Even before medieval times, the region had been characterized by a dense population, an unusually large number of free or semifree tenants, and the practice of partible inheritance, which resulted in a predominance of small holdings usually held in compact or near-compact blocks. The alienation of land was also less restricted by manorial lords in this region as manors became mere rent-collecting agencies. With the rise of population, the upturn in prices, the uncertain condition of foreign trade, and the harvest fluctuations of the late sixteenth and early seventeenth centuries, increasing pressure was brought to bear on salable East Anglian land.[7] While some of these factors made agriculture risky and encouraged overextended men to sell their land in order to cut losses, other circumstances in turn raised land values and rents. In the agriculturally productive area of Aveley, Essex, for instance, rent increased from two to nine shillings per acre between 1566 and 1651. In other districts of East Anglia the rise was even sharper, with a spectacular fourfold increase taking place in the first two decades of the seventeenth century. Enclosed areas appear to have carried higher rents, with the woodlands bearing the largest increases.[8] Men who would later settle in New England were aware of these trends. In Nayland, Suffolk, for instance, where future Watertown resident John Warren often served as a feoffee of town land, rental prices in the years before departure became increasingly steep.[9] Under these circumstances what better time could be found to buy

7. A number of these contemporary factors are discussed in more detail in chap. 6.
8. Thomas Barrett Lennard, "Some Essex Manors and Farms: And the Gradual Growth of an Estate during Tudor Times," *Essex Review*, XV (1906), 131–132; Spratt, "Agrarian Conditions in Norfolk and Suffolk," 214–215.
9. Compare Nayland Town Charity, Deeds and Related Papers, 2/10, 15, and *passim*, Nayland Town Charity Records, in custody of R. A. Brunton, Clerk, Nayland, Suffolk.

or let land, or, conversely, to sell it for the profit and purchase more, knowing that its value could only go up?

Consolidation and enclosure of land were characteristic of East Anglian communities, as we have noted. In Lavenham, Suffolk, an East Anglian cloth town where William Paine lived before moving to Ipswich, Massachusetts, the holdings of the parish church illustrate both processes. Bequests by wealthy merchants engaged in the cloth trade probably accounted for the size of the glebe, which contained 138 acres of land, a "Mansione" house, outhouses, yards, outyards, and gardens. The parsonage had 42 acres surrounding it that adjoined a second plot of "Ten akers." Next was a "wood" of 14 acres that appears to have been joined to the second plot, and then a "felde beyond the woode" of 13 acres, another "felde lying by the wood" of 7 acres, then "and other feld lyinge by the woode" of 12 acres, "One meadowe adjoyinge contaiyning five Akers," and a "feild adjoyning upon the Medowe" of 13 acres. Conceivably all eight plots, containing over 100 acres, may have been contiguous. If there was intervening land, it appears not to have functionally separated agricultural activities to any significant degree.[10]

Enclosure and consolidation of land thus were more advanced in Suffolk and Essex than in Hingham and other nearby Norfolk communities. There were no common-field strips as in Yorkshire and parts of the Wiltshire-Hampshire region. The term "fields" in the communal sense had lost any meaning here, as it was in the process of doing in the Norfolk wood-pasture region. Here, in fact, whole "fields" appear often to have been enclosed by one owner or by a small group of owners, and the location of a particular man's holdings was usually described in terms of nearby roads, ways, or other enclosures rather than by field names. Common land was still found in the woodlands of Essex and Suffolk, where it was used for herding, and along the marshy river and coastal areas of Essex, much of which was fresh or salt marsh or lands reclaimed from the river's reach. But cooperative farming was not the predominant land pattern that Ipswich and Watertown settlers brought with them as a common heritage from East Anglia.

Abraham Browne was one of the most influential men in shaping land

10. Lavenham terrier, 1633, 806/1/101, Bury St. Edmunds and West Suffolk Record Office, Angel Hill, Bury St. Edmunds, Suffolk, hereafter cited as West Suffolk R.O. For other examples showing similar enclosure and consolidation in places inhabited by future Ipswich emigrants, see Little Waldingfield terrier, 1636, Rattlesden terrier, 1627, 806/1/161, 124, West Suffolk R.O., and Great Yeldham and Tendring, Essex, terriers, summarized in Richard Newcourt, *Repertorium Ecclesiasticum Parochiale Londinense: An Ecclesiastical Parochial History of the Diocese of London* . . . (London, 1708–1710), II, 688, 576.

patterns in early Watertown. He was the only person who served on every committee chosen to divide land in the original grants. In his native village of Hawkedon, Suffolk, the church glebe contained arable enclosures of 3, 6, and 7 acres, some meadow and more woodland, and three enclosures of pasture of 2, 11, and 7 acres, respectively. According to the complaint recorded by the parson while making his list of lands, rents on the glebe lands had not kept pace with market conditions.[11] Both of these trends— the propensity to enclose and consolidate, and the rising prices and higher values that in turn encouraged the buying and selling of land—would become a part of the land system in Browne's new home.

A typical pattern of East Anglian land exchanges existed in Winthrop's Groton manor in Suffolk. Much of the land there had been held by the church until the dissolution of the monasteries. One late sixteenth-century rental gives an impression of the turnover in land occupation during the sixty years since the land had come into private hands. Since that earlier date the sale of land in Groton had been brisk, as a copyhold belonging to Philip Gosling indicated. The piece of land called "Dones" was "formerly in the Ten[ure] of Richd Bond and afterwd of Wm Smith and late of John Stickle."[12]

The character of the land parcels and the rapidity of exchanges allowed many East Anglian husbandmen and yeomen to consolidate their holdings into distinct enclosed farmsteads. About a generation and a half before Minister George Phillips and men such as Edward Howe and Simon Stone left Boxted, Essex, for Watertown, John Walker made a survey of the manor of Rivers Hall in Boxted. Walker's descriptions of the manor's customary holdings were accompanied by detailed maps of the lands. The illustrations below show the extent of consolidation in this manor by the late sixteenth century. Figure 6 represents the lands of Robert Fowle, which constituted one of the larger customary properties in the manor. His lands, labeled A, B, C, and D, amounted to 41 acres, 4 roods, and 58 perches, and all of this land, including some described as "fields," was in one compact holding. However, the smaller plots could easily be disposed of depending on circumstances.

11. Hawkedon terrier, 806/1/73, West Suffolk R.O. For other examples showing enclosure and consolidation in places inhabited by future Watertown emigrants, see the terriers for Boxford, 1627, and Bures St. Mary, 1633, 806/1/17, 18, West Suffolk R.O. The 1604 terrier for Great Bromley, Essex (T/B 142/5, Essex R.O.), the town from which several Watertown settlers came, lists almost 60 copyholds ranging from 1 to 50 acres. These were usually large parcels, a typical holding being somewhere between 10 and 20 acres.

12. Free and Copyhold Rents, Manor of Groton, Suffolk, 1597, E.3/10/114.2, West Suffolk R.O.

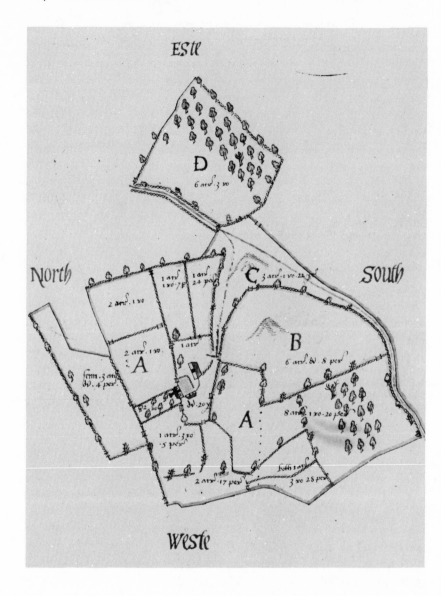

FIGURE 6. *From John Walker Senior's Survey of Rivers Hall, Boxted, Essex,
1586, D/DEI P1, Essex Record Office.*
(Courtesy Essex Record Office, County Hall, Chelmsford, Essex.)

The small plots delineated in figure 7 were occupied by three men. Parcels A through F all belonged to Thomas Peerce. The whole property was called "Sterlinges." These parcels are located in the upper center of the map. Parcels G through P belonged to Edward Milles. The total area was twice as large as Peerce's, amounting to more than 14 acres. Like all these single properties, the one occupied by Milles had a house on it that was "covered with tyles with dyvers Roomes mete for a Clother." Nuclear settlement such as was typical in common-field regions did not exist here. The third set of parcels, Q through S, was occupied by John Raynoldes, who held more than 10 acres. Like the other two men's properties, these parcels adjoined one another and formed one continuous farmstead.

The parcels in figure 8 were also held by three different occupants. The lands marked A contained over 18 acres and were rented by Steven Chillan for £6 a year. A small tenement and an acre lot labeled B were held by Joane Shelldrake, widow. Lands C through E were occupied by William Sickerlinge and contained about 21 acres. With the exception of parcel D all of his lands were adjoining. The different sized parcels indicate that they could be put to a greater variety of uses depending upon prevailing economic conditions. A husbandman could, for instance, convert his small close from pastureland to arable by himself if conditions warranted it.[13]

When Minister Phillips left this Essex town to settle in Watertown, he brought with him like-minded men from Boxted and from neighboring villages with similar land systems. The forty signers of the church covenant drawn up by Phillips on July 30, 1630, when the New England community was established, came almost entirely from Suffolk, Essex, or nearby counties. Over the course of the next ten years a total of twenty-seven men were appointed by the town to make allotments and other decisions involving land, and again, three-quarters of these individuals came from Essex and Suffolk, and all but two from nearby counties.[14] In selecting these men, the settlers of Watertown ensured the perpetuation of their particular land system on the new continent.

When they first arrived, the East Anglians of Watertown may have envisaged a different kind of land system. Having "escaped out of the pollu-

13. Survey of Rivers Hall, Boxted, Essex, 1586, D/DEI PI, Essex R.O.
14. Henry Dyer Locke, *An Ancient Parish: An Historical Summary of the First Parish, Watertown, Masstts.* (Watertown, Mass., 1930), ii–iii; Rev. Convers Francis, *An Historical Sketch of Watertown in Massachusetts, from the First Settlement of the Town to the Close of Its Second Century* (Cambridge, Mass., 1830), 134–135; Felt, *Ecclesiastical History of New England*, I, 138; *Watertown Recs.*, I, "Lands Grants Divisions Allotments Possessions and Proprietors' Book," 1–5. All citations to the *Watertown Recs.* hereafter will refer to vol. I, and all entries apply only to the meetings of the town and selectmen unless otherwise indicated.

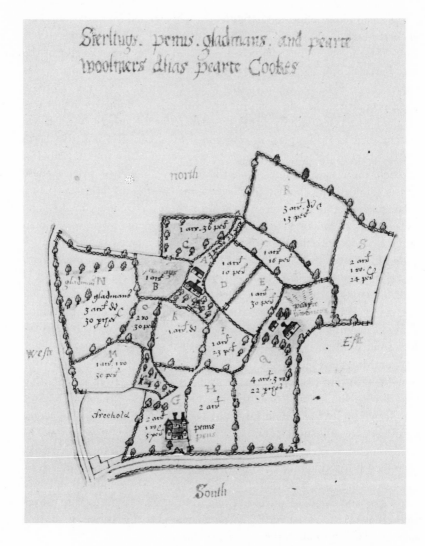

FIGURE 7. *From John Walker Senior's Survey of Rivers Hall, Boxted, Essex, 1586. (Courtesy Essex Record Office, County Hall, Chelmsford, Essex.)*

tions of the world," the settlers may have hoped to wash away all their old habits and attitudes. But in the end they were more able to "renounce all idolatry and superstition, all humane traditions and inventions whatsoever in the worship of God" than to alter drastically the practices affecting their livelihood. They may have insisted that their "reall intent [is] to sit down there close togither," but through a spectacular series of land divisions in-

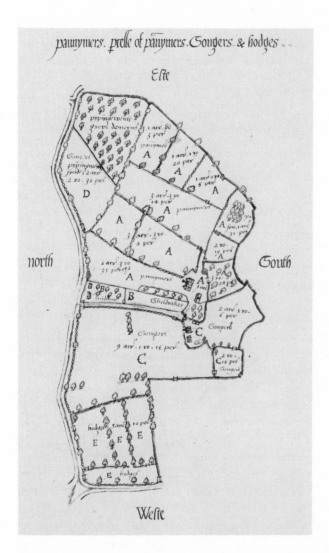

FIGURE 8. *From John Walker Senior's Survey of Rivers Hall, Boxted, Essex,*
1586. (Courtesy Essex Record Office, County Hall, Chelmsford, Essex.)

volving about two hundred men and over 16,000 acres, Watertown townsmen altered their original intent in less than a decade. In the process they
formed a community with more egalitarian land distribution than communities from the English North or West, and yet one in which the buying
and selling of land became an obsession. The Watertown land divisions
were larger than Rowley's common-field strips and formed compact

blocks. Common herding was practiced here, as it was in East Anglia, but no hint of common arable field regulations exists, except for the very earliest years when some direction was necessary to relieve confusion over grants. These large land divisions, together with the Watertown men's unrestrained interest in the local land market, combined to disperse the population onto still more remote, compact farmsteads where East Anglian farmers could engage in individual economic pursuits free from most town regulations.[15]

Land granting in Watertown commenced with the parceling out of house lots prior to 1634, when the records for the town began. Individual grants in this first division were never larger than 16 acres and averaged about 5 to 6. Because of their original small size and the East Anglian inclination to exchange and consolidate, the early proportions of these grants were quickly altered as larger properties were made from these smaller parcels. Jeremiah Norcross's house lot of 26 acres was actually composed of four smaller lots purchased from different persons. In like manner John Benjamin had a house lot of 60 acres, and Simon Stone had one of 50, of which only 12 acres had been formally granted to him.

Nine additional grants were made during the following years. Table 12 analyzes these land grants as they are recorded in the original land divisions. Compared with the distribution at Rowley, the Watertown grants were impressively large. In the "North Country" town less than 2,200 acres were granted, with the average size of the holdings just over 23 acres per settler. This was about the same size as the average holding at Hingham, Massachusetts, where the total acreage granted was only 3,191. To some degree, it seems that the more southern the origin of the population in England was, the larger the land grants were in Massachusetts. Newbury granted almost 8,000 acres, and each proprietor received an amount averaging slightly over 80 acres. In Ipswich the figure for total acreage granted was almost twice as high, 14,505 acres, and each individual received on the average 97 acres, which was close to the same amount of land as at Watertown.[16] While the amount of land granted was large, Watertown had the lowest concentration of land controlled by those in the highest economic levels of local society. Less than one-third of all the land

15. Francis, *Historical Sketch of Watertown*, 134–135; *Watertown Recs.*, 4 (Apr. 23, 1638).

16. Town records differ, and it is impossible to compare precisely the land grants of one town with another. The comparison here is approximate. The average Ipswich landholder probably held an additional 4 to 6 acres in a "planting lot" or "house lot," but they were never listed in terms of acreage in the town records.

The Ipswich figures are based on a list of 150 landholders that was compiled mainly in 1642, although a few of the names were added later. With the exception of a few small grants

TABLE 12. *Distribution of Land Grants within the Ten Original Divisions of Watertown, Massachusetts, ca. 1630–ca. 1642*

	No. of Landholders	Cumulative Acreage	% of Total Land Grants
Top 10%	21	5,546	30.7
Top 25%	53	10,574	58.6
Top 50%	105	15,512	85.9
Bottom 50%	105	2,542	14.1
Total	210	18,054	100.0

Note:
The median holding among Watertown landholders was 64 acres; the average holding was 86 acres. Of the 220 Watertown land grantees (the basis of table 4, above), 10 men left no record of their property holdings. This table is based on the remaining 210 landholders.

Source:
Compiled from *Watertown Records* . . . [title varies], 6 vols. in 5 (Watertown, Mass., 1894–1928), I, "Lands Grants Divisions Allotments Possessions and Proprietors' Book," 3–14.

was held by the top tenth of all townsmen. In communities from the North and West of England, the figure was closer to 50 percent.

The traffic in land sales in East Anglian Watertown and Ipswich was extraordinary.[17] On April 20, 1635, for instance, at least nine transactions were recorded in the Ipswich town records. The laxity with which Ipswich kept its land records will prevent forever any systematic analysis of the boom in land transactions there, but Ipswich deeds filed in county court during the first three decades of the town's existence reveal some

---

usually too imprecise to include in the figures, all grants were made before 1670, and in fact, most were made in the 1630s and early 1640s. These conditions basically conform to other town records examined here. Hingham's list of landholders, for instance, is made up mostly of those who entered the town prior to 1640, after which time immigration was greatly reduced. Newbury's list of proprietors was compiled in 1642. Likewise, land grants included here extend to the 1670 divisions in Hingham and to all land parceled out in the divisions as late as 1672 in Rowley. For the most part, therefore, the cutoff date that I have used to make these comparisons is approximately the same for all five towns.

17. When George Hadley sold his house lot to Samuel Boreman (Ipswich Town Recs., Jan. 12, 1640), for instance, the entry described the property as "lying on the South syde the Towne River bounded by an house lott, formerly granted to Phillip Challis on the East, and by a house lott, formerly granted to Robert Hayes on the Southwest, this houselott being formerly granted to John Wedgewood, as apeareth in this book folio 10, and by him sould to the sayd Geo. Hadlye." Ipswich land was often caught in the middle of a sea of land sales.

broad, comparative outlines, particularly in relation to the neighboring Essex County communities of Rowley and Newbury.

Before 1660, 104 deeds were filed involving Ipswich men and Ipswich land, twice as many as in Newbury and over ten times the number entered by Rowley men. Ipswich deeds involved 119 individuals in 206 exchanges, and suggest, when compared with the figures for the other towns, that buying and selling land was more broadly based in this East Anglian town since more men across the social and economic spectrum were involved in these transactions. A rough tabulation of the Ipswich deeds also indicates that in at least half of them a house lot or dwelling was sold, which reveals frequent movement inside the community, not merely the sale of isolated parcels of land on the fringes of the township. In 62 of the 104 deeds acreage was mentioned and in those cases the average was 28.9 acres per transaction. If one 2,200-acre purchase is excluded, the average drops only to 23.2 acres per deed. Excluding the atypical figures from the Ipswich, Newbury, and Rowley records, the average or normal Rowley transaction was slightly over 6 acres and the average Newbury transaction was 17.6 acres. In sum, in the East Anglian community there was considerably more trading activity in relation to population, and generally larger purchases. And in terms of the social and economic status of the purchasers, Ipswich drew from the middle rather than the upper ranks of local society more than either Rowley or Newbury did.[18]

By combining information from both town and county records for the period, some impression of the volume and scope of land transactions can be obtained. Some men were very actively engaged in the market, such as John Woodan, who bought eight parcels and sold nine, or Samuel Symonds, who purchased 300 acres of land and later sold over 700. Some men never received grants, such as Edward Harinden, who was still able to sell 150 acres in 1656 for £114, though George Hadley's rise from having no land at all to owning about 26 acres was more typical. Other East Anglians such as the Whipple brothers, John and Matthew, of Bocking, Essex, traded 216 and 140 acres, respectively, according to surviving records. Another East Anglian family, the Kimballs from Rattlesden, Suf-

18. Ipswich Deeds, I, 6–7, 20–21, 23–24, 30–33, 68–79, 83–85, 92–94, 121–126, 134–138, 147–150, 155–157, 160–161, 190–196, 198–208, 210–211, 238–239, 248–250, 254–256, 263–270, 276–279, 321–322, 327–328, 333–341, 360, 365–366, 369–370, 377–381, 397–398, 419–422, 426–427, 435–450, 459–463, 467–468, 492–495, 499–500, 513–515, 546–550, 561–572, 589–599, 606–607, 610–613, 625–629, 632–639, 642–645, 659–664, 666–667. Comparative estimated population figures (for 1647 and 1666) come from Wall, "Decline of the Massachusetts Franchise," *JAH*, LIX (1972–1973), 303–310.

folk, was also part of the Ipswich land market. Richard had received 40 acres and a house lot by grant but had increased his holdings to 107 acres by 1675. His son Richard, Jr., was granted only 6 acres in 1647 but managed to sell 30 only five years later. Finally, Thomas Kimball, though he never received a grant from the town, sold 26 acres of upland in 1655 and twenty-one years later had an estate of 422 acres worth £450.

At least twenty-eight Ipswich men bought or sold more than 100 acres of land during the first forty years of settlement, ranging from Richard Saltonstall's purchase of 2,200 acres, to the sale by Thomas Howlett, Jr., of 100 acres of ungranted property and a house. With the exception of the Perkinses, the Whittingham brothers, and Richard Saltonstall, nine out of every ten of the remaining men in the group of twenty-eight came from either Suffolk, Essex, or Hertfordshire, and all the rest originated from counties surrounding London, that is, from areas where the commercial value of agricultural land was widely recognized.[19]

Immigrants to Ipswich and Watertown came, for the most part, from a strictly defined region in East Anglia along the Stour River, which divides Essex from Suffolk, and from the boroughs of those counties and Hertfordshire. In contrast to Hingham, Norfolk, just to the north, the Stour River region and the neighboring boroughs were favorably positioned for commercial trade overseas and for taking advantage of the rising London food market. Ipswich and Watertown settlers' previous experience with this commercial milieu shaped their lives in Massachusetts. In England the forces of the market brought about competition for the available land and incessant buying, selling, and exchanging. In the New World, this pattern was reproduced in Ipswich and Watertown, where enclosed, consolidated family farms were quickly established, and the entangling common-field regulations of neighboring Rowley avoided.

Leadership Patterns and Local Government

Almost twenty years before the settlement of Ipswich, Captain John Smith saw great potential in Angoam, the Indian name for Ipswich, de-

19. Very helpful in the compilation of net land fluctuations in individual landholdings in Ipswich was Edward S. Perzel's Appendix 1, "Landholdings of the First Generation," in "The First Generation of Settlement in Colonial Ipswich, Massachusetts: 1633–1660" (Ph.D. diss., Rutgers– The State University, 1967), 242–313. Much of Perzel's discussion of land in Ipswich has been published as "Landholding in Ipswich," Essex Inst., *Hist. Colls.*, CIV (1968), 303–328.

scribing it as having "many rising hilles, and on their tops and descents many corne fields, and delightfull groves." There was much marsh grass for pasture "with many faire high groves of mulberrie trees and gardens; and there is also Okes, Pines, and other woods to make this place an excellent habitation." Edward Johnson referred to it some years later as "a very good Haven Towne" as well as having "very good Land for Husbandry, where Rocks hinder not the course of the Plow." The Plymouth Company considered planting their colony at Angoam before permanently settling further south.

This contemporary publicity, John Winthrop's own praise of the region (and the firsthand confirmation of it by John Winthrop, Jr.), and the success of the enterprising men who helped found the community in the early to mid-1630s helped to lure others there, and the town became, as a resident later described it, a place filled with great numbers of "both planters and other artificers."[20] The influx of large numbers of settlers, particularly the "artificers," led to economic differentiation and produced a highly stratified social structure. It was within this context that leadership patterns in Ipswich came to resemble those of the English boroughs that had been part of the English experience of leading Ipswich men. In the English boroughs and in Ipswich, Massachusetts, leadership was tied to wealth. In addition, and perhaps more important, Ipswich was a society well aware of its commercial capacities and promise.

Unlike other Massachusetts communities, Ipswich promoted business and commercial activities from the beginning and consciously fostered the town economy. In the first recorded town meeting, held in November 1634, well before most other towns looked into such matters, two men were given permission to build both a mill and a fishing weir. Several years later a "committee for furthering Trade among us" was established by Simon Bradstreet, Robert Paine, Daniel Denison, John Tuttle, Matthew and John Whipple, and Richard Saltonstall, who were in charge of "the putting up [of] B[u]oys, Beacons, and [the] providing of Salt[,] Cotton, sewing of hempe-seed [and] flax seed, and Cards wyer canes," which aided both commerce and "industrial" activity in the cloth trade. It was also agreed upon that a committee be appointed "with full power to dis-

---

20. Smith, *A Description of New England* . . . (London, 1616), in George Francis Dow, collector and annotator, *Two Centuries of Travel in Essex County, Massachusetts: A Collection of Narratives and Observations Made by Travelers, 1605–1799* (Topsfield, Mass., 1921), 6; Jameson, ed., *Johnson's Wonder-Working Providence*, 96; Joseph B. Felt, *History of Ipswich, Essex, and Hamilton* (Cambridge, Mass., 1834), iii–iv; Winthrop, *History of New England*, I, 98; Hubbard, *General History of New England*, 155.

pose [of] the little Neck for the advancing of Fishing." This group, as it turned out, was composed of many of the same men as the "trade" committee. Later, Daniel Hovey was granted liberty "to Biuld a wharfe against his ground he Bought of William Knowlton and also such Biulding as may tend to improvement thereof."[21]

The town was widely diversified in occupations outside of agriculture. Ipswich had over a dozen carpenters, at least as many leather workers engaged in every activity from tanning to saddlery and shoemaking, and half a dozen weavers. Many crafts and trades were represented in the town, ranging from coopers, butchers, and bakers to wheelwrights, blacksmiths, and tallow candlers. The town offered encouragement to other enterprises, for example when it granted liberty "to the Inhabitants with such others as shall joyne with them to set up a Bloomary for to make iron at Chebacco River," or when it allowed Samuel Appleton freedom to cut wood to operate the kiln of his malthouse.[22] None of the other four towns studied here left a record quite so filled with discussion and encouragement of crafts, trade, and commercial activities.

Some Ipswich merchants had direct business connections with England, most notably John Cogswell, but William Hubbard, Jonathan Wade, William Paine, and Jeremy Belcher, for instance, also traded with the British Isles, and some of the documentation of that activity is preserved in the local records. William Paine and William Bartholomew were often in Essex County court on matters pertaining to their commercial interests. Paine was involved in numerous cases: actions for debt over the ownership of ships; suits involving such products as wooden bolts and pipe staves, or a supply of fish for the London market; charges against him for the illegal sale of goods from Barbados; and even an action concerning the failure to deliver a parcel of moose skins. Paine's widespread New England enterprises ranged from sawmills in New Hampshire to ironworks in Lynn and Braintree.[23]

21. Ipswich Town Recs., Nov. 1634, Jan. 11, 1641, Feb. 14, 1660. A "company of adventurers" was formed in 1645 so that "whatever trade they may discover, shall be for their sole advantage twenty years." In the early years Ipswich also was engaged in a great deal of rivalry with Boston over its central trading position and pursued a political policy in the General Court aimed at reducing Boston's place in the colony. See Darrett B. Rutman, "The Mirror of Puritan Authority," in George Athan Billias, ed., *Law and Authority in Colonial America* (Barre, Mass., 1965), 160.

22. Felt, *History of Ipswich*, 94–110; Perzel, "First Generation of Settlement in Ipswich," 81–87; Ipswich Town Recs., Apr. 3, 1641, June 18, 1658.

23. Perzel, "First Generation of Settlement in Ipswich," 93. For some cases involving Paine and Bartholomew, see *Essex Co. Court Recs.*, I, 55, 64, 78, 87, 94–95, 95n, 98–101, 109, 112, 127–128, 139, 141, 147, 154–155, 161–162, 165, 175, 181, 183, 183n, 187, 204, 239, 259, 261, 263–264, 266n, 271, 278, 296, 303, 305, 326, 374, 403, II, 74, 81, 210.

A society with wide extremes in wealth soon emerged in Ipswich. A small group of men controlled a very high proportion of the town's resources, as compared to the other towns studied here. A select 10 percent of the settlers who arrived before 1640 controlled almost half of the total wealth in the community, as measured by estate inventories. The bottom 50 percent of the community shared only 12 percent of the total wealth (see table 13). Inventories ranged in value from those of merchants such as Jonathan Wade and Thomas Bishop, whose estates amounted to £7,326 10s. 8d. and £4,038 3s. 10d., respectively, to a few with a net indebtedness of 30 to 40 pounds. In Ipswich the richest eight men held almost half of the town wealth, whereas in Rowley and Newbury this group's share, the top decile, amounted to only a third, and in Hingham and Watertown, it was about a fourth. The top quartile in Ipswich held over two-thirds of

TABLE 13. *Distribution of Inventoried Wealth among 82 of the 170 Settlers in Ipswich, Massachusetts, Who Arrived before 1640 and Remained until at least 1660*

	No. of Inventories	Cumulative Wealth in £	% of Total Wealth
Top 10%	8	23,069/17/05	48.8
Top 25%	20	32,854/16/02	69.5
Top 50%	41	41,474/06/02	87.7
Bottom 50%	41	5,831/08/05	12.3
Total	82	47,305/14/07	100.0

Note:
   The median inventory among the 82 Ipswich settlers was £257/04/11, and the average inventory among them was £576/18. Of the 398 men who are known to have lived in Ipswich prior to 1660, 170 came to the town before 1640 and remained there until at least 1660. The cutoff date of 1640 was chosen because the end of the influx of new settlers occurred in 1639. See Edward S. Perzel, "Landholding in Ipswich," Essex Institute, *Historical Collections*, CIV (1968), 320. Of the 170 more or less permanent Ipswich inhabitants, 91 left inventories, but at least 9 of these appear suspiciously incomplete and have not been considered in this tabulation.

Sources:
   The names of the early settlers have been culled from: "Ipswich Proceedings," *New England Historical and Genealogical Register*, II (1848), 50–52; "Early Ipswich Families," *ibid.*, 174–177; Thomas Franklin Waters, *Ipswich in the Massachusetts Bay Colony*, 2 vols. (Ipswich, Mass., 1905–1917), I, Appendix A, "A Summary of the Names of the First Settlers from 1633 to 1649 . . . ," 490–494; D. Hamilton Hurd, comp., *History of Essex County, Massachusetts, with Biographical Sketches of Many of Its Pioneers and Prominent Men*, 2 vols. (Phila-

delphia, 1888), I, 570–571; and Edward S. Perzel, "First Generation of Settlement in Colonial Ipswich, Massachusetts: 1633–1660" (Ph.D. diss., Rutgers University, 1967), Appendix 2, "Vital Statistics," 314–376. Dates have been verified from James Savage, *A Genealogical Dictionary of the First Settlers of New England* . . . , 4 vols. (Boston, 1860–1862), and Charles Henry Pope, *The Pioneers of Massachusetts, A Descriptive List* . . . (Boston, 1900), among other sources. Inventories included in the table are: George Francis Dow, ed., *The Probate Records of Essex County, Massachusetts, 1635–1681*, 3 vols. (Salem, Mass., 1916–1920), I, 53–55, 60–61, 62–64, 87–91, 95, 97–98, 103–106, 108–109, 125–128, 151–152, 156–158, 163–165, 167–170, 173–174, 175, 190–191, 217–219, 222–225, 267, 282–284, 285–286, 306–308, 353, 392–393, 397–399, 439–441, II, 4–5, 18–19, 21–26, 34–37, 57–60, 63–73, 124–125, 138, 143–145, 166–168, 211–214, 235–237, 239–241, 315–317, 349–352, 387, 390–393, 426–429, III, 16–19, 43–45, 48–49, 59–62, 63–65, 74–76, 84–85, 160–162, 244–246, 250–252, 263–271, 294–297, 302–306, 379–382, 419–422; Bound Wills and Inventories, vol. 302, pp. 22, 94–95, vol. 303, pp. 91–92, 219, vol. 304, pp. 18–20, 28, 122–123, 211–212, 294–295, vol. 305, p. 74, vol. 307, pp. 107–108, vol. 308, p. 223, vol. 311, p. 23, and inventories on file, nos. 2303, 5523, 7549, 10073, 15855, Essex County Probate Office.

As suggested earlier with the experience of Rowley (chap. 2, n. 12, above), Ipswich inventories do not appear to be underrepresentative of the poor; if anything, they perhaps underemphasize the wealthy in this Essex County town. One town rate for 1648 has survived ("Ipswich Proceedings," *NEHGR*, II [1848], 50–52), and the table below has been constructed from this and from the 46 inventories of men on the list. The tax list included 161 individuals, and since the assessments were usually in full shilling amounts, the various economic divisions are the closest approximations possible. Only permanent men, that is, those who arrived before 1640 and did not move away (as well as can be determined from genealogical sources), form the basis of this table and have been used for the comparison. Permanent men account for 60% of all 1648 ratepayers. Nearly half of the rated men in the upper 50% category left town before their deaths; several others arrived after 1640. By contrast, nearly three out of every four men rated in the lower half remained in Ipswich throughout their lives. When permanent taxpaying inhabitants are compared with those who left inventories, it is clear that the wealthy were underrepresented: in the top decile inventories are less likely to occur almost three times as often than their proportion of the permanent taxpaying inhabitants would warrant. The same is true of the upper quartile, though less so. With these exceptions the proportions of extant inventories to permanent taxpaying inhabitants is almost at parity in other economic classifications, and the general conclusion would seem to be that, based on the 1648 rate, the distribution of inventoried wealth of settlers in Ipswich somewhat undervalues the disparities in wealth between the most affluent townsmen and all others.

Comparison of Extant Ipswich Inventories
with the Ipswich Tax Rate for 1648

Ratepayers	No.	Permanent Inhabitants Who Came before 1640	% of All Permanent Taxpaying Inhabitants	% of Extant Inventories among Taxpaying Inhabitants
Top 10%	12	6	6.1	2.2
Top 25%	47	25	25.5	17.4
Top 50%	83	41	41.8	39.1
Bottom 50%	78	57	58.2	60.9
Total	161	98	100.0	100.0

the community's resources, whereas in most of the other towns the figure was 10 to 15 percent less. The Ipswich figures might have shown even greater disparities in wealth if such affluent and influential individuals as John Winthrop, Jr., Richard Saltonstall, John Tuttle, Nathaniel Ward, and John Norton, and merchants William Bartholomew, William Hubbard, and William Paine had not eventually left the town.

Given this marked interest in furthering the commercial importance of the town, it is not surprising that Ipswich chose its selectmen from among the "principal inhabitants." One of these men, Samuel Symonds, described town society in Ipswich as one of a "more mixt condition" than in England, in which "the richer sort," though they owned less outward estate, had "the liberty of good government in their hands" and "the poorer sort (held under in England)" had "inlargement" of their property.[24] While Symonds and other prominent Ipswich men exaggerated the leveling tendencies in their town, they were perfectly correct about who ruled. Sixteen men served as selectmen for from six to nineteen years (terms) between 1636 and 1687. As a group their median inventory was £888 and it averaged £1,861 per selectman. Both of these figures were over three times higher than the town's as a whole.[25] With the exception of open-field

24. Samuel Symonds to John Winthrop, Jan. 6, 1647, in Waters, *Ipswich in the Massachusetts Bay Colony*, I, 515.

25. The Relationship between Wealth and Tenure in Office, Ipswich Selectmen, 1636–1687

Selectmen	No. of Years Served	Inventoried Estates in £
George Giddings	19	997/12/06
Daniel Denison	18	2,105/13/00
Robert Lord	16	631/15/03
Thomas Bishop	15	4,038/03/10
Thomas Burnham	15	778/16/01
John Whipple, Jr.	13	3,314/17/01
Jonathan Wade	12	7,326/10/08
Samuel Appleton	11	
Simon Stacey	9	664/05/11
William Goodhue	9	
John Andrews, Jr.	7	
Thomas Howlett	7	418/03/06
Daniel Epps	7	1,218/15/00
John Perkins	6	
Joseph Medcalfe	6	370/13/00
Robert Day	6	472/06/00

The table above is based on the following inventory sources: *Essex Co. Probate Recs.*, II, 18–19, 211–214, III, 63–65, 250–252; Bound Wills and Inventories, vol. 302, pp. 94–95, vol. 303, p. 219, vol. 304, pp. 11–15, 18–20, 55–56, vol. 305, p. 173, vol. 306, pp. 92–93, vol.

Rowley, wealth played some part in the leadership selection of other towns studied here. In Newbury and Hingham, however, the disparity in economic position between the rulers and the ruled was never so great as it was in Ipswich, and in the Norfolk town considerations like family ties played a more important role in determining who became the leading town officers.

Although family was not the basis of a "proprietary" right to office in Ipswich, the length of time that men served in a position apparently was. Many men served in the same offices a great number of times, compiling a wealth of experience. Service for the most active Ipswich selectmen usually began shortly after settlement and lasted until their deaths, or in some cases began later and often extended into the late seventeenth century. With the exception of the first several years, there were always men with long experience among the governing selectmen. During the 1660s the average number of years experience in office was 5.4 and this figure increased to 6.2 during the following decade.[26]

Frequent long terms in office and a restricted number of positions to be filled meant that a comparatively few men dominated officeholding. Only sixty-five men were elected to the position of selectman between 1636 and 1687, and seven of them, or one-tenth, controlled 108 out of 283 possible positions on the board, almost 40 percent of the total. Sixteen men, or a quarter of all selectmen, held 176, or 62 percent of the positions open over the fifty-year period. There was similar monopolization of other offices. On May 2, 1642, the position of "town treasurer," an office that seems only to have existed in Ipswich, was filled by Robert Paine, the wealthiest man in town. In addition to the position he apparently held throughout his life, he served as county treasurer from 1665 to 1683. He was also the chief patron and founder of the Ipswich grammar school, whose high-sounding board of "feoffees," another unique town institution, included other wealthy men, such as Paine's brother William, merchants William Bartholomew and William Hubbard, Major-General Daniel Denison, and Judge Samuel Symonds.[27] Unlike most communities, which merely appointed a master and approved his salary—if any school was established at

---

308, p. 223, and inventories on file, no. 7549, Essex County Probate Office. I am not claiming here that all wealthy men were selectmen. Some men of wealth were involved primarily with county or colony office, but others simply pursued their business activities.

26. See table 6 in chap. 2, above.

27. Ipswich Town Recs., May 2, 1642, Dec. 19, 1648 (published as "Ipswich Proceedings," *NEHGR*, II [1848], 50–52), Jan. 26, 1652; Abraham Hammatt, "Ipswich Grammar School," *NEHGR*, VI (1852), 64–71, 159–167.

all—the form that this institution took in Ipswich clearly shows again how leadership and public responsibility were left to a relatively small, economically and socially select group of townsmen.

As distinct from other towns, Ipswich employed several men who regularly took part in the administration of town affairs and whose functions set them apart as a class of "civil servants." Town constable Theophilus Wilson, who served from 1648 until shortly before his death in the 1680s, was one of them. He died with only a modest estate of £233 11s. 3d., considerably less than was typical of the wealth of the selectmen. Another such civil servant was Robert Lord, who served in a variety of capacities. Lord was town clerk from 1646 until his death in 1682, and was appointed as selectman over a dozen times. He was regularly chosen town marshal and was often in county court representing the town's interests as chief counsel. In 1652 he was appointed clerk of court for the county and two years later was made clerk of the writs for Ipswich. On February 23, 1644, Lord was "from this time forward" made responsible for recording the proceedings of the general town meeting as well as the freemen's and selectmen's deliberations. He was also appointed to record information about the personal estates of all inhabitants, which would be used for drawing up a new town rate, to "keepe the streets cleare of wood and timber," to sue various individuals for not paying their rates, to prosecute the constables for neglecting to bring in their accounts, to levy fines for absence from the yearly general town meeting, and to collect fines for acts committed contrary to town order.[28] For former borough men like Robert Lord of Sudbury, Suffolk, the performance of administrative duties in New England was merely a continuation of responsibilities exercised in old England where men "were expected to give life-long service to the government of the borough."[29]

Depending upon their special traditions of government and other local factors, the administration of seventeenth-century English boroughs varied in nature from tightly held organizations ruled by a close body to those in which the voice of the town's freemen was the determining factor. In much the same way, parish organization in East Anglian towns included a variety of forms, ranging from control by oligarchical groups to open town meetings. For Ipswich selectmen such as Robert Day and George Gid-

28. *Essex Co. Court Recs.*, I, 78, 109, 251, 266, 319, 367; Ipswich Town Recs., Feb. 23, 1644, Feb. 1645, Feb. 28, 1645, Sept. 21, 1646, [Oct.] 30, 1648, Feb. 12, 1649, and Mar. 26, 1649; A. C. Goodell, "A Biographical Notice of the Officers of Probate for Essex County, from the Commencement of the Colony to the Present Time," Essex Inst., *Hist. Colls.*, II (1860), 216.

29. Powell, *Puritan Village*, 44.

dings, who came from or had experience in the borough of St. Albans, Hertfordshire, their ideas about local government were shaped by their knowledge of this English borough.[30]

In St. Albans, government was run by a small self-perpetuating body, the mayor and aldermen. Exclusive control of government by this oligarchy began with the dissolution of the St. Albans abbey and the subsequent royal incorporation of the borough. The charter of 1553 established a governing body consisting of a mayor and eleven aldermen, and this body met regularly with the "Twenty-four," or assistants, to conduct borough business as the common council. The assistants were selected from the four craft guilds, representing forty-two separate trades and crafts, in St. Albans. Wardens from the guilds policed the borough and saw to it that none but freemen of the town were engaged in a trade and that those permitted to were carrying it on in a proper manner. Knowledge of infractions was brought to the mayor's court, composed of the mayor and aldermen. In addition to assistants and wardens, the charter provided for other officers, such as a steward, a recorder, two bailiffs, viewers of the market, constables, and viewers of each town ward.

With the declining power and influence of the medieval town guilds, the mayor and eleven principal burgesses, or aldermen, acquired even greater power. As long-standing members of the common council, their experience surpassed that of the assistants, though many of the latter had often been on the council for many terms, representing their company or trade. After 1633 the town received a new charter that went so far as to allow the mayor and principal burgesses to regulate the election of the guild members to the council. The highest position in borough government, the office of mayor, was filled on a strict rotation basis among the aldermen, which meant that each man served as mayor every twelfth year, unless the death of one of them intervened. Thus nearly every alderman between 1597 and 1643 served at least two terms in the position, and some, such as John Oxton, Thomas Rockett, and John Sanders, were elected three or four times. Deaths did interrupt this pattern occasionally, of course, but the aldermen formed a remarkably stable as well as powerful group throughout the early seventeenth century. In addition to serving a long tenure in office, mayors and aldermen were of necessity expected to be wealthy men. As the mayor's court observed in 1639, mayors ordinarily

30. For a discussion and examples of these various forms of local governmental administration, see Webb and Webb, *English Local Government: The Manor and the Borough*, 405–568, and *The Parish and the County*, 42–145, 173–276. For a more recent account of the increasingly oligarchic nature of English borough government, see Peter Clark and Paul Slack, *English Towns in Transition, 1500–1700* (Oxford, 1976), 126–140.

"sustained verie great charges" due to their expenses during their terms in office.[31] Wealth, increasing power, and long tenure were the characteristic features of the ruling group in St. Albans that men such as Robert Day and George Giddings helped transfer to the New World.

By far the greatest share of power in the borough was vested in the mayor and aldermen (or burgesses) sitting as the mayor's court. Our knowledge of this body's activities during the early seventeenth century is limited to the court book, some draft minutes, and mayors' accounts that still survive, but from them an outline of the scope and function of the court can be drawn. The court met four times a year, once with the council and townspeople in a session where the aldermen submitted two names from which they selected one for mayor. On other occasions the meetings were held in secret. Regulation of public nuisances preoccupied much of the business of the court. The various ward inspectors of the four town districts regularly reported disturbances that had taken place in the streets, and presentments were usually made on the offending parties. The mayor and aldermen were also in charge of education, that is, the appointment of new masters to the school. They handled town financial matters such as the leasing of tenements or stalls in the market. Above all, however, was their interest in the control and regulation of town trade. The mayor was by right of office allowed to fix the price of goods, and the mayor and burgesses prohibited trading by nonfreemen in the market and fined those who attempted to do so. In the process of regulating borough enterprise, the mayor and aldermen were not averse to furthering their own interests at the expense of lesser men. In 1606, for instance, various reports mentioned the existence of many unlicensed ale and tippling houses that provided "the cause of much drunkenness and looseness." Fearing a rise in the cost of fuel due to the increased consumption of wood for brewing, the mayor and aldermen ordered that in future only four beer brewers and two ale brewers should operate premises in the town. Four of those six were principal burgesses, and long explanations were given for the selection of the two others, both of whom received personal recommendations from court members.[32]

31. *Victoria Hist. of Counties, Hertfordshire*, II (1908), 481–482; Arthur Ernest Gibbs, *The Corporation Records of St. Albans, with Lists of Mayors, High Stewards, Members of Parliament, Etc.* (St. Albans, England, 1890), 54–71. For another example of an increasingly oligarchic borough from which Ipswich settlers came, see Thomas Cromwell, *History and Description of the Ancient Town and Borough of Colchester, in Essex*, 2 vols. (London, 1825), II, 438–439, 257–266.

32. The foregoing account has been compiled from the following records: Mayor's Court Book, 1586–1633; Draft Minute Book of the Borough Court, 1628–1629; Mayor's Accounts, 1626–1627, 1628–1629, St. Albans Public Library, Victoria Street, St. Albans, Hertford-

As in St. Albans, in the town of Ipswich, Massachusetts, men held varying degrees of political status. In the English borough, status ranged from the mayor, to the aldermen, assistants, wardens, and freemen, to nonfreemen. While not as complex as St. Albans, Ipswich men could be residents (or townsmen), commoners, freemen, leaders such as the selectmen, or a combination of several of these. Unlike the practice in Newbury and to a great extent that in Rowley, political rights in Ipswich were not necessarily tied to claims of common land. On the other hand, residence alone did not usually ensure the enjoyment of political and civil rights in town meeting, as it seems to have done in Hingham.

Beyond the lowliest status—inhabitant or townsman—a man could become a commoner or perhaps a freeman. Achieving the rank of commoner appears to have been relatively simple in early Ipswich. Many of the first inhabitants were made commoners; others became such when they purchased land containing common rights; and some directly applied for the right. However, the latter two procedures were only occasionally followed, and buying and selling of proprietors' rights never occurred as it did in Newbury. Still, the town was lax about declaring who was a commoner and who was not. It was not until March 15, 1660, that the use of commonage became severely restricted because of the increasing threat of overcrowding in the town. At that time it was ordered that "no house henceforth erected shall have any right to the comon land of this towne nor any person inhabiting such houses make use of any pasture timber or wood growing uppon any the said Common Lands" without the "Express leave and allowance of the towne first had and obtained."[33]

Initially, freemanship in the colony depended upon membership in the town church, but throughout the early period requirements for freemanship changed, and at the same time, certain privileges associated with this status were taken away.[34] What is significant about Ipswich is that there were fewer freemen in the town than commoners and inhabitants, and

---

shire. For other examples illustrating the workings of borough government in East Anglia, see: The Burghe of Bury St. Edmonds Constitucions and Statutes Made There for the Good Government of the Sayd Burghe the 18th Day of July: 5: Jacobi Ano Dm 1607, D14/2/1, West Suffolk R.O.; Schedule of By-Laws Appended to Roll for Court Held February 24, 1564, Court Roll of Bishops Hall, Chelmsford, 1560–1613, D/DM M7; Maldon Customs and Rules, ca. 1550, D/B3/1/3, and Notes on Maldon Privileges, ca. 1630, D/B/3/3/77, Essex R.O. As in St. Albans, all placed emphasis on trade and trading regulations as well as on the protection and perpetuation of certain groups within the borough.

33. Ipswich Town Recs., Feb. 28, 1642, June 1, July 3, 1639, May 12, 1642, Jan. 20, 1657, Apr. 8, 1665, July 19, 1666, Mar. 15, 1660.

34. The literature on the rights and role of the freeman in early Massachusetts is lengthy and its main points need not be discussed here. See articles listed on p. 39, n. 34, above.

that the freemen regarded themselves as different from the general population and participated in their own distinctive town meeting. Freemanship
in Ipswich entailed special functions and distinct status in town government. Of the over 250 men in the town in 1642, 111 were commoners and
only about 80 were freemen. The freemen usually met several times during the year, while the general or town meeting was held annually. The
gulf in political rights between town and freemen's meetings was so wide
that 33 Ipswich nonfreemen petitioned the General Court in 1658 asking
for the privileges of serving as jurymen, voting for selectmen, and voting
on rate assessments. Possibly the division between freeman and nonfree-
man was artificial in other towns, but in Ipswich nonfree status was a real
barrier to effective participation in town affairs.[35]

Business at the town meetings usually involved several general matters.
At the December 1648 meeting, for example, the topics under discussion
included construction of a rail fence between the town and neighboring
Rowley, selection of two men to supervise land exchanges, fencing of
land, and payment for damage done by the town to personal property. As
a great number of commoners attended this annual meeting, much of the
business normally concerned various types of land regulations.

The freemen met more regularly, and in cooperation with the selectmen
handled most of the important town affairs. Although in theory the pre-
ponderance of power was held by the freemen, much of the actual authority was passed on to the selectmen. Restrictions were occasionally imposed on the selectmen by the body of freemen, but it was recognized at
an early stage that more effective administration could be obtained by
granting initiative to the smaller group "to doe therein, whatsoever the
major part of the freemen might doe to bind the rest of the Towne." To
simplify their own affairs the freemen appointed committees, such as the
one "chosen to consider what is the best way to despatch Towne business,
[and] whether the quarter meetings may not be shortened," or another
chosen "to prepare for the next meeting of the freemen, what they shall
think meet for yearly maintenance and for the way of raysing of it." Much
of their responsibility, however, was delegated to the selectmen.[36]

The selectmen of Ipswich were usually referred to as the "7 men." Al-

---

35. Perzel, "First Generation of Settlement in Ipswich," 118–133; "The Voting Rights of
Freemen in 1658: A Petition from Some of the Inhabitants of Ipswich," Essex Inst., *Hist.
Colls.*, XXXVI (1900), 245–247.

36. Ipswich Town Recs., Jan. 3, 1643, Nov. 3, 1642. Ipswich's earliest minister, Nathaniel Ward, regarded the freemen as having too much power, which he thought was best
put in the hands of the selectmen. "I suspect both Commonwealth and Churches have dis-
cended to lowe already," he stated to John Winthrop in 1639; "I see the spirits of people

though no specific number was ever mentioned in any Massachusetts law, and the number of aldermen varied from one English borough to another, this figure is suggestive of the selectmen's role and stature in Ipswich town affairs. "Wherefore, brethren," admonished Acts 6: 3, "look ye out among you seven men of honest report, full of the Holy Ghost and wisdom, whom we may appoint over this business." On nearly every matter of local business, it was the selectmen who took charge, and conflict with town inhabitants over their power, such as was common in Hingham and New-bury, rarely occurred in Ipswich. Although governance of town land was not specifically within the selectmen's jurisdiction, they were allowed to make grants, which they were frequently called upon to do in the late 1630s. Later they were also allowed to sell land. The selectmen issued countless bylaws, ranging from the implementation of a new order on wolves to agricultural regulations. On March 11, 1648, for instance, the selectmen put into effect orders regulating cattle, building a gate, creating a passage at both ends of a bridge, making chimneys safe, appointing cow keepers, and establishing fines for owners of animals left on the common. The selectmen also appointed a number of town officers, for example to help settle land disputes, and minor officials such as cattle reeves, fence viewers, and pig keepers. The selectmen also had control over many of the town's financial affairs, including the power to set town and county rates. They occasionally used their authority to collect taxes and impose fines.[37] These men met regularly and often, and very few areas of town life were left unaffected by their actions.

Unlike Rowley and Newbury, Ipswich as an incorporated body often brought suit in Essex County court against its own inhabitants over issues in which the town felt it had a vital interest or a principle to protect. Actions were usually brought by the selectmen in the name of the "Town of Ipswich." The cases involved such matters as highway obstruction, non-payment of taxes, failure to complete the construction of public facilities like the local prison house, felling of trees on the common, and refusal to pay rates for the maintenance of the ministry. As was typical of East Anglian towns, Ipswich was also sensitive to the immigration of the poor

---

runne high and what they gett they hould. They may not be denyed their proper and lawfull liberties, but I question," he went on, "whether it be of God to interest the inferiour sort in that which should be reserved *inter optimates penes quos est sacire leges*." Waters, *Ipswich in Massachusetts Bay Colony*, I, 505–506.

37. See also Proverbs 9: 1, "Wisdom hath builded her house, she hath hewn out her seven pillars." Ipswich Town Recs., Feb. 20, 1637, but note restrictions of Jan. 3, 1643, Dec. 24, 1658; compare grants made in 1638 and 1639, such as Sept. 1, 1638, [June?] 11, 1650, [Mar.] 29, 164[5], Mar. 1646, Feb. 23, 1644, Feb. 1645, Nov. 25, 1645, Apr. 29, 1647.

into the township, and the selectmen brought individuals to court in order to prevent them from settling in the community. The "selectmen of Ipswich gave notice," their representative told the court, "to Daniel Grasier and John Morill, Irishmen, that they were not willing to receive them as inhabitants, and they not removing, complaint was made to this court."[38]

The cases brought before the county court often concerned the fundamental relationship between the governed and the governors. Questions of social disorder or land controversies in Newbury, for instance, never seemed to have attracted the interest and concern that basic governmental relationships created in Ipswich. One of the most significant of these cases, *Giddings* v. *Brown*, came before the Essex County court in 1657. The incident was touched off when George Giddings, who frequently served as an Ipswich selectman, and other residents refused to pay a special tax, the proceeds of which were to be used for building or buying a house worth one hundred pounds for the minister, Thomas Cobbett. Cobbett seems to have been a well-respected person with scholarly accomplishments. He succeeded John Norton, who had left two years before, and there is no evidence that the opposition pushed its case because of religious disagreements or personality differences. The lengthy and highly significant opinion of Judge Samuel Symonds, an East Anglian who lived in Ipswich himself, held that the town's order violated "a fundamental law" that prevented using public funds to acquire property for private use. "If noe kinge or parliament can justly enact and cause that one mans estate, in whole or in part, may be taken from him and given to another without his owne consent," Symonds declared, "then surely the major part of a towne or other inferior powers cannot doe it." The town complied with the order, and the following year it established a rate of one hundred pounds "to provide a Conveniant towne house to Remaine to posterity for the use of the ministery and being put and Delivered in sufficient and good Condition to be kept in Repaire by the present Inhabitant." In a related matter some time later, a town inhabitant refused to pay rates for military service, arguing that even "if a majority voted for it" he could not be held responsible "since the military officers were not chosen by the towns."[39] Clearly, the East Anglians' long familiarity with local govern-

38. *Essex Co. Court Recs.*, I, 78, 87, 112, 161, 129n, 319, as well as 40, 89, 109, 248, II, 26, 118, 280, 281 (compare Ipswich Town Recs., n.d., 1639, re Humphrey Griffin), 140, 440.

39. [Thomas] *Hutchinson Papers*, 2 vols. (Albany, N.Y., 1865), II, 1–25; David Tenny Kimball, *A Sketch of the Ecclesiastical History of Ipswich* (Haverhill, Mass., 1823); *Concise History of the First Church of Christ, in Ipswich, from Its Formation, A.D. 1834, to A.D. 1862* (Boston,

ment at the borough and town level encouraged this sort of questioning, which men from the open fields of Yorkshire or the mixed traditions of western England rarely bothered to formulate.

Like Ipswich, East Anglian Watertown elected men to long terms in office and allowed them broad, discretionary powers. Certainly the most striking feature about the records of public officeholding in Watertown is their evidence concerning the duration of tenure. In the course of fifty elections between 1634 and 1686, only 76 men filled the 379 available positions on the board of selectmen. Thus the average length of tenure was almost five years. Power was even more narrowly distributed, however, than these facts would indicate. The top 10 percent of the most frequently elected selectmen controlled 143 of the 379 positions; in other words, 8 men held almost 38 percent of the total positions available. The top 25 percent, or 19 men, controlled not just a majority, but almost two-thirds of all the positions, 62 percent of the total. In addition, certain key men were repeatedly elected to the board. Hugh Mason served for twenty-nine years, John Sherman for twenty-three, Thomas Hastings for twenty, Ephraim Child for sixteen, and at least sixteen other men served for seven years or more throughout this period. Invariably these men came from Suffolk and Essex, or counties near them. Among the twenty most frequently elected selectmen, three out of every four came from those two counties and nine out of every ten were from eastern England.

Watertown did not foster commercial enterprise like Ipswich did, nor was its social structure as stratified, but its board of selectmen was dominated by wealthy townsmen. Hugh Mason, who served twenty-nine terms, had the fifth largest estate in total value among the eighty-three surviving Watertown inventories from this period. Mason's estate was worth £692 13s. 9d. Thomas Hastings, who served twenty terms, had the fourth largest; Ephraim Child, who was elected sixteen times, the third; William Bond, who served twelve terms, had the eleventh largest; Henry Bright, who had ten years' experience on the board, had the sixth largest; and John Briscoe, whose estate was rated eighth among the inventories, served as selectman nine times. There were a number of cases in which the relationship between service as selectmen and wealth was not so closely tied, but rarely did the top quarter of the most frequently chosen selectmen

1862); Weis, *Colonial Clergy of New England*, 58; *Essex Co. Court Recs.*, II, 47, 66–67, 99; Ipswich Town Recs., Feb. 21, 1656, Feb. 10, 1657, June 18, 1658, Aug. 12, 1658, Dec. 24, 1658.

have inventories valued below the median wealth of the community.[40] Watertown's government was similar in its political and social structure to Ipswich's, and yet the former community did not have the same commercial orientation as Ipswich. This suggests that it was not simply the desire to replicate borough government that encouraged the characteristic leadership patterns of these towns. Government by oligarchy in local East Anglian parishes was becoming a common practice by the start of the seventeenth century. The movement was accelerated by Tudor and Stuart social legislation at the national level as well as by locals who wanted to take matters into their own hands as a result of the acute social dislocation experienced at this time in the region. Ministers and vestries frequently applied to ecclesiastical authorities for permission to create close vestries, or parish governments run by the minister and "the better sort of the parishioners," as one such request from Chigwell, Essex, phrased it. The petition, dated June 16, 1620, and drafted by the vicar, Emman Uty, and the vestry, complained that

> by the admitting of the parishioners of all sorts to their church meetings concerning the affairs of the church and parish there hath been much confusion and disorder at their said church meetings and by reason that some are ignorant or weak in judgment and others not so ready to yield to that which the better sort of the parishioners would determine and agree upon as . . . [what] should be the business could not be dispatched without much difficulty and trouble.

The petitioners asked the bishop of London to grant local authority to fourteen men of the vestry as well as to the minister and churchwardens. Any eleven of them and the vicar or his curate were to be considered "a full vestry to order dispose and manage all and single the affairs belonging to their church and parish which are to be done by their parish."

Two years later in Orsett, Essex, the parish curate, Abraham Arc, the churchwardens, and "other[s] of the ancientest and better sort of the parish" sent a similar request to the bishop, stating that there was "great confusion and disorder in their said parish at their church meetings by reason of the ignorance and weakness in judgment about matters of that nature of

---

40. Figures on Watertown officeholding were compiled from *Watertown Recs.*, *passim*; inventories are from Middlesex Bound Wills and Inventories, II, 91–93, V, 353–356, VI, 359–365, VII, 178–181, IX, 23–25, 321–323. Richard C. Simmons notes, from his study of the 207 men who held land in Watertown by 1650, that there was "a marked—though not an absolute—correlation between wealth in land on one hand and freemanship and officeholding on the other." "Freemanship in Early Massachusetts: Some Suggestions and a Case Study," *WMQ*, 3d Ser., XIX (1962), 427.

some of the parishioners that resort thither and by the dissent of the inferior and meaner sort of them there hath fallen out some disquietness and hinderance to the good proceedings which they desire should be in their said parish." They petitioned that "a certain number namely 10," in addition to the minister and churchwardens, should constitute a vestry "for the ordering and directing of such things belonging to their church as are to be done by the parish." "Named for the present" to be members of this body were "the most sufficient parishioners, two of whom are Churchwardens."[41]

Consolidation of local government in the hands of a few and in offices of importance besides the vestry was evident in other Suffolk and Essex parishes. In Polstead, Suffolk, for instance, an English town in the center of the area of greatest Suffolk emigration, the overseers of the poor and particularly the churchwardens were repeatedly selected from the same group of men. In the years prior to emigration, men such as William Allen and William Gage often served as churchwardens. In neighboring Nayland, Suffolk, from where Watertown men John Firman, Thomas Parish, Isaac Stearns, and John Warren came, lands controlled by the parish for the benefit of the poor were in the hands of a select few. Thomas Blythe, Edward Garrard, William Gladwyn, and James Marett repeatedly signed parish accounts involving these feoffments, and town business usually was left to "the churchwardens and overseers of the poor and the cheife of the inhabitants of Nayland." Certainly a man like John Warren, who as town feoffee handled indentures of lease for town lands and was responsible also for the disbursing of the proceeds to the town poor, was aware of the role that principal men were to play in local government when he settled in Watertown in 1630.[42]

41. T/A 485, Essex R.O., transcribed from the Vicar General's Books, Diocese of London, DL/C/341, June 16, 1620, fol. 163-v, June 29, 1622, fols. 268v–269, Greater London Record Office, County Hall, London. Writing in the 1880s, Edward Channing suggested that various parish offices "developed into the select vestry of later times and that it is the only institution which offers a suggestion as to the origin of the prudential men, townsmen, ten men or selectmen of early New England." *Town and County Government in the English Colonies of North America*, Johns Hopkins University Studies in Historical and Political Science, 2d Ser., X (1884), 20. Of course, select vestries did not simply "develop" throughout England, nor did they evolve uniformly throughout all regions at the same time. The close vestry may have been in the minds of members of the General Court when they enacted the general town legislation of 1636, but these men were never authorized by that local body with the same degree of power assumed by vestrymen in close English parishes. From whatever source the General Court derived the office of selectmen, men of East Anglian communities like Watertown and Ipswich put the office to more effective use, giving it added power and authority, than did inhabitants of other New England towns.

42. There is some general indication of this repetition in officeholding as well in West Suffolk parish register transcripts signed by churchwardens and calendared in "Records of

In nearby cloth towns, where the parish was also the center of local government, the affairs of the community were often controlled by a small self-perpetuating oligarchy. Such was the case in Braintree, Essex, which was ruled by "The Company of Four and Twenty," "a curious body," as the Webbs described it, "half-way between a gild and a municipal Court of Aldermen" as well as being a select vestry. The origins of this group, which was occasionally also referred to as the "24 Headboroughs," the "Town Magistrates," or the "governors of the Town," are obscure, but date back at least to the 1560s, seventy years before the departure to New England of so many from this Essex cloth town. By 1611 the "Four and Twenty" felt compelled to augment their already large role in the superintendance of town affairs by appealing to the bishop of London along the same lines as the vestries of Chigwell and Orsett, Essex, had. They explained that

> through the generall admittance of all sorts of Parishioners into their Vestries and Meetings for the public good of the saide Parishe, there falleth out great disquietness and hindrance to the good proceedings which they desire should be in their saide Parishe, by the Dissent of some evell disposed, and others of the inferiour and meanest sort of the parishioners and inhabitants of the Parish, being greater in number, and thereby more readie to crosse the good proceedings for the benefitt of theire Church and Parishe, then liable to further by counsell or otherwise the good thereof.

The petition thereafter suggested that "there might be a certain number, namely Twentie, besides the Vicar, Curate, or Minister, and the Churchwardens there for the time being, which might be appointed continually to be Vestrie-men, for the ordering and directinge of such thinges belonging to their Church, as are to be done by the Parishe." Most of this number were to be "Parishioners and Inhabitants . . . who are reputed to be the most sufficient of the said Parish, and of whom diverse of them have borne Office in the same Parishe" and "Parishioners of like place, sufficiencie, or estimation, may succeede them, to be chosen by the greater number of the said Vestrie-men." In September 1612, in a "faculty" (or formal instrument) the bishop appointed the men recommended in the petition

---

the Sudbury Archdeaconry," Suffolk Institute of Archaeology and Natural History, *Proceedings*, XI (1903), 252–266, though none cover a long, continuous period. The Polstead, Suffolk, churchwardens' accounts and lists of officers chosen at vestry meetings are contained in EL 158/1/1, West Suffolk R.O. The Nayland material is from Deeds and Related Papers, 2/*passim*, Town Accounts, 3/12 *passim*, and Bailiff's Accounts, 4/23, Nayland Town Charity Records, Nayland, Suffolk.

and warned others not to "intermeddle" with "such matters and business as doe belong to the said Church and Parishe."[43]

All of this concentration of power was established at the expense of the only other local authority in the town, the manorial court leet. The court leet gave the lord of the manor criminal and, to some extent, civil jurisdiction, with the power to enforce bylaws in most matters, including public health, property, agriculture, and highways. The manor lord also had some authority over poor law regulations. In Braintree, the court leet jury, which sought out and punished infractions, functioned in the early seventeenth century but it consisted mainly of men from the "Four and Twenty." The court leet did appoint some minor manorial officers, such as ale and flesh tasters, or sealers of leather, but the town's constables were appointed by them only after prior selection by the Four and Twenty. In fact, the Company of Four and Twenty agreed in their April 1629 meeting that all constables, churchwardens, and overseers of the poor would henceforth be "yearly elected out of the company," and five years later the town surveyors were chosen in that fashion, "being one of the company, every year as it falls to every one by turn." These officials—churchwardens, overseers, constables, and surveyors—also served as executive officers for the governing council, the Four and Twenty, so they not only absorbed the court leet in terms of personnel but also in the services it provided to the Essex town.[44]

The decline of the manorial court leet and the rise of the civil parish were brought about by various factors. One of the most important was Tudor and Stuart legislation that transformed the role of the parish in local affairs.[45] When the "statute for mending of highways" was enacted in 1555, for instance, the Marian parliament did not turn to the local manor to administer it, even though this institution had often supervised local roads through the court leet. The manor had become increasingly inadequate to handle this responsibility, and the parliament bypassed it for the better-defined and often territorially larger organ of government, the parish. From the standpoint of simple efficiency, the parish served better.

43. Philip Morant, *The History and Antiquities of the County of Essex* . . . , II (1768), 398n–399n; Webb and Webb, *English Local Government: The Parish and the County*, 221–227.

44. Minutes of the Company of Four and Twenty, D/P 264/8/3, Apr. 13, 1629, Apr. 7, 1634, Essex R.O.

45. The sheer number of statutes pertaining to the parish is itself a measure of change. Tate lists only 11 parliamentary acts referring to the parish prior to the reign of Henry VIII, while there were 58 enacted from that time until shortly before the migration of settlers to New England in the late 1620s and early 1630s. See W. E. Tate, *The Parish Chest: A Study of the Records of Parochial Administration in England* (Cambridge, 1946), Appendix 1, 315–316.

This was particularly true in eastern England where the manor was rarely coterminous with the parish and where court leet jurisdictions spread haphazardly over the territory within the parish boundaries. In Babergh hundred, Suffolk, for instance, there were ten manors in the parish of Stoke Nayland, six in Bures St. Mary, and eleven in Little Waldingfield, while in the hundreds nearby, the parishes of Hawkedon and Rattlesden, Suffolk, contained four and five manors respectively.

The highway act required parish constables, churchwardens, and "a number of the parishioners" to elect annually two men of the parish as surveyors. These men were to be in charge of "the works for amendment of the highways in their parish leading to any market-town." The constables and churchwardens were then required to set aside four days out of the year for road work and to announce them "openly in the church the next Sunday after Easter," after which time the parishioners themselves were to go about "amending of the said ways" according to their economic status in the community. The court leet still had a role in the new arrangement: it was to inquire into infractions and defaults committed by the parishioners. But the fines collected by the court leet were to be handed over to the churchwardens for use in the maintenance of the highways, and the churchwardens could rely upon the justices of the peace, if necessary, to have manorial officials account for the fines.[46]

The Elizabethan Poor Law of 1601 offers another example of the shift of authority to the parish. Because of its traditional concern with the poor, it was logical that the parish should assume the new secular charitable functions embodied in the poor law. According to this statute, from two to four "substantial householders" were to be nominated in the parish and appointed by two or more of the local justices of the peace to serve as overseers of the poor. The overseers were charged with finding work for children whose parents were unable to maintain them and for others who had no means of support. This task was implemented first through "taxation of every inhabitant, parson, vicar and other, and of every occupier of lands, houses, titthes impropriate, propriations of titthes, coal-mines, or saleable underwoods in the said parish"; this income was to be used for the relief of the lame, the impotent, the old, the blind, and others, as well as for funding the apprenticeship of children. The statute empowered the churchwardens and overseers to punish parish defaulters of the tax with the distress and sale of the offenders' goods; the overseers could also punish the poor who refused to work by imprisoning them.

46. "The Statute for Mending of Highways," 2 and 3 Philip and Mary, chap. 8 (1555).

The overseers and churchwardens were granted further powers. With the assent of local justices they had authority to bind children as apprentices, to use any waste or common in their parish to establish houses for the "impotent poor," provided they had the consent of the manor lord, and to place families (often more than one family together) in cottages or houses especially constructed for the parish poor.[47] Whereas at one time the ecclesiastical parish had been the sole agency of local charity for the poor and unfortunate, the civil parish now had the power to assess a sizable parish poor rate and was largely responsible for social welfare. In a matter of decades voluntary offerings had been transformed into compulsory rates.

In East Anglia at least, the decline of the court leet can be associated in large measure with the decreasing importance of the manor as a whole. Although many manors still operated in the region with the same vitality as those in the Wiltshire-Hampshire area or in the region around Rowley and Holme-on-Spalding Moor in Yorkshire, they were generally not located in those areas from which most settlers to New England came. In the extreme northwest corner of Essex, for instance, some manors continued to depend on communal regulation of agricultural matters. But by and large the manor did not play a large role in regulating farming activities in Essex and Suffolk, and this absence of superintendence was perpetuated by the town government of Watertown, Massachusetts.

Most East Anglian landholders, whether of free, lease, or copyhold lands, possessed closes of land, not open-field strips. They were therefore free to organize their own farming arrangements. Of course, some activities were still regarded as undesirable by the courts leet and offenses were entered on court rolls, but by the seventeenth century the number and variety of infractions had diminished. In Polstead, Suffolk, in the heart of the area of heavy emigration, a number of manorial estreats for the decade of the 1630s have survived. In October 1634, forty-seven of the fifty-four fines exacted were for nonattendance at the court leet. Of the remaining seven offenses, three involved obstruction of the highway "within the jurisdiction of this leet," one concerned the repair of a common footbridge, and three related to the failure to clear out watercourse ditches.[48]

47. "An Act for the Relief of the Poor," 43 Elizabeth, chap. 2 (1601). See also 39 Elizabeth, chap. 3 (1597). Many of these same responsibilities, as will be shown later, were assumed by the Watertown selectmen, though without express statutory direction.

48. Manor of Polstead Hall, estreats, 1634–1645, S1/1/6.1. West Suffolk R.O. Watertown settlers Simon and Gregory Stone of Great Bromley, Essex, shared a similar experience; see Great Bromley estreat roll, 1631, D/DU 40/12, Essex R.O. The influence of the court leet continued to decline in the long run too. Polstead customs from 1498 to the

The decline of the court leet, even in these ancillary areas, was indicative of widespread change throughout the region. A survey of the court rolls from twelve Essex manors between 1560 and 1640 shows a major decrease in the number of entries for the court leet. Excluding less significant entries such as lists of essoins (excuses for nonattendance), capital pledges, and payments of common fines, in 1560 approximately 215 entries were listed in the sessions court records for the twelve manors. By 1575 only 106 entries were listed, which was still the case in 1600. A quarter of a century later, though, the number had decreased to 39, where it remained in 1640. Thus over a period of eighty years the level of regulatory activity in these Essex manors had decreased by 80 percent, and, significantly, the variety of matters before the court had also declined.[49]

Even where the manor had been the center of jurisdiction and political authority as late as the sixteenth century, by the early-Stuart years many of its wider administrative powers had been lost through inactivity. A statement in the court rolls and survey of Aveley, Essex, in about 1623 summed up the transformation that had taken place there: "You shall fynde in the antient Roll fower tymes more presentmentes concerning the leet than in the later Rolls." In other Essex localities the manorial court simply dropped important functions or ceased operation. In Boxted, the English home of some Watertown settlers, no manorial bailiff was appointed in 1624 to regulate common grazing land, while in Great Yeldham, the former residence of other New England settlers, eleven inhabitants petitioned the quarter sessions for the appointment of new constables as the court leet had not met in years to elect them.[50]

Glorious Revolution indicate that there were more functioning manorial bylaws and better enforcement of them at the time Elizabeth became queen than at the start of the Stuarts' reign in the 17th century. Compare Polstead Hall, Extracts re Customs, 1498–1690, S1/1/7, West Suffolk R.O., in which progressively fewer matters were deemed worthy enough for extraction by the manorial steward over this time span and those that were, were usually concerned with only the manorial estate or commoning rights.

49. See Felix Hull, "Agriculture and Rural Society in Essex, 1560–1640" (Ph.D. thesis, University of London, 1950), especially chap. 10, 401–412.

50. D/DTh M-12, Essex R.O., as cited by Hull, "Agriculture and Rural Society in Essex," 411; Q/SBa 2/7, 82, and note, also, D/DRa M9, Essex R.O. Compare Theydon Mount, Essex, where in 1612 inhabitants complained to the court of quarter sessions that the manorial lord had designated one "poor man" of "very bad qualities" for the office of constable "without consent of the parishioners," a problem that existed, the justices believed, because the manorial court baron and court leet had not met for over 20 years. Carl Bridenbaugh, *Vexed and Troubled Englishmen, 1590–1642* (New York, 1968), 248–249.

Of course, manors varied widely in Essex, depending on many factors, from past history to geographic location. Many manorial courts leet in Essex had been quite vigorous in the 16th century. Compare the court rolls of Wanstead, 1–30 Elizabeth, D/DCw M1–5; Ruck-

As a result of the early enclosure of land in the Suffolk-Essex area, the manor became little more than a rent-collecting machine. The landholder was exceptionally free from manorial interference in economic affairs, and administratively the institution imposed few regulations. Although some courts leet survived with varying success, the upheaval of the Civil War and the Interregnum did near-fatal damage to the institution. Even before that time, many courts leet survived only by assuming the functions of a parish vestry, or by an unwitting fusion between the latter and its own functions, which was only possible in certain urban areas where the court leet and parish were coterminous.[51]

In the last half of the sixteenth century a national system of justice developed, based upon the ascendancy of the local justice of the peace, the establishment of petty sessions, and the creation and increasing significance of the officers of the civil parish. All these changes were made at the expense of manorial personnel. In addition to the rise of these new or expanded institutions, the economic upheaval that followed the suppression of the monasteries earlier in the century disturbed the traditional basis of many Suffolk and Essex manors, undermining both custom and privilege. In place of the manor the civil parish emerged, a nation-wide organization of voluntary officers responsible to the county government. These institutional changes had their sharpest test in the years immediately before the puritan migration and provided the model for local government that East Anglians brought with them when they settled in Watertown, Massachusetts.[52]

---

holts in Leyton, 9–37 Elizabeth, D/DCw M39; Bacons in Dengie, 1–40 Elizabeth, C/DP M1201; North Fambridge, 13–38 Elizabeth, D/DMj M3; Walden, 1 Henry VIII–32 Elizabeth; and even Wethersfield, 1–44 Elizabeth, D/DFy M18–21, Essex R.O. With the exception of the latter, all were located in the southeastern or southwestern parts of the county, usually in marshland areas where the manor continued to play an important part in the management of agriculture after 1600. Regardless of how active the manors were in matters of local social control, statutory enactments during Elizabeth's reign reduced their role in this sphere considerably, particularly where their influence was already on the wane.

51. This conterminous combination existed in Chelmsford, Essex. See Schedule of By-Laws Appended to Roll for Court held February 24, 1564, Court Roll of Bishops Hall, Chelmsford, 1560–1613, D/DM M7, Essex R.O. The Webbs discuss various examples at length. *English Local Government: The Manor and the Borough*, 64–126, 148–211.

52. See B. W. Quintrell, "The Government of the County of Essex, 1603–42" (Ph.D. thesis, University of London, 1965), 37–78. Two excellent examples of the workings of the parish vestry during the early 17th century are the Finchingfield vestry records, 1626–1634, D/P 14/8/1, and the Minutes of the Braintree Company of Four and Twenty, 1619–1636, D/P 264/8/3, Essex R.O. These records have been discussed in Allen, "In English Ways," 358–368. No Watertown or Ipswich men, however, came from either town. Records of select vestries or consolidated groups of men directing the affairs of East Anglian towns from which settlers to Watertown and Ipswich came are also available, but they are not as thorough. In

One does not find evidence for any Massachusetts town government of such sweeping powers and authority as were held by the select vestries in England. However, as we noted earlier, the "Town Act" of 1635, which formally established local authority in the Bay Colony, permitted considerably more variation at the community level than has been previously assumed. The act allowed town governments throughout the colony to grant lands and woods, to "make such orders as may concern the well ordering of their townes," provided they were not repugnant to those of the General Court, to lay fines and penalties for the breach of local orders, and to choose various officers. It was the prerogative of the community to decide how and by whom these various duties and responsibilities would be handled best.

Theoretically, the town meeting was the predominant body for administering town business and could have taken all local power to itself, except that which was statutorily given to the selectmen. On the other hand, there was nothing to stop the town meeting from delegating nearly all of its power to the selectmen. Year after year in Watertown the meeting elected the same experienced selectmen and relinquished authority to them, for instance giving "full power to the Seaven men to Consider in what way to give all men Satisfaction" concerning grants in the "Remote medowes," or agreeing that "the Select men shall Consider what is meete to be doone about repayring and Inlarging of the Meeteing howse," or settling a land controversy by allowing the selectmen to do "what the[y] shall in ther Judment think meet."[53]

In most cases, important matters of policy and judgment were referred to the Watertown selectmen. The town as a whole concerned itself only with the regular course of business, such as election of officers, approval of the annual rates, and confirmation of older bylaws that often had been

Little Waldingfield, Suffolk, for instance, affairs were decided upon "by the chief inhabitants of this parish" or "by the Overseers Churchwardens and chief inhabitants of the Towne." Their activities are noted in the Little Waldingfield Parish Book, 1629–1683, EL 158/1/1, West Suffolk R.O. Other accounts in other parishes of future Watertown and Ipswich inhabitants include Dedham, Essex, D/P 26/5/1, Essex R.O., and the meticulously detailed records of the Nayland Town Charity.

53. *Recs. of Mass. Bay*, I, 172; *Watertown Recs.*, 19 (n.d., 1650), 30 (Mar. 15, 1652), 40 (Jan. 1, 1655). Selectmen in the Bay Colony did not receive official recognition from the General Court until 1641, when freemen were acknowledged to have the right to choose a number of men "to order the planting or prudentiall occasions" of the town. William H. Whitmore, ed., *The Colonial Laws of Massachusetts, Reprinted from the Edition of 1660, with the Supplements of 1672* (Boston, 1889), 49. Yet they had been a vital force in Watertown government since the freemen of the town agreed on Aug. 23, 1634, the first entry in the recorded minutes, "that there shall be chosen three persons to be [   ] the ordering of the civil affairs in the town." Soon the number expanded to almost a dozen, then declined to seven. *Watertown Recs.*, 1.

made by the selectmen. What the East Anglian select vestries and the Watertown selectmen shared was the power of initiative in handling local governmental business. The English vestry was more secure since its authority derived from a bishop's faculty or from local custom, but the board of selectmen operated in much the same way through the consent of the inhabitants and freemen at large.[54]

When Watertown was first established, freemen's meetings were the occasion for the election of freemen as selectmen. By December of 1637, however, this meeting had evolved into a "general town meeting," where "inhabitants" as well as freemen seemed to have mingled. The difference in spheres of authority and power between the town meeting and the selectmen in Watertown was never finely drawn, and it was easy, consequently, for the selectmen to assert themselves in many situations. The records for the first five decades of settlement contain many examples of the selectmen's power. The town meeting "allowed" the selectmen to make decisions about such things as the repair and enlargement of the meetinghouse or the sale of town land. In other cases the town confirmed or "approved" bylaws drawn up by the selectmen, and on many occasions the selectmen called town meetings on their own initiative in order to inform townsmen of decisions they had made or of problems that had been dealt with.[55]

The Watertown selectmen were expected to deal with a wide gamut of problems. During a ten or twelve-year period in the mid-seventeenth century these town officials directed work on the repair of a town bridge and of the town pound, settled various land claims, granted land, inspected the town's boundaries, disposed of a personal estate and paid the deceased's debts, hired a keeper for the town herd, and settled a boundary dispute with neighboring Concord.[56] The range of duties expected of Watertown selectmen was actually wider and infinitely more detailed than

54. Of course, the parish oligarchies of East Anglia did not always wield powers so unilaterally as the "Four and Twenty" of Braintree. In Nayland, Suffolk, from where John Warren, one of Watertown's early selectmen, came, in addition to the exclusive group of churchwardens, overseers, and feoffees, a monthly meeting was assembled "by the consent of the inhabitants of Nayland" who fined themselves 12 pence for nonattendance. In Nayland and Watertown both a general and a select group of men governed, but the locus of authority was clearly in the hands of the smaller body. Nayland Town Charity, Feoffees Accounts, 4/25, Jan. 14, 1634.

55. *Watertown Recs.*, 30 (Mar. 15, 1652); 19 [n.d.], 61 (Jan. 18, 1659), 89 (Dec. 10, 1666), 146 (Jan. 26, 1680); 12 (Dec. 28, 1647), 32 (Oct. 18, 1653), 42 (Mar. 13, 1655), 46 (Nov. 11, 1656), 79 (Jan. 8, 1664), and note, 91 (Dec. 9, 1667).

56. *Ibid.*, 16 (Nov. 28, 1648), 17 (Jan. 16, 1649, Feb. 6, 1649), 37 (Feb. 14, 1654), 40 (Jan. 29, 1655), 67 (Nov. 12, 1660), 71 (Jan. 29, 1661).

these examples indicate. It is easy to understand how the strain might have compelled Hugh Mason to resign from the body in 1647, "burdened with the servis of the Towne," but the following year he was elected again by the town and nearly every other year afterwards for the next thirty. Aside from the intrinsic rewards for the long hours devoted to town business, the stature of the selectmen was recognized in concrete ways, too. In the seating plan for the meetinghouse (which was occasionally an important source of contention and jealousy in other towns), office came first, followed by age, estate, and "gifts."[57]

By contrast, the town meeting was rather routine, often brief, and rarely eventful. The meetings had become so cut-and-dried by mid-century that at one session in 1663 the townsmen outlined all the business that could be expected to come before the body at any time. According to that statement, the town meeting would normally be held annually on the first Monday in November, at which time the minister's salary, the town rate, and the schoolmaster's pay were to be agreed upon. At that time, too, the selectmen, constables, surveyors of the highway, and other officers would be chosen. The order of business also included "what els may be presented of publique Concernment," and although it was likely that several such issues might come before a typical meeting, they were usually handled with routine dispatch.[58]

During the decades before 1680 the town meeting convened two or possibly three times a year on the average, while the selectmen usually met about five to seven times annually; and as we have already noted, in their meetings the selectmen generally handled a greater volume of business concerning more significant and vital matters than the town meeting did. In addition, the experience accumulated by these boards during the early decades averaged six to eight years apiece for each selectman. It is not surprising then that the selectmen at one time or another affected nearly every aspect of life in the "East Anglian" towns of Massachusetts.

As an institution of local government, the selectmen performed several specific services for the town. Besides the various examples of lawmaking described above, the selectmen often found that in exercising local legislative power it became necessary for them to appoint minor officials to carry out their own enactments.[59] This was often done without the permission

57. *Ibid.*, 10 (Nov. 15, 1647), 47 (Nov. 17, 1656).
58. *Ibid.*, 78 (Dec. 4, 1663). Compare this with the vitality and effectiveness with which the selectmen handled town matters in their meeting a month later. *Ibid.*, 78–79 (Jan. 8, 1664).
59. For some additional examples of the selectmen's persistent use of lawmaking power, see *ibid.*, 17 (Feb. 6, 1649), and 44 (Jan. 14, 1656), which reconfirmed 41 (Feb. 27, 1655) and

of the meeting, but in other cases the town specifically delegated the power of appointment to the selectmen. In March 1651, without any order from the meeting, the selectmen made "articles of agreement" in the name of the town with Solomon Johnson, appointing him keeper of the town herd of dry cattle. In other cases, they appointed bylaw men in January 1652 and in February 1654, when it appeared the meeting had neglected to do so, and they named men to posts that had been created from bylaws of their own making. Richard Beers, for example, was chosen "in the Townes Behalfe" to prosecute John Toll of Sudbury for felling trees on the town's land, while several years later three men were chosen to "veiwe the Watercourse . . . and to Determin what is to be done in the case." That same year other men were appointed by the selectmen to take care of the town's ammunition, which was stored in the meetinghouse.[60]

The meeting's lack of initiative and vitality was also evident in its use of power over the purse. Watertown was well known throughout the colony for the small rebellion it instigated in the early 1630s over the issue of taxation and representation in the colony government. At the local level such items as town, ministerial, school, and special rates or assessments occupied town business. The guiding direction of the selectmen was evident throughout all the debates concerning rates, lists of town "charges," and other fiscal matters. When complaints were made that "wronge have benn done to men in Rateinge," it was the "7 men" who sought to rectify the situation by ordering that an "Invoyce," an assessment of the town's wealth, be made so that a new rate for each townsman based on his changing estate in the town could be compiled. The selectmen were also responsible for establishing the value of items assessed in townsmen's estates. In one instance the meeting attempted to tax town tradesmen, but when, as usual, it tried to turn the matter over to the selectmen they refused to initiate such a tax.

The town rarely tried to interfere, declaring as it did in 1655 that the "7 men shall rate by rules in Lawe [i.e., their own and the colony's] and acording to theer Discretion." Occasionally the selectmen went a step further and took matters more fully into their own hands, as they did in their meeting of January 3, 1660, when they "allowed" the rate of the minister's

were promulgated by the selectmen; 45 (Feb. 12, 1656), 52 (May 5, 1657), 56 (Apr. 13, 1658), and 86 ([town meeting] Nov. 6, 1665). This and other categories of selectmen's functions have been discussed in Lockridge and Kreider's "Evolution of Massachusetts Town Government," WMQ, 3d Ser., XXIII (1966), 549–574.

60. See, for example, Watertown Recs., 23 (Mar. 31, Dec. 2, 1651), 28 (Jan. 12, 1652), 32 (Oct. 18, 1652), 37 (Feb. 14, 1654), 82 (Aug. 30, 1664), 83 (Oct. 11, 1653), 85 (Feb. 7, 1665).

maintenance that had been passed on by the town three months earlier. A month later, on February 14, the selectmen "apon the apearance of more debts and other charges . . . saw cause to grant a [town] rate of fifty pounds," instead of the forty pounds agreed upon a short while earlier by the town. As with lawmaking and appointive powers, the town and selectmen shared the power of the purse, but just as with other functions, the "7 men" were able to use this authority more effectively and creatively.[61]

Another important indicator of the selectmen's role in Watertown government was their handling of judicially related matters. Like East Anglian parish officers, town selectmen were often appointed by their peers to "use there discretion in words to the moderating" of conflicts between townsmen. Selectmen also allowed townsmen "to present what they had to object" to when fines were exacted for town offenses; "thir respective pleas" were heard by the board, decided upon, and sometimes the fines were altered. The selectmen also held authority over minor town officers such as the constables, who were responsible for collecting and turning over the various town rates to the selectmen. In one instance, when Roger Willington gave "great dis[satis]faction" to the selectmen, two of their body were appointed "to deale with him to bring him to a more tollavable account or else to present him to the gradjury."

Selectmen played their most conspicuous judicial role in dealing with fines for infractions of bylaws and rates. One townsman was fined £1 6s. by the selectmen for not yoking and ringing his twenty-six hogs, and in February 1664 the hogreeves reported a total of £8 13s. 4d. in fines to their superiors, the board of selectmen, for violations of the hog, fence, and cattle bylaws. Perhaps most significant were the numerous fines exacted on townsmen by the selectmen for contempt of their authority. Although occasion for this was rare, the selectmen were not sparing in this use of their authority to the random few who refused to pay their rates, disobeyed a bylaw, or did not comply with a special request of the selectmen. John Livermore, for example, was fined 5s., a large sum by town "court" standards, for failure to appear before the seven men "apon warrant." In another case the selectmen chose two of their members to "take out the Exicution against the house and land" of John Brabrook "for payinge the debt due to the towne." The property was appraised and sold, and the accomplished act was accordingly "allowed and Confirmed by the Select-men."

61. Hubbard, *General History of New England*, 142; Francis, *Historical Sketch of Watertown in Massachusetts*, 21–22; *Watertown Recs.*, 13 (Jan. 25, 1648), 14 (Feb. 29, 1648), 43 ([town meeting] Dec. 10, 1655), 63 (Jan. 3, 1660), 65 (Feb. 14, 1660), 84 ([town meeting] Nov. 7, 1664), 89 (Feb. 22, 1667), 91 (Nov. 26, 1667), 91–92 ([town meeting] Dec. 9, 1667).

Whatever the infraction a townsman violated in early Watertown, if he obstructed settlement of the matter in any way, he could be quite certain of vigorous prosecution by the selectmen or their subordinates, the bylaw men.[62]

A final institutional function of the Watertown selectmen was the constant administrative attention they devoted to various local matters. These experienced men felt obliged to handle a vast number of activities. Besides dividing the ungranted town lands and establishing and enforcing agrarian bylaws, the selectmen engaged in a wide variety of administrative matters ranging from regulating ordinaries, establishing a town school, providing a house and land for the common herdsman, taking charge of the construction of a new meetinghouse, and countless other duties. Selectmen performed many of these tasks on their own initiative and often based on their own notion of what was best for the "town."

Only infrequently were they required to perform administrative duties at the "order" of the town meeting. As in England the parish or "town" was responsible for the maintenance of roads within its boundaries. Although the surveyors of the highways were usually appointed by the town meeting, they were, like other minor officers, occasionally chosen by the selectmen. In either case they were under the direction of that body. Unlike other towns where the selectmen's role was less conspicuous, in Watertown the surveyors could do very little on their own authority. The selectmen reminded townsmen from time to time that they were obligated to work on road repairs annually and that refusal to comply with the surveyors would result in the imposition of a fine. Selectmen even interfered with decisions made by the surveyors concerning the location and extension of roads through the town.[63]

Another sign of the effect of the administrative background of the East Anglian parish on Watertown selectmen was their preoccupation with such issues as settlement, apprenticeship, and related matters. The earliest page of the town records leaves no doubt as to how strong the English experience had been on town settlers and how significantly they would respond to old and familiar conditions on the edge of a new continent. The men of Watertown agreed on January 3, 1635, that "no man being for-

62. *Watertown Recs.*, 33 (Nov. 22, 1653), 37 (Oct. 14, 1654), 43 (Nov. 27, 1655), 44 (Jan. 21, Feb. 12, 1656), 45 (Mar. 1, 1656), 62 (July 6, 1659), 64 (Jan. 9, 1660), 76 (Dec. 15, 1663), 77 (Dec. 29, 1663), 79 (Jan. 19, 1664), 86 (Oct. 31, 1665), 92 (Sept. 22, 1668), 93 (Dec. 8, 1668).

63. For some examples, see *ibid.*, 3 (Feb. 16, 1638), 4 (Apr. 9, 1638), 18 (Nov. 2, 1649), 19 ([town meeting] Jan. 10, 1650), 37 ([town meeting] Oct. 14, 1654), 67 (Nov. 6, 1660); 3 (Dec. 29, 1637), 22 (June 7, 1651), 61 (Mar. 28, 1659), 66 (Sept. 4, 1660).

eigner . . . coming out of England, or some other Plantation, shall have liberty to sett downe amongst us, unles he first have the Consent of the Freemen of the Towne." Seven months later they were more explicit: "Whosoever being an Inhabitant in the Towne shall receive any person, or family upon their propriety that may prove chargeable to . . . the Towne shall maintaine the said persons at their owne charges, or to save the Towne harmeles."[64] As we shall see in chapter 7, growing concern with these and similar problems in the decades after 1660 signaled important changes in the towns of Massachusetts and initiated a shift from extreme local control to growing centralization of colony and provincial institutions.

Ipswich and Watertown both developed town governments that were remarkably similar, despite the urban character of life in the former and the agrarian features of the latter. Both towns had strong local leadership by men of long experience. In Ipswich the selectmen made a considerable effort to build up the commercial potential of the town. They encouraged industry and tried to attract outstanding individuals to settle there and recreate the kind of shire town that the English Ipswich represented to them. Watertown's efforts along this line were somewhat modest; it succeeded only in attracting one brickmaker, who was lured by the offer of town land. Nevertheless, the Watertown selectmen maintained the same grip on the community that we found in the select vestries of the East Anglian villages. Like in those English communities, the selectmen removed strangers, reprimanded idlers, cared for the old, and found work for the poor. Like those vestries the selectmen took surveys of their town, such as the one in 1660 to determine "the wants of some pore families, as likwise of there improvement of there times both concerning there soules, as of there bodies."[65] At the same time, the leadership in both New England towns actively encouraged economic individualism in the community by relinquishing control over the division of lands, by acting as a sort of land-transfer agent between buyers and sellers in Ipswich, and by visibly promoting land development and accurate surveying in Watertown. Such procedures were characteristic of East Anglian communities, where a heritage of enclosed-field farming traditionally had discouraged outside interference and encouraged land exchange.

64. *Ibid.*, 1 (Jan. 3, 1635), 1–2 (Aug. 22, 1635), and, note, 3 ([Dec.] 3, 1636). Selectmen were active in "warning out" strangers and making certain that townsmen were financially accountable for guests they entertained in their homes for extended periods. See, for examples, *ibid.*, 58 (Jan. 3, 1659), 62 (Aug. 22, 1659), 66 (Nov. 6, 1666), 83 (Nov. 1, 1664), 92 (Feb. 24, 1668).

65. *Ibid.*, 32 (Oct. 22, 1653), 70 (Jan. 8, 1661).

Part II

6 The Migration of Societies

HE comparisons that can be drawn between local societies in old and New England, as discussed in Part I, are only one aspect of the larger fact of the migration itself, which began when people decided to leave England and ended decades later when these same people or their heirs had succeeded in developing a new society of their own in early Massachusetts. In this chapter we will look at the first stage in this process by examining some of the conditions in England that encouraged migration. We have already seen that the special characteristics of each migrating society and the patterns of distinctive English regional cultures were transferred to and institutionalized in the New World. Little attention has been paid thus far, however, to developments later in the century. Chapter 7, therefore, will focus on the changes forced upon these Massachusetts villagers by new conditions in the mid- to late seventeenth century. It was at this point that many Massachusetts settlers experienced the beginnings of a society that extended beyond their particular New England town. The final phase of this process is discussed in chapter 8, which explores the emergence of centralization in Massachusetts as a colony and the rise of provincial bodies and county courts that would ultimately displace the town as the locus of power and authority in the lives of individual villagers. Paradoxically, it was the extreme local control of the separate English societies during the early decades of settlement that ultimately led to the necessity for broad control by extratown authority by 1700.

Two questions must be asked about the migration process: who migrates, and why? As we shall see, those questions cannot be answered in a general way. Different types of persons emigrated from different parts of England. In towns to the North and West, the emigrants were usually younger, often had some local prominence, often lived on the outskirts of local villages, and as they came from regions on the frontiers or fringes of the puritan movement, were probably regarded as a minority within the societies in which they lived. By contrast, emigrants from the South and East were usually older, came from more obscure backgrounds, lived in villages, and were puritans from a highly puritanized culture.

As to the causes of the movement to America, the English migration to these five Massachusetts towns in the 1630s cannot be explained by "laws" of migration or any uniform set of reasons. While certain factors may have been generally more important than others, none explains every particular migration satisfactorily. Each society appears to have been affected by different forces; some "causes" that deeply affected some communities were nonexistent or of little importance in others.[1]

We can never adequately know the circumstances that propelled any individual to emigrate, although a few, years after their exodus, recorded their understanding of why they left. It is possible, however, to explore the specific characteristics of migrant groups, particularly groups as homogeneous in origin and background as many of those that came to Massachusetts. Historians have isolated a number of motivations for the puritans' departure from England in the 1630s, ranging from religious persecution and economic distress at home to a yearning for a "better" life, for intellectual freedom, and for a different climate and more land. Certain possible causes can immediately be eliminated in the case of the settlers of the five New England towns studied here, however. These were not desperate groups of people. They came from regions with long-standing traditions, and they had confidence in their own economic abilities and resourcefulness. These were not people who were "pushed" to the New World by miserable circumstances in the Old.

The two most widely accepted broad explanations of the migration are the religious, and the economic. Yet each of these must be sharply qualified by local factors when individual cases are examined. We find that, characteristically, although a religious or economic cause appears to have been the dominant impetus behind particular migrations, so many modifying circumstances existed in each case that the significance of the single broad explanation is greatly reduced. At the time of the Rowley migration, for instance, there was little economic distress in Yorkshire, yet any religious explanation for the exodus must be modified by a recognition of particular factors such as the charismatic qualities of the local puritan religious leaders, kinship and social ties with the people who had left earlier, and even the location of the emigrants' dwellings in their Yorkshire villages. Such factors may have been closely tied to puritanism itself, but they are also separate variables and were not necessarily present in other

1. Even recent studies of other, more modern migrations that contain greater documentation have failed to produce an overarching model for migration employing economic, geographic, demographic, and social psychological variables. See, for instance, Sune Åkerman, "Theories and Methods of Migration Research," in Harald Runblom and Hans Norman, eds., *From Sweden to America: A History of the Migration* (Minneapolis, Minn., 1976), 19–75.

emigration centers in different English regions. In other places, the heart of East Anglia along the Stour River, for instance, conditions were very different at the time of emigration. Both economic and religious motives existed, but as we shall see, they were operative in different ways than in Yorkshire. Through an examination of the local factors behind the decision to migrate in each of the five regions we have studied, we should be able to arrive at a better understanding of the influence of such factors in relation to the general explanations.

Rowley

In some respects the emigrants who went to Rowley, Massachusetts, provide a classic example of migration during the puritan exodus. These Yorkshire settlers had been under the influence of the new religion for relatively few years, were inspired by a charismatic leader, and were the victims of a sudden change in ecclesiastical policy. But in other English localities the causes of migration were quite different.

Rowley parish was probably an important center of puritan activity for the entire East Riding area. Ezekiel Rogers, rector of Rowley, was well known among diocesan authorities by the mid-1630s for his dissident beliefs and practices. The diocesan cause papers from 1634 bear witness to a series of "straing preachers" known to have preached in Rogers's parish beginning in the late 1620s. In 1635 the churchwardens were charged with various nonconformist activities, including permitting "divers and sundry persons" to preach in the parish. They admitted that "Mr. Ellis of Beverley, Mr. Osgroby, Mr. Simpson of Sancton, Mr. Nelson of Feraby, Mr. Mason of Ellinton, Mr. Constable of Everingham, Mr. Hamon of Hartswell and one Mr. Atkinson being strange preachers did all and every one of them preach severally at the parish church of Rowley in the Year of our Lord God 1634." In addition, the churchwardens were held responsible for a new loft that had been constructed in the church to seat the overflow of nonparishioners attracted to Rowley to hear puritan sermons. Rogers was known outside his parish as well, since he often met in conventicles "with other preists or ministers of the word of God or some other persons" at other places within the diocese, and his activities were probably also known to laymen as far away as Bradford and Leeds.[2]

2. Office c. Churchwardens of Rowley, R. VII. H. 2106 (especially articles 9, 10, and the reply to 9), and Office c. Ezekiel Rogers, Rector of Rowley, R. VII. H. 2069 (especially article 12), Cause Papers, Diocese of York, Borthwick Inst. Hist. Res. It is true that Hull and Bev-

This minister, who played such a pivotal role in the migration of the Yorkshire group, was born in 1590 in Wethersfield, Essex, the son of Richard Rogers, also a well-known puritan minister. He matriculated at Cambridge in 1604, graduating from Christ's College in 1608. He then went to Hatfield Broad Oak, Essex, for about twelve years, where he served as chaplain to the family of Sir Francis Barrington, an active puritan leader. In 1621 Sir Francis presented Rogers with the living at Rowley, quite likely, as Cotton Mather later suggested, "in hope that his more lively ministry might be particularly successful in awakening those drowsy corners of the north."[3]

The neutrality or sympathy toward puritanism that characterized the views of Archbishops Matthew Hutton (1594–1606) and Tobias Matthew (1606–1628) of York, shifted after 1630 to sustained opposition under Richard Neile (1631–1641). This change in policy had a devastating effect on the newly puritanized region. By one estimate, the number of puritan ministers in Yorkshire in 1640 was only two-thirds what it had been seven years previously. Although Rogers later stated that he was suspended for not reading "that accursed book which allowed sports on God's holy day," the official records indicate more subtle and widespread activities. Charged in 1635 with having met "at unlawfull and secrete assemblies or conventicles" and having at that time "made prayers of your owne fancie and invention and made sermons exhortacions repeticions and expositions of sermons and by way of expoundinge vented dangerous and schismatic opinions contrarie to the Canons and discipline of the church of England," Rogers admitted only that he had "used to make repiticions of sermones of

---

erley had a long tradition of puritanism, stretching back well into the 16th century. But aside from these urban strongholds and a few isolated rural pockets like Hackness, which were for the most part located in the northern part of the East Riding, puritanism did not spread out into the countryside until the 1620s, when puritan gentry began to fill many parishes such as Rowley, Holme, and nearby Aughton with puritan ministers. See "List of Puritan Clergy," Roland A. Marchant, *The Puritans and the Church Courts in the Diocese of York, 1560–1642* (London, 1960), 222–294, and John Newton, "The Yorkshire Puritan Movement, 1603–1640," Congregational Historical Society, *Transactions*, XIX (1960–1961), 5. Similar concentrations of puritanism were typical in other parts of the North Country, where large areas were virtually unaffected. See R. C. Richardson, *Puritanism in North-West England: A Regional Study of the Diocese of Chester* (Totowa, N.J., 1972), 7–9, 13–15. Several puritan gentry in or near Holme and Rowley such as Sir William Constable and Sir Matthew Boynton could have shaped and directed the puritan emigration, but in the end it was left to Rogers to organize the movement. J. T. Cliff, *The Yorkshire Gentry from the Reformation to the Civil War* (London, 1969), 306–308.

3. Mather, *Magnalia Christi Americana*, I, 409 (italics excluded); John Anthony Newton, "Puritanism in the Diocese of York (Excluding Nottinghamshire) 1603–1640" (Ph.D. thesis, University of London, 1955), 259n.

his owne upon Sundayes in the after noones in his own house to his own family and others who have commed." Rogers's intention to leave the Yorkshire parish in order to escape Neile's antipuritan policy must have been widely known for several years before he was finally excommunicated. A personal pique against his patron, Sir Francis Barrington, for not allowing Rogers to name his successor once he had made his intentions known, became a second reason for leaving.[4]

In other Yorkshire parishes ecclesiastical persecution produced similar results. Joseph Haworth, vicar of Batley (1602–1635) in the West Riding, was presented in 1633 for singing "psalmes after the lessons instead of Reading the hymnes." Nearby Bradford was an important center of puritan activity in the West Riding, but by 1633 strong and persistent ecclesiastical pressure was applied to discontinue a series of very successful puritan "Exercises" (worship services) and conferences. Similar events in their own communities or some knowledge of Rogers's travail against ecclesiastical authorities may have encouraged Humphrey Reyner, Matthew Boyes, and Joseph and Maximilan Jewett to follow Rogers to New England.[5]

Despite the distance and isolation of lonely Yorkshire parishes, there were several integrating elements in the lives of these North Country emigrants. The influence of Rogers himself, and the effects of ecclesiastical policy on him and throughout the archdiocese generally were, of course, paramount. Social and economic ties across parish boundaries may have been important, too, though surviving evidence is scanty. Several future settlers held land in the parishes of other people who emigrated. The Barkers of Holme owned land in Rowley, and the Northends of Little Weeton in Rowley parish controlled some of the manor lands in Cottingham. The puritan Barringtons, patrons of Rowley parish, were the lords of one of the Cottingham manors, Cottingham Sarum.[6]

4. Daniel Neal, *The History of the Puritans; or, Protestant Non-conformists, from the Reformation in 1517, to the Revolution in 1688* . . . , 5 vols. (London, 1822), II, 285–286; Newton, "Puritanism in the Diocese of York," 450; William Stickney Ewell, "Rowley of the Massachusetts Bay Colony," in *1639–1939: The Tercentenary Celebration of the Town of Rowley* (Rowley, Mass., 1942), 154; Office c. Ezekiel Rogers, R.VII.H. 2069, article 12 and reply, Cause Papers, Diocese of York, Borthwick Inst. Hist. Res.; Marchant, *Puritans and the Church Courts in the Diocese of York*, 274, 96–102.

5. Office c. Joseph Haworth, Vicar of Batley, R.VI.B.4, Cause Papers, Diocese of York, Borthwick Inst. Hist. Res.; Newton, "Puritanism in the Diocese of York," 34–35.

6. Bargains and Sales, DDHA/4/24/48–50 (1621), Univ. of Hull; Surveys of the Three Manors, Cottingham Powes, Cottingham Richmond, and Cottingham Westmorland, Royal Contract Estates, Mar. 29, 1627–Apr. 1, 1630, R.C.E. Rentals, Box 2.8, Corporation of London Record Office, Guildhall, London; Robert Burton to Thomas Barrington, Oct. 29, 1643, vol. 2647, Egerton MSS.

Rowley, Massachusetts, became a traditional society of orderly, established ways in spite of its inhabitants, who were much younger overall than the East Anglians who founded Ipswich, Watertown, and Hingham. Although complete information is unavailable, surviving records indicate that 61 percent of the original landowners of Rowley were between eighteen and thirty-three years of age in 1635, and many of the others were even younger.[7] Any youthful disdain for orderly, established ways must have been of negligible significance since Rowley became one of the most traditional societies among Massachusetts communities. One of the reasons for this conservatism may have been the lack of strong economic discontent among the inhabitants as a motivating desire to leave their former Yorkshire parishes. Surviving local records contain little evidence of overwhelming economic distress at the time.[8] Consequently, the Yorkshire emigration included many of the more well-to-do men from the marshes and wolds, men who undoubtedly preferred things in New England to remain as they had been in the North Country.

In Batley in the West Riding, for instance, Humphrey Reyner, Sr., father of the emigrant of the same name, must have been regarded as a man of wealth and influence, for he was named a trustee of the Batley grammar school in 1612. The other trustees were men of some distinction and the group as a whole was responsible for the administration of lands that formed the school's original endowment. Humphrey Reyner, Sr., proba-

7. Compiled from various sources including Blodgette, comp., and Jewett, ed., *Early Settlers of Rowley*; Banks, *Planters of the Commonwealth*; and others.

8. The only general instance of economic (crop) difficulties in the East Riding during the 1630s occurred in the spring of 1638, at the very moment these Yorkshire men were leaving for New England. *Cal. State Papers, Domestic, 1637–1638*, 347–348. Even this fact, too late to have had much, if any, impact on the emigrants, seems to have affected other parts of the Riding, not just the region surrounding Holme-on-Spalding Moor. The number of deaths recorded in the parish registers of Holme and nearby villages appears to have been only slightly, if at all, affected in 1638, and deaths were relatively constant in the other years of the decade, compared to Hingham, for instance, discussed later in this chapter. "Parish Registers of Holme," *Holme Parish Magazine* (1931), unpaginated; James Foord, transcriber, and A. B. Wilson-Barkworth, ed., *The Register of Kirk Ella, Co. York*, Parish Register Society, XI [London, 1897], 23–45; Arthur T. Winn, ed., *The Registers of the Parish Church of Cherry Burton, Co. York, 1561–1740* (Yorkshire Parish Register Society, *Publications*, XV [Leeds, 1903]), 20–27; John Charlesworth, ed., *The Parish Register of Bubwith, Baptisms and Burials 1600–1767, Marriages 1600–1753* (Yorkshire Parish Register Society, *Publications*, LXXXVI [Leeds, 1928]), 2–21. Of course, the East Riding did not escape the increased number of deaths experienced throughout the North in the early 1620s. While records for those years in Rowley and Holme have not survived, the printed records for the neighboring parishes referred to above, unlike others cited by Appleby, show a rise in burials but none necessarily attributable to either plague or famine. Andrew B. Appleby, *Famine in Tudor and Stuart England* (Stanford, Calif., 1978), 147, 153.

bly served in other public capacities, among them as a member of the sessions jury in the West Riding quarterly courts.[9]

Thomas Crosby and his son, Simon, both of whom emigrated from Holme-on-Spalding Moor, were among the wealthiest men in that parish. Thomas's father, Anthony, an ambitious and energetic yeoman, had acquired considerable property in the Holme area before 1599 and bequeathed to his son "all and singular my lands whatsoever lying and being in Holme in Spaldingmore and the libertyes thereof." Thomas enhanced his position by marrying Jane Sotheron, the daughter of William Sotheron, who according to the 1609 lay subsidy tax was the wealthiest man in the parish. By 1640 Thomas ranked with Sotheron's son, John, as one of the highest-rated men in Holme. The backgrounds of other Yorkshire emigrants were similar.[10]

Hingham

On the surface the background and motives of the emigrants from Hingham appear similar to that of the Rowley group. As in Rowley there was contention between episcopal authorities and the local minister, Robert Peck. In addition, economic distress had appeared in the region, a second and powerful motive for migration. But one purely local factor suggests a new and different explanation for this migration.

In chapter 3 we touched briefly on the distinctive economy of central Norfolk and noted how the region was susceptible to periodic crop failure common to the "woody part of Norfolk." During the two decades before the exodus harvests gradually diminished in Norfolk as well as throughout England. From 1610 to 1620 the harvests were on the whole average, but they started to worsen in the early 1620s. The first disastrous harvest occurred in 1622 and was repeated again the next year. The dearth of 1630 began a decade in which only one harvest in ten was good, instead of the usual four. In early March 1631, a couple of years before the first Hing-

9. Sheard, *Records of the Parish of Batley*, 149–150, 153, 159; *West Riding Sessions Records*, II, *Orders, 1611–1642, Indictments, 1637–1642*, Yorkshire Arch. Soc., *Record Series*, LIV (1915), 185, 319.

10. Eleanor Davis Crosby, *Simon Crosby the Emigrant: His English Ancestry, and Some of His American Descendants* (Boston, 1914), 13, 15, 29, 146–152; J. G. Bartlett to Mrs. William Sumner Crosby, Pittsburgh, Calif., Mar. 28, 1913, Bartlett Collection, Carton 3 (Chandler, Crosby), New England Historic Genealogical Society Library, Boston; Bargains and Sales, DDHA/4/63 (1634), Univ. of Hull; E.179/204, 401; 8 James I, Harthill Wapentake (Holme and Wilton Beacons), P.R.O.

ham arrivals in Massachusetts, the Norfolk sheriff reported that the price of corn in the county was "deemed excessive." The wheels of Stuart social policy then began to move. In actuality, the prices of wheat, rye, barley, and malt had risen twofold between the fall of 1628 and the winter of 1630, and would climb far higher in the next few years. General complaints, such as Henry Spelman's tract, "Reasons against a General Sending of Corne to the Marketts in the Champion parte of Norfolk," directed justices to investigate profitable grain exportation to foreign ports at a time when the greatest need was at home. Officials also looked into the engrossing and hoarding of grain and considered means to regulate the prices more directly. Maltsters were condemned for cornering existing supplies, and poor relief was instituted in the affected areas. The depression in the clothing and knit-stocking industries doubly hurt the rural wood-pasture areas.[11]

How greatly was Hingham affected by these economic troubles? The evidence is incomplete and indirect. The wood-pasture economy usually produced an adequate grain supply as well as a great variety of other products. The decline in the cloth industry was certainly more damaging there than it was in areas that had other handicraft occupations and were not so dependent on foreign markets. The people of Hingham and surrounding towns probably also suffered from the depredations of Dunkirk privateers who preyed on the East Anglian coast and interfered with shipments of butter and cheese to London during the late 1620s and early 1630s. Whatever the specific effects of these difficult conditions on the town of Hingham, Norfolk, a general sense of insecurity was pervasive in this area, much like what Alan Everitt has found in other wood-pasture regions.[12] On the one hand, manorial control here was weak, major gentry few, and small, independent family farmers proportionately greater than elsewhere. Such circumstances heightened a sense of independence and a tendency to dissent from authority. On the other hand, a dense population, an agriculture likely to be more vulnerable to natural catastrophe than in other regions, and a necessary dependence upon by-employment (non-

11. See W. G. Hoskins, "Harvest Fluctuations and English Economic History, 1620–1759," *Ag. Hist. Rev.*, XVI (1968), 15–31, especially 19–20. For examples of contemporary conditions in Norfolk, see *Cal. State Papers, Domestic, 1619–1623*, 377, 418, 491–502, *1628–1629*, 336, *1629–1631*, 22, 41, 56, 175, 206, 266, 275, 396, 419, 485, 525, 545, *1631–1633*, 32, 46, 50, 62, 68, 71, 77, 97, 116, 169, 191, 271, 357, *1633–1634*, 385, *1635*, 10, *1637–1638*, 216, *1638–1639*, 5. For references to northern Norfolk's abundant grain production and profitable overseas trading, see *ibid.*, *1619–1623*, 91, 361, 549, *1629–1631*, 68, and *1635*, 34. There is reason to believe that under normal circumstances the district around Hingham, Norfolk, produced enough grain for its own consumption. See *ibid.*, *1623*, 361, 549.

12. See, particularly, Everitt, *Change in the Provinces*, 22–23, 36.

agricultural sidelines) frequently led to instability, to various forms of social protest, and to an intense religious evangelicalism.

Ket's rebellion in 1549, for example, was centered in the Hingham region as were the "risings" of 1569 and 1570; among others, the vicar of Hingham, William Cantrell, was tried for his part in the 1549 rebellion. Enclosure and evictions in Norfolk also led to social protest at various times throughout the sixteenth century.[13] The same capricious and interdependent factors were present in the 1630s—the lack of a self-sufficient agriculture, the shift in demand for goods made by cottage industry, and the encroachment on the land by a few large farmers at the expense of many small, independent ones.

Vicar Cantrell's spirit of dissent, reform, and independence was carried on by Hingham's puritan minister, Robert Peck. Peck's travails, while reflecting this regional dissent and mirroring the life of another charismatic religious leader, Ezekiel Rogers, also show, as we shall see shortly, that his influence on emigration was actually minimal. We do not know when Peck began his activities against conformity, but it was undoubtedly within a short time after his installation in 1605. Local historians have referred to him as "a man of a very violent schismatical spirit" who "pulled down the rails, and levelled the altar and the whole chancel a foot below the church," alterations that remain to this day. The Pecks and families allied to them were descended from several generations of religious nonconformists. Lawrence Peck, a "grave minister," preached among those fleeing the persecution of Queen Mary in the mid-sixteenth century while they remained "together in the woods and secret places as they could." Eventually, during Elizabeth's reign, this Peck became the preacher at Fressingfield, Suffolk, a place that later sent many settlers to Dedham, Massachusetts.[14]

Like Ezekiel Rogers in Yorkshire, Robert Peck held private religious meetings in his own home. Bishop Samuel Harsnett required all those who attended these meetings to confess their errors on pain of excommunication. Later, in 1623, when citizens of Norwich complained to the House of Commons about Harsnett's conduct in this and other matters, the bishop stood firm. In defense of himself he stated that Peck had been

13. Neville Williams, "The Risings in Norfolk, 1569 and 1570," *Norfolk Arch.*, XXXII (1961), 73–81; Leadam, "The Inquisition of 1517," Royal Hist. Soc., *Trans.*, N.S., VII (1893), 127–218.

14. Blomefield, *Topographical History of Norfolk*, II, 424–425; Tanner MSS, vol. 180, fols. 24b–25a. The account of Peck that follows is taken, in part, from John J. Waters, "Hingham, Massachusetts, 1631–1661: An East Anglian Oligarchy in the New World," *Journal of Social History*, I (1967–1968), 351–370.

sent to him by local justices for holding a conventicle at night. Peck had filled the parish with strange opinions such as that "the people are not to kneel as they enter the church; that it is superstition to bow at the name of Jesus; and that the church is no more sacred than any other building." The bishop had nothing to say about Peck's life and doctrine, being concerned only with his nonconformity. He also noted that Peck had been convicted of holding conventicles in 1615 and 1617, and that in 1622 he had been arrested in his house with twenty-two of his neighbors for the same reason.[15]

The situation worsened for Peck after the installation of a new bishop, Matthew Wren, in the mid-1630s. When Peck failed to attend a synod at Norwich in 1635, the chancellor of the diocese, Dr. Clement Corbett, and, indirectly, the new Bishop Wren seized their chance to punish him with excommunication. The deprived minister appealed this decision to the chancellor, who agreed to absolve Peck if he would subscribe to certain specified articles. As before, Peck was not charged with deviation from doctrine, but only from certain forms of conduct. In order to gain redemption from church officials, Peck would have to wear his surplice, constantly use his Book of Common Prayer, read the second service at high altar, and adhere to various other articles.[16]

With Peck's refusal, Corbett's next step was to sequester the annual "living" or salary of the parish, which was worth £160 yearly, and promptly "putt in what curates . . . [he] pleased to the vexacion both of parson and parishioners." For a year and a half Peck remained in the town, probably ministering to his followers in his house or in secret, much as he had done for several decades. Newly appointed curates of St. Andrew's parish had a most difficult time with Peck's stubborn parishioners. Shortly after Peck's removal, Edward Agas, the new vicar at Hingham, complained to his superior that he had found "divers of the parishioners there very factious and refractory to the government of the Church" and that, in particular, some had left their own parish church to go "to a neighbour towne to heare a godly minister preach," as some townsmen would describe it later. Two "Chiefe" culprits, Isaac Pitcher and Thomas Taylor, were warned to dis-

15. Brook, *Lives of the Puritans*, III, 263–264.

16. Accounts of the actions against Peck are contained in Samuel Peck's petition to the House of Commons in behalf of his father, n.d., Tanner MSS, vol. 220, fol. 145, and in The Humble Peticon of the Inhabitants of the Poore Ruinated Towne of Hingham in the County of Norfolk, 1640, *ibid.*, vol. 220, fols. 54–56. See also Rawlinson MSS, d 1092, Bodleian Library, Oxford; and Dr. Richard Nykke, bishop of Norwich, to William Hare, Tanner MSS, vol. 106, fol. 39b.

continue their wanderings, and when they failed to do so, Agas excommunicated them. The two began a countersuit in the puritan-controlled court of arches against the new curate, but Archbishop William Laud quickly quashed it.[17]

Other attempts were made to subvert the chancellor's actions. "Young" Samuel Peck officiated at the Hingham church in the fall of 1636, but before Corbett could serve process on him, the son of the "old Fox" had slipped back into Essex and outside the chancellor's jurisdiction. Parishioners secured the services of puritan Thomas Tofte, a "godly minister," to be their curate, until Corbett cited him in the consistory court, which took away his license to preach. Another curate hired after this incident was also suspended by the court. Subversion, therefore, had only limited success. A year and a half after Peck's excommunication, the chancellor passed sentence and deprived him of his parish for "non residency," although he had remained in Hingham the entire time. Finally, Corbett threatened Peck with an action from the court of high commission, and with this, plus Peck's unsuccessful court attempts to combat the bishop and chancellor, the minister, with his family and "many households in that and other towns adjacent," departed for New England.[18]

This religious account and the preceding economic explanation are persuasive but not entirely adequate analyses of the Hingham migration. Peck's puritanism may have been a significant mobilizing force, but Hingham's migration to New England began four years before he was excommunicated. Moreover, Peck only reluctantly went to Massachusetts and certainly would not have left England had he not been under severe pressure to do so. Samuel, Peck's son, referred to his parents as having been

17. See Tanner MSS, vol. 220, fol. 54, and Collection of Letters and Papers Relating to the Visitation of the Diocese of Norwich Ann. 1635–8, with Some Few Relating to the Clergy Brought against Dr. Matt. Wren, Bp. of Norwich, An. 1640. Extracts from the Letters of Dr. Clement Corbett, Chancellor of Norwich to Dr. Matt. Wren, Bp. of Norwich, Giving an Account of the Visitation, May 3, 7, June 9, 1637, and Mar. 7, 1638, ibid., vol. 68, fols. 3, 16b, and 21a; The Humble Petition of Edward Agas, Feb. 14, 1638, State Papers Domestic, Charles I, 16/382, no. 14, P.R.O. For religious agitation in neighboring Wymondham during this period, see Cal. State Papers, Domestic, 1627–1628, 137, and 1636–1637, 223.

Puritan Michael Metcalf of Norwich appeared to have suffered a similar fate in the archdeacons' and bishops' courts "concerning the matter of Bowing as well as for other matters of like consequence" and for "innovations now forced upon" him by Wren and Corbett. He later settled in Dedham, Massachusetts. See his letter, "To All the True Professors of Christs Gospel within the City of Norwich," Jan. 13, 1637, from Plymouth, England, in NEHGR, XVI (1862), 279–284.

18. Corbett to Wren, Nov. 4, 1636, Tanner MSS, vol. 68, fol. 3, and see n. 16 above.

made "exiles in their old age," and detailed arrangements were made for the care of family property remaining in Hingham.[19] As soon as favorable conditions were restored several years later, Peck returned to his Norfolk parish. The migration to new Hingham was led principally not by Peck, but by the Edmund Hobart family, whose son Peter grew up in old Hingham under the ministry of Peck, graduated from Peck's Cambridge college, Magdalene, and served the new town as its minister.

Similarly, economic conditions in the region during the 1620s and 1630s did not exactly coincide with social changes in the town. Hingham men, as we have seen, preserved long-standing traditions of independence and resourcefulness and had confidence in their ability to survive economic difficulty. Economic conditions go far toward explaining the general sense of uncertainty and insecurity exhibited by these wood-pasture men, but the increasing death rate, the decline in the number of births, and the rarity of marriages in Hingham after 1620 (as revealed in the Hingham parish register) cannot be attributed to the rise of famine in the community. Another factor was at work.

This mysterious phenomenon was the rise of plague in the central Norfolk market town. Outbreaks occurred in Norwich, only eighteen miles away, in 1625–1626, 1631, and 1637–1638, and were so severe in the neighboring town of Wymondham in 1631–1632 that even the distant parish of Stockton in the southeast part of the county sent the afflicted town thirteen shillings that year for its poor. But outside of a few official papers and local references in Norfolk, there has been little discussion of plague as a cause for migration, and only recently has the problem been given extensive attention in the writing of English local history.[20]

There is some indication that Hingham was relatively stable demographically from about 1550 until the third decade of the seventeenth century, a condition characterized by steady, upward birth and marriage rates

19. *Joseph Peck and Others* v. *Robert Peck Clericus and Others in Hingham and Elsewhere*, Norfolk Feet of Fines, C.P. 25 (2)/463, 13 Charles I, Hilary Term, P.R.O.

20. George Alfred Carthew, "Extracts from a Town Book of the Parish of Stockton, in Norfolk; Containing the Churchwardens' (and incidently, other) Accounts, from 1625 to 1712 Inclusive," *Norfolk Arch.*, I (1847), 171–172.

For a discussion of the interconnections among population, death, and disease, see: "Did the Peasants Really Starve?" in Laslett, *World We Have Lost*, 107–127; Pierre Goubert, *Beauvais et le Beauvaisis de 1600 à 1730* (Paris, 1960); E. A. Wrigley, "Mortality in Pre-Industrial England: The Example of Colyton, Devon, over Three Centuries," *Daedalus*, XCVII (1968), 546–547; and Michael Drake, "An Elementary Exercise in Parish Register Demography," *Econ. Hist. Rev.*, 2d Ser., XIV (1961–1962), 434–436. Two works of recent and particular importance are J.F.D. Shrewsbury, *A History of Bubonic Plague in the British Isles* (Cambridge, 1970), and Andrew B. Appleby, "Disease or Famine? Mortality in Cumberland and Westmorland, 1580–1640," *Econ. Hist. Rev.*, 2d Ser., XXVI (1973), 403–432.

and a leveling or declining death rate. Undoubtedly there were a number of deficient harvests during this period, but no evidence indicates that in Hingham they were of devastating proportions. The Norfolk county justices of the peace, who were responsible for relief efforts during such critical periods, reported some difficulties during 1572, 1577, 1581–1583, and major problems as a result of high grain prices and scarcity in late 1585 to 1587 and 1597 to 1598, but the evidence suggests that the greatest toll of misery and death was in other sections of the county.[21]

This impressionistic evidence from the late Tudor period is confirmed for the first twenty years of the following century by data extracted from the extant Hingham parish registers, which begin in 1601.[22] Until about 1618 the number of marriages and baptisms continued to increase, and, at the same time, the number of burials never exceeded the number of baptisms. But between 1618 and 1625, and particularly after 1625 for about fifteen years, sharp changes in these patterns occurred. In 1625, for the first time in the seventeenth century the number of recorded burials exceeded the number of baptisms, and after a brief dip this continued throughout the 1630s. Moreover, the number of marriages in Hingham declined from 1620 through mid-century (see graphs 1 and 2). Baptisms, roughly equivalent to the number of births, slipped from 49 in 1618 to 29 in 1634, or 59 percent of the former level. Even more dramatic trends are evident in the number of marriages, which in 1631 were at 14 percent of their level in 1620. In 1625 (and later in 1635 and 1639) the number of deaths increased nearly threefold from that just a few years earlier.

By itself the plague may not have been a powerful enough factor to account for the migration, but coming after a long period of relative demographic calm in the community, the crisis of 1625 must have had an unhinging effect. When the plague made its next appearance in neighboring Norwich and Wymondham in 1631 and 1632, accompanied by a slowly rising number of deaths in Hingham after a brief decline in 1629, the

21. *Cal. State Papers, Domestic, 1547–1580*, 449, 452, *1581–1590*, 4, 59, 105, 292, 301, 338, 382, 403, *1591–1595*, 401, *1598–1601*, 16. Distress was felt in 1586 in Wayland hundred in the nearby Breckland region, which supported a different agricultural system, but most reports came from diverse parts of the county like Hatcham, near Lynn, in western Norfolk where in 1597, 24 men "upon their own authority, stayed a ship laden with corn bound for Gainsborough, and forcibly unloaded her." Like all regions in Norfolk outside of the specialized grain-growing areas of the north, Hingham obviously felt the effects of the poor harvest, but as these records suggest, the town experienced no serious, vocal distress. Most important, there is also no mention of the plague in Hingham or its environs during the latter half of the 16th century.
22. Hingham Parish Records, 1601–1666, Hingham Parish Chest, St. Andrew's Church, Hingham, Norfolk.

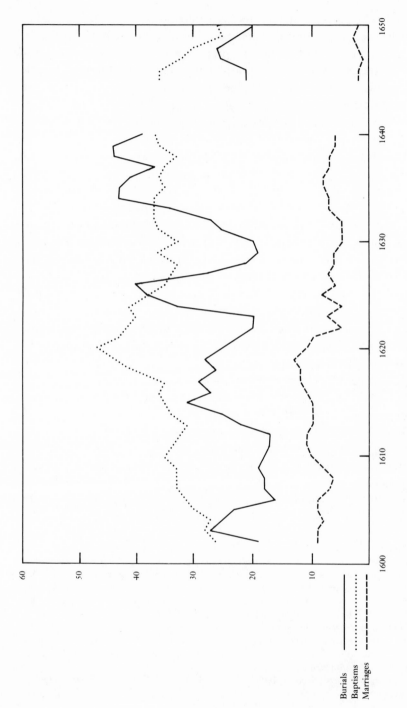

GRAPH 1. *Recorded Baptisms, Burials, and Marriages in Hingham, Norfolk, 1602–1650, Based on a Three-Year Moving Average*

Burials ——————
Baptisms ·················
Marriages ─ ─ ─ ─ ─

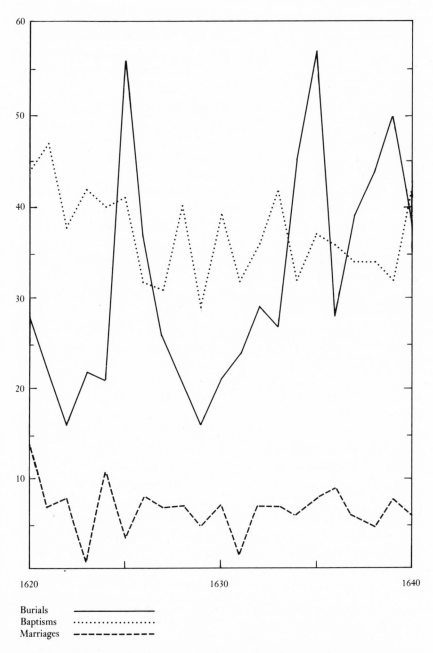

GRAPH 2. *Recorded Baptisms, Burials, and Marriages in Hingham, Norfolk,*
1620–1640

motivation to emigrate must have been heightened. Thus, the combination of plague and religious, economic, and kinship factors probably explains the Hingham migration. The entire migration occurred between 1633 and 1638, years in which the number of deaths from the recurrence of the plague was either increasing or at its peak.

The plague that erupted in central Norfolk in the 1620s and 1630s was itself not simply a consequence of poor harvests and famine. It was a separate element in the lives of Hingham residents and as such a separate motivating force for leaving the Norfolk region. The plague, which was probably of the bubonic variety, struck most heavily during the period between late spring or early summer and the end of the year, while deaths attributable to starvation or to diseases caused by malnutrition were usually highest in late winter and spring. In addition, children, widows, and the elderly, the people least likely to have a proper diet, were not especially prominent in the parish burial statistics, which suggests that unusual causes were involved. Moreover, the number of conceptions and marriages decreased less than would be expected if famine and famine-related diseases were at work. Finally, the prices of grains do not correlate with the sharp increases in deaths from 1625 to 1640. Prices, of course, changed from year to year, but during the critical or crisis years—1625, 1634, 1635, and 1639—they were not unusually high at the national level, or in the East Anglian and Norfolk regions, except in the first of those years. Even in 1625, however, the increase was modest, perhaps 5 to 10 percent, compared with 1621 and 1622 when prices rose 100 percent or more.[23]

An examination of the group of Hingham families that actually left for Massachusetts offers a final perspective on the causes of the migration. A most striking characteristic of the Hingham emigrants, which distinguishes them from the Yorkshire group that settled Rowley, was their age. For instance, only 31 percent of the men in Hingham were between the ages of eighteen and thirty-three in the base year 1635, whereas Rowley had twice that percentage of men in this age group. The age distribution

23. Lists containing national averages and lists of prices paid by Cambridge colleges are contained in J. E. Thorold Rogers, comp., *A History of Agriculture and Prices in England* . . . (Oxford, 1886–1902), V, 170–288. The Norwich and Norfolk Record Office contains records of the Norwich Assize of Bread from the mid-16th century to 1627, though unfortunately the document is usable only to 1616. The record office also temporarily houses the Thetford borough records, which contain price lists for the period to 1626 when the series ends. Neither price series reveals any correlation between grain prices and the deaths recorded in Hingham.

of the early Hingham settlers was fairly evenly proportioned. About as many men were in their twenties as were in their thirties or forties. Like Rowley, the Hingham migration was one of families, but it was not primarily composed of the young.[24] Kinship ties within Hingham and surrounding towns must have been a powerful force in encouraging families such as these to go to New England.

Even over relatively great distances, kinship or social ties to Hingham influenced the decisions of several individuals. Matthew Hawke, who came from Cambridgeshire, a county adjoining Norfolk to the west, may have been the son of John Hawke and Mary Cooper, who were married in Hingham on January 7, 1613, and soon thereafter left the parish. Others who lived in Norfolk County at some distance from Hingham had ties with the parish stretching back several decades. Thomas Thaxter, who had lived in Brigham, Norfolk, had a child baptized at St. Andrew's in 1618, although both he and his father later moved to Norwich. In Norwich William Ludkin, a son or brother of George Ludkin (some of whose children were baptized in Hingham), became apprenticed to a locksmith in 1619. Thaxter and the Ludkins had migrated to Hingham, New England, by the late 1630s.

In sum, several conditions affected the people of Hingham who eventually settled in New England. The wood-pasture regions of East Anglia were highly puritanized, and the persecution of the minister Robert Peck for nonconformist beliefs probably induced many of his puritan followers to leave Norfolk. Significantly, however, few of those parishioners who were directly charged with nonconformity later emigrated. Other local puritans were instrumental in the Hingham exodus. Peter Hobart, whose family lived in Hingham and who later became the minister in the new community, was serving as a preacher in Haverhill, Suffolk, in the early 1630s. He was influenced by such distinguished figures as John Norton and Thomas Shepard who embarked for Massachusetts in 1635, and in turn may have persuaded men in his home parish to leave. At least one important puritan, John Haynes of Copford Hall, Essex, who served as governor of Massachusetts Bay and later of Connecticut, was connected with Hingham, Norfolk. Years before his emigration he had married into the Thornton family of local renown and had lived in the parish peri-

---

24. Compiled from various sources including George Lincoln, ed., *History of the Town of Hingham, Massachusetts*, 3 vols. in 4 (Hingham, Mass., 1893), II and III, *passim*; Banks, *Planters of the Commonwealth*; and various individual genealogies and sources, most of which are listed in Appendix 2 of this volume.

odically before his departure. Such social or kinship ties, as well as other factors such as the plague, must have had a significant bearing on the eventual migration.

Newbury

Unlike Rowley and Hingham, Newbury, as we have seen, was never able to govern itself effectively during the early years after its establishment. Religious and civil difficulties in Newbury were probably rooted in earlier differences among the "West Country" men who settled the community. One man whose purposes and actions illustrate such differences was Richard Dummer of Bishopstoke, Hampshire, who came to New England in 1632. A man of considerable wealth, he, along with "Richard Saltonstall and divers other gentlemen in England," wanted to establish a region within the commonwealth that would be devoted to the profitable livestock-rearing activities that were common in his part of Hampshire. In May 1635 the General Court created the plantation of Newbury, and on July 8 it granted "a convenient quantity of land [to be] sett out by Mr. Dumer and Mr. Bartholmewe, within the bounds of Neweberry, for the keepeing of the sheepe and cattell that came over in the Dutch shipps this yeare" and further granted that the land was "to belonge to the owners of the said cattell." [25] Dummer soon left for England after hiring a group of men, many from Marlborough, Wiltshire, to tend the livestock in his absence. While he was away his cattle-raising enterprise took a turn for the worse. Thomas Coleman, who among others was in charge of "the keeping of certain horses, bulls and sheepe in a general stock for the space of three years," proved "exceedingly negligent in discharging the trust committed to him, . . . by reason whereof many of the said cattle are dead already and more damage likely to accrue." Undaunted, Dummer returned to Newbury in the summer of 1638. [26]

Other men, differing in outlook, interest, and background, arrived, according to extant ship lists, on the only four ships that carried Newbury

25. Banks, *Planters of the Commonwealth*, 94; *Recs. of Mass. Bay*, I, 146, 149. Emery Battis has suggested that Dummer was persuaded to join a New England venture, the "Plough Company" or "Company of Husbandmen," through "his kinsman" Stephen Bachiler, whom the company had hired for ministerial services. Both arrived in New England from Hampshire in the same year on different ships (Banks, *Planters of the Commonwealth*, 96). The company, however, disbanded. Whatever connection did exist between the two men, they both failed to follow Massachusetts orthodoxy, though only Dummer was involved in the Antinomian Controversy in the 1630s. See Battis, *Saints and Sectaries*, 278n.

26. *Recs. of Mass. Bay*, I, 155.

settlers from the Wiltshire-Hampshire region to New England. The first was the *Mary and John*, which sailed with the Reverend Thomas Parker and his group from Southampton on March 24, 1634. Parker, his cousin James Noyes, and another relation, Reverend Joseph Avery of Romsey, Hampshire, came with a large number of "river men" from Hampshire and open-field settlers from eastern Wiltshire and Hampshire. It is possible that while Dummer and Parker were together in New England in 1635, Dummer had persuaded Parker to join the Newbury settlement as minister. In any event, Parker and his group settled in Newbury the following spring.

After the first group of settlers arrived, events occurred in rapid order. On June 3, 1635, a second group sailed on the *James* of London from Southampton and a month later Dummer's livestock were delivered. The passengers on the *James* included a diverse group of people, including "laborers" from Marlborough, some of whom had been hired by Dummer, men such as Thomas Brown and Hercules Woodman from Christian Malford in western Wiltshire, immigrants from the New Forest region in southeastern Wiltshire such as John Pike and John Musselwhite, and a number of Joseph Avery's congregation from Romsey, Hampshire. With the exception of the latter group from Romsey, and Dummer's livestock men, it is hard to determine what prompted so many men from scattered places in the two-county area to converge in Southampton and sail to New England. Kinship may have played a part, at least among those living along the common border of the two counties, and word about departing ships may have been a factor among puritan congregations throughout the more remote reaches of western Wiltshire. Unlike Hingham emigrants, however, a number of men from distant localities did not have the comfort of friends and neighbors leaving en masse for the New World.[27]

27. The four ship lists are conveniently found in Banks, *Planters of the Commonwealth*, 110–113, 135–139, 195–198, and 198–200. Kinship was obviously an important factor among many chalk-country settlers from the Wiltshire-Hampshire border area, especially among the religious leadership of the community, which was composed of four ministers who were related. Parker was related to the Noyes, Avery, and Woodbridge families as cousin, brother-in-law, and uncle, respectively. James Noyes's mother, Ann Parker Noyes, in her will of Mar. 7, 1657, left some of her estate to her son-in-law, Thomas Kent of Upper Wallop, from where the Richard Kents came (Henry E. Noyes and Harriette E. Noyes, eds., *Genealogical Record of Some of the Noyes Descendants of James Nicholas and Peter Noyes* [Boston, 1904], I, 5, hereafter cited as *Noyes Genealogy*). Undoubtedly other kinship ties existed prior to departure for New England. Many emigrants from the same village or subregion certainly knew each other and possibly some from neighboring subregions were acquainted. For example, John Emery of Romsey, a weaver, may have been the same man listed in the Bishopstoke entry fines in 1632 with Richard and Stephen Dummer, local residents there. See P.R.O. transcripts, 120/7, Hampshire R.O.

The third group of Newbury settlers left Southampton three years later in April of 1638. Most were from the Test River valley region in Hampshire, which stretches from Southampton to the northwestern border of the county. Not all the passengers of the *Confidence* later settled in Newbury, some deciding instead to join East Anglians in organizing the town of Sudbury in 1639. The final group, which included the Dummers, sailed in May 1638 on the *Bevis* and was comprised almost wholly of Hampshire men from the Test and Itchen rivers region. These four boatloads of settlers from diverse Wiltshire-Hampshire regions, as we have earlier observed, quickly demonstrated how equally diverse their concepts of religion, agriculture, and social life were.

If Newbury settlers were unable to rely upon friends and family for aid in contending with the problems of emigration, they at least had the advantage of youth in making the transition. Among the ninety-one men who became proprietors of the town in 1642 whose ages can be determined, over three-quarters were between eighteen and thirty-three, and most of these men were in their twenties. Some were in their thirties, but few migrated who had passed their fortieth birthday. In contrast, the Hingham emigrants were fairly evenly distributed in age from twenty to forty-nine, while among the settlers of Rowley about three out of every five men were between eighteen and thirty-three.[28]

Despite their youth and unlike their East Anglian counterparts, many Newbury settlers had English backgrounds of local social prominence. In 1632 Richard Dummer was a wealthy enough member of his parish to rent out a close of land called "Five Acres," which produced an annual return of forty shillings that he gave to the poor at Michaelmas and on Lady Day. In 1653 Thomas Dummer, probably Richard's oldest son, gave additional rent monies of forty shillings for "Poor Close" to be distributed among the parish poor on the same holidays. The family of James and Nicholas Noyes had owned the estate of Hatherdean in Weyhill, near Cholderton, Wiltshire, since the previous century. Their father, Robert, was even able to exchange a debt owed him on rents in Cholderton for the next "avoidance," or right to fill a parish ministerial vacancy, "for and towards the advancement of one of the sones . . . being a living worth 100 marks yearly and more." Shortly thereafter the Noyes family was given

28. Like the age comparisons of settlers made for the other Massachusetts towns studied here, the base year for comparison is 1635, the midpoint during the decade of the Great Migration. For Newbury, it is compiled from several sources including Coffin, *Sketch of the History of Newbury*, 293–322; Banks, *Planters of the Commonwealth*; *Essex Co. Court Recs.*, *passim*; and various individual genealogies and sources, most of which are listed in Appendix 3 herein.

this right permanently as advowson, or patron of the parish, which they held until near the end of the seventeenth century.[29] Evidence from inventories and tax records suggests that other Newbury settlers came from relatively notable backgrounds. John Rolfe, father of emigrant Henry Rolfe, died in Landford, Wiltshire, in 1625. His inventory amounted to £103 10s. 4d., which was a reasonably good estate for the New Forest region. Other Newbury settlers or their fathers (where they can be traced) figured prominently in the lay subsidy tax lists of the period. Peter Weare, very likely the father of emigrant Nathaniel Weare, had the highest assessment for land in the Brokenborough, Wiltshire, lists in the 1620s. In one case Weare paid an assessment that was three times higher than those of all but one of his neighbors. The names of both John and his son Henry Rolfe were on the Whiteparish subsidy list of 1628, and Thomas was on one two decades earlier. Stephen and Richard Kent appear in several Hampshire subsidy returns. Richard Kent, listed in Upper Wallop, was rated in the middle range of those assessed in 1622, and Stephen Kent was rated third out of eleven men. It seems very likely that a Thomas Kent of Nether Wallop who died in 1605 with an inventory of £200 18s. 7d., one of the highest in the region, was the father of both Richard and Stephen Kent.[30]

None of these men seems to have been wealthy enough to invest in a large-scale, livestock-raising enterprise such as Dummer and his associates initiated, but these records suggest, insofar as they have been examined, that there were more men in Newbury with comfortable backgrounds than in Hingham. Of course not all the early settlers of Newbury were well-off. John Musselwhite from Landford, Wiltshire, arrived as a "laborer" and died in 1670 leaving an estate of £30 4s. 4d., the second poorest man among all the proprietors inventoried. Others like Henry Rolfe, a Wiltshire neighbor of Musselwhite's, did not fare as well as they might have. The son of John Rolfe, noted above, Henry came from a moderately wealthy family for the region, but died in 1643 with an estate of only £153 8s. 6d., which was low by Newbury, Massachusetts, standards. His early death may explain why his inventory was thirty-seventh in value of fifty-

29. *Victoria Hist. of Counties, Hampshire*, III, 310; *Noyes Genealogy*, I, 3–4; "Records of Wiltshire Parishes. Cholderton," *Wiltshire Notes and Queries*, II (1896), 105–110, especially 106, referring to Petition, Proceedings in Chancery, Cc 11, no. 59 (1599).

30. E.179/175/485 (9 James I), 491 (19 James I), 510 (1 Charles I), 512 (5 Charles I), 513 and 519 (4 Charles I); E.179/199/356 (3 James I), 366 (7 James I), 369 (8 James I), 370 (7 James I), 378 (22 James I), 381 (1 Charles I), 383 (2 Charles I), 395 (4 Charles I), 398 (4 Charles I), P.R.O.; Thomas Kent, inventory, Winchester Archdeaconry Court Wills, 1605, Hampshire R.O.

one. Though Newbury was a society with marked economic inequalities, it was also one that did not stand still. Newbury men seemed to put a premium on material acquisitiveness, and unless men like Rolfe grasped opportunities when they could and outdid their rivals, they were apt to be bypassed.[31]

The nature of and circumstances behind the Newbury migration were very different from Hingham's experience. Religion appears to have played a much different and less influential role as a cause for migration. Unlike the situation in Norfolk and York, puritans and other groups were not systematically persecuted or harassed in the Wiltshire-Hampshire region. Possibly this explains in part why fewer people migrated from this region than, for instance, from East Anglia. Puritanism was a more moderate, reforming force in Wiltshire-Hampshire than it was in the East, in addition to being newer, more dispersed, and less institutionalized. Kinship, social, and some religious congregational ties played an important part in the migration of "fielden" men from eastern Wiltshire and western Hampshire. Nevertheless, the primary motivations for leaving the wood-pasture region of western Wiltshire appear to have been declining economic opportunities, the depression in the cloth trade, and similar causes mentioned earlier. Finally, many West Countrymen had displayed signs of economic importance in their local English villages, a trait shared by few who moved to new Hingham and by none who remained there.[32]

Ipswich and Watertown

Although the settlers of Ipswich came from a slightly different area of England than the settlers of Watertown, and emigrated at a different time, the English experiences of the two groups were in most ways similar. Many Ipswich men migrated to Massachusetts Bay in 1634, four years after the major group that settled in Watertown. The Ipswich settlers also

31. *Essex Co. Court Recs.*, IV, 291; *Essex Co. Probate Recs.*, I, 21–22.
32. W. H. Mildon, "Puritanism in Hampshire and the Isle of Wight from the Reign of Elizabeth to the Restoration" (Ph.D. thesis, University of London, 1934), 6–10, 42–44, 64–65, 103, 122–123; Edmund Parsons, "The Andover Woollen Industry," Hampshire Field Club and Arch. Soc., *Papers and Procs.*, XVI (1945), 178–184; Romsey Corporation Records, Add. MSS 26774, I, fol. 76a. Winchester bishops shared the puritans' enthusiasm by warmly approving two of their most important aims in the region, Sabbatarianism and preaching, and in the puritan-influenced river towns both activities received the sanction of local law. For a discussion of economic problems in western Wiltshire, see pp. 87–89, above.

were drawn from a much larger area, which included not only Suffolk and Essex, but also the boroughs of Hertfordshire, just to the west of East Anglia and north of London. Even so, the background and experiences of settlers from all three counties were in many ways alike prior to their departure.

Whether they had lived in villages, in towns, or in boroughs, Ipswich and Watertown inhabitants generally came from a roughly triangular area in East Anglia that stretched from the mouth of the river Stour in the east, west to Haverhill in western Suffolk, and north to Bury St. Edmunds. A great number of them came from towns on or near the Stour, which divides Essex and Suffolk, or its tributaries. The center of these two East Anglian migrations was the wood-pasture region around Babergh hundred, Suffolk, which was south and east of the borough of Sudbury along the river. The distinctly urban character of Ipswich, Massachusetts, which has been discussed previously, was partially the result of the presence of settlers from Hertfordshire boroughs, principally St. Albans and Bishop Stortford, and from several urban centers in East Anglia, especially Colchester, Chelmsford, and Bocking, Essex, and Lavenham, Suffolk.[33]

At least two major causes were behind the migration to New England from this region of England. Economic reverses, particularly in the cloth trade, and, somewhat paradoxically, economic vitality in agriculture followed by a sharp decline in production from poor harvests led to a widespread social dislocation in central East Anglia, beginning in the decade preceding the Great Migration and continuing throughout the 1630s. In addition, there was a sharp change in ecclesiastical policy in the area despite decades of relative calm from which the puritans had benefited while institutionalizing changes in their local parishes.

The central East Anglian, or Suffolk-Essex-Hertfordshire region, was one of the most important industrial and commercial agricultural areas in early seventeenth-century England. The region, in fact, was the premier industrial district of fifteenth- and sixteenth-century England and was only starting to decelerate in the 1620s and 1630s. It was not until the end of the seventeenth century that the area was in full-scale decline.[34] Lo-

33. The English places of origin for the original 111 commoners of Ipswich, Massachusetts, in 1642, and those for the grantees of the first division of land on July 25, 1636, in Watertown, Massachusetts, are listed in Appendixes 4 and 5 of this study.

34. For example, "the Suffolk cloth industry was, however, declining and by 1693 it could be stated that the manufacture of cloth had almost disappeared from the county." Bowden, "Wool Supply and the Woollen Industry," *Econ. Hist. Rev.*, 2d Ser., IX (1956–1957), 50n.

cated in "a profittable and commodious scituation," even remote inland villages here were close to the sea, for navigable rivers, particularly in Suffolk, reached far into the interior. East Anglia was also on the mainline of continental trade, a factor that encouraged not only commercial but also manufacturing enterprise, especially clothmaking, in boroughs, towns, and villages along the many rivers. East Anglian cloth was sent in East Anglian ships as far as Russia and the eastern Mediterranean. Trading was not, however, limited to what foreigners would buy, but extended to London itself via coastal traffic, inland rivers, and overland routes. East Anglians from the Stour valley region and other enterprising men in neighboring Hertfordshire sold a large portion of their cloth to the city, but probably more important was their role in supplying the capital with agricultural produce.[35] Increasing demand for farm goods in the seventeenth century rapidly outstripped existing land resources in the central East Anglian area, a circumstance that contributed to a galloping increase in the price of land.

The three-county area could be economically dynamic when conditions were right, but it was also vulnerable to economic and social catastrophe. Social dislocation was caused by a variety of factors. The health of the clothmaking industry was dependent upon fluctuations in the conditions of foreign trade. The food supply was often insufficient if harvests in this wood-pasture region were poor. In such cases, grain had to be imported from the large-scale, capitalistic farming regions of eastern Suffolk and northern Norfolk, and often this grain found more profitable markets on the Continent. Finally, the past history of East Anglia, the attractiveness to immigrant poor of employment in the cloth industry, and the lack of strong manorial control all contributed to the area's dense population. With industrial decline and food scarcity, the numerous poor only exacerbated the magnitude of these problems. All of them combined in the 1620s and 1630s to produce an economic depression of serious proportions in East Anglia.

When depression hit the whole clothmaking industry, it sent men of moderate means, such as the weavers of Braintree and Bocking, Essex, "into great extremity and want and [they were] not able to maintain their poor wives and children" because of the lack of work. This affected large numbers of people, which "in our neighbour towns amounteth to thirty thousand persons and upwards [who] dependeth only by weaving and

35. For a fuller discussion of East Anglian commercial agriculture, see Allen, "In English Ways," 236–242.

spinning, and now are utterly put out of their work for the most part of them." Many people other than weavers were also hurt indirectly. Even Braintree's efforts to employ several dozen families with work in the cloth trade during the depression year of 1629 did not stop the complaint that many more people were still seeking work. Essex justices summed up conditions perceptively in 1631 when they reported that "the poor suffer much in respect of the high prices of corn, yet they are in far greater misery in the most populous parts of the country [county], by reason that the clothiers forbear to set the weavers on work"; the potential employers claimed that they were unable to sell the finished cloth in the depressed market.[36]

With mounting unemployment and poor harvests, obtaining a constant food supply was one of the most serious concerns in the three-county region. Calls of alarm most often came from the wood-pasture lands of the middle section of Suffolk, north central Essex and the forests to the west, and eastern Hertfordshire, the very areas from which many puritans emigrated. During the scarcity of 1621–1623, all of these county subregions were affected, including such urban areas as Bury St. Edmunds, Ipswich, and other cloth and trading centers. In the puritan hundreds of Cosford and Babergh, Suffolk, it was reported that since "the stores of corn will hardly suffice" and "some of the towns being very populous, and the prices high and still rising," relief for the poor and "suppression of vagrants and alehouses" had been ordered. In February 1622 justices leveled warrants against the churchwardens and overseers of the poor in John Winthrop's Groton and the neighboring towns of Boxford and Edwardston on the grounds that "the aged and impotent poor are not relieved in such comfort and sufficient manner as their necessity requireth, and that the other sort of poor which are of able bodies to work are in great distress and many of them likely to perish."

Throughout the twenties complaints were also registered about large groups of wandering poor and about the particular problems of the urban poor, such as at Hertford, Hertfordshire, in 1629. By December 1630, the East Anglian food supply was again seriously in trouble and justices allotted farmers specified quantities of corn that "each person weekly should carry to market at the clothing towns of Coggeshall and Witham and how much at the boroughs of Colchester and Maldon." Matters worsened from 1630 to 1631. In Nayland, Suffolk, for instance, the English town from

36. Essex County Quarter Sessions Records, Q/SR 226/120, 121, Essex R.O.; *Cal. State Papers, Domestic, 1631–1633*, 14.

which such Watertown settlers as John Firman, Isaac Stearns, and John Warren came, townsmen petitioned to the lord treasurer that "their distressed estate, for want of corn, is so great that most of the inhabitants are ready to perish." The community implored him "for Christ's sake, and the love he bears the town, to take some course for their relief."

In 1631 and 1632 conditions also deteriorated in the eastern Hertfordshire countryside and in such county boroughs as St. Albans, Hertford, and Bishop Stortford where a number of puritan families were preparing to leave for Ipswich, Massachusetts. In St. Albans, for instance, prosecutions against bakers for underweight bread were not uncommon during a time of dearth, and well-established plans for poor relief of city residents were in force. Discussion among local justices, county sheriffs, and the king's council on how to deal with the distressing conditions continued until after the middle of the decade and then gradually tapered off. In the process, local officials were concerned not only with the allocation of foodstuffs but also with public health, the safety of inhabitants from marauding vagabonds, and the problem of encampment on town property by landless wanderers.[37]

The malnutrition resulting from food shortages was probably the greatest cause of disease throughout these decades and may have been a factor when local justices were required to take measures against the "plague" in Sudbury in 1626, the outbreak of smallpox in neighboring Lavenham in 1635, and a great "infection" in Bury St. Edmunds two years later. In these cases, Suffolk justices were often required to institute a general assessment on already impoverished inhabitants to pay for relief efforts.[38] Probably more tedious and never ending for local officials, however, were the countless cases throughout these decades that involved the policing of beggars and vagabonds. The towns were constantly on guard to prevent these poor folk from attempting to settle in towns and become charges on the parishes' poor relief rolls. The responsiveness of local officials to such crises suggests the high regard villagers from this area had for local of-

37. For some details on the conditions in the three-county area, its food supply, and corresponding social dislocations, see *Cal. State Papers, Domestic, 1619–1623*, 361, 465, 484, 490, 548–549, *1627–1628*, 72, 133, 536, *1628–1629*, 495–496, 560, *1629–1631*, 415, 417, 476, 484–485, 549, 268, 342, 480, 493, 539, 546–547, 508, *1631–1633*, 14, 190, 191, 39, 7, 36, 28, 97, 128, 129, 131, 132, 176, 188, 210, 224, 240, 249, 251, 264, 268, 318, 344, 349, 449, 518, 572, 37, 44, 49, 68, 86, 97, 108, 213, 305, 341, 425, 434, *1633–1634*, 163, 222, 221, 50, 51, 71, 80, 240, 244, 294, 305–306, 381, 490, 534, 560, *1635*, 264, 417, *1637–1638*, 545, *1639*, 531; Historical Manuscripts Commission, *Thirteenth Report, Part IV* (London, 1892), 439. Note, also, *Cal. State Papers, Domestic, 1635–1636*, 11–12.

38. *Winthrop Papers*, I, 331–332; *Cal. State Papers, Domestic, 1637*, 282–283; Lavenham list of assessments (1635), 1531/7/1, (1), (2), West Suffolk R.O.

ficeholding, a factor no less significant, as we have seen, among East Anglian villagers in Watertown and Ipswich, Massachusetts.

The itinerant poor were very much in evidence in the populous wood-pasture region of Suffolk and Essex as well as in the eastern part of Hertfordshire and that county's urban centers. The contemporary Suffolk antiquary Robert Reyce stated, "It is by common experience tried" that "the greatest number of the poor" were found "where the clothiers doe dwell or have dwelled" in the urban towns, and that the next greatest number were in the wood-pasture rural areas "where the meaner sort doe practise spinning of thred linnen and other such like womens imploy-ments." There was more poverty here than on the East Anglian coast or nearer London, and evidence of its extent was found in urban centers as well as in rural communities.[39]

The region's economic well-being deteriorated under conditions associated with the pressure of large populations. Wood-pasture regions were generally thickly inhabited and from 1500 to about 1650 the region as a whole experienced a striking population increase. Sixteenth-century lay subsidy taxes, and seventeenth-century ship money assessments, hearth taxes, and the Compton ecclesiastical census of 1676 all testify to the scope of the increase as well as to the surprising mobility of workers from one cloth town to another. Babergh hundred, Suffolk, and adjoining Essex hundred of Hinckford, both wood-pasture areas along the Stour River and in the center of emigration for many Watertown and Ipswich, Massachusetts, settlers, were possibly the two most densely populated hundreds in the two-county area in the early seventeenth century.[40] John Winthrop, who was lord of Groton manor in Suffolk prior to his departure to the Bay Colony, was well aware of the impact of population pressures in this area. "This lande grows wearye of her Inhabitantes," he penned in arguing for a New England plantation, "so as man which is the most pretious of all Creatures, is neer more vile and base, then the earthe they treade upon, and of lesse prise among us than an horse or a sheepe." While man's own value diminished in East Anglia, competition for land became stronger,

39. Robert Reyce, *Suffolk in the XVIIth Century: The Breviary of Suffolk by Robert Reyce, 1618; Now Published for the First Time from the MS. in the British Museum, with Notes by Lord Francis Hervey* (London, 1902), 57; Susan E. Cunningham, "Changes in the Pattern of Rural Settlement in Northern Essex between 1650 and 1850" (M.S. thesis, Victoria University of Manchester, 1968), 27.

40. I. G. Doolittle, "Population Growth and Movement in and around Colchester and the Tendring Hundred, 1500–1800" (thesis submitted for the Emmison Prize, 1970), T/Z 13/132, Essex R.O.; "The Condition of the Archdeaconries of Suffolk and Sudbury in the Year 1603," Suffolk Inst. Arch. and Nat. Hist., *Procs.*, XI (1903), 1–46.

"many men spending as much labour and coste to recover and keepe some-times an acre or towe of Land, we would procure them many c [hundred] as good or better in another Countrie."[41]

Matters were further complicated by the small number of major resident gentry in the region. As in Norfolk, most were situated in the champion country, which was suited to large-scale agricultural enterprise. In Suffolk the equivalent region was located toward the east. Lesser gentry like John Winthrop, to be sure, lived on their own small manors in the wood-pasture region, but unlike the wealthier families in eastern Suffolk who took part in county affairs as justices of the peace and members of the traveling assizes, the minor gentry only occasionally served as "cheife constables" in the affairs of the local hundred. The absence of major men contributed to the weakening of the manor as an institution in the region and made it easier for the ever-expanding number of homeless poor to take over forest land as squatters and, in time, to overpopulate the countryside.

The origins and early development of East Anglian puritanism have been the subject of intensive study by a number of historians of the Tudor and Stuart period.[42] East Anglia's commercial life helped expose the area to European Protestantism as early as the mid-sixteenth century. In 1556 men in Dedham, Essex, were indicted for aiding and abetting a preacher of "heresies and schismatic sermons." Two decades later in nearby Bocking, Essex, the spirit of the new religion had so caught up local inhabitants that one man exclaimed despairingly that "it was never mery in Ingland sithen [since] the scriptures were so comonly preched and talked upon." This kind of protest was overshadowed by the great number of East Anglians who diligently attended the village or town sermons and would often meet afterward at dinner or other social occasions to "reason upon" them.[43]

The most notable characteristic of the area by the early seventeenth century was that puritanism had become for many a routine way of life. Unlike the situation in the North or the West, for instance, in East Anglia evangelical fire was noticeably absent. While in new territories its doctrines and practices might spread rapidly across the isolated moors and marshes, forests and pastures, in much of the area east of London one of

41. John Patten, "Village and Town: An Occupational Study," *Ag. Hist. Rev.*, XX (1972), 1; Cunningham, "Changes in the Pattern of Rural Settlement in Northern Essex," 27; *Winthrop Papers*, I, 297, II, 112, 114, 129, *passim*.

42. For some examples, see Usher, ed., *Presbyterian Movement in the Reign of Queen Elizabeth* (Camden Soc., *Pubs.*, 3d Ser., VIII [London, 1905]); and Collinson, *Elizabethan Puritan Movement*.

43. Q/SR 2/15, Q/SR 65/61, and note Q/SR 196/124, Essex R.O.

puritanism's main effects was that it helped to consolidate relations between the parish or town and the manorial lord. As Bishop Wren of Norwich commented to Archbishop Laud, puritan "lectures abounded, especially in Suffolk. Not a bowling green, or an ordinary could stand without one, and many of them were set up by private gentlemen at their pleasure." The small towns and manors of East Anglia were not the only places where puritanism flourished, for as another observer noted, the boroughs of Essex "consist mostly of Puritans" as did many cloth and market towns in Suffolk and Hertfordshire.[44] Only when ecclesiastical authority attempted seriously to undercut this relationship in the 1630s did many puritans begin to question how their institutional arrangements might best be maintained.

In the early seventeenth century, there was little apparent persecution in East Anglia. Visiting ministers and wandering preachers were commonplace and conventicles were well attended, but they rarely raised ecclesiastical condemnation. Adam Winthrop, father of the Massachusetts Bay colonizer, frequently noted in his diary that traveling preachers had visited neighboring parishes to speak. He wrote in 1607, for instance, that in "the last of December Mr. William Amyes [Ames] preached at Boxford uppon the 80 psalme and first verse pie et docte," and such entries were repeated on a monthly or weekly basis. A little later, however, Adam's son John became aware of the growing obstacles that confronted these itinerants in the East Anglian wood-pasture country. The young Winthrop's "Common Grievance Groaning for Reformation," originally written in 1624, cited some problems for puritans even in the region not openly hostile to the new persuasion. He noted that "many [were] Unjustely Traduced for Conventicles" and reported "the Suspension and Silencing of Many painfull learned ministers for not Conformitie in some poynts or ceremonies and refuseinge subscription directed by the late canons." Finally, Winthrop was clearly upset at the practice of "ponishinge the subjecte for goeing to another Parish to hear a sermon when there is none in there owne parish."[45]

For three-quarters of a century there had been an unsettled and uneasy coexistence between national religious orthodoxy and local puritan prac-

---

44. *Cal. State Papers, Domestic, 1636–1637*, 223, *1640*, 608–609.

45. "Diary of Adam Winthrop," *Winthrop Papers*, I, 39–145 *passim*, 243–247; and John Winthrop, "Common Grievance Groaning for Reformation," *ibid.*, 295–310 *passim*. For a perspective on the broader puritan lay and clerical community extending beyond parish bounds, see Patrick Collinson, "Lectures by Combination: Structure and Characteristics of Church Life in 17th-Century England," Institute of Historical Research, *Bulletin*, XLVIII (1975), 182–213.

tice. One of the more important insulating forces for the latter, as Bishop Wren had pointed out, was the role that the local puritan gentry played in maintaining their control over religious activities. Richard Rogers of Wethersfield, Essex, whose son Ezekiel brought many emigrants from the East Riding to Massachusetts Bay, was often in violation of ecclesiastical regulations, but through the intervention of local gentry he managed to hold onto his parish for decades. According to him, the archbishop of Canterbury "protested none of us should Preach without conformity and Subscription. I thanke God I have seen him eate his Words as Great and as Peremptory as he was." About thirty weeks after being silenced by Archbishop John Whitgift in 1583, Rogers was reinstated by Sir Robert Wroth, a local manorial lord, who "writ in favour of me, and bad[e] me Preach and he would beare me out, and so I have continued . . . to the end of Archbishop Whitgifts Life." On other occasions Rogers was excommunicated, but the matter was cleared up each time. Other cases involving the Essex minister came before the high commission and the consistory court, but men such as Sir Robert Jermyn from Suffolk always saw to it that the matter was allowed to "sleape."[46]

Another factor that weakened episcopal control over localities in East Anglia was geographical. Many East Anglians who settled in Watertown and Ipswich came from the area of the Stour River valley, which not only divided the counties of Suffolk and Essex but was also an ecclesiastical boundary. Richard Rogers's Wethersfield parish was in the diocese of London and consequently on the remote fringes of the bishop's territory, and similar communities in Suffolk across the river were in the southernmost part of the bishop of Norwich's domain.

Although ecclesiastical policy was normally kept in check by means described above, local puritan autonomy in the region appears to have been severely curtailed between 1629 and 1634, years which, coincidentally, witnessed severe social and economic dislocation in the region. For the most part ecclesiastical action was directed against particular individuals. In 1629 proceedings were initiated to remove Thomas Hooker from his Chelmsford, Essex, parish, and a year later Daniel Rogers, lecturer of Wethersfield, Essex, was deprived of his. Shortly thereafter the church directed its attention westward to Ware, Hertfordshire, where ecclesiasti-

---

46. M. M. Knappen, ed., *Two Elizabethan Puritan Diaries by Richard Rogers and Samuel Ward* (Chicago, 1933), 29–31, 100; and compare E. Hockliffe, ed., *The Diary of the Rev. Ralph Josselin 1616–1683* (Camden Soc., *Pubs.*, 3d Ser., XV [London, 1908]), and Savage, *Gen. Dict.*, III, 564.

cal commissioners charged the local vicar, Charles Chauncey, with "the omission of Athanasius's Creed, the Lesson from the Old Testament, the Litany, the Surplice, the cross in Baptism," and similar offenses. The commission also noted "various speeches" from the "pulpit and elsewhere, in praise of the Puritans, in disparagement of the authority of the church, and in anticipation of changes likely to ensue in church and state, in expectation whereof [Chauncey] asserted that some families were preparing to go to New England." Although Chauncey immediately denied any nonconformity and "explained away" speeches "attributed to him," he and Thomas Hooker eventually left for Massachusetts.[47]

In such communities along or near the Stour as Dedham, Wethersfield, Manningtree, Finchingfield, and Colchester, official inquiries were made concerning the lecturers of Essex, while in other places conventicles were suppressed. In Great Bromley, where Watertown settlers Gregory and Simon Stone and Edward Howe came from, the churchwardens' account book reveals fines of 5s. 4d. paid "at the Court for our absolution being excominicate," £3 10s. "for making of the rayle att the Communion Table," and 2s. 4d. "for stefyinge [certifying] into the Cort for getting up the rayle" and "for bring[ing] the rayle from Colchester." Evidently the churchwardens had been excommunicated for neglecting to replace the communion rail after it had been torn down, a practice puritans heartily encouraged. The ecclesiastical visitation to several parishes near Great Bromley in northeast Essex in the year 1633 demonstrated just how far apart both sides were. The detailed listing of every single departure from conformity, whether great or small, testified to the degree to which authorities planned to carry their reform as well as to the inability of puritan communities to accept those changes.[48] These attacks, coupled with the growing economic uncertainties and accompanying social dislocations of

47. *Cal. State Papers, Domestic, 1629–1631*, 92, 391, 233.

48. For some other aspects of puritanism in the Suffolk, Essex, and Hertfordshire area, see: *ibid.*, *1619–1623*, 41, *1623–1625*, 285, *1629–1631*, 186, 98–99, 274, 240, *1631–1633*, 108, 255, 341, 352, 492, *1633–1634*, 239, 480–481, 450–451, 113, 281, *1635*, 528; Rev. H. H. Minchin, "The Churches of Great and Little Bromley," Essex Archaeological Society, *Transactions*, N.S., VIII (1903), 292–293; J. Gardner Bartlett, *Gregory Stone Genealogy: Ancestry and Descendants of Dea. Gregory Stone of Cambridge, Mass., 1320–1917* (Boston, 1918), 43; W. E. Layton, "Ecclesiastical Disturbances in Ipswich during the Reign of Charles I," *East Anglian; or Notes and Queries in Subjects Connected with the Counties of Suffolk, Essex and Norfolk*, N.S., II (1887–1888), 209–211, 257–259, 315–317, 373–374, 405–406; Robert Peters, *Oculus Episcopi: Administration in the Archdeaconry of St. Albans, 1580–1625* (Manchester, England, 1963), 26–28, 34, 82, and *passim*; Tanner MSS, vol. 68, fol. 225; D/ACV/5, Essex R.O.

the late 1620s and early 1630s, made it inevitable, as John Dane, an Ipswich, Massachusetts, immigrant, put it, that "thare was a great cuming to nu ingland."[49]

Dane's narrative of his life in England and Massachusetts, a remarkable and rare document, links together some of the social and religious elements behind the East Anglian migration by men of modest means and expectations. In the first place, the Dane family was characterized by a rootlessness that was primarily a result of the itinerant, insecure, and impermanent nature of John's father's employment as a tailor.[50] At an early age, John recalled, his family moved from Berkhamsted to Bishop Stortford in Hertfordshire. His father went off "to finesh matters" but stayed longer than expected and his mother, growing increasingly upset and uncertain, "met with sum wants and was trobeled and weapt." John followed in his father's trade and was constantly on the move. At eighteen he left home, he recalled, "to seke my fortin" and went first to Berkhamsted, then to the borough of Hertford, and finally settled in the Essex woods at "wood Ro grene, on hatfild forrist."

Dane seems to have grown up in a puritan household, but as a young man he gave himself "mutch of dansing and staying out and heatting myself and lying in haymowes." When he left home his mother warned him that "goe whare you will, god he will find you out." He did manage to avoid the pitfalls associated with women and seems to have worked hard at his various jobs, but according to his own account, for at least several years he lived a somewhat aimless life. In Hertford, Dane went to hear a puritan minister preach "consarning prayer." The next Sunday he avoided going to church, but while walking in a meadow that morning he was suddenly stung in his finger, which "paind me mutch." Subsequently the pain and swelling increased and even his shoulder became enlarged. Lying in his room he "toke [his] . . . bybell and lokt over sum instructions my father had Ret, and I weapt sorly." He prayed, asking that his sin be pardoned and his arm healed. Finally he went to a "surgin" who described his condition as "*the take*," which meant that "it was taken by the provedens of god." "This," Dane exclaimed, "knoct home on my hart what my mother said, *god will find you out*." Now, it seemed, he was ready to commit himself to reforming his life.

His resolution lasted only a short while, however, and Dane resumed his former pastimes and pleasures. One Sunday he decided to walk miles

49. John Dane, "A Declaration of Remarkabell Prouedenses in the Corse of My Lyfe," *NEHGR*, VIII (1854), 149–156.

50. *Suffolk Deeds*, Liber I, 340.

to hear a nonpuritan minister rather than attend local services. Again he was stung on the same finger and in the same place, and now he concluded that surely "god had found me out." This second "sign" was powerful enough to induce him to "goe and work Jurney work thorow all the Counties in ingland, to walk as a pilgrim up and downe on the earth," but instead he became a servant to the Barringtons of Hatfield Broad Oak, Essex, the same puritan family that had employed Ezekiel Rogers as a household minister and had later given him charge of the parish they held in Rowley, Yorkshire. While in the Barrington household Dane "cept companie with the choises[t] Christions," and even after he had married and was no longer under their immediate influence, he remained in the Essex woods working as a tailor in the same puritan community.

When the puritan exodus took place, Dane decided to follow, he said, for two reasons. The change, he felt, would protect him from the temptations that beset him while living in England, though he found later in life that there was also "a devell to tempt, and a corupt hart to deseve" in New England. But Dane was also affected by those around him. When John Norton, who was curate in Bishop Stortford, Hertfordshire, where Dane's father resided, left for New England, Dane was not far behind; when Norton left Roxbury, Massachusetts, for the ministry at Ipswich, Dane also went there since he "had a mynd to live under him." Because Dane had been influenced in the past by signs, prayer, and prophecy, his last act before leaving England is of particular interest. Upon deciding to emigrate he returned home to discuss his plans with his parents, who at first "showd themselfs unwilling." Then young Dane "hastily toke up the bybell, and tould [his] . . . father if whare I opend the bybell thare i met with anie thing eyther to incuredg or discouredg that should settell me." Opening the book his eyes fell upon the verses of Isaiah 52: 11–12, which he later paraphrased as "Cum out from among them, touch no unclene thing, and I will be your god and you shall be my pepell." After that demonstration his parents no longer opposed him and instead encouraged his plans for departure. Moreover, as soon as they were able, they also left for New England.[51]

Many of the East Anglians who went to New England probably had experiences similar to Dane's. Some men were forced to become mobile, going from town to town in search of employment in their trade. If they

---

51. Dane, "Declaration of Remarkabell Prouedenses," *NEHGR*, VIII (1854), *passim*. On the role of prayer, prophecy, the use of the Bible, and interpretation of other "signs" in Tudor and Stuart England, see Keith Thomas's useful study, *Religion and the Decline of Magic* (New York, 1971).

were dependent upon the land for a living, their future was equally uncertain, varying with the fortunes of trade and industry. In addition, Dane lived in the two strongholds of puritan influence, the boroughs and forest communities of the area. And like so many other East Anglians, Dane was sufficiently influenced by the preaching of local puritan ministers in these towns and boroughs to follow them when conditions worsened during the early 1630s.

Most emigrating East Anglian puritans were mobilized for migration from one of five different types of social groups—household, neighborhood, church, family, or those formed from more broadly based networks of economic and social ties. Household connections were important, as the passenger lists for emigrating East Anglians show. Whole entourages of servants and assistants from wealthy and even moderately well-to-do families often went to Massachusetts.[52] Neighborhood influence was another important factor among those who emigrated. Most Watertown and Ipswich immigrants, as has been discussed, came from towns and villages like Bocking and Lavenham, or Dedham and Nayland, which were all located in south central Suffolk or the north central region of Essex, and in many cases were located along the Stour River.

As important as these types of social groups were, other intimate ties often existed among East Anglians. Within towns, members of the same church congregation formed close bonds. Closer still were kinship ties of marriage and blood, as well as the personal, business, economic, or social relationships with other people from surrounding towns that can be documented by extant records. Religious harassment and economic uncertainty in East Anglia might have been sufficient reasons to emigrate, but the final resolution for potential emigrants came from the knowledge that they would be joined by like-minded relatives and friends. As a result, emigration became almost a chain reaction in the region. Personal factors probably played a smaller part for the settlers from the North and West who decided to emigrate. In those regions emigrants were drawn from a larger area and came from widely scattered locations. In East Anglia, however, the bonds of friendship and ties of blood and marriage were a powerful inducement to the irresolute and the timid.

Richard Kimball, for instance, married Ursula Scott about fifteen years before they left for New England, but the union probably also influenced their respective brothers-in-law, Thomas Scott and Henry Kimball, as well as other family members, to come and live in Watertown and

52. For the detailed passenger lists, see Banks, *Planters of the Commonwealth, passim.*

Ipswich. John Waite of Wethersfield, Essex, settled in Maldon, Massachusetts, in the 1630s and was probably urged by or had himself encouraged his sister and his brother-in-law, Robert Lord, of Sudbury, Suffolk, to settle in Ipswich, Massachusetts. The same may have been true for Martin Underwood, who married into the Fiske family, George Giddings who wed the daughter of John Tuttle, or William Hammond who was a brother-in-law of William Paine.[53]

The church congregation as a group often was the source of the inclination to emigrate from East Anglia. As a result of the leadership of charismatic ministers, the church "congregation" often became a more intimate group than the local parish or village neighborhood. In most cases people from surrounding towns were inspired by a minister from the area and joined his congregation in services and conventicles. The future ministers of Watertown and Ipswich, George Phillips of Boxted, Essex, and John Rogers of Assington, Suffolk, both had a reputation for drawing sympathetic individuals from the surrounding countryside into religious worship. It was said of the latter's father, John Rogers of Dedham, by an anti-puritan superior, Chancellor Corbett, that "he hath troubled all the country these 30 yeeres, and dyd poyson all these partes for x myle rounde abowte that place."[54]

53. Henry F. Waters, *Genealogical Gleanings in England*, 2 vols. (Boston, 1901), II, 1413; Deloraine-Pendre Corey, "The Waite Family of Malden, Mass.," *NEHGR*, XXXII (1878), 188; Joseph Hunter, "Suffolk Emigrants: Genealogical Notices of Various Persons and Families Who in the Reign of King Charles the First Emigrated to New England from the County of Suffolk," Mass. Hist. Soc., *Colls.*, 3d Ser., X (1849), 158; "Notes and Queries," *NEHGR*, XLV (1891), 85; Bond, *Watertown Genealogies*, I, 269–270. For examples of other families, including the Winthrops, the Morse and Sherman cousins of Dedham, Essex, the Wards and Rogerses of Wethersfield, Essex, and the Bradstreets, originally from Suffolk but residing in Lincoln, see Joseph James Muskett, ed., *Evidences of the Winthrops of Groton, Co. Suffolk, England, and of Families in and near That County, with Whom They Intermarried* ([Boston], 1894–1896), *passim*; G. Andrews Moriarty, Jr., "Genealogical Research in England," *NEHGR*, LXXXIII (1929), 285–293; Rev. David Sherman, communicator, "The Sherman Family," *ibid.*, XXIV (1870), 64–67; Thomas Townsend Sherman, "The Early English Shermans," *ibid.*, LXVI (1912), 324–325; Henry F. Waters, communicator, "Genealogical Gleanings in England," *ibid.*, L (1896), 414–417; Knappen, ed., *Two Elizabethan Puritan Diaries*, 24; J. G. Bartlett, "Genealogical Research in England," *NEHGR*, LXV (1911), 74. Numerous other examples of blood or marriage ties among Watertown and Ipswich settlers prior to departure from England can be found by careful readings of Charles Henry Pope, *The Pioneers of Massachusetts, A Descriptive List, Drawn from Records of the Colonies, Towns and Churches, and Other Contemporaneous Documents* (Boston, 1900); Savage, *Gen. Dict.*; and Bond, *Watertown Genealogies*.

54. Robert Reyce to John Winthrop, Mar. 1, 1636, as cited by Waters, communicator, "Genealogical Gleanings in England," *NEHGR*, XLI (1887), 182–183; and note *Cal. State Papers, Domestic, 1633–1634*, 450–451, in which Henry Dade, commissary of Suffolk, wrote to Archbishop Laud that many were leaving for New England because they were "discon-

Social and economic ties, other than those formed in town or church, also probably broadened the emigration. Simon Stone of Great Bromley, Essex, held enough land in distant Boxted, Essex, to be assessed in the lay subsidy there in 1629. His connection with Boxted may have acquainted him with its minister, George Phillips, and perhaps with Edward Howe. All three later removed to Watertown, Massachusetts. William Hubbard, who lived in Tendring, Essex, leased land called "Whipples farm" miles away at Stondon Massey, Essex. This farm may have been owned or occupied originally by the Whipple brothers, John and Matthew, of Bocking, Essex. Significantly, the rector of Stondon Massey, Nathaniel Ward, later served as the first minister in Ipswich, where the Whipples and Hubbards came to live.[55] We may never know for certain the elusive details about the relationships of the men in these examples, but what is certain is the regularity with which emigrating men from East Anglia maintained social and business relationships over considerable distances in the decades before the 1630s.

These kinship and other relationships helped mobilize men for migration from East Anglia, a migration that differed from the movement from the North or the West where settlers were characteristically younger and economically better-off. Robert Reyce, Suffolk antiquary and friend of John Winthrop, probably echoed familiar arguments against emigration when he stated to the future colony leader that "plantations ar for yonge men, that can enduer all paynes and hunger. . . . These remote partes wyll not well agree with your yeeres, whiles you are heere you wyll be ever fytter by your understandinge and wysdome to supplye theere [young men's] necessities."[56] Such arguments, however, apparently failed to discourage many of Reyce's fellow East Anglians who, like John Winthrop, were well beyond the age recommended for emigrating to the New England wilderness.

This apparent disregard for "yeeres" was reflected in the age composition of early Watertown settlers. When the *Elizabeth* sailed from Ipswich, Suffolk, on April 30, 1634, it carried twenty-eight men, most with families, many of whom would eventually come to live in Watertown. While the average age of these Watertown men in 1635 was almost thirty-five

---

tented with the government of the Church of England," and that "the breeders of these persons" included Samuel Ward of Ipswich and a Mr. Patton of Wolvestone, who have "caused this giddiness" in "those parts" of the county.

55. E.179/112/638, 4 Charles I (1629); Lexden, Tendring, and Thurstable hundreds, Essex, P.R.O.; Rev. E.H.L. Reeve, *Stondon Massey, Essex* (n.p., n.d.), 71.

56. Robert Reyce to John Winthrop, Aug. 12, 1629, *Winthrop Papers*, II, 105–106.

years and the median age thirty-three, the group was fairly evenly distributed between the ages of twenty and fifty. This small group on the *Elizabeth* reflected Watertown as a whole. In 1635 the ages of first-generation male settlers ranged from eleven to seventy-seven years, but they were fairly well distributed among those in their twenties, thirties, and forties. As a whole, the group was slightly younger than the tightly knit emigrants from Hingham, Norfolk, where only a third of the men were in their young mature years, eighteen to thirty-three. In Watertown about 40 percent of the townsmen fit into this category. Still, this was much less than the figure for Rowley, where the group between eighteen and thirty-three accounted for 61 percent of all male settlers and where most of the others tended to be even younger. In Newbury the figure was higher yet. There, three out of every four male settlers whose ages can be determined were between eighteen and thirty-three. Most of these men were in their twenties while few emigrated who had passed the age of forty.[57] Men in East Anglian Watertown were apparently not deterred by age but instead were emboldened to leave home by kinship and neighborhood ties.

On the whole the men from East Anglia who migrated to towns such as Watertown and Ipswich appear to have been from the middle or lower classes in their native region. Unlike those in Hingham, however, the leaders of these New England towns had been fairly prominent back home, according to English indicators of wealth and local position. John Stower, an early Watertown selectman, originated from the manorial class at Old Hall, Parham, Suffolk. Edmund Sherman of Dedham, Essex, another early Watertown selectman, in 1610 donated a large charitable contribution to the town of Dedham that included a schoolhouse with a yard and garden, and a dwelling house for the "Writing-Master" employed to instruct local children. The wealth of other East Anglians was revealed in more indirect ways. Two men were indicted and appeared before court for breaking into future emigrant Gregory Stone's house and stealing the sizable sum of £86 in money.[58]

The same conclusion about the wealth and status of certain emigrating

57. Compiled from various sources including Banks, *Planters of the Commonwealth*, Bond, *Watertown Genealogies*, and individual genealogies and sources, most of which are listed in Appendix 5 of this book. Age apparently did not deter later remigration from Watertown to surrounding Massachusetts communities or to Connecticut.

58. Norman C. P. Tyack, "Migration from East Anglia to New England before 1660" (Ph.D. thesis, University of London, 1951), 55; *Victoria Hist. of Counties, Hertfordshire*, III, 302; Morant, *History and Antiquities of Essex*, II, 247; Queen's Bench Indictments, Ancient 698, pt. i, 23, T/Z 428, Essex R.O.

East Anglians can be derived from the listings in English lay subsidy tax rolls. For town after town one finds the names of men who later would be prominent in town affairs in Watertown or Ipswich. Such men as Simon Stone and Edward Howe of Boxted, Edmund Sherman of Dedham, Matthew Whipple of Bocking, Giles Firman of Sudbury, John Goodrich of Bury St. Edmunds, William Paine of Lavenham, and Thomas Parish of Nayland seem to have retained their social positions in New England. In other cases fathers or relatives of emigrating sons or nephews were listed. These included John Gage of Polstead, father of William; Thomas Hammond of Hawkedon, who may have been the father of William Hammond; and Robert Browne of Hawkedon, uncle of Richard and Abraham Browne.[59] But the names of the men on lay subsidy lists were far fewer than the total number of emigrants from these towns in the 1630s, confirming, along with other evidence, that many more of the East Anglian emigrants came from lower or middle-class origins. In contrast, we have seen that a large degree of men from the North and West came from relatively influential backgrounds. Leaders and other individuals alike from these regions appeared on subsidy tax lists or exhibited other indications of local social prominence, despite their relative youth.

The comparatively small number of wealthy emigrants from the East Anglian region is not surprising, for as we have seen, the wood-pasture lands throughout much of England produced societies less economically stratified than the commercial open-field country. East Anglia was populated predominantly by small, family farmers who produced grain, raised livestock, and engaged in clothmaking as a cottage industry. Few inventories have survived for the decades immediately preceding the Great Migration, but later records give ample evidence of economic conditions.[60] Urban cloth towns like Lavenham, the great medieval woolen center in the heart of the emigration region, were marked, as was noted in the last

59. E.179/112/626, Hinckford hundred, Essex; E.179/112/638, Lexden, Tendring, and Thurstable hundreds, Essex; E.179/183/498, Babergh hundred, Suffolk; E.179/183/503, Risbridge hundred, Suffolk; E.179/183/504, Thedwestry hundred, Suffolk; all dated 4 Charles I (1629) and in the P.R.O., representing a dozen and a half emigrant communities on the eve of colonization. Tyack has also found evidence from different sources to conclude that most East Anglian emigrants had their social origins in the middle or lower classes. Few, Tyack maintains, were of the manorial or yeoman class. See "Migration from East Anglia," 76–77.

60. Suffolk and especially Essex, unlike other counties in England, have few surviving inventories for the 17th century, particularly during the decades near the Great Migration. A check of manuscript wills of men who lived in seven Essex communities that contributed settlers to Watertown and Ipswich, Massachusetts (listed in F. G. Emmison, ed., *Wills at Chelmsford, 1400–1858*, 3 vols. [London, 1958–1969], II, *1620–1720, passim*), revealed no inventories accompanying them. About three dozen scattered inventories from various parts of Essex exist in a number of collections of documents at the Essex Record Office, but only a

chapter, by relatively greater economic disparities. Some 56 percent of the town's wealth, as recorded in inventories from the 1660s, was in the hands of one man out of every ten, while 85 percent of it was held by a quarter of the population. As might be expected, rural county towns and villages contained fewer extremes in wealth. The men whose inventories formed the top tenth of the town's wealth in Little Waldingfield, Suffolk, controlled only 31 percent of the town's resources, and that percentage was even lower in Polstead. Even the relatively large cloth village of Nayland showed only modest differentiation. There, the top decile controlled only 25 percent and the upper quartile controlled 48 percent of the town's wealth, while the top half held slightly over three-quarters.[61]

The distribution of wealth that was developing in Watertown, Massachusetts, at the same time was more or less like that in the town of Nayland (see table 14). Most of the estates in these East Anglian villages, like those in Watertown, were modest in value, few being spectacularly large or exceedingly small. The wealthiest estate in Nayland was valued at a little over £258 while the median inventory was about £66. By contrast, society in the West of England was highly stratified economically, even in wood-pasture areas like Whiteparish, Wiltshire. In that community, it will be recalled, the upper tenth of the population controlled over twice as much wealth, 56 percent, as measured by extant inventories, as the same groups in Nayland and in Watertown did, while the top quarter in Whiteparish held close to 70 percent as opposed to Watertown's and Nayland's figures of about 50 percent. In Whiteparish estates ranged from one valued at £722 to another assessed at a meager £2 12s. 10d. The median inventory, rated at £35 3s., was about half that in Nayland.[62]

few apply to the north central region of the county, where most emigrants resided. Other Essex inventories for the period from ecclesiastical sources will become more easily available once they are housed at Guildhall Library, London. See Alan Macfarlane, *Witchcraft in Tudor and Stuart England: A Regional and Comparative Study* (London, 1970), 315.

Suffolk records are, at present, somewhat better. Inventories at Ipswich exist for 1582–1584, 1590, and 1685, while those at Bury are more extensive and consecutive: 1570–1576, 1617, 1625, 1640, 1650, 1652, 1660–1747. See Camp, *Wills and Their Whereabouts*, 71–72, and the much less useful Samuel Tymms, ed., *Wills and Inventories from the Registers of the Commissary of Bury St. Edmund's and the Archdeacon of Sudbury* (Camden Soc., *Pubs.*, XLIX [London, 1850]). Inventories discussed here include some of the scattered 17th-century Essex records and Archdeaconry of Sudbury Probate Inventories, Ac. 540/1–40 (1640), Ac. 592/5–14/*passim* (1660–1669), West Suffolk R.O.

61. Archdeaconry of Sudbury Probate Inventories, Ac. 592/5–14/*passim* (1660–1669), West Suffolk R.O. The towns studied were Lavenham, Rattlesden, Nayland, Assington, Polstead, and Little Waldingfield, Suffolk.

62. *Ibid.*, Ac. 592/6/41, 72, 7/79, 101, 152, 224, 229, 8/28, 102, 191, 9/29, 169, 10/175, 12/19, 94, 99, 112, 13/184, 14/64, 88.

TABLE 14. *Distribution of Inventoried Wealth among 83 of 125 Watertown, Massachusetts, Settlers Who Arrived before 1644 and Remained until at least 1660*

	No. of Inventories	Cumulative Wealth in £	% of Total Wealth
Top 10%	8	5,987/12/01	26.5
Top 25%	21	12,362/05/04	54.7
Top 50%	42	18,377/13/03	81.4
Bottom 50%	41	4,210/06/03	18.6
Total	83	22,587/19/06	100.0

Note:
The median inventory among the 83 Watertown settlers was £239/10, and the average inventory among them was £272/02/11.

Sources:
In "The Early Settlers, Their Residences, and the Migrations," Henry Bond lists 285 men who had lived in Watertown prior to 1644 (*Family Memorials: Genealogies of the Families and Descendants of the Early Settlers of Watertown, Massachusetts . . .* [Boston, 1855], 1004–1016). Several names can be added to Bond's original list, bringing the total number to about 293. Of these, 168 (or over half) moved from the community by 1660, while 125 remained. Of those who stayed, 83 left inventories when they died. The inventories included in the table are from Bound Wills and Inventories, I, 24–25, 41–42, 44–46, 107–110, 116, 168, 233–235, 245–248, II, 2–4, 8–9, 77–78, 81–83, 89, 91–93, 165–166, 209–210, 250–252, 263–265, 283–284, 286–287, 290, III, 62, 120–122, 168–170, 204–211, 291–295, 377–380, 391, IV, 31–33, 50–52, 100–101, 121–122, 144–145, 178–179, 185–188, 200–202, 203–206, 270–271, V, 32, 69–70, 207, 230–232, 282–283, 353–356, 389–390, 393–396, 508–509, VI, 128–132, 157–159, 188–190, 226–228, 267–269, 278–279, 284–285, 295–296, 304–305, 327–328, 359–365, 380–383, VII, 32–33, 84–87, 161–162, 178–181, 199–201, 221–222, VIII, 51–54, 168–169, 482–483, IX, 23–25, 288–289, X, 650–652, XII, 260–261, XXVIII, 10–11, Middlesex County Probate Office, East Cambridge, Mass.

From a study of these five early Massachusetts towns we can glean a relatively clear picture of the types of men who migrated to New England. Those from the North and the West of England were usually young, had been socially prominent in their former English communities, and probably had been regarded as minorities within the English societies in which they lived prior to migration. This combination of attributes was sufficiently harmonious to maintain the most traditional of societies, such as Rowley. At least it appears not to have been the explosive combination of factors that so fragmented the town of Newbury. The men from East Anglia who migrated to America typified the society from which they came. Most were older men of modest means, and as the example of Hingham indicates, they formed societies of middling men in which the class structure and conservative ways of the parent community could be reestablished and maintained. In commercial and urban Ipswich, those who had figured prominently in local English society or had come from places such as cloth towns and boroughs where the economic structure was marked by inequalities retained and perpetuated their social positions.

Why the people in these five towns came to New England is less easily answered. There was no single cause, and even the explanation, so often cited by historians, that a combination of economic decline and religious persecution were the main inducements, must be modified by taking into account purely local factors. Economic decline can be ruled out altogether in some areas, particularly the champion regions of Yorkshire and Wiltshire-Hampshire, but economic depression was severe in western Wiltshire and the Essex-Suffolk region, especially in the cloth towns. On the other hand, religious persecution varied according to local episcopal policy. Discrimination was not evident in the Wiltshire-Hampshire region to any extent, most likely because the conservative aims of puritans there were goals the local dioceses could maintain as well. Even in Hingham, where puritans clashed with religious authority, migration began several years before Minister Peck became involved in the situation that eventually led to his excommunication. Further south in Suffolk and Essex, it must also be remembered, the clergy rather than the parishioners were touched by the changes in ecclesiastical policy in the late 1620s and early 1630s. Did men who left for ostensibly religious reasons do so because of the persecution of their religious leaders, because of firsthand experience with ecclesiastical authority, or for the more personal reason that countless friends and neighbors in a church congregation had decided to go?

Examination of these two traditionally accepted "causes" for migration point out the importance of taking local factors into account. Above all, we must realize that men affected by these larger economic and religious elements and by local circumstances still maintained a strong desire to continue to live as they always had. We have seen this, in previous chapters, in their retention of social, economic, and institutional practices. The puritan migration was also characterized by the kinds of social groupings that it mobilized for the move to the New World. While such social ties as household, neighborhood, church, and interfamily connections were not unique to the puritans, they were not widely evident in other seventeenth-century migrations like those to Maryland and Virginia. On the other hand, in later migrations outside factors weakened the influence that such ties had on the retention of familiar ways. Without this web of personal connections, born in England and nurtured in New England, the puritans' migration and the communities that they founded might never have been so distinctive.

7 A Contrapuntal Life

HE inhabitants of our five Massachusetts towns had essentially reproduced what they wanted—the ordering of life as they knew it before their emigration. They had recreated the diversity of local England in the New England countryside. Their new home was made particularly appealing, moreover, by the absence of several undesirable English features. In America, control at the county or colony level was relatively weak, and Massachusetts townsmen exercised considerable independence in the development of land systems, agricultural methods, and governmental forms. They were also unencumbered, at least at first, by a privileged aristocracy and a class of despised poor, for neither of these groups migrated in numbers large enough to influence the shape of these New England communities created by middling Englishmen. In addition, settlers had the opportunity to exercise a distinctive American freedom, the liberty to move on. Geographical mobility, of course, existed in England at this time, particularly in wood-pasture regions, but in New England it was possible, through moving, to establish new communities made up of like-minded souls.[1] Finally, among the advantages found in America, in many Massachusetts towns political power rested on the consent of the inhabitants. This notion of government by consent was not unknown in local English society, but the full implementation of the principle was impossible there.[2]

1. For examples, see E. E. Rich, "The Population of Elizabethan England," *Econ. Hist. Rev.*, 2d Ser., II (1950), 247–265, especially 263–264; John Harrison and Peter Laslett, "Clayworth and Cogenhoe," in H. E. Bell and R. L. Ollard, eds., *Historical Essays, 1600–1750, Presented to David Ogg* (London, 1963), 157–184; and Julian Cornwall, "Evidence of Population Mobility in the Seventeenth Century," Institute of Historical Research, *Bulletin*, XL (1967), 143–152.

2. My general argument here is that few outside factors had the power to redirect the older ways immigrants knew from their experiences in various parts of England. As we have seen, a number of indigenous factors also contributed to the perpetuation of traditional ways. The two most important were homogeneity, the sine qua non of continuity, and a similar environment to that with which they were familiar in old England. As Winthrop himself commented after arrival in New England, "for the country itself, I can discern little difference between it and our own" (John Winthrop, *The History of New England from 1630 to 1649*, ed. James Savage, 2 vols. [Boston, 1825–1826], I, 375). There were differences, of course, but agricultural inventories discussed in previous chapters indicate that New England settlers

It would be excessive to claim that these characteristics were uniquely American. In part they were the result simply of the absence of particular English constraints. Yet as the decades wore on, even those English characteristics that were brought over intact began to fade, and an unmistakably "American" society took shape. In the process, Massachusetts, by the mid-eighteenth century, became a much more centralized colony than it had been one hundred years earlier.

Although the autonomy of the early Massachusetts towns has been noted before, little attention has been paid to the conditions that made this independence possible. As we have noted, the main factor was the lack of effective government at the colony level. Despite the contrary claims in much of the historical literature, which portrays a system of centralized and unified power exercised by the government at Boston over both secular and ecclesiastical affairs of the towns, it is evident that the colony's central institutions developed slowly at first.[3] The hierarchy of institutions found in the seventeenth century evolved in piecemeal fashion, conditioned by particular events and immediate problems.[4] The town was a viable organization from the first months after settlement, even though it was not given legal definition or powers by the General Court until early 1636. The intermediate unit of government, the county and its court, was not created until the following decade in 1643, and many other interstitial judicial bodies were sporadically established by the General Court throughout most of the seventeenth century only as the need arose.[5]

---

were nevertheless able to continue old practices. To these factors should be added several others, which have been summarized recently in T. H. Breen, "Transfer of Culture: Chance and Design in Shaping Massachusetts Bay, 1630–1660," *NEHGR*, CXXXII (1978), 3–17. The inability of the New England settlers to exploit the area to produce either staple crops or mineral wealth further insulated early settlers from change. The absence of Indian, foreign, or intercolonial threats, as well as the weak Bay Colony government (the latter discussed in this chapter) were also important, while the longevity of the migrating generation and the constant contact between settlers through their civil (and religious) institutions, as we have seen, only helped to maintain older ideas concerning social, economic, and political life.

3. Some studies have focused on government at the colony level, often drawing only on (and because of) the printed colony records. Compare Charles J. Hilky, "Legal Development of Colonial Massachusetts, 1630–1686," *Columbia Studies in History, Economics and Law*, XXXVII, no. 2 (1910); compare also, George Lee Haskins, *Law and Authority in Early Massachusetts: A Study in Tradition and Design* (New York, 1960), 59–60, 68–69, 76.

4. Compare James Willard Hurst, *Law and Social Process in United States History* (Ann Arbor, Mich., 1960), 62–75.

5. *Recs. of Mass. Bay*, I, 172 (towns); I, 169–170, II, 28, 38, 84 (county courts); I, 239, 264, II, 81, 162–163, 188–189, 192–193 (interstitial courts). Courts that had some jurisdiction over townsmen were established as early as 1636 (*ibid.*, I, 169), but they did little to alter the nature of local society in the ways I have been describing.

Even after such institutions were developed, it was some time before they became fully operative, and consequently it was even longer before they began to affect the lives and actions of townspeople in significant ways. A chronological listing of estate inventories in Essex County from 1635 to 1700, for example, indicates that before 1652 the county court neither proved a consistently high number of wills nor filed many inventories, even though the quarterly county courts had handled these functions in a haphazard way since 1636.[6] In about 1640, a practicing lawyer, Thomas Lechford, complained about the lack of trial records, the failure to use legal precedents, and the practice of trial de novo at every appellate stage. Lechford also made a long list of recommendations for improvements in the courts, none of which were implemented.[7]

When the colony government did try occasionally to interfere at the local level, it generally failed to enforce its will upon the localities, an outcome that revealed not only its impotence but also the ineffectiveness of intermediate institutions, such as the county courts and constables, that could carry out the desires of a central authority. Although the General Court rarely intervened in strictly local matters, it felt compelled for some unexplained reason to attempt during the early years to establish and maintain agricultural regulations for the towns. It was not until 1647, when the General Court finally realized the futility of trying to manage this aspect of local life, that it officially shifted the burden back to the towns, which had actually carried it all along.[8] There are also some instances recorded in which the Court considered intervening on behalf of townsmen in disputes with town governments over land claims, but such examples are rare.[9] More important than actions directed toward subordinating the independence of the towns were those that expanded local power. Many enactments of the General Court during the first two decades of settlement strengthened both the town and its inhabitants.[10]

6. William I. Davisson and Dennis J. Dugan, "Economic History Research: Essex County, Massachusetts" (paper presented at the Essex Institute Historical Seminar, Salem, Massachusetts, June 29–30, 1971), 17–18. Prior to the establishment of the shire system in 1643, the court handled 1.5 inventories per year. Between 1643 and 1652, it processed slightly over 9 per year, and in the 10 years after 1652, 18 per year. Size and age structure of county populations might account for *some* of this difference, but as material in earlier chapters indicates, Massachusetts did not have as excessively young a population as, for instance, Virginia had. There is a considerable number of cases of recorded deaths without accompanying wills and inventories in the first two decades of settlement.

7. Lechford, *Plain Dealing*, 85–87.

8. *Recs. of Mass. Bay*, I, 86, 106, 119, 148, 150, 157, 181–182, 187–189, 215, 221, 238–239, 255, 272, 293–294, II, 14–15, 190, 220–221.

9. *Ibid.*, I, 267.

10. *Ibid.*, I, 183, 216–217, 240–241, II, 28, 39, 49, 195, 208, 284.

The early General Court did fine towns for various offenses, but the circumstances in each case belie the notion that there was an effective central government. Most of the fines in the early period were imposed between June 1638 and June 1641, during the Pequot War, and many of the specific infractions appear to have involved war-related activities. In fact, most were merely instances during the crisis of war in which the General Court threatened fines as a means of compelling towns to perform actions. There is an important difference, however, between imposing a penalty and actually carrying it out. Few of the town fines were ever collected and many were remitted, nor is there evidence that the Court's will was carried out.[11] The fact is, that with the exception of this three-year interval, the Court rarely attempted to compel the towns to obey its laws and, indeed, the sheer volume of the Court's own pressing legislative business would have prevented it from doing more in any case.[12]

The only local officer directly responsible to the colony government was the constable, who was required to handle many detailed and time-consuming matters. The colony offered him little encouragement for his troubles and yet held him responsible for any problems that arose. This situation undoubtedly affected his sense of duty. The constable was expected to bring infractions before the county court, but that institution was itself only in its infancy.[13] During the early years, the court was conducted by itinerant personnel vague in their understanding of local problems and conditions. During the first ten years for which surviving records of the Middlesex County court exist, 1649 to 1659, only half (47 percent) of the judges sitting in sessions actually resided in the county. In the last decade under the first charter, however, 94 percent of them came from one of the county's towns.[14]

Besides the deficiencies of colony-level governmental and judicial institutions, the centralizing influence of the law and legal personnel was also absent. This is not to say that law in the Bay Colony was merely "a rude, popular summary kind," as Paul S. Reinsch put it.[15] Massachusetts

11. *Ibid.*, II, 27, I, 136, 283, 297, 310, 317, II, 75, 80, 150, 168, 262; compare Jules Zanger, "Crime and Punishment in Early Massachusetts," *WMQ*, 3d Ser., XXII (1965), 471–477.

12. *Recs. of Mass. Bay*, I, 276, II, 16–17, 188, 279.

13. *Ibid.*, I, 160, 179, 214, 241, 302, II, 123, 150–151, 223–224. For examples of fines imposed upon constables for negligence of duty, see *ibid.*, I, 134, 220, 284, 301.

14. Based on the 111 sessions of the Middlesex County court in which judges are listed, 1649–1686, Middlesex County Court Records, Middlesex County Courthouse, East Cambridge, Massachusetts, as well as on biographical information in Savage, *Gen. Dict.*, and Pope, *Pioneers of Mass.*

15. Paul Samuel Reinsch, "English Common Law in the Early American Colonies," Uni-

townsmen lived in a world of customary law, which was recognized by Coke as an important source of English law, and was, in the words of a modern authority, "just as much an integral part of the living law . . . as the statutes or the common law."[16] Most men in England in the seventeenth century still lived in rural areas away from the influence of or need for the national court system. They seldom required the services of trained lawyers, and they were not likely to carry disputes beyond the manor or borough, or hundred or county courts. Life in Massachusetts was little different. There were very few lawyers or men with legal experience among the founders of the colony and none of any stature until after 1700. Those few men in the early years who had formerly served in legal positions in England were seldom available to fill responsible capacities below the highest levels of Massachusetts government.[17] Legal talent or training did not filter down to the county or town level and, in any case, would not have been relevant there.

English law from the central courts seems rarely to have been recognized, let alone acted upon, even at the colony level in seventeenth-century Massachusetts. Little of the great flood of law reports that were published during the Protectorate reached Boston until the latter decades of the century, and there are few signs that lawyers made use of any of these reports before 1700. One finds no indication that Coke's *Reports* or Glisson's *The Common Law Epitomiz'd*, both of which were published or reprinted in several English editions during the 1650s, were ever used in the colony until a half century or more later.[18] Furthermore, published

versity of Wisconsin, *Bulletin*, no. 3 (Economics, Political Science, and History Ser., II, no. 4 [1899]), 399–400. Compare Haskins, *Law and Authority in Early Massachusetts*, ix.

16. Edward Coke, *The First Part of the Institutes of the Laws of England: Or, a Commentary upon Littleton*, 1st American ed., from the 19th English ed., 2 vols. (Philadelphia, 1853), I, 11b; George E. Woodbine, "The Suffolk County Court, 1671–1680," in David H. Flaherty, ed., *Essays in the History of Early American Law* (Chapel Hill, N.C., 1969), 196, 199 (reprinted from *Yale Law Journal*, XLIII [1936], 1036–1043).

17. Emory Washburn, *Sketches of the Judicial History of Massachusetts from 1630 to the Revolution in 1775* (Boston, 1840), 50–53; Joseph Willard, *An Address to the Members of the Bar of Worcester County, Massachusetts: October 2, 1829* (Lancaster, Mass., 1830), 24, 25–26, 27–30; Samuel Eliot Morison, ed., with an introduction by Zechariah Chaffee, Jr., *Records of the Suffolk County Court, 1671–1680*, 2 vols. (Colonial Society of Massachusetts, *Collections*, XXIX–XXX [Boston, 1833]), I, xxvi–xxvii, hereafter cited as *Suffolk Co. Court Recs.*

18. There are occasional early references to law books in the colony, such as to the six that the General Court ordered on Nov. 11, 1647—*Coke on Littleton*, the *Book of Entries*, *Coke upon Magna Charta*, the *New Terms of the Law*, Dalton's *Justice of the Peace*, and *Coke's Reports* (*Recs. of Mass. Bay*, II, 212). During the early decades of settlement, however, Massachusetts Bay was probably much like neighboring Plymouth, where no law books were listed in the 93 inventories filed with the General Court between 1633 and 1659 (Rose T. Briggs, "Books of the Pilgrims, As Recorded in Their Inventories and Preserved in Pilgrim Hall," *Old-Time New*

sources or guides to the law for laymen were not printed in Massachusetts or the other colonies until the late 1680s.[19] The absence of centralizing, uniform legal influences and the weakness of colony institutions during most of the first charter period make it easy to understand why local law and custom flourished in Massachusetts Bay communities for such a long time.

New England towns were also distinguished from those in contemporary England by the peculiar ease with which government by consent was able to evolve in America. Government by consent was certainly not novel in English experience, and it would be a mistake to assume that its adoption in New England was a sharp departure from practices at home. Peo-

England, LXI [1970], 41–46; compare Henry M. Dexter, "Catalogue of Elder Brewster's Library," Mass. Hist. Soc., *Procs.*, 2d Ser., V [1889], 37–85). It is surprising that such leaders as Thomas Dudley and John Winthrop, Jr., who subsequently moved to Connecticut, owned only a couple of books that might be classified as legal. See "Gov. Thomas Dudley's Library," *NEHGR*, XII (1858), 355–356, and "Catalogue of the Winthrop Library," in *Alphabetical and Analytical Catalogue of the New York Society Library* (New York, 1850), 491–505.

In addition to the paucity of legal listings in early inventories there is very little evidence that English law books were imported for some time after the enormous output of legal materials in England during the 1650s. In this decade alone almost as many new common law reports were published as had been before 1650, one-fifth of all those printed from 1550 until 1776. See John William Wallace, *The Reporters, Chronologically Arranged: With Occasional Remarks upon Their Respective Merits*, 3d ed. (Philadelphia, 1855). Nothing from scattered Boston bookshop invoices and inventories before 1684 indicates that a steady importation of important reports and treatises had begun (Worthington Chauncey Ford, *The Boston Book Market, 1679–1700* [Boston, 1917], 88–153, 153–154, 163–182). By the end of the 17th century some lawyers began to rely heavily on legal treatises, but by the middle of the next century emphasis was placed on case law from the reports. "Francis Brinley," *NEHGR*, XII (1858), 75, and George B. Reed, *Sketch of the Life of the Honorable John Read, of Boston, 1722–1749* (Boston, 1879), 17–18.

For another large inventory of law books in the provincial period, see George L. McKay, with an introduction by Clarence S. Brigham, *American Book Auction Catalogues, 1713–1934: A Union List* [including supplements of 1946 and 1948] (New York, 1966 [orig. publ. 1937]), 40. Compare the lack of legal sources, despite Sewall's many years on the bench, in Steward Stokes, comp., "Books Owned by Samuel Sewall (1652–1730), in the Prince Collection, Rare Book Room, Boston Public Library," typescript, Rare Book Room, Boston Public Library. Note also Thomas Goddard Wright, *Literary Culture in Early New England, 1630–1730* (New Haven, Conn., 1920), 174–175. Whatever size Massachusetts law libraries may have been by the mid-18th century, none could rival some of those in Virginia and in New York. See Charles Warren, *A History of the American Bar* (Boston, 1911), 161–162, and Paul Mahlon Hamlin, *Legal Education in Colonial New York* (New York, 1939), 171–200.

19. Eldon Revare James, "A List of Legal Treatises Printed in the British Colonies and the American States before 1801," *Harvard Legal Essays Written in Honor of, and Presented to Joseph Henry Beale and Samuel Williston* (Cambridge, Mass., 1934), 159–211. The exception here was *The Laws and Liberties*, which was gradually accepted as a legal guide in Massachusetts communities during the decade of the 1660s. See the discussion later in this chapter and in chapter 8.

ple in Stuart England were not incapable of directing their own lives. The most illuminating example is Hingham, where in both the English parish and the New England town the approval of the town meeting was an essential element of government. In other Massachusetts towns, such as Ipswich and Watertown, where practices were less controlled by the town meeting, the tacit consent of the townsmen was still necessary for choosing leaders and instituting government. Moreover, the principle of consent was not tied to the Norfolk woods or to wood-pasture country generally, but became important even in highly manorialized areas when men were forced, by necessity, to govern themselves. As in New England in a similarly lordless environment, self-government developed naturally in the English countryside.

Consider the example of Shrewton, Wiltshire, only a dozen or so miles away from James and Nicholas Noyeses' parish of Cholderton. In Shrewton the manor was dismembered in 1596, and farmlands were sold to various ambitious local yeomen. Within three years, however, such "divers disorders" had "been commited to the great hurt and detriment of the greater pt of the frehoulders tenants and commoners," and such a "breache of christia[n] charities and peace of the neighborhode" had been created, that a series of orders was drawn up at the "earnest persuasion" of the local vicar, Nicholas Barlowe, for the "better gov'ment and quiet estate of all." Seventeen orders were formulated and signed by twenty-three freeholders, tenants, and commoners in the order of their "quality," and all the bylaws were enforced through an institution much like the manorial court baron that had operated in the years before dismemberment. Some men had taken advantage of the chaotic situation for their own material well-being, but "bycause we have heard by olde men and find by antient records in divers coppies of court roule that no freholder tenant or commoner [had by] . . . right kept any wuther beaste [wether sheep] in the fields of Shrewton or [a part of Shrewton called] Net, untill of late years they have usurped the same," all were accordingly prohibited from leaving their sheep there to feed.

For the most part these seventeen orders, promulgated by "common consent" of men living in a manorless village, prohibited the use of the fields for various livestock, stinted or limited their number in the "feeldes downes and other commons," and required common herding or flocking. A herdsman was to be "provided nominated and appointed by the most voyces of the freeholderes tenants and commoners to keepe all the swyne in Shrewton." Other orders authorized by the "voyces of the frehoulders tenantes or commoners of Shrewton and Nett" provided for sufficient hay for all the village sheep "in the extremitie of winter" and established the mechanism for nominating and choosing a hayward. Judging from one farm account book and inventory, this system of "manorless" regulation did not discourage productive, enterprising agriculture. In addition, the dismemberment of the manor did not result in drastic changes in the lives of inhabitants; it neither instituted enclosure of the fields nor put an end to the system of common rights. The records of bylaw infractions and fines thirty years later testify to the vigorous administration that common men could give to local regulations even without such formal institutions as manors, courts, stewards, and bailiffs.[20]

The practice by ordinary seventeenth-century Englishmen of establishing local government by common consent was certainly not unusual, no matter where they lived. What separated the manorless governments of the forest or chalk-country regions of England from the Massachusetts towns, however, was the possibility in America for working out the long-term implications of government by consent. Three of the towns studied here present three different examples. In rapidly growing Ipswich, where land-hungry men swallowed up the countryside, consolidated their holdings, and moved to remote parts of the town, it soon became inevitable that many of the inhabitants would want to form separate societies. In England such men would have had to become a dissenting minority within the community; in New England they were able to build a new and independent town based on common consent. In Newbury, where violent disagreement was common, a different outgrowth of government by consent appeared. In this "western English" society full rights were possible at first only for proprietors. What happened, then, when the proprietors became a distinct minority in a town steadily rising in population? The exercise of government by consent led to a redefinition of town citizenship. Finally, in Watertown, where the community was unable to handle its problems by itself, self-government eventually brought about greater dependence on the General Court and other colony-wide institutions. In-

20. Rev. Canon Bennett, "The Orders of Shrewton," *Wiltshire Arch. Mag.*, XXIII (1886), 33–39; Kerridge, "Note Book of a Wiltshire Farmer," *ibid.*, LIV (1952), 416–428; Shrewton court paper, Apr. 20, Oct. 22, 1630, 121/1, Wiltshire R.O.

Of course, this was not the only experiment in local self-government of this kind before men from western England left for Massachusetts. For example, in Ibthorpe, a hamlet in the parish of Hurstbourn Tarrant, Hampshire, not far from many of the Test River manors that contributed so many of Newbury's settlers, the people were "the Lords of their own Manor" and exercised their manorial rights in the exclusive use of common land there, in addition to the right of pasturage in Hurstbourn common that they shared with Hurstbourn men. Webb and Webb, *English Local Government: The Manor and the Borough*, 133n–134n.

side the town, power shifted from the selectmen to the town meeting. Each of these cases can be profitably examined in more detail.

One of the characteristics of the New England towns established by settlers from East Anglia was the rapid enclosure and consolidation of landholdings that occurred in them. This characteristic was also evident in Newbury and probably in many other early Massachusetts communities. In towns such as Ipswich and Watertown, which inherited a strong tradition of land trading, this ingrained tendency was all the more accelerated by the large supply of unclaimed land and the absence of manorial entry fines. To use the example of Watertown, where the land records are more accurate than in Ipswich, between the time that the final "general" grants were made in 1638 and the first town "inventory" of personal landholdings was taken, over 50 percent of the townsmen had gained additional parcels of land through trade and barter. We cannot be exactly certain when the first inventory was completed, but evidence seems to indicate that it might have been as early as 1639, though 1642 is a more probable date. Whatever the exact moment, the transformation of land into a marketable commodity was well established within two to four years after the last "general" grant was made (see table 15). About 40 percent of the landholders had either enlarged or reduced their holdings by 20 or more acres during this brief period, and for four-fifths of the inhabitants some change at least had occurred in their ownership of land. Part of the increase in land transactions was the result of the departure of some of the original grantees, who left to join new communities elsewhere. Those who stayed behind found these departures an ideal opportunity to consolidate or increase their holdings. Others who remained wished to sell off unwanted or unneeded parcels of land, and they apparently found buyers quickly. Whatever the reason or circumstance, only one man in five did not increase or decrease his landholdings during this half decade, and a later town "inventory" reveals a continuation of this trend.[21]

All of this real estate activity had specific consequences. First of all, such transactions encouraged the continual outward expansion of settlement, a practice that eventually came up against colony law. Fear of Indian attack probably prompted the General Court to pass a statute in 1635

21. *Watertown Recs.*, 17–67, and a second inventory from 1644, 69–146. Land sales in Watertown did not lead to concentration of holdings among fewer and fewer individuals, however. Analysis of the first town inventory indicates that despite the high turnover of land indicated in table 15, the upper 10% of the landholders controlled only 31% of all Watertown land, the top 25% only 57%, and the upper 50% a little over 86%. These were increases of little over 1% in each category from the percentages of holdings in the original grants.

TABLE 15. *Changes in Landholding in Watertown, Massachusetts,*
ca. 1638–ca. 1642

Net Turnover in Landholdings (in acres)	No. of Landholders[a]	% of Landholders[a]
over 200	4	2.6
101–200	14	9.1
51–100	21	13.6
21–50	22	14.3
1–20	61	39.6
0	32	20.8
Total	154	100.0

Note:
[a] Includes only landholders who held original grants and are listed in the first town inventory for Watertown.

Source:
Compiled from *Watertown Records . . .* [title varies], 6 vols. in 5 (Watertown, Mass., 1894–1928), I, "Lands Grants Divisions Allotments Possessions and Proprietors' Book," 3–14, 17–57.

that prohibited the building of dwelling houses farther than a half mile from the meetinghouse, the center of town. But Watertown was successful in petitioning the General Court to grant it an exception in 1639, and a year later the rule was repealed.[22] The healthy land market in Watertown also led to speculation by outsiders. Throughout the lists of grantees are the names of men, such as Edmund Angier, John and William Baker, Thomas and John Brigham, and John Knight, who probably never lived in the community. It would appear that already during the first decade of its existence the close homogeneous community, founded on a basis of mutual consent, was changing. Men who in the East Anglian woods might have spent a lifetime building up a compact farmstead accomplished the same thing in Massachusetts in a matter of years. The rapid turnover in land also encouraged geographical mobility. Stimulated by the economic opportunities around them, the colonists were willing to risk relocation. All of these outcomes distinguished life in New England from that in old England.

22. *Recs. of Mass. Bay,* I, 157, 181, 257, 291.

In Ipswich, as in Watertown, the exchanges of land tended to draw many inhabitants away from the town center. Samuel Maverick noted in 1660 that Ipswich "hath many Inhabitants, and there farmes lye farr abroad, some of them severall miles from the Towne." Even by 1645 the system for assessing town rates took into account the distances inhabitants might be living and working from the town center. Two years earlier, only a decade after settlement, the town granted Michael Cartwright 10 acres of land next to another 10 acres he already owned on the Rowley town line, and several months later it granted Daniel Denison a 200-acre farm on the opposite town boundary "between this Towne and Salem or Jeffrey's Creeke." Settlement had reached two ends of the township before the end of 1643.[23]

In the same year, the Ipswich inhabitants who lived far from the town center at "New Meadow," or Topsfield as it later was known, petitioned the General Court for the liberty to settle a village there, since they had paid for their own minister during the preceding two years. Two years later the new village appealed to the General Court for permission to be excused from contributing to the support of the Ipswich minister. Topsfield finally received the corporate status of a separate town in 1650, the first division of a township to occur in Massachusetts Bay from within an original town grant.[24] This was a momentous development. People had simply moved away from the town center and then had found it difficult to take advantage of services, although they were still required to pay for them through their rates. Had there been less flexible local institutions and less free land, as was the case in England, these men would have found it impossible to break away and form new, legitimate societies.

In Newbury in the decades after 1660 more serious difficulties arose, and land problems were again the cause of them. In some New England communities, such as Ipswich, "proprietorship" never figured very greatly. In fact, any distinction between landholders and nonlandholders in terms of rights to land was virtually nonexistent in Ipswich. The 1642 list of "commoners," or those entitled to use as yet undivided town lands, almost doubled by 1664 and surpassed that mark by 1679.[25] In Newbury, on the other hand, the ninety-one proprietors chosen in 1642 remained an exclusive group who did not easily relinquish their control over town lands or

23. Dow, *Two Centuries of Travel in Essex County*, 27; Ipswich Town Recs., Feb. 10, 1645, July 18, 1643, and Oct. 12, 1643.

24. *Recs. of Mass. Bay*, II, 48, 135, 144, 258, and generally, Felt, *History of Ipswich*, 70.

25. Ipswich Town Recs., Feb. 28, 1642, Feb. 16, 1665, and Feb. 18, 1679. The last list has been published as "Materials for the History of Ipswich," *NEHGR*, VII (1853), 77–79.

town government. From almost the beginning the freeholders (or proprietors) and the town were regarded as nearly synonymous. In town meetings, therefore, proprietors voted for fellow proprietors to be selectmen, who then managed the town when the meeting was not in session. By the early 1650s, however, many new men had entered the town. Some had bought proprietors' rights, but many others who attended town meetings had not. One of the first instances of recognition of changing relationships in the town occurred in 1651, when the town meeting ordered the selectmen neither to "sell nor give away any of the Townes land or Timber wth out the Townes Consent and to Look that the Freeholds may have theyr priviledg and such as have not a Freehold that they should have no Liberty in the Common." The town further ordered that all titles to land must be verified to determine who held "a priviledg of a Freehold." Social distinctions among the town's inhabitants were now apparent. Proprietorship, which had originally been open to many, was now becoming a way to divide and separate men in this New England community. The very term "town meeting," which formerly had been clear enough, now required explanation. "A meeting of the freemen" no longer casually meant "a meeting of the freeholders," and "a meeting of the freeholders and proprietors" differed from "a meeting of the freeholders and inhabitants," "a general towne meeting," or "a legall town meeting." The nature, object, and competence of a particular town meeting came to be judged by the type of person who attended it.[26] The dividing factor was land proprietorship, but it would be several decades before the issue was faced directly and resolved.

In the meantime other events were occurring in Newbury that helped move the issue of land proprietorship closer to the center of attention. Newbury men were in an advantageous position at the mouth of the Merrimack River valley for developing a healthy trade with the hinterlands of Massachusetts and New Hampshire. In addition, these enterprising settlers from western England with an eye for profit quickly began to invest in trade with the West Indies. As early as 1655 Captain Paul White had been granted an area for a wharf, a wharf house, and a dock on the river, though little of the construction took place until the late 1670s and early 1680s. By then, "in consequence of the largeness of the town and the frequent concours of vessels," the inhabitants found it necessary to petition the General Court to provide for a special magistrate. During the 1670s the town supported at least three cattle commons and five flocks of sheep,

26. Newbury Town Recs., Mar. 1, 1651; *Essex Co. Court Recs.*, I, 329; Newbury Town Recs., Jan. 10, 1652, Feb. 23, Jan. 10, 1653.

all managed by town herdsmen, as meat production for the West Indies trade increased remarkably. Nothing on this scale had been attempted earlier in Newbury. Fishing also became an important enterprise with heavy sales to the Caribbean islands. Timber regulations began to appear frequently after 1660 as materials for building ships and making pipe staves for casks and hogsheads used up much common wood. In addition, the commercial activity attracted settlers to Newbury, with attendant overcrowding and diminution of resources. It is no wonder that in 1669 the town met to determine "the just liberties and privileges of the true proprietors" regarding timber, fencing, feed for cattle, and firewood, "for the prevention of utter ruin therein both for present and future generations."[27]

Despite the shortage of divided, available land for new inhabitants of Newbury, the proprietors in the late 1670s attempted to divide the common among themselves. The nonproprietors successfully opposed this effort, however, and in 1684 a compromise was proposed by the proprietors. The nonproprietors remained unsatisfied and no action occurred. Two years later the nonproprietors took the initiative, demanding a greater proportion of the common lands. They based their claims on the equal rate of taxation in Newbury for nonproprietors and proprietors alike and on their service as soldiers in King Philip's War. Only after six months of laborious committee work was a compromise agreement finally reached on October 20, 1686. Under this agreement, 6,000 acres of the upper common, almost as much as had been divided among the original inhabitants in the early decades, were to be distributed among both groups: half of this acreage was to be given to the proprietors in equal shares and the other 3,000 acres were to be divided "among all such inhabitants of this town and freeholders as have paid rates two years last past, proportionable to what each man paid by rate to the minister's rate in the year 1685." The division made, controversy came to an end. Several pastures were created for old and "new" proprietors later in the year, and new divisions involving considerable acreage were made in 1702 and 1708.[28] The issue and its solution in Newbury included at least two important departures from typical procedures in English society. It was clear that an exclusive and restrictive status like that of proprietorship could be superseded in the new society. Men could simply leave and establish or join new commu-

27. Newbury Town Recs., Apr. 25, 1655, Mar. 4, 1678, Sept. 20, 1678, Jan. 5, 1681; Dow, *Two Centuries of Travel in Essex County*, 26–27; Massachusetts Archives, CXII, 328 (Oct. 11, 1681); Coffin, *Sketch of the History of Newbury*, 114; Currier, *History of Newbury*, I, 116, 119; Newbury Town Recs., Mar. 21, 1679, Apr. 19, 1677, Mar. 14, 1682, Mar. 26, 1665, May 21, 1669.

28. Newbury Town Recs., May 21, 1679, Mar. 23, Oct. 20, 1686.

nities, but town inhabitants could also, by sheer weight of numbers, over-come vestiges of older rights if necessary. The events in Newbury also suggest that new economic and social factors could significantly alter tra-ditional relationships within Massachusetts society.

Other communities besides Newbury were similarly affected by such changes. By the latter decades of the seventeenth century many Mas-sachusetts towns were contending with social problems. Ipswich had to cope with the realization after 1660 that "the Comon Lands of this towne are over Burthened by the multiplying of dwelling houses" of squatters.[29] By the early 1650s the same problems that had preoccupied the vestrymen in East Anglian parishes on the eve of emigration were pressing for the attention of selectmen in Watertown. And the evidence indicates that New England towns, like English parishes, were not totally equipped to handle the situation by themselves. Increasingly, the assistance of colony-level government was needed, thereby diminishing the individual re-sponses of the communities. Towns began to accept and even welcome the intervention of the General Court in the late decades of the century, with the result that they gave up many of their unique customs and preroga-tives. In Watertown, for instance, growing reliance on the central govern-ment reduced the system of leadership by town selectmen to a state of desuetude.

At mid-century it had been by the authority of the selectmen alone rather than by that of the town meeting or General Court that disputes were settled, problems investigated, and relief administered to the town poor. Individual cases were treated with a great deal of interest and atten-tion. Samuel Benjamin was brought before the selectmen in the early 1650s "for Idelnes By Mr Norcros which Did two evidently apeare by his ragged Clothes and Divers Depts [debts]." In the likelihood that such be-havior eventually would make men town charges, selectmen sought ways to make people more self-sufficient. In another case, two selectmen were appointed to go to "Sister Baall, and there to acquaint her that it is the mind of the Select men, that she sett her selfe to the Carding of two Skaines of Cotton or sheeps wooll and her daughter to spin it, wth other Business of the family and this to be her daily taske, the wch if she refuse, she must exspect, to be sent to the howse of corection." Warnings of this kind were not always so severe, but potential town charges were not treated lightly. Hugh Parsons was "Sent For" by the selectmen upon "Complaint" and "advised to imploy his time to the better providing For his Family," and

---

29. Statements concerning 17th-century land pressure in Ipswich are noted in Ipswich Town Recs., Mar. 15, 1660, n.d., 1668, and ca. 1678–1679.

"for his incouragment" to that end, they granted his family a supply of grain to see them through the winter.[30] In some cases fees were arranged for the care of elderly townspeople, while in others, where wants were not so great, the selectmen might buy a cow for those in need or supply them with grain or firewood.[31]

By 1660, however, the selectmen's responsibilities began to change. Selectmen had always been involved in apprenticing children, not only for the benefit of the child but more often to give destitute parents relief from the care and expense of maintenance. Apprenticeship cases, like poverty cases, dot the records of selectmen's meetings.[32] But after about 1660, apprenticeship and related cases involving town children reflected wider demands. Children began to be bound out not only in response to obvious local economic or welfare needs, but also because the town felt the necessity of acting in accordance and compliance with colony law. As early as 1656 when Jonathan Phillips appeared before the seven men "to give answere of his loosse living," it was ordered that his mother should be notified of his conduct and that he should be placed under her "gover[n]ment, or otherwise to despose of him to some such place or way, that may in able the town to give ansere to the law."[33]

Soon Watertown selectmen were enforcing other colony laws. According to a General Court law of 1642, they were responsible for moral and educational instruction in the town, though it was not until the end of 1665 that the selectmen agreed to go two by two throughout the town "to exsamin how children are taught to reade: and instructed in the grounds of religion and the Capitall laws." In 1669 each of the seven men and the two constables were given "a Coppy of the lawes in printe: viz the bookes sent to the towns Divers years past: as also to each a Coppy of thos papers sent last up." Before long the changes in the locus of legal authority and the increased degree of social superintendence from outside the town became evident. By 1674 the selectmen agreed that two of their number

should go about the town to see that children wear taught to Read the Inglish tung and that they wear taught sum authordox cattycize and to see that Each man heave in his house a coppy of the capitall

30. *Watertown Recs.*, 33 (Dec. 13, 1653), 49 (Dec. 11, 1656), 50 (Feb. 3, 1657), 60 (Jan. 18, 1659), 64 (Jan. 31, 1660).

31. For examples, see *ibid.*, 40 (Jan. 29, 1655), 49 (Dec. 11, 1656), 56 (Apr. 13, 1658), 78 (Dec. 4, 1663), 87 (Aug. 31, Sept. 27, 1666), 89 (Dec. 4, 1666), 104 (Jan. 3, 1671).

32. For some examples, see *ibid.*, 47 (Nov. 19, 27, 1656), 51 (Feb. 3, 1657), 52 (Mar. 11, 1657), 92 (Sept. 22, 1668).

33. *Ibid.*, 49 (Dec. 11, 1656), 103–104 (Dec. 13, 1670), 105 (Mar. 3, 1671), 107 (Sept. 2, 1671), and *passim*.

lawes for which End the select men agrede thear should be coppyes procured by captin mason at the printturs and thay to be paid for out of the town Reat and the man above menshioned to cary them along with them to such of the inhabitanc as heave none.[34]

The selectmen's acceptance of the authority of the General Court after 1660 and their desire to comply with the Court's laws were developments that gradually contributed to the diminution of the selectmen's role in Watertown government in the late seventeenth century.

Like the parish officers in East Anglia, the selectmen of Watertown increasingly came to rely upon aid and direction from outside the town in administering poor relief and dealing with other social ills.[35] At the same time, because of the growing complexity of politics in the community, the selectmen were also losing power in relation to the town meeting. More and more the meeting bypassed the selectmen in favor of ad hoc committees that were appointed to look into or resolve particular matters coming to the town's attention. Administrative matters that were formerly delegated to the selectmen were now parceled out by the town meeting to various districts or precincts of the town, each of which had its own tax, militia, and church officers, as well as recording clerk. In consequence of these changes, selectmen's meetings became less frequent and more routine in content.

34. *Ibid.*, 86 (Dec. 12, 1665), 95 (n.d.), 121 (Dec. 1, 1674), and *Recs. of Mass. Bay*, II, 8–9. For evidence that the town was under outside pressure, note the business in the selectmen's meeting previous to the first quotation above (*Watertown Recs.*, 86 [Nov. 21, 1665]), in which "the two Cunstables weare Chosen to take care of the youth upon the Saboth days and other times of publique worshipe: in refferance to the order of Courte." For some examples of compliance and enforcement of colony laws by Watertown selectmen, see *ibid.*, 93–94 (Jan. 12, 1669), 102 (Nov. 29, 1670), 103 (Dec. 13, 1670), 104 (Jan. 3, 1671), which all refer to families and the education of children; 62 (Apr. 12, 1659), 83 (Oct. 11, 1664), involving sumptuary legislation enacted by the selectmen "in refference to the Law concerning the eccesse in apparrell"; 136 (Dec. 10, 1678), in which the selectmen quickly responded to a General Court order regarding a rate for Harvard College. Deference to the authority of the General Court and its laws was not restricted to the selectmen, however. See, for example, *ibid.*, 144 (Jan. 5, 1680), when the town meeting "voated that the select men at the Towne charge are to procure two hundred coppies of those severall laws respecting the worke of the tithing men and there worke which the law requirs of them and to be for the severall Inhabitants use."

35. See, for examples, Suffolk County Quarter Sessions Records, 1639–1651 Order Book, 105/2/1, Ipswich and East Suffolk Record Office, County Hall, Ipswich, Suffolk, Rattlesden, 46r, Nayland, 77v, Little Waldingfield, 7v, Sudbury, 130v, Capel St. Mary, 150r, Polstead, 81v, 107r and v, 157r, Hawkedon, 143r, Lavenham, 38v, 76v, 85v, 117r, 119r, 127r, 138v, Bures St. Mary, 65v, 112v, 119v, for reaction in emigrant towns to problems involving settlement laws and land use; see Stoke Nayland and Bures St. Mary, 99v, 112r, Capel St. Mary, 11r, Great and Little Wenham, 75v, Polstead, 157v, Lavenham, 45v and

As late as the 1670s, townsmen had seemed content to leave troublesome decisions to the same experienced selectmen that they continued to elect year after year. In 1676, for instance, the meeting asked the selectmen to hire a schoolmaster "as cheap as they can," and three years later they asked them to establish some bylaws that would alleviate "the disorderliness of cattle and swine and the multitude of sheep in the town."[36] But this pattern was entirely altered within the next forty years. The selectmen ceased to make town bylaws after 1680. They also lost control over the setting of rates and over the use of the proceeds. In addition, they were not always able to persuade the town meeting to make the appropriations they requested.

As the meeting became the focal point of community life in Watertown, the resolution of issues depended on the popular vote and on suffrage qualifications rather than on the judgment of those with long experience serving in local institutions. The emergence of the town meeting as a political force was itself a factor that paradoxically contributed to the loss of local autonomy, for, inevitably, Watertown was compelled to appeal to and rely upon higher authority for settling disputes when local issues engendered unresolvable agitation. Thus, in Watertown as in other communities, a variety of new political and social developments combined to alter local character. Not only was the central government actively legislating in the area of local government, but local governments were themselves encountering problems they could not handle alone.[37] Such shifting relationships within the towns, and between the towns and the provincial government, resulted in communities that by 1750 were very different institutions from those founded over a century earlier.

The New World offered Massachusetts immigrants a chance to reproduce in rough form the life that had prevailed in their native English villages, from the land system to local government. By and large they followed the patterns that they knew from direct experience at home. Yet, necessarily, whatever the goals or ambitions of the settlers, the American environment both imposed unexpected constraints and opened up new opportunities. In contrast to the political conditions in their native re-

---

138v, for cases of appeal to the county court by East Anglian towns for enforcement of town orders; and B. W. Quintrell, "Government of Essex, 1603–42," 37–38.

36. *Watertown Recs.*, 127 (Nov. 6, 1676), 142 (Nov. 3, 1679).

37. For a discussion of this transfer of power from selectmen to the town meeting, see Lockridge and Kreider, "Evolution of Massachusetts Town Government," *WMQ*, 3d Ser., XXIII (1966), 557–563.

gions, life in New England offered nearly complete local control, with little fear or expectation of intervention from outside higher authority. Moreover, New England communities were protected from the social difficulties that would inevitably have arisen had there been a significant migration of either the very rich or the very poor.

Yet there were problems inherent in the very nature of these New World societies. If they were founded upon consensus, what would prevent men who were dissatisfied with conditions in any given town from physically leaving in order to form a separate township? The process of fission had both distinctive and constructive consequences, but in either case it represented an important departure from English local life. In addition, the trend toward the establishment of private farms probably occurred at a generally more accelerated pace than would have been possible in England and was accompanied by a remarkable increase in land exchanges within some New England villages. As we have seen, older, limited conceptions of "proprietorship" were overthrown by the greater numbers of nonproprietors in the community, a situation without parallel in late seventeenth-century England. In the process the older landholding practices of the towns were greatly altered and, in some communities, within a short span of years almost as much acreage as was in the original grants was channeled into private hands.

The land market was not the cause of all these transformations of English society in the New World. The inhabitants of Massachusetts towns became increasingly unable to handle certain social problems within their own communities and gradually came to need, accept, and rely upon colony law. In some towns, for example Watertown, this change greatly altered customary relationships, such as that between the selectmen and the town meeting. On the other hand, the assertion of higher authority over Massachusetts towns restored an arrangement like that found in England, where justices of the peace, and hundred, petty sessions, and quarter sessions courts supervised the activities of townsmen. As a result, government in New England during the final decades of the seventeenth century and the early years of the eighteenth came to resemble more closely the distinctive hierarchical organization of provincial England.

8 Epilogue: An Eighteenth-Century Perspective

HE inevitable inconsistencies between the requirements of English local law and custom and the opportunities offered by the American environment eventually led, as we have just seen, to modifications in landholding practices, in the notion of community consent, and in concepts of town leadership and government as perceived by early seventeenth-century Englishmen. These changes, however, were merely forerunners of the more profound alterations that occurred in the period after 1680. While the full story of this forgotten middle period in Massachusetts's colonial history remains to be written, it is possible to sketch here briefly the contrast between the character of early town life and that of the later colonial, or provincial, period. Most apparent in this contrast is the changing institutional relationship between the town and the colony, especially through the colony's agency, the county court. Patterns of land use and agricultural production diverged significantly from the practices established following settlement. Lastly, colony-wide social and cultural influences diminished the distinctiveness of individual towns. No longer did town culture as fashioned by the early founders and inhabitants determine governmental, social, or economic policy.

Even a casual look at town records after 1680 reveals that town orders after that date had become a more or less static code of well-tried rules, formulated years earlier but by the beginning of the eighteenth century only remotely related to current concerns. Not only had the town's initiative gradually waned, but its customary legal practices—once as distinctive and individualistic as the local experiences of its first settlers—had become regularized and routinized. External factors, such as the effort of the General Court to impose its authority over the local governments, encouraged this trend. Increasing use was made in the towns of legal "guides" or treatises, a process that eroded local officers' concepts of their duties.

In Watertown, for instance, outside authority was willingly accepted. As we noted in the preceding chapter, a deliberate effort was made there to provide the means of basic legal education for the inhabitants. Town records contain countless instances of the selectmen directing that the town's children should be taught the laws of the land and, at times more specifically, the "Capital Laws" of the colony.[1] By the end of the seventeenth century the concern that all should know the provincial law, and the notion that there were specified and "correct" methods of solving local problems and enforcing colony law came out explicitly. At a meeting of the selectmen in 1697 former town officers were required to return the copies of the provincial laws they had used during their year in office, making the volumes available "with in one weeke after the Election of the town officers for the use of such as shall be Choosen to the offices above named."[2]

By 1690, as the Watertown records show, the pattern was becoming unmistakably clear; Massachusetts towns were well on their way to losing their distinctiveness. By 1700 few new town bylaws were passed, and routine, day-to-day business had come to dominate town meetings. Even though the towns were growing more complex, requiring new policies and new decisions, the passage of statutes concerning taxes, roads, and paupers took up most town business, whereas other types of problems were left unconsidered or were handled by private groups. With the dawn of the provincial era in the 1690s, local problems were beginning to be addressed by outside authority as was increasingly the case in the course of the eighteenth century.

An examination of the Newbury bylaws demonstrates the growing supervision of local affairs from outside. The town meeting of May 21, 1669, outlined the duties of selectmen, designating to them many responsibilities. The selectmen were empowered to call the town meeting, order the "business for the herds," set the minister's rate, prohibit the felling of town trees for transport, make town, county, and colony rates, repair the meetinghouse, pound, and stocks, "looke that all strangers that come into the Towne, . . . depart in due season," and to draw up the town accounts at the end of the year. The provision concerning migrating strangers, which had been inspired by the settlement law enacted by the General Court on May 30, 1660, and by the obvious pressure on land resources caused by newcomers taking advantage of Newbury's economic opportunities, was the only item on the 1669 list of selectmen's responsibilities

1. *Watertown Recs.*, I, 68 (Dec. 5, 1660), 70 (Dec. 31, 1660), 95 (ca. Apr. 11–June 3, 1669), 121 (Jan. 1, 1675), 123 (Aug. 31, 1675), 144 (Jan. 5, 1680), 86 (Dec. 12, 1665), 104 (Jan. 3, 1671), 124 (Oct. 8, 1675), II, 17 (Apr. 11, 1684).
    2. *Ibid.*, II, 115 (June 25, 1697).

that was created in response to outside demands. Even that problem could have been handled by Newbury on its own.

Six decades later on March 14, 1727, the responsibilities of Newbury selectmen were again outlined in the town meeting records. Their duties at this date not only reveal a deterioration in the initiative expected of town officers, but also the effects of social currents touching the province as a whole over which the town had no direct control. The town had become institutionally subservient to the provincial government's policies, as the 1727 list of selectmen's duties suggests. It was expected that the selectmen:

1. Keep the Towns pound in repair.
2. Observe the directions in the Law relating to the admission of inhabitants into Towns and . . . warn out all strangers according to the directions in the Law and prosecute all such as do not depart when so warned.
3. Supply the wants of the poor.
4. Bind out the children of the poor as the Law directs.
5. Observe the directions in the Law relating to reputed drunkards, common tipplers and such as mispend their time and estates in publick houses and prosecute such as transgress the Laws in that case.
6. Set to work such as live idle and disorderly lives as the Law directs.
7. Take care of and improve the estates of such as are neither able to take care of or improve them themselves that they may be preserved for the maintenance of such persons as need may require as the Law directs.
8. Be aiding and assisting to Tything men and other officers in suppressing of vice, prophaness and immorality and vigorously exert themselves herein as the Law directs.
9. Give not their approbation for any to renew or have a licence for the keeping of publick houses but to such as are qualified as the Law directs.

Only the first and third provisions were independent of provincial regulations. All other items were drawn up in accordance with what the "Law directs," which meant colony-wide rather than town law. Town officers gradually lost independent responsibility for the town they were elected to serve. They had become simply caretakers of colony-wide policies.[3]

3. Newbury Town Recs., Oct. 12, 1670; Currier, *History of Newbury*, I, 112–114.

Even before 1700 life in New England towns had changed dramatically from the days when a minister such as Newbury's Thomas Parker was able to admonish inhabitants to resolve conflicts within the community in accordance with Matthew 18: 17. Similarly, the time had passed when it seemed reasonable for Dedham's covenanters to solve problems merely by agreeing "That if at any time difference shall arise betweene Parties of our said Towne. that then such partie and parties shall presently Referre all such difference. Unto some one. 2 or 3. others of our said societie to be fully accorded and determined."[4] By the beginning of the eighteenth century the community's role in the arbitration of differences between townsmen seems to have diminished greatly.

The early stages of this development can be seen in the record of civil cases in Middlesex County court from 1649 to 1686. During the first five complete years of the court records, 1650 to 1654, about 35 percent of all cases involved litigants residing in the same town, while about 65 percent were from different towns. During the last five years under the First Charter, 1682 to 1686, the figures were nearly reversed, and only 36 percent of all cases originated in disputes between parties from different towns (see table 16).

We do not know how effective pastoral exhortations or town covenants were in suppressing controversies within the towns or channeling them to local arbiters. Few disputes, it seems, reached the intermediary level of government, the county court, during the early years. There is reason to believe, as Thomas Haskell has found for the New Haven court during this period, that the litigants were generally of a higher status group than the population at large and were bringing suit against individuals from towns other than their own. The same litigants were often involved in a number of suits concerning large sums of money, goods, or lands. By the 1670s, however, county court cases increasingly consisted of ordinary individuals suing their own towns and town officers. Other cases involved disputes with fellow townsmen (often for slander or assault) or controversies among family members over wills and estates. Inheritance cases, like some of the other suits, often reached across town boundaries. Although the character of litigation was to change considerably during the provincial period, it was already clear by 1680 that local disputes were no longer

4. Article 3, Dedham town covenant of 1636, in Don Gleason Hill, ed., *The Early Records of the Town of Dedham, Massachusetts* (Dedham, Mass., 1886–1899), III, 2. According to one contemporary source, it was unnecessary to take civil actions beyond local authorities. See Hubbard, *General History of New England*, 159.

TABLE 16. *Town Origins of Civil Court Cases in Middlesex County, Massachusetts, 1649–1686*

	Litigants from Same Town		Litigants from Different Towns		
	No.	% of Total	No.	% of Total	Total Cases
1649–1659	66	33.6	125	65.5	191
1660–1663	30	40.5	44	59.5	74
1671–1679	86	60.6	56	39.4	142
1680–1686	79	57.2	59	42.8	138
Total	261	47.9	284	52.1	545

Sources:
   Compiled from Middlesex County Court Records, 1649–1699, 4 vols., Middlesex County Courthouse, East Cambridge, Mass. Identification of the litigants' residences is from James Savage, *A Genealogical Dictionary of the First Settlers of New England . . .* , 4 vols. (Boston, 1860–1862), and Charles Henry Pope, *The Pioneers of Massachusetts, A Descriptive List . . .* (Boston, 1900). The comparatively few cases (10 to 15%) for which no residence has been identified have been excluded from the table.

strictly matters for local arbitration. Individuals sought settlements outside the harmony of the "accommodative" consensus of the early Massachusetts town.[5]

Perhaps more integral to the lives and livelihoods of the inhabitants of the towns studied here were changes in agricultural life. The early settlers of these towns established fairly self-sufficient agricultural societies that were a continuation of distinctive English regional differences in specialization. Each town developed at a different pace, and some, like Newbury, as we have seen, became trading centers for commercial agriculture. By 1690 Newbury had devoted five commons to raising sheep in an elaborate

5. Thomas L. Haskell, "Litigation and Status in a Puritan Commonwealth: New Haven, 1640–1670" (unpublished paper, Stanford University, 1968), 23 (graph 1), 24, 52, 55. On this changing nature of litigation in the county courts, David T. Konig has noted a similar transition in his study of land transactions, attendant disputes, and the resulting systemization of land law. See "Community Custom and the Common Law in Seventeenth-Century Massachusetts," *American Journal of Legal History*, XVIII (1974), 137–172.

foldcourse system with a capacity for about five thousand head. Despite such auspicious beginnings, Newbury never became an important sheep-raising center, but instead concentrated on shipbuilding and commerce.[6] Like many other communities in Essex County and eastern Massachusetts that had produced agricultural surpluses before 1670 or 1680, however, output began to decline precipitously thereafter. Although much of our current knowledge of early Massachusetts agriculture is based on figures derived from the export and import trade, which tell us nothing of the importance and volume of intracolony commerce, it is still possible to mark the decline of local agriculture from roughly 1700 to 1720 when those trade figures begin to show Massachusetts's dependence upon other colonies for foodstuffs that they had formerly been able to supply for themselves.[7]

The towns in this study were undergoing an agricultural revolution of sorts, though of a different nature than the one then in progress in England, where land use was shifting from permanent tillage and permanent grassland to a more flexible and efficient system of permanently cultivated arable in which temporary tillage and temporary grass leys (pasture) were alternated.[8] Convertible husbandry of this sort did not come to Massachusetts until after the Revolution. Inventories and other contemporary evidence reveal some signs of change in Massachusetts, such as a shift to better grasses and the introduction of new crops, including turnips,

6. Coffin, *Sketch of the History of Newbury*, 137, 139, 143. On Newbury interest in shipbuilding and trading from the late 17th through the mid-18th century, see Currier, *History of Newbury*, I, 476–477, 479–480, 481–482, 484.

7. The transition is illustrated in two different accounts by visitors, that of Edmund Randolph, in his 1676 report to the Privy Council, and that of Edmund Andros 14 years later. Randolph found Massachusetts farmers numerous and wealthy, men who took advantage of their livestock and produce for trade with other colonies and countries. Andros, on the other hand, described Massachusetts, the most populous of the colonies, as containing "one of the smallest and poorest tracts of land, and produces least of all the Colonies for exportation." Inhabitants had no livestock or grain beyond their own needs, but he thought the country was well suited for extensive sheep raising (*Hutchinson Papers*, II, 219, 230–231; *Calendar of State Papers, Colonial Series, America and West Indies, 1689–1692* [London, 1901], 255). For some 17th-century export figures, see Bidwell and Falconer, *History of Agriculture*, 43–44. For the general decline in Massachusetts agriculture before the Revolution, as measured by coastal export and import figures, see Max George Schumacher, "The Northern Farmer and His Markets during the Late Colonial Period" (Ph.D. diss., University of California, Berkeley, 1948), published in the Arno Dissertations in American Economic History Series, ed. Stuart Bruchey (New York, 1975), 21–30; David Klingaman, "Food Surpluses and Deficits in the American Colonies, 1768–1772," *Jour. Econ. Hist.*, XXXI (1971), 563–564; and James F. Shepherd and Samuel H. Williamson, "The Coastal Trade of the British North American Colonies, 1768–1772," *ibid.*, XXXII (1972), 788–793.

8. Kerridge, *Agricultural Revolution*, 181.

tobacco, and potatoes, but none of these crops were grown in substantial amounts, and little effort was made to use them advantageously as English farmers did.[9] Towns such as Newbury and Rowley were in fact undergoing not just a decline; they were also abandoning the mixed-farming tradition and economy that the earliest settlers had brought with them. In its place evolved an agricultural system almost totally devoted to grazing. Whereas harvests in these towns had once produced sizable surpluses that could be sold in the larger towns or overseas, by the eighteenth century agriculture engaged a smaller number of men and women on a full-time basis, and the food supply depended more and more upon outside resources.

Given the limited potential of the soil in eastern Massachusetts, it seems unlikely in any case that new farming methods would have been able to arrest the changes occurring in town agricultural economies during the latter part of the seventeenth and the early decades of the eighteenth century. The earliest settlers had staked out the most promising tillage lands, which were probably already deteriorating in fertility by the early eighteenth century. New lands granted by the towns required too much labor to be transformed into plowlands, if they were suitable at all. With rising town populations, less area was devoted to tillage in both relative and absolute terms. The agricultural landscape, as William Douglas observed in the 1740s, had changed to one dominated by pastures and orchards.[10]

The change in land use in both Newbury and Rowley probably began in the late seventeenth century or the first decades of the eighteenth. As late as 1688 only 3,771 acres had been set to productive use by Newbury's proprietors and grantees, but during the next century a total of over

9. On English crop innovations, see generally E. L. Jones, "Agricultural and Economic Growth in England, 1660–1750: Agricultural Change," *Jour. Econ. Hist.*, XXV (1965), 1–18. Newbury, Rowley, and Ipswich inventories were examined for the decades 1700–1709, 1730–1739, and 1750–1759, from among the Essex County probate records. For some examples illustrating these crop changes, see Essex Bound Wills and Inventories, vol. 316, pp. 469–471, vol. 329, pp. 225–226, 453–455, vol. 330, pp. 264–265, vol. 331, pp. 404–405, 434–435, vol. 335, pp. 52–53, vol. 336, pp. 445–446. In Hingham, see, for instance, town meeting, May 16, 1694, Hingham Mass. Town Recs. Shifts to pasturage, more extensive livestock production, the rising importance of orchards, cider, and rum, some of which are discussed later in the text or mentioned in tables, are all evident in these inventories, particularly among those investigated for the latter years. While it is arguable that some men imported and used English grasses in the years immediately following settlement (Josselyn, *Account of Two Voyages to New-England*, 144), it was not until the 1730s and later that cultivated grasses were commonly mentioned in estate inventories and valuation lists.

10. William Douglas, *A Summary, Historical and Political, of the First Planting, Progressive Improvements, and Present State of the British Settlement in North America . . .* , 2 vols. (Boston, 1748–1753, [1757]), I, 537.

TABLE 17. *Changes in Land Use in Newbury and Rowley, Massachusetts, between the Seventeenth and Eighteenth Centuries (in Percents)*

	Newbury		Rowley	
	1688	1781	ca. 1650	1771
Plowland	35	8	30–36	11
Meadow	40	19		
Pasture	25	54	16–22	54
Mowing		12		9
Woodland		6		
Fresh Marsh			24	11
Salt Marsh			24	15

Sources:
Compiled from Benjamin P. Mighill and George B. Blodgette, eds., *The Early Records of the Town of Rowley, Massachusetts*, I, *1639–1672* (Rowley, Mass., 1894), 1–51; Town Valuation, 1771, Massachusetts Archives, CXXXII, 27–36, State House, Boston; Walter Lloyd Jeffries, communicator, "Town Rate of Newbury, Mass., 1688," *New England Historical and Genealogical Register*, XXXII (1878), 156–164; Essex Valuations, 1781, Dane Papers, Massachusetts Historical Society, Boston. No earlier valuation, ca. 1758–ca. 1771, for instance, exists for Newbury in this period. Similarly proportioned figures were recorded in a 1773 town valuation in Hingham. See George Lincoln, ed., *History of the Town of Hingham, Massachusetts*, 3 vols. in 4 (Hingham, Mass., 1893), I, pt. ii, 181–182.

20,000 acres came into individual ownership, much of which was divided shortly after 1700.[11] A comparison of the proportions of land used for various purposes in the 1688 and 1781 valuations of Newbury indicates that plowland dramatically decreased from one-third to less than 10 percent of the land. Pasturage during the same period doubled to over 50 percent of all land used by Newbury residents. In neighboring Rowley, which had a different agricultural economy than Newbury, tillage declined between the mid-seventeenth century and the decade of the Revolution at the same rate as in Newbury, while pasturage doubled and probably trebled during the same period (see table 17).

As these figures indirectly suggest, the differences in agricultural practices between Newbury and Rowley, so evident in the seventeenth century, had diminished. Change, however, was not restricted to these two communities. Broad regional agricultural economies came to dominate the

11. Newbury Proprietors' Records, II, 47–125.

TABLE 18. *Proportional Land Use in Massachusetts Counties, 1751 (in Percents)*

County	Orchards	Plowland	Mowing	Pasture
Suffolk	3	11	35	51
Essex	2	6	34	58
Middlesex	3	20	44	33
Hampshire	2	55	37	6
Worcester	3	22	53	22
Plymouth	3	21	34	42
Barnstable		24	19	57
Bristol	4	21	33	42
York	1	10	43	46
Dukes		7	8	85
Nantucket		12	13	75
Colony-wide Averages	2.5	18.0	36.6	42.9

Source:
Compiled from "Valuation of the several Counties in the Provce. of Mass. Bay. in 1751," Miscellaneous Bound MSS, 1749–1755, Massachusetts Historical Society, Boston.

colony by the middle of the eighteenth century, if not earlier. By 1750 in nearly every coastal county in the colony, pasturage occupied half or more of all the land. In the central regions of Massachusetts, such as Middlesex County, farmers devoted a third of their land to pasturage and about one-fifth to tillage. In the Connecticut River valley, land use was almost totally the reverse of the ratios in coastal areas. There, arable amounted to well over half of the land while pasturage was restricted to only about 6 percent of the land area (see table 18). Farmers in Essex County towns and along other stretches of the Massachusetts coast were no longer able to maintain in 1750 the broad range of farming alternatives their predecessors had when they engaged in mixed-farming agriculture a century earlier. The new, dependent pastoral economy produced little exportable surplus, and from a preliminary examination of valuation records for some of the towns studied here, it appears that proportionate to population, fewer men were financially involved in agriculture on the eve of the Revolution than had been a century before.

By 1700 most Massachusetts communities could no longer be described as hamlets or villages that contained within themselves nearly all the activities of daily life. Changing social and cultural factors also helped diminish distinctive characteristics of Massachusetts towns, as these communities became more complex and variegated during the century after 1650. Analysis of the first comprehensive Massachusetts census of 1765 reveals that 52 percent of its approximately two hundred towns had populations in excess of one thousand by that date, and, of more fundamental importance, 72 percent of the colony's population lived in these larger, more complex communities.[12]

One of the more visible effects of population growth demonstrated much earlier than 1765 was an increase in town dissension and discord, a process that usually culminated in partitioning or in the creation of new town units out of the older communities. Evidence does suggest that population factors and imperial policy were the basic determinants of town formation and that the desire for "accommodation or separation" by the town itself was merely an effect.[13] The pressure of rising generations probably produced a continual demand for community development in the eighteenth century, but during certain periods, such as the 1740s and 1750s, external restrictions were placed on towns wishing to divide for the sake of internal harmony. Governor William Shirley, among others, was well aware that new units of representation only strengthened the Massachusetts legislature at the expense of the royal governor, and he often vetoed bills creating new townships.[14] By the 1760s and 1770s existing towns were divided and new towns created from unincorporated lands in unprecedented numbers. After the general act of incorporation of towns

12. Compiled from Evarts B. Greene and Virginia D. Harrington, *American Population before the Federal Census of 1790* (New York, 1932), 21–30. On changes in settlement patterns and the widening geographical separation of New England inhabitants in the 18th century, see Edna Scofield, "The Origin of Settlement Patterns in Rural New England," *Geographical Review*, XXVII (1938), 652–663, and Glenn T. Trewartha, "Types of Rural Settlement in Colonial America," *ibid.*, XXXVI (1946), 568–580, especially 577–579. Compare also François Jean Chastellux, *Travels in North America, in the Years 1780, 1781 and 1782*, trans. anon., 2 vols. (London, 1787), I, 20; Richard L. Bushman, *From Puritan to Yankee: Character and the Social Order in Connecticut, 1690–1765* (Cambridge, Mass., 1967), 54–72; and J. M. Bumsted, "A Caution to Erring Christians: Ecclesiastical Disorder on Cape Cod, 1717 to 1738," *WMQ*, 3d Ser., XXVIII (1971), 414, 438. For a differing view, see Zuckerman, *Peaceable Kingdoms*, 8, 24, 33–35, 116, 154, 219, 221, 229, 239, 254, 255.

13. Edwin Scott Gaustad, *The Great Awakening in New England* (New York, 1957), 114; J. M. Bumsted, "Religion, Finance, and Democracy in Massachusetts: The Town of Norton as a Case Study," *JAH*, LVII (1970–1971), 820, 821. Compare Bushman, *From Puritan to Yankee*, 83, 66–67, 291–293.

14. See Bernard Bailyn, *The Origins of American Politics* (New York, 1968), 81–82, and Robert E. Brown, *Middle-Class Democracy and the Revolution in Massachusetts, 1691–1780* (Ithaca, N.Y., 1955), 69–77.

became law in 1774, thirty-five new towns were established by the end of the following year (see table 19).

The Great Awakening and the related rise of denominationalism were other factors that divided communities. Some towns were able to maintain a single church by keeping diverse religious loyalties in check; in other cases the whole community became either Old or New Light. Until new studies of separate towns or regions are made, we cannot know how individual towns were able to deal with changing and divisive religious sentiments, or how closely these disputes came to the core of community life.[15] The few recent studies we have do indicate that the religious controversies associated with the Great Awakening did affect community harmony.[16] In addition, in the decades prior to the Revolution, whole areas of Massachusetts, centering in Middleborough and Rehoboth, stretching west across the southern tier of towns to the Connecticut River, and reaching a number of Berkshire communities by the 1770s, developed Separatist and Baptist splinter churches.[17]

Finally, in the category of new social problems, some mention should be made of the increasing burden placed on local communities by poor migrants. While the wandering poor were already a problem for seventeenth-century communities, the magnitude of the disorder and the threat to community resources experienced in the following century were far greater. Greater geographic mobility, the rise of a permanent class of transient poor, the decline in residential stability, and widespread economic difficulties were all factors that led towns to discourage migrants from settling in their communities, in order to avoid the responsibilities of poor relief. A tabulation of Worcester County "warnings out" from 1737 to 1788 shows that 56 percent of the cases occurred between 1762 and 1767 and 80 percent of them took place in the fourteen-year span between 1754 and 1767.[18] The increase in migration and "warnings out" during the pe-

15. Morgan, "New England Puritanism: Another Approach," *WMQ*, 3d Ser., XVIII (1961), 236–242.

16. Compare, for example, Bumsted, "Religion, Finance, and Democracy in Massachusetts," *JAH*, LVII (1970–1971), 817–831, "A Caution to Erring Christians," *WMQ*, 3d Ser., XXVIII (1971), 413–438, and, for Connecticut, his "Revivalism and Separatism in New England: The First Society of Norwich, Connecticut, as a Case Study," *ibid.*, 3d Ser., XXIV (1967), 588–612; and James Walsh, "The Great Awakening in the First Congregational Church of Woodbury, Connecticut," *ibid.*, XXVIII (1971), 543–562.

17. Compiled from Weis, *Colonial Clergy of New England*, 239–280.

18. Francis E. Blake, *Worcester County, Massachusetts, Warnings, 1737–1788* (Worcester, Mass., 1899). This tabulation is based on the 20 towns (of 40 listed) that were established in the county before 1740. Only the individual or family head, rather than each person re-

TABLE 19. *The Creation of Massachusetts Towns from Older Communities, 1630–1800*

	No. of Towns Created	Towns Created from Older Towns		Plymouth Colony Included		
					From Older Towns	
		No.	% of Total	No. of Towns Created	No.	% of Total
1630–1639	17			24		
1640–1649	12	5	41.7	16	5	31.3
1650–1659	7	1	14.3	8	2	25.0
1660–1669	7	3	42.9	11	3	27.3
1670–1679	6	2	33.3	8	2	25.0
1680–1689	2			6		
1690–1699	6	1	14.3	8	2	25.0
17th-century totals	57	12	21.0	81	14	17.3

	No. of Towns Created	Towns Created from Older Towns	
		No.	% of Total
1700–1709	5	1	20.0
1710–1719	19	10	52.6
1720–1729	16	12	75.0
1730–1739	21	14	66.7
1740–1749	5	3	60.0
1750–1759	3	1	33.3
1760–1769	28	6	21.4
1770–1779	58	45	77.6
1780–1789	17	15	88.2
1790–1799	15	12	80.0
18th-century totals	187	119	63.6

Source:
Compiled from material in *Historical Data Relating to Counties, Cities and Towns in Massachusetts* ([Boston], 1966). The data do not include those towns that later became part of Maine.

riod coincides with the last colonial war and its aftermath, and with the financial burdens placed upon communities by the General Court during and after the hostilities.[19] The towns' resistance to the migrants appears to have been motivated almost entirely by economic concerns.[20]

The towns' reliance upon the provincial settlement laws and the enforcement of them through the county courts epitomized the changing nature of government in eighteenth-century Massachusetts. No longer capable of handling many of the problems with which they were beset—problems that were in fact no longer confined within town boundaries—local communities sought relief from higher levels of government. Inhabitants could not now rely on traditions of cooperation within the towns and on unity in facing the outside. The day was past when the town's powers were jealously guarded and when inhabitants found not only their values, but most of their social and economic relationships as well, all within one local setting.[21] The number of lawsuits that crowded the

corded as having been warned out, has been used for the tabulation. For similar results in two other Massachusetts counties, see Douglas Lamar Jones, "The Strolling Poor: Transiency in Eighteenth-Century Massachusetts," *Jour. Soc. Hist.*, VIII (Spring 1975), 28–54; and for the changing nature of transiency from the 17th to the 18th century, see Jones, "Geographic Mobility and Society in Eighteenth-Century Essex County, Massachusetts" (Ph.D. diss., Brandeis University, 1975), especially 20, 55, 153–156. As in other aspects of 18th-century life, the warnings out system, though initiated by the town, made the community even more dependent upon the county courts and General Court. Hendrik Hartog, "The Public Law of the County Court: Judicial Government in Eighteenth Century Massachusetts," *American Journal of Legal History*, XX (1976), 282–329, especially 292–299.

19. Compare Edward M. Cook, Jr., "Social Behavior and Changing Values in Dedham, Massachusetts, 1700 to 1775," *WMQ*, 3d Ser., XXVII (1970), 568, 569; Kenneth A. Lockridge, "Land, Population and the Evolution of New England Society," *Past and Present*, no. 39 (1968), 72–73, and "Afterword, 1970," in Stanley N. Katz, ed., *Colonial America: Essays in Politics and Social Development* (Boston, 1971), 485–491; and Allan Kulikoff, "The Progress of Inequality in Revolutionary Boston," *WMQ*, 3d Ser., XXVIII (1971), 399–400.

20. Petitions in the Massachusetts Archives 9-volume "Town Series" encourage an economic explanation. Beginning in the 1730s and continuing until the Revolution, a great number of towns petitioned the Court for aid to help paupers, so that the towns would be relieved of the expense. At about the same time, towns seeking permission to tax unincorporated land virtually flooded the General Court with petitions. Caught in the dilemma between a decreasing proportion of taxes available for local needs and a steadily increasing demand for their use throughout the provincial period, the towns probably had little choice but to direct petitions for help to the General Court.

21. Kenneth Alan Lockridge, "Dedham 1636–1736: The Anatomy of a Puritan Utopia" (Ph.D. diss., Princeton University, 1965), 329–330, 339–341; Sidney V. James, "Colonial Rhode Island and the Beginnings of the Liberal Rationalized State," in Melvin Richter, ed., *Essays in Theory and History: An Approach to the Social Sciences* (Cambridge, Mass., 1970), 165–185. Compare also L. Kinvin Wroth, "Possible Kingdoms: The New England Town from the Perspective of Legal History," *Am. Jour. Legal Hist.*, XV (1971), 318–330.

courts in the eighteenth century suggests the change in sentiment that had taken place.[22] In Middlesex County the number of civil cases multiplied tenfold between the first and fourth decades of the eighteenth century, from an average of seven to seventy-five per quarter session, an increase that far exceeded any estimated population rise for the corresponding period. The decline in reliance on local arbitration could not be more dramatic.

The growing resort to personal litigation sprang from a variety of factors, not the least of which were the changing economic conditions and the increase in social discord discussed earlier. This discord was channeled into legal action partly because of the declining cost of legal services or fees after 1700. In the seventeenth century fees probably remained quite high, though no schedule of them has ever been published and only several appear to have been prescribed by law. One fee, for example, required payment of 18d. (though it was soon more than doubled to 3s. 4d.) for every action tried before the lowest rung in the court system, the "small causes" men who were nominated by the town to hear local cases involving debt, trespass, or damage not exceeding twenty shillings. In another instance the General Court complained about the "very burthensome" number of petitions brought before it, and declared that in "all petitions for abatements of fines or mittigation of offences" or those that "concerne controversies betwixt person and person, towne and towne," and those "for debts betwixt party and party, brought from Quarter Corts, or that concerns appeales" the petitioners or litigants were to pay ten shillings outright "besides the charges of the Corte borne." The commissioners' court of Boston in 1652 charged an equally high fee for entering an action in cases involving more than forty shillings.

Behind the high fees was the General Court's desire to discourage a large number of cases from coming into the courts "uppon slender grounds." It also continually sought ways of reducing the case loads of civil suits by shifting jurisdictions and making appeals more difficult to obtain. After 1650 there was also a growing reliance upon court fees to cover court ex-

22. Felt, *Ecclesiastical History of New England*, I, 236; *Recs. of Mass. Bay*, II, 3, 181–182; Lechford, *Plain Dealing*, 86; John M. Murrin, "The Legal Transformation: The Bench and Bar of Eighteenth-Century Massachusetts," in Katz, ed., *Colonial America*, 417; Powell, *Puritan Village*, 108; *Suffolk Co. Court Recs.*, I, xxxvi–xxxviii; Washburn, *Judicial History*, 52, 190–191, 169, 169n; Emil Oberholzer, Jr., "The Church in New England Society," in Smith, ed., *Seventeenth-Century America*, 152–153; Cook, "Social Behavior," *WMQ*, 3d Ser., XXVII (1970), 574–575; and compare Françoise Alexandre la Rouchefoucauld-Liancourt, *Travels through the United States of North America, the Country of the Iroquois, and Upper Canada in the Years 1795, 1796, 1797; with an Authentic Account of Lower Canada*, 2d ed., 4 vols. (London, 1800), II, 343–344.

penses. Judging from what we know of the fees under the First Charter, they varied little from those that were enacted in 1693 when the first, detailed provincial list was approved of by the General Court.[23]

Although court fees under the new schedule remained constant for the first four decades of royal government (1686–1726), events in the provincial era led to a gradual reduction in these costs. It is likely that the increasing number of civil suits brought by Massachusetts men in the provincial years was encouraged by the massive depreciation of currency. The story of currency in these years was "full of difficulty" even for its most interested and authoritative student, Andrew McFarland Davis, but certain conclusions may be drawn about the declining value of money. Provincial currency remained relatively stable until about 1710. By 1727, however, it had depreciated by half in terms of its value in silver. Later, in 1735, "New" tenor was established at the same value as "lawful money" (and by 1740 it was three times the value of "Old" tenor), but by 1750 had depreciated by almost half. Even as early as 1720, John Colman, who twenty years later founded the Land Bank, stated that "the vast Number of Law Suits" of the period was occasioned by "the miserable Effects" of an unstable currency. From 1750 until the Revolution, currency remained relatively stable, but the effects of forty years of uncertainty were reflected in the values of various provincial currencies. One shilling of sterling, for instance, was worth ten shillings of "Old" tenor, 2s. 6d. of "New" tenor, and 1s. 4d. of "lawful" Massachusetts money.[24]

Coupled with the decline in the "real" costs of legal services for inhabitants that resulted from the devaluation of currency was the reduction in the fees themselves. The fee schedule remained basically unchanged until 1742 when the General Court reasserted its interest and prerogative over such matters, due probably in no small part to former Governor Jonathan Belcher's disastrous attempts to remove the influence of the land bankers from that body. That year the Court established a new set of fees that, though slightly more structured, were reduced by one-half almost straight

---

23. During the first charter period (to 1686), several acts concerning the costs of legal services in the courts and related matters were enacted by the General Court. See *Recs. of Mass. Bay*, I, 169–170, 176, II, 208–209, 261–262, 279, III, 82, 167, 184, 340–342, IV, pt. i, 104–105, 154, 134–135, 287. For an analysis of the structure of colonial and provincial Massachusetts courts, see Joseph H. Smith, ed., *Colonial Justice in Western Massachusetts, 1639–1702: The Pynchon Court Record, an Original Judge's Diary of the Administration of Justice in the Springfield Courts in the Massachusetts Bay Colony* (Cambridge, Mass., 1961), 65–88.

24. Andrew McFarland Davis, *Currency and Banking in the Province of the Massachusetts-Bay*, 2 vols. (New York, 1900–1901), I, *Currency*, 88, 90; Brown, *Middle-Class Democracy*, 83–87. Compare the inflationary conditions in neighboring Connecticut discussed in Bushman, *From Puritan to Yankee*, 136, and Appendix 3, 297.

across the schedule and were payable, reaffirming previous Massachusetts practice, "in bills of credit, emitted for the supply of the treasury the last year, or *in other province bills*, or gold [and] silver in proportion (*at the choice of the payer*)."

This measure was reenacted over and over again for the next twenty years or more, ensuring legislative prerogative in such matters. During that period only one major set of changes occurred and this happened in the 1750 act. At that time fees were increased by about two-thirds of what they had been in 1693. Some were raised three-quarters of that rate. These increases were relatively insignificant, however, since between the continuing decline in the value of the currency and the absolute lowering of fees, provincial litigants in 1750 were probably paying one-sixth of the cost in their court battles that litigants in 1700 had been required to pay. It was no wonder then that at mid-century William Douglas of Boston declared that "the Smallness of Court-Fees, multiply Law-Suits, and is a snare for poor People to become litigious."[25]

Middlesex County is probably a fairly representative indicator of the meaning of these social and legal changes in provincial Massachusetts. Predominantly rural, with a moderately large population by 1765, and dating back to the earliest years of settlement, the county was neither exposed to the somewhat different legal-cultural influence that affected the Plymouth Colony and the Connecticut River valley counties, nor was it a relatively new, frontier, underpopulated area as were a number of counties in central and western Massachusetts before the Revolution. But by 1775 the county contained an equal number of communities that had been created in the eighteenth century as had been created in the seventeenth, and

25. The three provincial fee laws used here are from *The Acts and Resolves, Public and Private, of the Province of the Massachusetts Bay* . . . , 21 vols. (Boston, 1869–1922), hereafter cited as *Mass. Acts and Resolves*: "An Act for Regulating Fees," I, 84–88 (1692–1693, chap. 37); "An Act for Establishing and Better Regulating Fees within This Province," III, 13–18 (1742–1743, chap. 5), italics added; and "An Act for Establishing and Regulating Fees of the Several Officers within This Province, As Are Hereafter Mentioned," *ibid.*, 525–531 (1750–1751, chap. 8). Other provincial fee laws enacted through 1768 include the following, all in *Mass. Acts and Resolves*: I, 72–76, 184–185, 222–223, 287, 324–325, 374, 467, II, 463–464, 655–656, 938–939, III, 101–107, 176–181, 253, 328–333, 656–662, 983, 1032–1038, IV, 213–214, 291–298, 743–751, 1022–1023, VII, 10–11, IX, 175, 683. See also, Bailyn, *Origins of American Politics*, 114–117; "The Distressed State of the Town of Boston, etc. Considered in a Letter from a Gentleman in the Town, To His Friend in the Countrey," reprinted in Andrew McFarland Davis, ed., *Colonial Currency Reprints, 1682–1751*, 4 vols. (Boston, 1910–1911), I, 398–408; and Douglas, *Summary of the British Settlements*, I, 517–518, 517n.

Douglas, in the statement quoted in the text, recognized that it was the court of common pleas, particularly with its low fees, that encouraged litigation among private individuals and generally served "without much Pleadings, only to transmit [cases] to the Superior or Provin-

thus can serve as a measure of certain changes characteristic of both older and younger areas. The records of civil cases during the period from 1700 to 1750 show a steep relative decline in the number of suits involving litigants from the more urbanized areas of the county, that is, from Charlestown and Cambridge, and from Boston men sued in Middlesex courts.[26] In 1700 nearly 55 percent of all civil litigants were from one of these three communities, whereas by 1750 their representation in the court had declined to only slightly above 20 percent. No longer were the courts so monopolized by the localistic concerns of the county's leading towns. At the beginning of the century, in nearly all cases in which one of the parties was an inhabitant of Cambridge, Charlestown, or Boston, the other party was also from one of these localities. By 1730 this trend had been totally reversed, and the second party most often came from more rural parts of the county. At the same time, throughout the first half of the century the ratio of farmers to professionals and tradesmen as litigants in court cases remained the same, even though the ratio for the locale of parties had changed. Both factors indicate that a more dispersed commercial and interdependent economy had developed well before 1750.[27]

The number of civil suits involving parties from the same town also declined. It will be recalled that throughout the seventeenth century an in-

---

cial Court." Functionally, common pleas might serve the opposite purpose, too. In "An Act for Preventing Unnecessary Expence of Time in the Attendance of Petit Jurors, on the Several Courts of Justice, and for the Enlarging Their Fees, and the Allowance to Witnesses in Civil Cases," provincial lawmakers recognized that many unnecessary suits were brought forth "frequently (especially in the courts of common pleas)" to be privately settled outside of the courtroom (*Mass. Acts and Resolves*, II, 463–464 [1727–1728, chap. 10]). Increasingly lower legal service fees made both uses especially attractive to men seeking to settle both large and small disputes. Douglas also suggested that the rapidly increasing number of local officials may have encouraged many Massachusetts men to resort to them to settle matters, after which they often appealed their cases to higher tribunals. "It has hither to be too much a Practice," he commented, "to multiply the Number of the Justices of the Peace (this amongst other Inconveniencies, as an old Country Justice well observed) 'Depreciates the former Credit of a Justice, as the multiplying of our publick Bills of Credit, depreciates our Currency.' May not Act of Assembly be made from Time to Time, to *limit* the Number of Justices in each County, and their *Qualifications* be under some *Regulation*?" Similar comments were penned by Englishman Joseph Bennet at this time. See Mass. Hist. Soc., *Procs.*, 1st Ser., V (1860–1862), 120–121.

26. Records of the Inferior Court of Common Pleas, 11 vols., 1692–1780, Middlesex County Courthouse.

27. "Urbanization implies changes . . . that follow from the increased involvement of the members of rural communities in sets of activities, norms, and social relationships that reach beyond the limits of their own localities." Charles Tilly, *The Vendée* (Cambridge, Mass., 1964), 11–12.

creasing number of civil cases had been originating from within the same town. In Middlesex County this trend culminated in the 1680s when about 64 percent of the disputes were between inhabitants of the same town. By 1700, only 42 percent were intratown conflicts and by 1730 this proportion had been pared in half. There is some evidence that part of this decline was due to what appears to have been a lack of conflict within new towns, since intratown disputes were three or four times more likely to occur in old, seventeenth-century Middlesex County towns than in eighteenth-century ones. But the decline in intratown disputes implied much more. The increasing number of cases between relatively urbanized Charlestown-Cambridge-Boston and Middlesex rural areas suggests that the barriers of town self-sufficiency were breaking down and that new unities were being created along lines of trade.

The predominant trend in litigation during the eighteenth century was toward suits involving parties from different towns. In 1700 only two out of every five parties came from different towns, but by 1730 it was four out of five. Throughout these years nearly half of these suits involved litigants from adjoining communities. Individuals became increasingly dependent in their economic relationships upon people from outside the local community. In addition, between 1700 and 1730 there was a corresponding fourfold increase in the number of Middlesex cases involving litigants from communities separated by more than the distance of one intervening (that is, adjacent) town, and a decline of about one-third in the number of cases involving litigants separated by only one town. In short, the geographic relationship of the parties in civil suits—particularly those involving loans, produce, or trade—increasingly extended beyond the confines of a single town. Most likely a suit would be between individuals from adjoining communities, but by 1730 it was equally likely that a suit would involve individuals living at a great distance, either within Middlesex or within the province as a whole.

Finally, the decline of the town as an effective lawmaking institution and the emergence of the county placed greater interest in the county magistracy, making the office, as it had in England, an important upward channel for men with talent and influence. It had become in Hampshire County according to one recent study "a self-conscious elite, bound by family, marriage, and economic interests," which by 1750 was virtually closed to outsiders.[28] And unlike in Connecticut and Rhode Island, for

28. Ronald Kingman Snell, "The County Magistracy in Eighteenth-Century Massachusetts: 1692–1750 (Ph.D. diss., Princeton University, 1971), iii–iv; John Adams, *A Defence of the Constitutions of Government of the United States of America, against the Attack of M. Turgot* . . .

instance, justices in Massachusetts "were not appointed for every town regardless of size or importance."[29] For other positions in the legal system, living in less than a substantial town had become a severe handicap to appointment in the eighteenth century. In Essex, Suffolk, and Middlesex counties, three-quarters of all the provincial appointments to the court of common pleas came from Salem, Ipswich, Boston, Charlestown, and Cambridge, the largest communities in the counties. In Hampshire and Bristol counties such families as the Pynchons, Dwights, Williamses, and Leonards held most of the positions on this court. Even in the fast-rising legal profession, a change of location to the shire town or to Boston became a necessity.[30]

Increasingly after 1700, towns could no longer be described as simply units of local government isolated from colonial power as they had been before 1660. Towns had become variegated and complex institutions. No longer, too, did the town and its meeting serve as a creative lawmaking body; it had become more a consensus-building and caretaking one. Towns had reached their limit of effective authority before the beginning of the eighteenth century, and by 1700 daily life went beyond its confines and moved the townsman increasingly into the centralizing social web of the law and economy by way of different institutions, personnel, and interests.

Dated the Twenty-Second Day of March, 1778, 3 vols. (Philadelphia, 1797), I, 110–111; William H. Whitmore, *Massachusetts Civil List for the Colonial and Provincial Periods, 1630–1774* (Albany, N.Y., 1870), 6.

29. Edward M. Cook, Jr., "Local Leadership and the Typology of New England Towns, 1700–1785," *Political Science Quarterly*, LXXXVI (1971), 586–608. In Middlesex and Bristol counties, to cite two other examples, one can find a similar consistency of selection. The Prescott, Russell, Danforth, Reed, and Tyng families had from four to seven members as justices during the provincial period and the Churches, Leonards, Popes, Richmonds, and Williamses were as equally well represented in Bristol. See Whitmore, *Massachusetts Civil List*, 126–152.

30. Washburn, *Judicial History*, 319–385; Cook, "Local Leadership," *Pol. Sci. Qtly.*, LXXXVI (1971), 586–608; Murrin, "Legal Transformation," in Katz, ed., *Colonial America*, 426–427, 429–433; compare Zuckerman, *Peaceable Kingdoms*, 91–92.

Appendixes

With the exception of Appendix 2, each of the lists of settlers below is a representative and significant sample of the early inhabitants several years after the founding of each of the communities studied here. Names used for these appendixes are listed as they were written in the contemporary documents and are sometimes followed by variant spellings, in brackets, taken from other sources (genealogies, town histories, and other records). The names have been alphabetized in all five appendixes. Asterisks are used to designate less permanent settlers, those who moved from the community before 1660. Occasionally these are followed by a question mark, which indicates that evidence is scanty or nonexistent and does not indicate whether the individual left the town or not. Without wills, inventories, or other contemporary documentation, the assumption is that the settlers in question moved on. In other places, question marks have been used to indicate a less than certain connection between a documentary source and an emigrant. Often, for instance, one cannot be absolutely certain that a child recorded in English baptismal records is actually the son or daughter of an emigrant, even though there are many indications to support such a conclusion. When any doubt exists, a question mark has been inserted. A bracketed asterisk following a name indicates that the settler returned to England before 1660. Occasionally the ship and point of embarkation for a settler are listed under Place of Origin when his or her specific English home is unknown, on the supposition that he or she came from a nearby location.

Appendix 1

English Origins of the Original Landholders of Rowley, Massachusetts

Name	Place of Origin	Reference
1. George Abbot		
2. William Acy	Cottingham, Yorkshire (children baptized 1626, 1627, 1630, 1632, 1636)	Banks, *Top. Dict.*, 185; Hazen, "Yorkshire Origins," 136–137; Cottingham parish register, Humberside R.O.
3. James Barker	born Stragewell or Stradishall, Suffolk	Blodgette, comp., and Jewett, ed., *Early Settlers of Rowley*, 15.
4. Thomas Barker	Holme-on-Spalding Moor, Yorkshire	Hazen, "Yorkshire Origins," 136; Jewett, "Beginning of Rowley," 35.
5. Mr. William Bellingham (husband of Elizabeth Wiull)	manor of Brombye Wood, Lincolnshire; parish of Aisthorpe, Lincolnshire; married in Rowley, Yorkshire, May 29, 1634	Hazen, "Yorkshire Origins," 135; Townshend, "Bellingham Sketch," 381–382.
6. Matthew Boyes[*]	Leeds, Yorkshire (baptized 1611)	Banks, *Top. Dict.*, 187; Bartlett, "Genealogical Research," 385–386; cf. "Lane Family Papers," 106.
7. John Boynton (brother of William, below)	Knapton, Yorkshire; Holme-on-Spalding Moor, Yorkshire?	Banks, *Top. Dict.*, 187; cf. Hazen, "Yorkshire Origins," 139; no proof of latter location but notation in document in Holme parish chest.
8. William Boynton (brother of John, above)	Knapton, Yorkshire; Holme-on-Spalding Moor, Yorkshire?	Banks, *Top. Dict.*, 187; cf. Hazen, "Yorkshire Origins," 139; no proof of latter location but notation in document in Holme parish chest.
9. Edward Bridges*		
10. Sebastian Brigham[*]	Holme-on-Spalding Moor, Yorkshire (children baptized 1635, 1637)	Jewett, "Beginning of Rowley," 35; Holme parish register, Humberside R.O.
11. Jane Brockelbank [Brocklebank]	Rowley, Yorkshire	Banks, *Top. Dict.*, 188.
12. John Burbank		

Name	Place of Origin	Reference
13. Mr. Edward Carlton[*]	born Beeford, Yorkshire; Barmston and Hornsea, Yorkshire	Hazen, "Edward Carlton," 3–46; Hazen, "Ellen Newton," 3–18; Hazen, "Yorkshire Origins," 138.
14. Hugh Chaplin	Bradford, Yorkshire?; Hemingbrough, Yorkshire?	Savage, *Gen. Dict.*, I, 360–361; but cf. Hazen, "Yorkshire Origins," 138; no proof of latter location but notation in document in Holme parish chest.
15. Peter Cooper		
16. Constance Crosby	Holme-on-Spalding Moor, Yorkshire	Blodgette, comp., and Jewett, ed., *Early Settlers of Rowley*, 92; Crosby, *Simon Crosby*, 62–63; Prindle, "Crosby Sisters," 248.
17. Thomas Dickinson	Gildersome, Yorkshire?	"Lane Family Papers," 110.
18. John Dresser		
19. Thomas Elithorp	Holme-on-Spalding Moor, Yorkshire (children baptized 1633, 1634)	Hazen, "Yorkshire Origins," 136; Holme parish register, Humberside R.O.
20. Jane Grant (widow of Thomas Grant)	Cottingham, Yorkshire (married 1624; children baptized 1625, 1631, 1634, 1637)	Hazen, "Yorkshire Origins," 136–137; Cottingham parish register, Humberside R.O.
21. John Harris (son of Thomas of Charlestown; brother of Thomas and William, below, and Daniel; cousin of Ezekiel Rogers?)	father sailed with Winthrop Fleet, but origin unknown	Banks, *Planters of the Commonwealth*, 71; Blodgette, comp., and Jewett, ed., *Early Settlers of Rowley*, 137–138.
22. Thomas Harris* (son of Thomas of Charlestown; brother of John, above, William, below, and Daniel; cousin of Ezekiel Rogers?)	father sailed with Winthrop Fleet, but origin unknown	Banks, *Planters of the Commonwealth*, 71; Blodgette, comp., and Jewett, ed., *Early Settlers of Rowley*, 142n.
23. William Harris* (son of Thomas of Charlestown; brother of John and Thomas, above, and Daniel; cousin of Ezekiel Rogers?)	father sailed with Winthrop Fleet, but origin unknown	Banks, *Planters of the Commonwealth*, 71; Blodgette, comp., and Jewett, ed., *Early Settlers of Rowley*, 142n.
24. John Haseltine (brother of Robert, below)	Holme-on-Spalding Moor, Yorkshire	Blodgette, comp., and Jewett, ed., *Early Settlers of Rowley*, 142; Yorkshire Wills, vol. 30, p. 373 (1607), Borthwick Inst. Hist. Res.

Name	Place of Origin	Reference
25. Robert Haseltine (brother of John, above)	Holme-on-Spalding Moor, Yorkshire	Blodgette, comp., and Jewett, ed., *Early Settlers of Rowley*, 142; Yorkshire Wills, vol. 30, p. 373 (1607), Borthwick Inst. Hist. Res.
26. Michael Hopkinson		
27. Robert Hunter	Cottingham, Yorkshire?	Hazen, "Yorkshire Origins," 136–137.
28. William Jackson	Hunsley, Rowley parish, Yorkshire (Rowley churchwarden, 1622; child baptized, 1637)	*Ibid.*, 135; Rowley parish register, Bishop's Transcripts, Borthwick Inst. Hist. Res.
29. John Jarrat		
30. Joseph Jewett (brother of Maximilan, below)	Bradford, Yorkshire	Blodgette, comp., and Jewett, ed., *Early Settlers of Rowley*, 168n, 186; Moriarty, "Jewett," 185.
31. Maximilan Jewett (brother of Joseph, above)	Bradford, Yorkshire	Blodgette, comp., and Jewett, ed., *Early Settlers of Rowley*, 168n, 186; Moriarty, "Jewett," 185.
32. George Kilbourne	baptized Wood Ditton, Cambridgeshire; lived in Wethersfield, Essex?	Banks, *Planters of the Commonwealth*, 119; *Recs. of Rowley*, viii; Savage, *Gen. Dict.*, III, 19.
33. Francis Lambert	Holme-on-Spalding Moor, Yorkshire (married 1630; children baptized 1633, 1636)	Hazen, "Yorkshire Origins," 136; Jewett, "Beginning of Rowley," 35; Holme parish register, Humberside R.O.
34. Thomas Leaver		
35. Thomas Lilforth*		
36. Thomas Mighill		
37. Mr. John Miller*	attended Gonville and Caius College, Cambridge	Blodgette, comp., and Jewett, ed., *Early Settlers of Rowley*, 242.
38. Thomas Miller*		
39. Mr. Thomas Nelson	Cottingham, Yorkshire (1626); Rowley, Yorkshire (wife Dorothy buried Sept. 27, 1637)	Hazen, "Yorkshire Origins," 135; Wilbour, "First Wife of Thomas Nelson," 82; Rowley parish register, Bishop's Transcripts, Borthwick Inst. Hist. Res.
40. John Newmarch*		
41. Thomas Palmer	Holme-on-Spalding Moor, Yorkshire?	Yorkshire Wills, vol. 35, p. 492 (1619), vol. 37, p. 446 (1623), Borthwick Inst. Hist. Res.

Name	Place of Origin	Reference
42. Francis Parrat	Sutterton, Lincolnshire	Banks, *Top. Dict.*, 96.
43. John Remington*		
44. Humphrey Reyner	born Gildersome, Batley, Yorkshire; wife's land in Edgeton, Yorkshire; brother's land in Gildersome	Blodgette, comp., and Jewett, ed., *Early Settlers of Rowley*, 321; Coddington, "Rayner Family," 11; "Lane Family Papers," 105, 109, 237; Savage, *Gen. Dict.*, III, 513.
45. Mr. Ezekiel Rogers	born Wethersfield, Essex; Rowley, Yorkshire	Savage, *Gen. Dict.*, III, 559–560.
46. Mr. Henry Sandys*		
47. William Scales	Rowley, Yorkshire?	Scales, ed., "Descendants of William Scales," 42, but no proof.
48. Mrs. Margery Shove (mother of Rev. George Shove of Gatton, Surrey)		Banks, *Top Dict.*, 167 (Banks MSS); Pope, *Pioneers of Mass.*, 414.
49. Hugh Smith		
50. John Spofford	Rowley or Kirk Ella, Yorkshire?; Cherry Burton, Yorkshire?	Sunderland, "John Spofford," 174; no proof of latter location but notation in document in Holme parish chest.
51. Margaret Stanton		
52. William Stickney	Cottingham, Yorkshire (children baptized 1633, 1635, 1637)	Hazen, "Yorkshire Origins," 136–137; Cottingham parish register, Humberside R.O.
53. Thomas Sumner	Rowley, Yorkshire?	Lea, "Lost Registers of Rowley," 307n, 312n.
54. Richard Swan		
55. Thomas Tenny		
56. Richard Thorley*	probably Holme-on-Spalding Moor, Yorkshire (child baptized 1628)	DDHA 4/3 (2); Holme parish register, Humberside R.O.
57. John Trumble		
58. Richard Wickham		
59. William Wild*		

The names of the original landholders were compiled from Benjamin P. Mighill and George B. Blodgette, eds., *The Early Records of the Town of Rowley, Massachusetts*, I, *1639–1672* (Rowley, Mass., 1894), 1–6.

Almost a dozen other early landholders can be traced to origins in East Riding communities. These include: Richard Clark, John Pickard, and perhaps John Scales (Rowley); Thomas Crosby, John Johnson, John Palmer, and probably Richard Longhorne (Holme-on-Spalding Moor); Margaret Cross and Ezekiel Northend (Ripplingham, Rowley parish); possibly Edward and John Sawyer (Cottingham); Nicholas Jackson (Hunsley, Rowley parish); and Jeremiah Northend (Little Weeton, Rowley parish). It is possible that other settlers came originally from Holme or Rowley, but parish records from 1601 to 1628 are missing for Holme and none exist for Rowley.

PRINTED SOURCES FOR APPENDIX I

Charles Edward Banks, *The Planters of the Commonwealth: A Study of the Emigrants and Emigration in Colonial Times: To Which Are Added Lists of Passengers to Boston and to the Bay Colony, the Ships Which Brought Them; Their English Homes, and the Places of Their Settlement in Massachusetts, 1620–1640* (Boston, 1930); Banks, *Topographical Dictionary of 2885 English Emigrants to New England, 1620–1650*, ed. Elijah Ellsworth Brownell (Philadelphia, 1937), cited as Banks, *Top. Dict.*; Joseph Gardner Bartlett, "Genealogical Research in England," *New England Historical and Genealogical Register*, LXI (1907), 385–386; George Brainard Blodgette, comp., and Amos Everett Jewett, ed., *Early Settlers of Rowley, Massachusetts: A Genealogical Record of the Families Who Settled in Rowley before 1700 with Several Generations of Their Descendants* (Rowley, Mass., 1933); John Insley Coddington, "The Rayner Family of Batley, Co. York, England, and of New England," *NEHGR*, CIX (1955), 5–11; Eleanor Davis Crosby, *Simon Crosby the Emigrant: His English Ancestry, and Some of His American Descendants* (Boston, 1914); Tracy Elliot Hazen, "The Ancestry of Ellen Newton, Wife of Edward Carlton of Rowley, Mass.," *NEHGR*, XCIV (1940), 3–18; Hazen, "The English Ancestry of Edward Carlton of Rowley, Mass.," *NEHGR*, XCIII (1939), 3–46; Hazen, "New Light on the Yorkshire Origins of Rowley Founders," in *1639–1939: The Tercentenary Celebration of the Town of Rowley* (Rowley, Mass., 1942), 131–139; Amos Everett Jewett, "The Beginning of Rowley, Massachusetts," *ibid.*, 30–37; "Lane Family Papers," *NEHGR*, XI (1857), 102–112, 231–241; J. Henry Lea, "Transcripts of the Lost Registers of Rowley, Co. York, England," Essex Institute, *Historical Collections*, XLIV (1908), 305–312; Benjamin P. Mighill and George B. Blodgette, eds., *The Early Records of the Town of Rowley, Massachusetts*, I, *1639–1672* (Rowley, Mass., 1894), cited as *Recs. of Rowley*; G. Andrews Moriarty, "Gleanings from English Records—Jewett," *NEHGR*, CIII (1949), 185; Charles Henry Pope, *The Pioneers of Massachusetts, A Descriptive List, Drawn from Records of the Colonies, Towns and Churches, and Other Contemporaneous Documents* (Boston, 1900), 414; Paul W. Prindle, "The Yorkshire Ancestry of the Three Crosby Sisters of Rowley, Mass.," *NEHGR*, CXIX (1965), 243–248; James Savage, *A Genealogical Dictionary of the First Settlers of New England, Showing Three Generations of Those Who Came before May, 1692, on the Basis of Farmer's Register*, 4 vols. (Boston, 1860–1862), cited as Savage, *Gen. Dict.*; John Scales, ed., "Some Descendants of William Scales of Rowley, Mass., 1640," *NEHGR*, LXVI (1912), 42–54; Jeremiah Spofford, "A Family Record of the Descendants of John Spofford, and Elizabeth, His Wife, Who Came from England to America, and Settled at Rowley, in 1638," *NEHGR*, VIII (1854), 335–344; F. H. Sunderland, "Notes—Who Was the John Spofford Who Accompanied the Rev. Ezekiel Rogers in 1638?" *NEHGR*, XCIX (1945), 174; Charles Hervey Townshend, "Bellingham Sketch," *NEHGR*, XXXVI (1882), 381–386; Benjamin F. Wilbour, "Note on the First Wife and Parentage of Thomas Nelson of Rowley, Mass.," *NEHGR*, CXXVIII (1974), 82.

Appendix 2

English Origins of Pre-1640
Hingham, Massachusetts, Settlers

Name	Place of Origin	Reference
1. Bezowne Allen*	King's Lynn, Norfolk	"Cushing's Record," 27.
2. Joseph Andrews* (son of Thomas, below)	Devon	Lincoln, ed., *History of Hingham*, II, 10–11.
3. Thomas Andrews (father of Joseph, above)	Devon	*Ibid.*
4. William Arnold*	born Cheselbourne, Dorset, 1587	Drowne, "Arnold Family," 435; Savage, *Gen. Dict.*, I, 67.
5. Jonah Austin*	Tenterden or Staplehurst, Kent	French, "Austen," 165–166; Pope, *Pioneers of Mass.*, 24; Savage, *Gen. Dict.*, I, 81.
6. George Bachor [Bacon?]	sailed on *Increase*, from London, 1635	Banks, *Planters of the Commonwealth*, 148.
7. Nathaniel Baker (brother of Nicholas, below)		Savage, *Gen. Dict.*, I, 98.
8. Nicholas Baker* (brother of Nathaniel, above)	A.B., 1631–1632, A.M., 1635, St. John's College, Cambridge	*Ibid.*
9. Thomas Barns	Hingham, Norfolk (baptized 1617)?	*Ibid.*, 122; Hingham parish register, St. Andrew's parish, Hingham, Norfolk.
10. Clement Bates (father of Clement, below)	All Hallows, Lydd, Kent	Lincoln, ed., *History of Hingham*, II, 38; Pope, *Pioneers of Mass.*, 38.
11. Clement Bates (son of Clement, above)	All Hallows, Lydd, Kent?	Lincoln, ed., *History of Hingham*, II, 38.
12. Richard Baxter* (servant of Francis James, below)	Hingham, Norfolk	"Cushing's Record," 26.
13. John Beale, Sr. (husband of Nazareth Turner)	Hingham, Norfolk (married 1630; child baptized 1635)	"Cushing's Record," 26; Hingham parish register.
14. John Benson, Sr.*?	Gonsham or Caversham, Oxford; sailed on *Confidence*, from Southampton, 1638	Pope, *Pioneers of Mass.*, 46; Savage, *Gen. Dict.*, I, 168.
15. Richard Betsome*	Bridgeport, Dorset	Hale, ed., *Lechford Note-Book*, 289.

Name	Place of Origin	Reference
16. Benjamin Bosworth* (probably brother of Jonathan, below)	Coventry, Warwick	Pope, *Pioneers of Mass.*, 59; Savage, *Gen. Dict.*, I, 216.
17. Jonathan Bosworth* (probably brother of Benjamin, above)	Coventry, Warwick?	Savage, *Gen. Dict.*, I, 216.
18. James Buck	Hingham, Norfolk (child baptized 1615?)	"Cushing's Record," 26; Hingham parish register.
19. William Buckland*	Essex?	Banks, *Planters of the Commonwealth*, 68.
20. James Cade*	Northam, Dorset	Bartlett, "Cade or Cady," 61; Savage, *Gen. Dict.*, I, 327.
21. Thomas Chaffee*		Savage, *Gen. Dict.*, I, 352.
22. Henry Chamberlin [Sr.?], blacksmith*	Hingham, Norfolk (children baptized 1632, 1633, 1635)	"Cushing's Record," 26; Lincoln, ed., *History of Hingham*, II, 121; Hingham parish register.
23. Henry Chamberlin [Jr.?], shoemaker	Hingham, Norfolk (baptized 1635?)	Ward, "First Settlers," 251; Hingham parish register; Suffolk Co. Probate Recs., XII, 250.
24. Old Chapman?		Egan, ed., "Hobart Journal," 12; Pope, *Pioneers of Mass.*, 94.
25. Thomas Chubbuck	Hingham, Norfolk (child baptized 1632)	"Cushing's Record," 25; Hingham parish register.
26. Thomas Clap*	Venn Ottery, Devon	Pope, *Pioneers of Mass.*, 100–101.
27. Thomas Collier	Reading, Berkshire?	Adams and Watkins, "Reading," 60.
28. Anthony Cooper*	Hingham, Norfolk	"Cushing's Record," 25.
29. Josiah Cooper*	probably Hingham, Norfolk	Suffolk Co. Probate Recs., XII, 263.
30. Thomas Cooper*	Hingham, Norfolk (baptized 1607?; married 1634; children baptized 1634, 1637?)	"Cushing's Record," 26; Hingham parish register.
31. William Cotherill [Cockerill?]*	(daughter Martha Cackram born Hingham, Mass., 1638?)	Egan, ed., "Hobart Journal," 11; Savage, *Gen. Dict.*, I, 415.
32. William Cotherum [Cockram? Cockraine? Cockerum?] [*]	Southold, Suffolk (daughter Martha Cackram born Hingham, Mass., 1638?)	Adams, "Framingham," 198; Egan, ed., "Hobart Journal," 11; Lincoln, ed., *History of Hingham*, II, 134; Pope, *Pioneers of Mass.*, 106–107; Savage, *Gen. Dict.*, I, 415.

Name	Place of Origin	Reference
33. Matthew Cushing (husband of Nazarethe Pitcher; brother of Theophilus, below?)	Hingham, Norfolk (married 1613; children baptized 1619, 1621, 1623, 1625)	"Cushing's Record," 26; Hingham parish register.
34. Theophilus Cushing (brother of Matthew, above?)	Hingham, Norfolk	"Cushing's Record," 25; Pope, *Pioneers of Mass.*, 126.
35. John Cutter [Cutler?]*	Sprowston, Norfolk	"Cushing's Record," 27.
36. Thomas Dimock*	Chesterblade, Somerset	Banks, *Top. Dict.*, 140 (Banks MSS); Savage, *Gen. Dict.*, II, 51.
37. Vincent Druce*		Savage, *Gen. Dict.*, II, 74.
38. Anthony Eames*	Fordington, Dorset	Banks, *Top. Dict.*, 33; Savage, *Gen. Dict.*, II, 89.
39. Thomas Ensign*	Cranbrook, Kent? (daughter, Hannah, baptized in Hingham, Mass.)	Egan, ed., "Hobart Journal," 13; Hall, "Miscellaneous Notes," 87; Savage, *Gen. Dict.*, II, 125.
40. John Farrow	Hingham, Norfolk	"Cushing's Record," 26.
41. John Fearing (servant of Matthew Hawke, below)	Cambridgeshire	*Ibid.*, 27.
42. Adam Foulsham [Folsom] [*] (younger brother of John, below)	Hingham, Norfolk (baptized 1621?; or children baptized 1621, 1623?)	*Ibid.*; Davis, *Able Lunt*, 146; Folsom and Chapman, "Folsom Family," 207; Savage, *Gen. Dict.*, II, 178; Hingham parish register.
43. John Foulsham [Folsom]* (husband of Mary Gilman; older brother of Adam, above)	Hingham, Norfolk (married 1636)	"Cushing's Record," 26; Davis, *Able Lunt*, 145; Folsom and Chapman, "Folsom Family," 207, 212; Hingham parish register.
44. Daniel Fox*?		Pope, *Pioneers of Mass.*, 174; Ward, "First Settlers," 251.
45. Stephen Gates* (husband of Ann Veare)	Norwich, Norfolk?; Hingham, Norfolk (married 1628)	"Cushing's Record," 26; Fuller, "Gates Family," 401; Hingham parish register.
46. Henry Gibbs (servant of Edmund Hobart, Sr., below)	Hingham, Norfolk	"Cushing's Record," 25.
47. Thomas Gill		Savage, *Gen. Dict.*, II, 254.
48. Edward Gilman* (husband of Mary Clark)	born Caston [Coston?], Norfolk, 1587; Hingham, Norfolk (married 1614; children baptized? 1615, 1617, 1626, 1630, 1633, 1634)	Davis, *Able Lunt*, 151–160; Hingham parish register.

Name	Place of Origin	Reference
49. Jarvice Gould* (servant of Clement Bates, Sr., above)	Kent? sailed on *Elizabeth*, from London, 1635	Savage, *Gen. Dict.*, II, 285.
50. Thomas Hammond*	Lavenham, Suffolk (baptized 1587)	Battell, "Benjamin Hammond," 28; Bond, *Watertown Genealogies*, I, 269–270; Lincoln, ed., *History of Hingham*, II, 286.
51. Matthew Hawke	Cambridgeshire	"Cushing's Record," 27; Lincoln, ed., *History of Hingham*, II, 294.
52. William Hersye [Hersey]		Savage, *Gen. Dict.*, II, 406–407.
53. Thomas Hill		Ward, "First Settlers," 251.
54. Anthony Hilliard*		Lincoln, ed., *History of Hingham*, II, 331–332.
55. Edmund Hobart, Sr. (husband of Margaret Dowe; father of Joshua, Peter, Thomas, and Edmund, Jr., below)	Hingham, Norfolk (born ca. 1570; married 1600)	"Cushing's Record," 25; Lincoln, ed., *History of Hingham*, II, 334; Hingham parish register.
56. Edmund Hobart, Jr. (husband of Elizabeth Elmer; son of Edmund, Sr., above; brother of Joshua, Peter, and Thomas, below)	Wymondham, Norfolk; Hingham, Norfolk (baptized 1603; married 1632)	"Cushing's Record," 25; Lincoln, ed., *History of Hingham*, II, 334; Hingham parish register.
57. Joshua Hobart (son of Edmund, Sr., above; brother of Edmund, Jr., above, Peter and Thomas, below)	Hingham, Norfolk (baptized 1614)	"Cushing's Record," 25; Lincoln, ed., *History of Hingham*, II, 336; Hingham parish register.
58. Mr. Peter Hobart (son of Edmund, Sr., above; brother of Edmund, Jr., Joshua, above, and Thomas, below)	Hingham, Norfolk (baptized 1604); Haverhill, Suffolk; Magdalen College, Cambridge, 1625	"Cushing's Record," 25; Weis, *Colonial Clergy*, 108; Hingham parish register.
59. Thomas Hobart (son of Edmund, Sr., above; brother of Edmund, Jr., Joshua, and Peter, above)	Wymondham, Norfolk; Hingham, Norfolk (baptized 1606)	"Cushing's Record," 25; Lincoln, ed., *History of Hingham*, II, 336; Hingham parish register.
60. Nicholas Hodsdin [Hodges?]*		Savage, *Gen. Dict.*, II, 440; Pope, *Pioneers of Mass.*, 234.
61. Thomas Huet [Hewett] (brother of Rev. Ephraim Huet of Wraxall, Warwick)	Stockenham, Lincolnshire?	Banks, *Top. Dict.*, 97; Savage, *Gen. Dict.*, II, 490–491.

Name	Place of Origin	Reference
62. Joseph Hull*	Crewkerne, Somerset?; Weymouth, Dorset	Banks, *Top. Dict.*, 141; Lincoln, ed., *History of Hingham*, II, 360; Pope, *Pioneers of Mass.*, 247.
63. Richard Ibrook	Hingham, Norfolk	Banks, *Top. Dict.*, 118; Savage, *Gen. Dict.*, II, 516.
64. Nicholas Jacob (cousin of Thomas Lincoln, weaver, below)	Hingham, Norfolk	"Cushing's Record," 25.
65. Francis James (probably brother of Philip, below)	Hingham, Norfolk	*Ibid.*, 26; Lincoln, ed., *History of Hingham*, II, 379.
66. Philip James (probably brother of Francis, above)	Hingham, Norfolk (child baptized 1635)	"Cushing's Record," 26; Lincoln, ed., *History of Hingham*, II, 379.
67. Thomas Johnson*	sailed on *Hopewell*, from London, 1635?	Savage, *Gen. Dict.*, II, 557–558.
68. Robert Jones	Reading, Berkshire?	Banks, *Top. Dict.*, 135; Lincoln, ed., *History of Hingham*, II, 386–387.
69. Thomas Jones*	Elsing, Norfolk; Caversham, Oxford?; sailed on *Confidence*, from Southampton, 1638?	Adams and Watkins, "Reading," 60; Crandall and Coffman, "From Emigrants to Rulers," 127; Lincoln, ed., *History of Hingham*, II, 386–387; Savage, *Gen. Dict.*, II, 566.
70. Thomas Josselyn*	Roxwell, Essex?; Barham, Suffolk; sailed on *Increase*, from London, 1635	Banks, *Top. Dict.*, 51, 149; Lincoln, ed., *History of Hingham*, II, 395.
71. George Knights	Barrow, Suffolk	"Cushing's Record," 26; Savage, *Gen. Dict.*, III, 36.
72. Andrew Lane (son of William of Dorchester; brother of George, below)		Savage, *Gen. Dict.*, III, 50–51, 53.
73. George Lane (son of William of Dorchester; brother of Andrew, above)		*Ibid.*, 52.
74. Richard Langer		*Ibid.*, 55.
75. Thomas Lawrence		Lincoln, ed., *History of Hingham*, II, 426; Savage, *Gen. Dict.*, III, 63.
76. William Layre [Large? Longe?]*	Hingham, Norfolk? (William Longe married 1606?; children baptized? 1612, 1614, 1617, 1619, 1622, 1625, 1629, 1635)	"Cushing's Record," 25; Savage, *Gen. Dict.*, III, 56; Hingham parish register.

Name	Place of Origin	Reference
77. John Leavitt		Lincoln, ed., *History of Hingham*, II, 428; Savage, *Gen. Dict.*, III, 69–70.
78. [Thomas] Liford [Linford] (wife Ann died in Hingham, Mass.)	Yarmouth, Norfolk?	Egan, ed., "Hobart Journal," 11; Pope, *Pioneers of Mass.*, 287; Savage, *Gen. Dict.*, III, 90.
79. Samuel Lincoln	Hingham, Norfolk (baptized 1622)	"Cushing's Record," 26; Lincoln, ed., *History of Hingham*, II, 459; Hingham parish register.
80. Stephen Lincoln (brother of Thomas, husbandman, below)	Wymondham, Norfolk	"Cushing's Record," 27; Lincoln, ed., *History of Hingham*, II, 476.
81. Thomas Lincoln, cooper		Lincoln, ed., *History of Hingham*, III, 3.
82. Thomas Lincoln, husbandman (brother of Stephen, above)	Wymondham, Norfolk	"Cushing's Record," 27; Lincoln, ed., *History of Hingham*, III, 15–16; Pope, *Pioneers of Mass.*, 286.
83. Thomas Lincoln, miller*		Lincoln, ed., *History of Hingham*, III, 20.
84. Thomas Lincoln, weaver (cousin of Nicholas Jacob, above)	Hingham, Norfolk	"Cushing's Record," 25; Lincoln, ed., *History of Hingham*, III, 21.
85. Nicholas Lobdin* [Lobden]		Lincoln, ed., *History of Hingham*, III, 24; Savage, *Gen. Dict.*, III, 102.
86. John Lord*		Savage, *Gen. Dict.*, III, 115.
87. Thomas Loring*	Axminster, Devon?	*Ibid.*, 118–119.
88. Aaron Ludkin* (son of George, below)	Norwich, Norfolk; Hingham, Norfolk (baptized 1618)	*Ibid.*, 128–129; Hingham parish register.
89. George Ludkin* (father of Aaron, above; probably brother of William, below)	Norwich, Norfolk; Hingham, Norfolk (children baptized 1618, 1621)	"Cushing's Record," 25; Savage, *Gen. Dict.*, III, 129; Hingham parish register.
90. William Ludkin (probably brother of George, above)	Norwich, Norfolk	"Cushing's Record," 25; Millican, ed., *Freemen of Norwich*, 232; Savage, *Gen. Dict.*, III, 129.
91. George Marsh	Hingham, Norfolk?; Ipswich, Suffolk? (both doubtful)	Banks, *Top. Dict.*, 156 (Banks MSS); Lincoln, ed., *History of Hingham*, III, 56; Savage, *Gen. Dict.*, III, 154.
92. Abraham Martin* (died 1643)		Savage, *Gen. Dict.*, III, 161.

Name	Place of Origin	Reference
93. Widow Martin		Ward, "First Settlers," 250.
94. John Merrick [Morrick]		Lincoln, ed., *History of Hingham*, III, 70; Savage, *Gen. Dict.*, III, 198.
95. Thomas Minard [Mayer]*	Hapton (or Happen) Hall or Hempnall (Hemenhall), Norfolk	"Cushing's Record," 27; Lincoln, ed., *History of Hingham*, III, 71; Whitney, ed., *Cushing's Minutes*, 10–11.
96. Edward Mitchell* (servant of Philip James, above)	Hingham, Norfolk	"Cushing's Record," 26; Savage, *Gen. Dict.*, III, 219.
97. Jeremiah Moore*	Wymondham, Norfolk	"Cushing's Record," 27; Savage, *Gen. Dict.*, III, 228.
98. John Morfield* (servant of James Buck, above)	Hingham, Norfolk	"Cushing's Record," 26; Savage, *Gen. Dict.*, III, 231.
99. Adam Mott*	Cambridge, Cambridgeshire	Savage, *Gen. Dict.*, III, 247.
100. Thomas Nichols	Coggeshall, Essex	Pope, *Pioneers of Mass.*, 329.
101. William Norton [Notter? Knowlton?]		Egan, ed., "Hobart Journal," 11; Pope, *Pioneers of Mass.*, 332.
102. Richard Osborne*		Savage, *Gen. Dict.*, III, 318.
103. John Otis*	Glastonbury, Somerset	*Ibid.*, 323; Waters, *Otis Family*, 5–6.
104. Samuel Packer [Packard]*	Wymondham, Norfolk	"Cushing's Record," 27; Savage, *Gen. Dict.*, III, 327.
105. John Palmer* (husband of Mary Fit? [doubtful])	Hingham, Norfolk? (married 1609?); sailed on *Elizabeth*, from Ipswich, 1634?	Pope, *Pioneers of Mass.*, 341–342; Savage, *Gen. Dict.*, III, 341; Hingham parish register.
106. Stephen Payne*	Great Ellingham, Norfolk	"Cushing's Record," 26; Savage, *Gen. Dict.*, III, 335.
107. Thomas Paynter*		Savage, *Gen. Dict.*, III, 338.
108. Mr. Joseph Peck* (son of Robert, brother of Nathaniel, below)	Hingham, Norfolk (baptized 1610?; child buried 1636)	"Cushing's Record," 26; Savage, *Gen. Dict.*, III, 381–382; Hingham parish register.
109. Nathaniel Peck* (son of Robert, below, brother of Joseph, above)	Hingham, Norfolk (baptized 1614)	Pope, *Pioneers of Mass.*, 351; Savage, *Gen. Dict.*, III, 382; Hingham parish register.
110. Robert Peck[*] (father of Joseph and Nathaniel, above)	born Beccles, Suffolk, 1580; rector, Hingham, Norfolk, 1605–1638	"Cushing's Record," 26; Weis, *Colonial Clergy*, 161.
111. David Phippen* (father of Joseph, below)	Weymouth or Melcombe Regis, Dorset?	Savage, *Gen. Dict.*, III, 418.

Name	Place of Origin	Reference
112. Joseph Phippen* (son of David, above)	Weymouth or Melcombe Regis, Dorset?	*Ibid.*, 419.
113. Edmund Pitts (brother of Leonard, below)	Hingham, Norfolk (married 1619; children baptized? 1620, 1635, 1637)	"Cushing's Record," 27; Hingham parish register.
114. Leonard Pitts* (brother of Edmund, above)	Hingham, Norfolk	"Cushing's Record," 27; Pope, *Pioneers of Mass.*, 363.
115. William Pitts* (servant of Philip James, above)	Hingham, Norfolk	"Cushing's Record," 26; Savage, *Gen. Dict.*, III, 443.
116. John Porter*	Dorset	Lincoln, ed., *History of Hingham*, III, 115; Savage, *Gen. Dict.*, III, 461.
117. John Prince*	East Shefford, Berkshire	Savage, *Gen. Dict.*, III, 487.
118. Frances (Pitcher) Ricroft (husband John died 1634)	Hingham, Norfolk (married 1624)	"Cushing's Record," 26; Pope, *Pioneers of Mass.*, 478; Hingham parish register.
119. William Ripley	Hingham, Norfolk	"Cushing's Record," 27; Savage, *Gen. Dict.*, III, 543; but note Wymondham Survey, E315/360, P.R.O.
120. George Russell	Hawkhurst, Kent; sailed on *Elizabeth*, from London, 1635	Savage, *Gen. Dict.*, III, 590.
121. Henry Rust*		*Ibid.*, 595.
122. Richard Sanger		Ward, "First Settlers," 250.
123. Elizabeth Sayer	Hingham, Norfolk	"Cushing's Record," 26.
124. Mary Sayer	Hingham, Norfolk	*Ibid.*
125. Ephraim Searle* (son baptized Hingham, Mass., 1638)		Egan, ed., "Hobart Journal," 10.
126. Thomas Shaw*		Savage, *Gen. Dict.*, IV, 65–66.
127. Robert Skouling* (related to Francis Schuldeham, gentleman, of Hingham, Norfolk?)	Hingham, Norfolk	"Cushing's Record," 26.
128. John Smart*	Norfolk	*Ibid.*, 27; Savage, *Gen. Dict.*, IV, 108.
129. Francis Smith*		Lincoln, ed., *History of Hingham*, III, 152.
130. Mr. Henry Smith*	Hapton (or Happen) Hall or Hempnall (Hemenhall) Norfolk	"Cushing's Record," 27; Lincoln, ed., *History of Hingham*, III, 152–153.
131. Ralph Smith*		Lincoln, ed., *History of Hingham*, III, 152.

Name	Place of Origin	Reference
132. Ralph Smith	Hingham, Norfolk	"Cushing's Record," 25; Lincoln, ed., *History of Hingham*, III, 152.
133. William Sprague (brother of Ralph and Richard of Charlestown)	Upway, Devon?; Fordington, Dorset?	Banks, *Top. Dict.*, 33; Pope, *Pioneers of Mass.*, 429; Savage, *Gen. Dict.*, IV, 154, 156.
134. John Stevens		Ward, "First Settlers," 250.
135. John Stodder		Lincoln, ed., *History of Hingham*, III, 191.
136. George Strange*	Littleham, Devon; wife's lands in Northam, Devon	Banks, *Top. Dict.*, 24 (Banks MSS); Lincoln, ed., *History of Hingham*, III, 224; Pope, *Pioneers of Mass.*, 438.
137. John Strong*	Taunton, Somerset?	Lincoln, ed., *History of Hingham*, III, 225; Savage, *Gen. Dict.*, IV, 225–226; Strong, "John Strong," 294 (no proof, however)
138. Thomas Sucklin* (servant of Francis James, above)	Hingham, Norfolk	"Cushing's Record," 26.
139. John Sutton, Sr.*	Attleborough, Norfolk	*Ibid.*
140. John Thaxter (son of Thomas, below)	Brigham, Norfolk	Pope, *Pioneers of Mass.*, 450; Savage, *Gen. Dict.*, IV, 274–275.
141. Thomas Thaxter (father of John, above)	Brigham, Norfolk; Hingham, Norfolk? (child baptized 1623)	Pope, *Pioneers of Mass.*, 450; Savage, *Gen. Dict.*, IV, 274–275; Hingham parish register.
142. John Tower	Hingham, Norfolk (baptized 1609)	"Cushing's Record," 26; Lincoln, ed., *History of Hingham*, III, 251–252; Hingham parish register.
143. John Tucker		Savage, *Gen. Dict.*, IV, 338.
144. John Tufts*?	Hingham, Norfolk	"Cushing's Record," 26.
145. Thomas Turner* (son of Humphrey of Scituate, Mass.)	sailed on *Hopewell*, from London, 1635	Savage, *Gen. Dict.*, IV, 348.
146. Henry Tuttle	Norfolk	"Cushing's Record," 27.
147. Joseph Underwood* (brother of Thomas, below)		Savage, *Gen. Dict.*, IV, 359.
148. Thomas Underwood* (brother of Joseph, above)		*Ibid.*
149. Thomas Wakely		*Ibid.*, 387.

Name	Place of Origin	Reference
150. William Walker	sailed on *Elizabeth*, from London, 1635?	Ward, "First Settlers," 251.
151. William Walton*	Seaton, Devon? Emmanuel College, Cambridge?	Pope, *Pioneers of Mass.*, 477; Savage, *Gen. Dict.*, IV, 404–405.
152. Samuel Ward*		Savage, *Gen. Dict.*, IV, 412–413.
153. Edward Wilder (son of Widow Wilder, below?)	Shiplake, Berkshire?; Shiplock, Oxfordshire?	*Ibid.*, 549.
154. Widow Martha Wilder (mother of Edward, above?)	Shiplake, Berkshire?; Shiplock, Oxfordshire?	Adams and Watkins, "Reading," 60; Pope, *Pioneers of Mass.*, 497; Savage, *Gen. Dict.*, IV, 549.
155. John Winchester*	sailed on *Elizabeth*, from London, 1635	Pope, *Pioneers of Mass.*, 505; Savage, *Gen. Dict.*, IV, 592.
156. Ralph Woodward	Dublin, Ireland	Pope, *Pioneers of Mass.*, 514; Savage, *Gen. Dict.*, IV, 646.
157. Isaac Wright	Norfolk (baptized Hingham, 1629?); came with his wife and Henry Tuttle	"Cushing's Record," 27; Savage, *Gen. Dict.*, IV, 656; Hingham parish register.

This listing of settlers was compiled from "Daniel Cushing's Record," *New England Historical and Genealogical Register*, XV (1861), 25–27; Andrew H. Ward, "First Settlers of Hingham," *NEHGR*, II (1848), 250–251; George Lincoln, ed., *History of the Town of Hingham, Massachusetts*, 3 vols. in 4 (Hingham, Mass., 1893), II and III; Solomon Lincoln, Jr., *History of the Town of Hingham, Plymouth County, Massachusetts* (Hingham, Mass., 1827), 40–49.

PRINTED SOURCES FOR APPENDIX 2

Oscar Fay Adams, "Our English Parent Towns—Framingham," *New England Historical and Genealogical Register*, LVII (1903), 193–198; Adams, with notes by Walter Kendall Watkins, "Our English Parent Towns—Reading," *NEHGR*, LX (1906), 57–61; Charles Edward Banks, *The Planters of the Commonwealth: A Study of the Emigrants and Emigration in Colonial Times: To Which Are Added Lists of Passengers to Boston and to the Bay Colony, the Ships Which Brought Them; Their English Homes, and the Places of Their Settlement in Massachusetts, 1620–1640* (Boston, 1930); Banks, *Topographical Dictionary of 2885 English Emigrants to New England, 1620–1650*, ed. Elijah Ellsworth Brownell (Philadelphia, 1937), cited as Banks, *Top. Dict.*; J. Gardner Bartlett, "Genealogical Research in England—Cade or Cady," *NEHGR*, LXVIII (1914), 61; Philip Battell, "Descendants of Benjamin Hammond," *NEHGR*, XXX (1876), 28–32; Henry Bond, *Family Memorials: Genealogies of the Families and Descendants of the Early Settlers of Watertown, Massachusetts, including Waltham and Weston; to Which is Appended the Early History of the Town* (Boston, 1855), cited as Bond, *Watertown Genealogies*; Louis C. Cornish, *The Settlement of Hingham, Massachusetts* (Boston, 1911); Ralph J. Crandall and Ralph J. Coffman, "From Emigrants to Rulers: The Charlestown Oligarchy in the Great Migration," *NEHGR*, CXXXI (1977), 3–27, 121–132, 207–213; "Daniel Cushing's Record," *NEHGR*, XV (1861), 25–27; Walter Goodwin Davis, *The Ancestry of Abel Lunt, 1769–1806, of Newbury, Massachusetts* (Portland, Me., 1963); Henry T. Drowne, "Mr. Somerby's Genealogy of the Arnold Family," *NEHGR*, XXXIII (1879), 432–438; C. Edward Egan, ed., "The Hobart Journal," *NEHGR*, CXXI (1967), 3–25, 102–127, 191–216, 269–294; Nathaniel S. Folsom and Jacob Chapman, "The Folsom Family," *NEHGR*, XXX

(1876), 207–231; Elizabeth French, "Genealogical Research in England—Austen," *NEHGR*, LXVII (1913), 161–166; Benjamin A. G. Fuller, "The Gates Family," *NEHGR*, XXXI (1877), 401–402; Edward Everett Hale, Jr., ed., *Note-Book Kept by Thomas Lechford, Esq., Lawyer, in Boston, Massachusetts Bay, from June 27, 1638, to July 29, 1641* (American Antiquarian Society, *Transactions and Collections*, VII [Cambridge, Mass., 1885]), cited as Hale, ed., *Lechford Note-Book;* Virginia Hall, "Miscellaneous Notes," *NEHGR*, LXVI (1912), 87–88; George Lincoln, ed., *History of the Town of Hingham, Massachusetts*, 3 vols. in 4 (Hingham, Mass., 1893), cited as Lincoln, ed., *History of Hingham;* Solomon Lincoln, Jr., *History of the Town of Hingham, Plymouth County, Massachusetts* (Hingham, Mass., 1827), 40–49; Percy Millican, ed., *The Register of the Freemen of Norwich, 1548–1713: A Transcript, with an Introduction, an Appendix to Those Freemen Whose Apprenticeship Indentures Are Enrolled in the City Records, and Indexes of Names and Places* (Norwich, Eng., 1934); Charles Henry Pope, *The Pioneers of Massachusetts, A Descriptive List, Drawn from Records of the Colonies, Towns and Churches, and Other Contemporaneous Documents* (Boston, 1900); James Savage, *A Genealogical Dictionary of the First Settlers of New England, Showing Three Generations of Those Who Came before May, 1692, on the Basis of Farmer's Register*, 4 vols. (Boston, 1860–1862), cited as Savage, *Gen. Dict.;* Caleb Strong, compiler, and Edward Strong, contributor, "Elder John Strong and His Descendants," *NEHGR*, XXIII (1869), 294–296; Andrew H. Ward, "First Settlers of Hingham," *NEHGR*, II (1848), 250–255; John J. Waters, Jr., *The Otis Family in Provincial and Revolutionary Massachusetts* (Chapel Hill, N.C., 1968); Frederick Lewis Weis, *The Colonial Clergy and Colonial Churches of New England* (Lancaster, Mass., 1936); William Arthur Whitcomb, contributor, and Howard Oaken French, compiler, "Sutton Family," *NEHGR*, XCI (1937), 61–68; Henry Austin Whitney, ed., *Extracts from the Minutes of Daniel Cushing, of Hingham, with a Photograph of His Manuscript, Entitled, A List of the Names of Such Persons as Came out of the Town of Hingham, and Towns Adjacent, in the County of Norfolk, in the Kingdom of England, into New England, and Settled in Hingham, in New England* (Boston, 1865), cited as Whitney, ed., *Cushing's Minutes*.

Appendix 3

English Origins of the Ninety-One Original Proprietors of Newbury, Massachusetts, December 7, 1642

Name	Place of Origin	Reference
1. Walter Allen*		
2. Giles Badger (brother of Nathaniel and Richard, below)	Westbury on Severn, Gloucester?	Banks, *Top. Dict.*, 58.
3. Nathaniel Badger (brother of Giles, above, and Richard, below)	Westbury on Severn, Gloucester?	Savage, *Gen. Dict.*, I, 93.
4. Richard Badger (brother of Giles and Nathaniel, above)	Westbury on Severn, Gloucester?	*Ibid.*
5. Christopher Bartlet[t] (brother of John, below)	Wiltshire-Hampshire?	Brown, "Bartlett Family," 192–204; Pope, *Pioneers of Mass.*, 36.
6. John Bartlet[t] (brother of Christopher, above)	Wiltshire-Hampshire? (sailed on *Mary and John* with Parker group, from Southampton, Mar. 1634)	Banks, *Planters of the Commonwealth*, 112; Brown, "Bartlett Family," 192–204; Pope, *Pioneers of Mass.*, 36.
7. Richard Bartlet[t] (father of John and Christopher, above)	Wiltshire-Hampshire?	Brown, "Bartlett Family," 192–204; Pope, *Pioneers of Mass.*, 36.
8. Nicholas Batt	Devizes, Wiltshire	Banks, *Planters of the Commonwealth*, 137; Drake, "Founders of New England," 333; Pope, *Pioneers of Mass.*, 39; Savage, *Gen. Dict.*, I, 140.
9. William Berry		
10. Thomas Blumfield		
11. John Bond*		
12. George Browne (related to Richard, below?)	Wiltshire-Hampshire? (sailed on *Mary and John* with Parker group, from Southampton, Mar. 1634)	Banks, *Planters of the Commonwealth*, 112.
13. Mr. James Browne	Southampton, Hampshire	Coffin, *History of Newbury*, 297; Drake, "Founders of New England," 333.
14. Richard Browne (related to George, above?)	Wiltshire-Hampshire? (sailed on *Mary and John* with Parker group, from Southampton, Mar. 1634)	Banks, *Planters of the Commonwealth*, 112.

Name	Place of Origin	Reference
15. Thomas Browne	Christian Malford, Wiltshire	*Ibid.*, 136; Coffin, *History of Newbury*, 295; Pope, *Pioneers of Mass.*, 74–75.
16. Joseph Carter[*]	London?	Hale, "Thomas Hale," 373; Pope, *Pioneers of Mass.*, 89.
17. John Cheney	Waltham Abbey, Essex?	Banks, *Top. Dict.*, 53 (Banks MSS).
18. Mr. John Clark*	London	Pope, *Pioneers of Mass.*, 102.
19. Robert Coker	Wiltshire-Hampshire? (sailed on *Mary and John* with Parker group, from Southampton, Mar. 1634)	Banks, *Planters of the Commonwealth*, 112.
20. Thomas Coleman*	Marlborough, Wiltshire	*Ibid.*, 136. Coffin, "Coleman Family," 347; Coffin, *History of Newbury*, 298; Drake, "Founders of New England," 333.
21. Thomas Cromwell*		
22. Mr. John Cutting*	London?	Banks, *Top. Dict.*, 104.
23. Thomas Davis*	Marlborough, Wiltshire	Banks, *Planters of the Commonwealth*, 137; Coffin, *History of Newbury*, 300; Drake, "Founders of New England," 333; Pope, *Pioneers of Mass.*, 133.
24. Thomas Dow*		
25. Mr. Richard Dummer (brother of Stephen, below)	born Bishopstoke, Hampshire; South Stoneham, Hampshire?	Banks, *Planters of the Commonwealth*, 200; Banks, *Top. Dict.*, 63 (Banks MSS); Coffin, *History of Newbury*, 301; Savage, *Gen. Dict.*, II, 79; P.R.O. Transcripts 120/7, Hampshire R.O.
26. Mr. Stephen Dummer[*] (brother of Richard, above)	Bishopstoke, Hampshire	Banks, *Planters of the Commonwealth*, 200; Pope, *Pioneers of Mass.*, 146; P.R.O. Transcripts 120/7, Hampshire R.O.
27. John Emery	Romsey, Hampshire	Banks, *Planters of the Commonwealth*, 138; Drake, "Founders of New England," 333; Pope, *Pioneers of Mass.*, 156.
28. Richard Fitts		
29. William Franklin*	Wiltshire-Hampshire? (sailed on *Mary and John* with Parker group, from Southampton, Mar. 1634)	Banks, *Planters of the Commonwealth*, 111.

Name	Place of Origin	Reference
30. John Fry*	Basingstoke, Hampshire	*Ibid.*, 199; Drake, "Founders of New England," 336; "Pedigree of Frye," 226.
31. Samuel Gile*		
32. John Goff		
33. Mr. Edmund Greenleaf*	Ipswich, Suffolk?; Brixham, Devon	Appleton, "Greenleaf Ancestry," 299–300; Banks, *Top. Dict.*, 155; Willis, *History of the Law of Maine*, 522.
34. Thomas Hale	Watton at Stone, Hertfordshire	Greenlaw, "Hale," 186; Hale, "Thomas Hale," 370.
35. Nicholas Holt*	Romsey, Hampshire	Banks, *Planters of the Commonwealth*, 138; Coffin, *History of Newbury*, 305; Drake, "Founders of New England," 333; Pope, *Pioneers of Mass.*, 455.
36. Abel Huse		
37. John Hutchins*		
38. William Ilsley	Nether Wallop, Hampshire	Banks, *Planters of the Commonwealth*, 198; Banks, *Top. Dict.*, 63.
39. John Kelly	Newbury, Berkshire	Coffin, *History of Newbury*, 306.
40. Richard Kent, Jr.	Upper Wallop, Hampshire (child baptized 1632?); Nether Wallop, Hampshire	Banks, *Planters of the Commonwealth*, 111; Banks, *Top. Dict.*, 63 (Banks MSS); Nether Wallop parish register, Parish Recs., vol. 1, Hampshire R.O.
41. Stephen Kent* (brother of Richard, Sr.)	Nether Wallop or West Tytherley, Hampshire	Banks, *Planters of the Commonwealth*, 197; Banks, *Top. Dict.*, 63.
42. John Knight (brother of Richard, below)	Romsey, Hampshire	Banks, *Planters of the Commonwealth*, 138; Coffin, *History of Newbury*, 307; Drake, "Founders of New England," 333; Pope, *Pioneers of Mass.*, 273; Savage, *Gen. Dict.*, III, 36.
43. Richard Knight (brother of John, above)	Romsey, Hampshire	Banks, *Planters of the Commonwealth*, 138; Coffin, *History of Newbury*, 307; Drake, "Founders of New England," 333; Savage, *Gen. Dict.*, III, 38.
44. Richard Littlehale*	Wiltshire-Hampshire? (sailed on *Mary and John* with Parker group, from Southampton, Mar. 1634)	Banks, *Planters of the Commonwealth*, 112.

Name	Place of Origin	Reference
45. Mr. John Lowle [Lowell] (son of Percival, below)	Portbury, Somerset?	Lowell, *Lowells of America*, 7.
46. Mr. Percival Lowle [Lowell] (father of John, above)	Portbury, Somerset	Banks, *Top. Dict.*, 144 (Harleian MSS, 1559).
47. Henry Lunt	Wiltshire-Hampshire? (sailed on *Mary and John* with Parker group, from Southampton, Mar. 1634)	Banks, *Planters of the Commonwealth*, 111.
48. John Merrill	Wherstead, Suffolk	Banks, *Top. Dict.*, 164.
49. Mr. [John] Miller*		
50. William Moody	King's Samborne, Hampshire; sailed on *Mary and John* with Parker group, from Southampton, Mar. 1634	Banks, *Planters of the Commonwealth*, 110; Banks, *Top. Dict.*, 60 (Banks MSS).
51. William Mors[e] (brother of Anthony Morss, below)	Marlborough, Wiltshire	Banks, *Planters of the Commonwealth*, 136; Coffin, *History of Newbury*, 311; Savage, *Gen. Dict.*, III, 242.
52. Anthony Morss [Morse] (brother of William Morse, above)	Marlborough, Wiltshire (children baptized at St. Peter's 1626, St. Mary's 1628)	Coffin, *History of Newbury*, 311; Pope, *Pioneers of Mass.*, 320.
53. John Musselwhite	Landford, Wiltshire	Banks, *Planters of the Commonwealth*, 138; Bartlett, ed., "Whittier," 254; Coffin, *History of Newbury*, 311; Drake, "Founders of New England," 333; Savage, *Gen. Dict.*, III, 258.
54. Mr. James Noyes (brother of Nicholas, below; cousin of Thomas Parker, below)	born Cholderton, Wiltshire, 1608	Banks, *Planters of the Commonwealth*, 112; Coffin, *History of Newbury*, 312; Noyes, "Noyes Pedigree," 36.
55. Nicholas Noyes (brother of James, above; cousin of Thomas Parker, below)	Cholderton, Wiltshire	Banks, *Planters of the Commonwealth*, 112; Noyes, "Noyes Pedigree," 36.
56. Mrs. [John] Oliver	Bristol, Gloucester	Banks, *Top. Dict.*, 55–56; Coffin, *History of Newbury*, 312.
57. John Osgood*	born Andover, Hampshire; Wherwell, Hampshire (daughter baptized 1634)	Coffin, *History of Newbury*, 313; Field, "Family of Osgood," 24.
58. Henry Palmer* (related to William, below?)		

Name	Place of Origin	Reference
59. William Palmer* (related to Henry, above?)	Great Ormsby, Norfolk?	Pope, *Pioneers of Mass.*, 342.
60. Mr. Thomas Parker (cousin of James and Nicholas Noyes, above)	born Cholderton, Wiltshire; Newbury, Berkshire; Mildenhall, Wiltshire	Appleton, "Parkers of America," 337; Banks, *Planters of the Commonwealth*, 111; Noyes, "Noyes Pedigree," 36.
61. Joseph Peasley*		
62. John Pemberton*	Lawford, Essex	Waters, "Genealogical Gleanings," XXXIX, 61–73.
63. John Pike, Sr.* (father of John, Jr., below)	Whiteparish, Wiltshire; Landford, Wiltshire	Banks, *Planters of the Commonwealth*, 138; Bartlett, ed., "Pike," 260; Coffin, *History of Newbury*, 314; Drake, "Founders of New England," 333; *Pike Family*, 31–32.
64. John Pike, Jr. (son of John, Sr., above)	Whiteparish, Wiltshire (baptized 1613); Landford, Wiltshire	Banks, *Planters of the Commonwealth*, 138; Bartlett, ed., "Pike," 260; Whiteparish register, 830/1, Wiltshire R.O.
65. Francis Plummer	London?	Coffin, *History of Newbury*, 315.
66. John Poor	Thornbury, Gloucester?; Landford, Wiltshire	*Ibid.*, 314; Thurston, "Thurston of Newbury," 249–250.
67. Mr. Edward Rawson*	born Gillingham, Dorset; London	Coffin, *History of Newbury*, 316; Pope, *Pioneers of Mass.*, 379.
68. Henry Rolfe	baptized Whiteparish, Wiltshire, 1585	Bartlett, ed., "Rolfe," 250–251.
69. John Russ*		
70. Samuel Scullard	Hampshire? (married daughter of Richard Kent, Sr., before emigration)	Savage, *Gen. Dict.*, III, 12.
71. Mr. Henry Sewell*	Coventry, Warwick	Coffin, *History of Newbury*, 317; Pope, *Pioneers of Mass.*, 407.
72. Anthony Short (brother of Henry, below)	Wiltshire-Hampshire?	Savage, *Gen. Dict.*, IV, 88–89.
73. Henry Short (brother of Anthony, above)	Wiltshire-Hampshire? (sailed on *Mary and John* with Parker group, from Southampton, Mar. 1634)	Banks, *Planters of the Commonwealth*, 111.
74. Thomas Silver		

Name	Place of Origin	Reference
75. Thomas Smith	Romsey, Hampshire	*Ibid.*, 138; Coffin, *History of Newbury*, 318; Drake, "Founders of New England," 333; Pope, *Pioneers of Mass.*, 424.
76. Anthony Somerby (brother of Henry, below)	Little Bytham, Lincolnshire	Coffin, *History of Newbury*, 318; Pope, *Pioneers of Mass.*, 425; Newbury Town Recs.
77. Henry Somerby (brother of Anthony, above)	Little Bytham, Lincolnshire	Pope, *Pioneers of Mass.*, 425.
78. Mr. John Spencer[*]	Kingston, Surrey?; London; Wiltshire-Hampshire? (sailed on *Mary and John* with Parker group, from Southampton, Mar. 1634)	Banks, *Planters of the Commonwealth*, 111; Coffin, *History of Newbury*, 318; Waters, "Genealogical Gleanings," XLIV, 390–391.
79. John Stevens* (probably brother-in-law of Widow Stevens, below)	Caversham, Oxfordshire	Adams and Watkins, "Reading," 60; Banks, *Planters of the Commonwealth*, 197; Savage, *Gen. Dict.*, IV, 186, 190.
80. Widow [William] Stevens	Gonsham, Oxfordshire; Caversham, Oxfordshire	Pope, *Pioneers of Mass.*, 434; Savage, *Gen. Dict.*, IV, 189–190.
81. John Swett	Wymondham, Norfolk?	Banks, *Top. Dict.*, 122.
82. William Thomas	Great Comberton, Worcester	Savage, *Gen. Dict.*, IV, 282.
83. Daniel Thurston	Thornbury, Gloucester?; Wiltshire?	Coffin, *History of Newbury*, 314; Thurston, "Thurston of Newbury," 249–250.
84. William Titcomb	baptized Ogbourne St. George, Wiltshire, 1620	Titcomb, *Descendants of William Titcomb*, 5.
85. Abraham Toppan	possibly Calbridge, Coverham, Yorkshire?; departed from Yarmouth, Norfolk	Coffin, *History of Newbury*, 320; Todd, "Toppan Lane," 434; but see Tappan, "Tappan Family," 66, and "Tappan Genealogy," 48.
86. Henry Travers[*]	Wiltshire-Hampshire? (sailed on *Mary and John* with Parker group, from Southampton, Mar. 1634)	Banks, *Planters of the Commonwealth*, 111.
87. Nicholas [Nathaniel] Weare	Brokenborough, Wiltshire	Banks, *Top. Dict.*, 177 (Banks MSS); Savage, *Gen. Dict.*, IV, 441.
88. William White*	Beaminster, Dorset; sailed on *Mary and John* with Parker group, from Southampton, Mar. 1634	Banks, *Planters of the Commonwealth*, 112; Banks, *Top. Dict.*, 30 (Banks MSS).

Name	Place of Origin	Reference
89. Mr. John Woodbridge (nephew of Thomas Parker, above; cousin of James and Nicholas Noyes, above)	born at Stanton, near Highworth, Wiltshire, 1613	Banks, *Planters of the Commonwealth*, 110; Coffin, *History of Newbury*, 322; Talcott, "Woodbridge Family," 292.
90. Archelaus Woodman (brother of Edward, below)	Christian Malford, Wiltshire	Banks, *Planters of the Commonwealth*, 136; Coffin, *History of Newbury*, 322; Drake, "Founders of New England," 333; Waters, "Genealogical Gleanings," XXXIX, 61–73.
91. Mr. [Edward] Woodman (brother of Archelaus, above)	Christian Malford, Wiltshire; Corsham, Wiltshire	Coffin, *History of Newbury*, 322; Pope, *Pioneers of Mass.*, 513; Waters, "Genealogical Gleanings," XXXIX, 61–73.

The names of the 91 original proprietors were compiled from the Newbury Proprietors' Book, Town Clerk's Office, Newbury, Mass.

In addition to the original proprietors, many other individuals from Wiltshire-Hampshire came to and left Newbury before the 1642 proprietors' list was compiled or arrived too late to be included. Among them were: Stephen Bachiler (Barton Stacy, Hampshire); Nicholas Easton (Lymington, Hampshire); Joseph Parker (Romsey, Hampshire); Hugh March and Anthony Sadler (West? Tytherley, Hampshire); Hugh Monday and Nicholas Wallingford (Nether Wallop, Hampshire); William Gerrish (Melksham, Wiltshire?); John Saunders (Whiteparish, Wiltshire); and Henry Jacques (Stanton, Wiltshire).

PRINTED SOURCES FOR APPENDIX 3

Oscar Fay Adams, with notes by Walter Kendall Watkins, "Our English Parent Towns—Reading," *New England Historical and Genealogical Register*, LX (1906), 57–61; William S. Appleton, "The Greenleaf Ancestry," *NEHGR*, XXXVIII (1884), 299–301; Appleton, "Parkers of America," *NEHGR*, XXXII (1878), 337; Charles Edward Banks, *The Planters of the Commonwealth: A Study of the Emigrants and Emigration in Colonial Times: To Which Are Added Lists of Passengers to Boston and to the Bay Colony; the Ships Which Brought Them; Their English Homes, and the Places of Their Settlement in Massachusetts, 1620–1640* (Boston, 1930); Banks, *Topographical Dictionary of 2885 English Emigrants to New England, 1620–1650*, ed. Elijah Ellsworth Brownell (Philadelphia, 1937), cited as Banks, *Top. Dict.*; J. Gardner Bartlett, "Genealogical Research in England—Rolfe," *NEHGR*, LXVI (1912), 244–252; Bartlett, ed., "Genealogical Research in England—Whittier," *NEHGR*, LXVI (1912), 252–257; Bartlett, ed., "Genealogical Research in England—Pike," *NEHGR*, LXVI (1912), 257–261; John Coffin Jones Brown, "Newbury and the Bartlett Family," *NEHGR*, XL (1886), 192–204; Joshua Coffin, "Coleman Family," *NEHGR*, XI (1857), 347; Coffin, *A Sketch of the History of Newbury, Newburyport, and West Newbury, from 1635 to 1845* (Boston, 1845); Samuel G. Drake, "The Founders of New England," *NEHGR*, XIV (1860), 297–359; Osgood Field, "A Contribution to the History of the Family of Osgood," *NEHGR*, XX (1866), 22–28; William Prescott Greenlaw, "Notes—Hale, Dowsett, Kirby, Cranfield," *NEHGR*, LXIV (1910), 186, cited as Greenlaw, "Hale"; Robert S. Hale, "Thomas Hale of Newbury, Mass., 1637: His English Origin and Connections," *NEHGR*, XXXV (1881), 367–376; Delmar Rial Lowell, comp. and ed., *The Historic Genealogy of the Lowells of America from 1639 to 1899* (Rutland, Vt., 1899); James Atkins Noyes, "Noyes Pedigree," *NEHGR*, LIII (1899), 35–43; "Pedigree of Frye," *NEHGR*, VIII (1854), 226–227; Charles Henry

Pope, *The Pioneers of Massachusetts, A Descriptive List, Drawn from Records of the Colonies, Towns and Churches, and Other Contemporaneous Documents* (Boston, 1900); *Records of the Pike Family Association of America* (Auburndale, Mass., 1940), cited as *Pike Family*; James Savage, *A Genealogical Dictionary of the First Settlers of New England, Showing Three Generations of Those Who Came before May, 1692, on the Basis of Farmer's Register*, 4 vols. (Boston, 1860–1862), cited as Savage, *Gen. Dict.*; Mary K. Talcott, "Genealogy of the Woodbridge Family," *NEHGR*, XXXII (1878), 292–296; Herbert Tappan, "English Ancestry of the Toppan or Tappan Family of Newbury," *NEHGR*, XXXIII (1879), 66–68; Tappan, "The Tappan (or Toppan) Genealogy," *NEHGR*, XXXIV (1880), 48–57; Ariel S. Thurston, "Thurston of Newbury," *NEHGR*, XLII (1888), 249–250; Gilbert Merrill Titcomb, *Descendants of William Titcomb of Newbury, Massachusetts, 1635* (Ann Arbor, Mich., 1969); W. C. Todd, "Notes and Queries—Toppan Lane, Newburyport, Mass.," *NEHGR*, XXVI (1872), 434; Henry F. Waters, "Genealogical Gleanings in England," *NEHGR*, XXXIX (1885), 61–73, XLIV (1890), 383–398; William Willis, *A History of the Law, the Courts, and the Lawyers of Maine, from Its First Colonization to the Early Part of the Present Century* (Portland, Me., 1863).

Appendix 4

English Origins of Ipswich, Massachusetts, Commoners, 1642

Name	Place of Origin	Reference
1. William Addams* [Adams]	sailed on *Elizabeth and Ann*, from London, May 1635	Banks, *Planters of the Commonwealth*, 156; Pope, *Pioneers of Mass.*, 11.
2. John Annyball [Annable] (servant of John Whittingham, below)	Boston, Lincolnshire	Pope, *Pioneers of Mass.*, 19.
3. Mr. Samuel Appleton	Little Waldingfield, Suffolk (baptized Aug. 1586); Reydon, Suffolk	*Ibid.*, 20; Savage, *Gen. Dict.*, I, 61; Waters, "Genealogical Gleanings," XXXIX, 66, 67; E. 3/1/2-9, Exy. 4/W.5/80, 82, 544/3, West Suffolk R.O.
4. William Averill*?	Broadway, Worcester	Dow, "William Averill," 133.
5. Henry Bachellor	Dover, Kent	Banks, *Planters of the Commonwealth*, 189; Pope, *Pioneers of Mass.*, 25; Savage, *Gen. Dict.*, I, 87.
6. Robert Beauchamp*?		
7. Jeremy Belcher	sailed on *Susan and Ellen*, from London, May 1635	Banks, *Planters of the Commonwealth*, 132.
8. Thomas Berry*?		
9. Richard Betgood*	Romsey, Hampshire; London?	Adams and Watkins, "Reading," 60; Banks, *Planters of the Commonwealth*, 198; Pope, *Pioneers of Mass.*, 48; Savage, *Gen. Dict.*, I, 175.
10. Thomas Bishop	brother lived in Kingston, Surrey	Pope, *Pioneers of Mass.*, 51–52.
11. Thomas Boreman [Sr.] [Boardman, Boarman]		
12. Thomas Bracey	Wootton, Bedfordshire	Banks, *Top. Dict.*, 3 (Banks MSS).
13. Humphrey Bradstreet (cousin of Simon, below)	Capel St. Mary, Suffolk	Banks, *Planters of the Commonwealth*, 119–120; Bartlett, "Bradstreet of Capel," 74.

Name	Place of Origin	Reference
14. Mr. Simon Bradstreet* (cousin of Humphrey, above)	born Horbling, Lincolnshire; A.B., 1620; A.M., 1624, Emmanuel College, Cambridge	Banks, *Planters of the Commonwealth*, 67; Dean and Dudley, "Descendants of Bradstreet," 312–313; Greenwood, "Bradstreet's Ancestry," 169; Pope, *Pioneers of Mass.*, 64; Savage, *Gen. Dict.*, I, 326.
15. Thomas Brewer*		
16. John Browne [Sr.]	Great or Little Baddow, Essex	Banks, *Planters of the Commonwealth*, 130; Savage, *Gen. Dict.*, I, 270.
17. Mathias Button*		
18. Lionel Chute [Choate]	Dedham, Essex	Pope, *Pioneers of Mass.*, 100.
19. John Clark, Sr.* (father of John, Jr., below)	Westhorpe, Suffolk?; Groton, Suffolk?	Banks, *Planters of the Commonwealth*, 69; Matthews, "Alumni Founders," 20; Moriarty, "Clarke-Cooke-Kerrich," 273, 279; Tyack, "Migration from East Anglia," App. 1, ix (Banks, *Winthrop Fleet*, 66).
20. John Clark, Jr.*? (son of John, Sr., above)	Westhorpe, Suffolk?; Groton, Suffolk?; Colchester, Essex?	French, "Genealogical Research," LXIV, 138; Matthews, "Alumni Founders," 20; Moriarty, "Clarke-Cooke-Kerrich," 273, 279–280; Tyack, "Migration from East Anglia," App. 1, ix (Banks, *Winthrop Fleet*, 66); Waters, "Genealogical Gleanings," XLVI, 318; cf. *Winthrop Papers*, III, 199–200.
21. Thomas Clark, Sr.	Westhorpe, Suffolk?	Moriarty, "Clarke-Cooke-Kerrich," 273–280; Savage, *Gen. Dict.*, I, 392, 398, 401.
22. John Cowley*? [Cooley?]		
23. Robert Cross		
24. Isaac Cummings		
25. Francis Dane* (son of John, Sr., brother of John, Jr., below)	Berkhamsted, Hertfordshire; baptized Bishop Stortford, Hertfordshire, 1615; matriculated King's College, Cambridge, 1633	Morison, *Founding of Harvard*, 374; Pope, *Pioneers of Mass.*, 129; Savage, *Gen. Dict.*, II, 6.
26. John Dane, Sr. (father of Francis, above, and John, Jr., below)	Bishop Stortford, Hertfordshire; Berkhamsted, Hertfordshire	"John Dane's Narrative," 148; Pope, *Pioneers of Mass.*, 129.

Name	Place of Origin	Reference
27. John Dane, Jr. (son of John, Sr., brother of Francis, above)	Bishop Stortford, Hertfordshire; Berkhamsted, Hertfordshire; Hatfield Broad Oak, Essex; probably born Little Berkhamsted, Hertfordshire	"John Dane's Narrative," 148; Pope, *Pioneers of Mass.*, 129; Tyack, "Migration from East Anglia," App. 1, lxxiii; Walne, "Emigrants from Hertfordshire," 18–19.
28. John Davis	sailed on *Increase*, from London, Apr. 1635	Banks, *Planters of the Commonwealth*, 149.
29. Robert Daye	Stanstead Abbot, Hertfordshire	*Ibid.*, 159; Savage, *Gen. Dict.*, II, 27.
30. Thomas Dorman		
31. William D[o]uglas* (of New London, Conn.; wife was daughter of Thomas Mable of Ringstead, Northampton)		Savage, *Gen. Dict.*, II, 63.
32. Thomas Emerson		
33. William Fellows	St. Albans, Hertfordshire	Banks, *Planters of the Commonwealth*, 143; Pope, *Pioneers of Mass.*, 163.
34. Mr. Giles Firman[*] (related to Thomas, below?)	Sudbury, Suffolk; Emmanuel College, Cambridge, 1629	Adams *et al.*, "Sudbury," 182; Banks, *Planters of the Commonwealth*, 73; Bartlett, "Parmenter," 176; Dean, "Giles Firman," 52–56; Hunter, "Suffolk Emigrants," 168; Morison, *Founding of Harvard*, 378–379; Pope, *Pioneers of Mass.*, 166; Savage, *Gen. Dict.*, II, 160; Waters, "Genealogical Gleanings," XXXVIII, 72.
35. Mr. Thomas Firman (related to Giles, above?)		Savage, *Gen. Dict.*, II, 160.
36. Reginald Foster	Exeter, Devon?	Foster, "Fo(r)ster Descendants," 83.
37. Thomas French	Assington, Suffolk?	Banks, *Top. Dict.*, 149; Banks, *Winthrop Fleet*, 71; Waters, *Genealogical Gleanings*, II, 954; cf. *Winthrop Papers*, III, 199–200.
38. John Gage*	Polstead?, Suffolk	Banks, *Planters of the Commonwealth*, 69; Banks, *Winthrop Fleet*, 71; Savage, *Gen. Dict.*, II, 220; cf. Gage, "John Gage," 254.
39. Edmund Gardner*?	sailed on *James*, from London, July 1635	Banks, *Planters of the Commonwealth*, 152.

Name	Place of Origin	Reference
40. George Giddings	St. Albans, Hertfordshire; Clapham, Bedford	*Ibid.*, 141; Drake, "Founders of New England," 303–304; Pope, *Pioneers of Mass.*, 186.
41. William Goodhugh [Goodhue]	Tonbridge, Kent	Banks, *Top. Dict.*, 84 (Banks MSS).
42. Henry Greene*	Great Bromley, Essex	Morison, *Founding of Harvard*, 380.
43. Thomas Hart (servant of John Browne, above)	Baddow, Essex	Banks, *Planters of the Commonwealth*, 130.
44. Andrew Hodges		
45. James Howe	Hatfield Broad Oak, Essex	"John Dane's Narrative," 153n; Savage, *Gen. Dict.*, II, 475.
46. Thomas Howlett	South Elmham?, Suffolk	Banks, *Planters of the Commonwealth*, 74; Banks, *Top. Dict.*, 161 (Banks MSS).
47. Mr. William Hubbard*	Tendring [hundred?], Essex; Little Clacton, Essex	Banks, *Planters of the Commonwealth*, 169; Pope, *Pioneers of Mass.*, 245; Savage, *Gen. Dict.*, II, 486; Waters, "Genealogical Gleanings," XLI, 180.
48. Richard Huttley [Hatley]	sailed on *Hopewell*, from London, 1635?	Savage, *Gen. Dict.*, II, 377.
49. John Jackson	St. Mary White Chapel, London	Monnette, "Jackson," 84; but cf. Banks, *Planters of the Commonwealth*, 155, 169, 178.
50. Richard Jacob	Wiltshire-Hampshire? (sailed on *Mary and John*, from Southampton, Mar. 1634)	Banks, *Planters of the Commonwealth*, 112.
51. Frances Jurdan [Francis Jordan]		
52. Richard Kimball	Rattlesden, Suffolk	Adams and Watkins, "Chelmsford," 335; Banks, *Planters of the Commonwealth*, 118; Bartlett, "New England Colonists," 331–332; Pope, *Pioneers of Mass.*, 269; Standish, "Helen Kimball," 115; Waters, "Genealogical Gleanings," LII, 247–248.
53. Henry Kingsbury*	Groton, Suffolk; Boxford, Suffolk?	Banks, *Planters of the Commonwealth*, 75; Banks, *Top. Dict.*, 149 (Banks MSS); Savage, *Gen. Dict.*, III, 28.

Name	Place of Origin	Reference
54. Robert Kinsman	Wiltshire-Hampshire? (sailed on *Mary and John*, from Southampton, May 1633)	Banks, *Planters of the Commonwealth*, 111; Pope, *Pioneers of Mass.*, 272.
55. Alexander Knight	Chelmsford, Essex	Adams and Watkins, "Chelmsford," 378; Savage, *Gen. Dict.*, III, 35; Vincent, "True Relation," 41; Q/SR 211/51, 52, 253/89, 265/38, 288/9, Essex R.O.
56. Mr. [William] Knight	Binfield, Berkshire?	Banks, *Top. Dict.*, 5 (Banks MSS).
57. John Kno[w]lton (brother of Thomas and William, below)	Canterbury, Kent?	Pope, *Pioneers of Mass.*, 275.
58. Thomas Kno[w]lton (brother of John, above, and William, below)	Canterbury, Kent?	Banks, *Top. Dict.*, 76; Pope, *Pioneers of Mass.*, 275.
59. William Kno[w]lton (brother of John and Thomas, above)	Canterbury, Kent?	Pope, *Pioneers of Mass.*, 275.
60. William Lampson		
61. Roger Langton*		
62. John Lee (father of Thomas, below?)	a John Lea sailed on *Francis*, from Ipswich, Suffolk, Apr. 1634	Banks, *Planters of the Commonwealth*, 121; but see Savage, *Gen. Dict.*, III, 71.
63. Thomas Lee (son of John, above?)		Pope, *Pioneers of Mass.*, 282.
64. Edward Lumas [Loomis]	Braintree?, Essex; sailed on *Elizabeth*, from London, Apr. 1635, or on *Susan and Ellen*, from London, May 1635	Adams and Watkins, "Braintree," 275; Banks, *Planters of the Commonwealth*, 132, 147; Pope, *Pioneers of Mass.*, 291; Savage, *Gen. Dict.*, III, 111.
65. Richard Lumpkin	Boxted, Essex	Savage, *Gen. Dict.*, III, 130.
66. Thomas Manning		
67. Joseph Medcalfe		
68. Joseph Mosse [Morse] (father of Joseph of Watertown, Mass.)	Boxted, Essex (baptized 1576); Dedham, Essex	Moriarty, "Morse," 70, 292–293; Savage, *Gen. Dict.*, III, 239.
69. Robert Mussey [Muzzey]	South Stoneham, Hampshire	Banks, *Top. Dict.*, 62 (Banks MSS).
70. Thomas Newman	Wiltshire-Hampshire? (sailed on *Mary and John*, from Southampton, Mar. 1634)	Banks, *Planters of the Commonwealth*, 111.

Name	Place of Origin	Reference
71. Mr. John Norton*	Bishop Stortford, Hertfordshire (born 1606); High Lever, Essex; A.B., 1624, A.M., 1627, Peterhouse, Cambridge	Morison, *Founding of Harvard*, 392; Pope, *Pioneers of Mass.*, 331–332; Savage, *Gen. Dict.*, III, 291–292.
72. Christopher Osgood	Marlborough, Wiltshire	Banks, *Planters of the Commonwealth*, 110; Field, "Family of Osgood," 25, 27.
73. Mr. William Payne [Paine]*	Lavenham, Suffolk	Adams *et al.*, "Sudbury," 184; Banks, *Planters of the Commonwealth*, 150; French, "Payne," 251–252; Moriarty, "Richard Payne," 183–184; Moriarty, "Payne," 82; Pope, *Pioneers of Mass.*, 340; Waters, "Genealogical Gleanings," L, 127.
74. Moses Pengry [Pingry]	Gloucester, Gloucestershire; Upton Bishop, Hereford	Aspinwall, *Early History of Boston*, 326.
75. Jo[hn] Perkins, Sr. (father of John, Jr., below)	Hilmorton, Warwick; Newent, Gloucester? (sailed on *Lyon*, from Bristol, Gloucester, Dec. 1630)	Banks, *Planters of the Commonwealth*, 93; Drake, "Perkins Pedigree," 315; "Family of Perkins," 213–215; Whitmore, "Gleanings," 294.
76. John Perkins, Jr. (son of John, Sr., above; father of John III, below)	Hilmorton, Warwick; Newent, Gloucester? (sailed on *Lyon*, from Bristol, Gloucester, Dec. 1630)	Banks, *Planters of the Commonwealth*, 93; Drake, "Perkins Pedigree," 315; "Family of Perkins," 213–215; Whitmore, "Gleanings," 294.
77. John Perkins [III] (son of John, Jr., above)	Hilmorton, Warwick; Newent, Gloucester?	Drake, "Perkins Pedigree," 315; "Family of Perkins," 213–215; Savage, *Gen. Dict.*, III, 396; Whitmore, "Gleanings," 294.
78. Allen Perley	St. Albans, Hertfordshire	Banks, *Planters of the Commonwealth*, 143; Pope, *Pioneers of Mass.*, 355.
79. John Pettis [Pettice]		
80. Henry Pynder [Pindar]	Cottingham, Yorkshire	Banks, *Planters of the Commonwealth*, 132; Banks, *Top Dict.*, 186 (Banks MSS); Savage, *Gen. Dict.*, III, 438.
81. Samuel Podd*?	sailed on *Susan and Ellen*, from London, May 1635	Banks, *Planters of the Commonwealth*, 132.
82. John Proctor*	sailed on *Susan and Ellen*, from London, May 1635	*Ibid.*, 131.

Name	Place of Origin	Reference
83. Mark Quilter	Stoke Nayland, Suffolk; Assington, Suffolk	French, "Quilter," 189–190.
84. Joseph Redding		Banks, *Planters of the Commonwealth*, 80.
85. Mr. Nathaniel Rogers	Bocking, Essex; Assington, Suffolk (1630); born Haverhill, Suffolk, 1598; A.B., 1617, A.M., 1621, Emmanuel College, Cambridge	Adams *et al.*, "Sudbury," 184; Chester, "Rogers Genealogy," 495–496, 498; Bartlett, "Genealogical Research," LXIII, 356–358; Morison, *Founding of Harvard*, 398; Pope, *Pioneers of Mass.*, 390; Savage, *Gen. Dict.*, III, 564; Waters, "Genealogical Gleanings," XLI, 158–159; *Winthrop Papers*, I, 560.
86. Thomas Rolison [Rowlandson, Rawlinson] [Sr.]*		
87. Thomas Safford		
88. Mr. Richard Saltonstall, Jr. [*]	Huntwick, Yorkshire	Pope, *Pioneers of Mass.*, 398.
89. John Satchell [Shatswell]		
90. Richard Sc[h]ofield*	sailed on *Susan and Ellen*, from London, May 1635	Banks, *Planters of the Commonwealth*, 132; Pope, *Pioneers of Mass.*, 403.
91. Thomas Scott	Rattlesden, Suffolk	Banks, *Planters of the Commonwealth*, 118; Bartlett, "New England Colonists," 331–332; Waters, "Genealogical Gleanings," LII, 247–248; Waters, *Genealogical Gleanings*, II, 1413; E. 3/10/85.2, 37.4, West Suffolk R.O.
92. Theophilus Setchell [Shatswell]*		
93. Richard Smyth [Smith]	Shropham, Norfolk	Pope, *Pioneers of Mass.*, 423; Savage, *Gen. Dict.*, IV, 130.
94. Thomas Smyth [Smith]		Savage, *Gen. Dict.*, IV, 134.
95. Simon Stacye [Stacy]	Bocking, Essex	Banks, *Top. Dict.*, 40 (Banks MSS); Q/SR 272/42, 59, 274/10, 276/34, 279/27, 284/13, T/G6/4, Essex R.O.
96. Marke Symonds	Suffolk	Banks, *Top. Dict.*, 54 (Banks MSS).

Name	Place of Origin	Reference
97. Mr. Samuel Symonds	Great Yeldham, Essex	Adams *et al.*, "Sudbury," 184; Pope, *Pioneers of Mass.*, 445; Savage, *Gen. Dict.*, IV, 246; Waters, "Genealogical Gleanings," XL, 304–305; *Winthrop Papers*, II, 118n, III, 111.
98. Mr. Jo[hn] Tuttle[*]	St. Albans, Hertfordshire	Banks, *Planters of the Commonwealth*, 141; Pope, *Pioneers of Mass.*, 466.
99. Jonathan Wade	Northampton, Northamptonshire?; Denver, Norfolk?	Patch, "Abstracts on File," 23; *Recs. of Mass. Bay*, III, 154; Savage, *Gen. Dict.*, IV, 377–378.
100. Daniel Warner (son of William; brother of John)	Boxted, Essex?	Savage, *Gen. Dict.*, IV, 418, 420; cf. Banks, *Top. Dict.*, 40.
101. Richard Wattles*? [Wattlin?]	sailed on *Francis*, from Ipswich, Suffolk, Apr. 1634	Banks, *Planters of the Commonwealth*, 123; Pope, *Pioneers of Mass.*, 482.
102. Thomas Wells	Boxted, Essex; Colchester, Essex?; sailed on *Susan and Ellen*, from London, May 1635	Banks, *Planters of the Commonwealth*, 132; Banks, *Top. Dict.*, 40 (Banks MSS); *Essex Co. Probate Recs.*, II, 69.
103. John Whipple	Bocking, Essex	Bartlett, "Historical Intelligence," 449; Waters, *Genealogical Gleanings*, I, 465–466.
104. Matthew Whipple	Bocking, Essex	Adams and Watkins, "Braintree," 276; Q/SR 125/11, 131/10, 136/9, 148/110–113, 173/104, 188/73, D/DU203/6, Essex R.O.
105. William White*	London? sailed on *Mary and John*, from Southampton, Mar. 1634	Banks, *Planters of the Commonwealth*, 112; Savage, *Gen. Dict.*, IV, 515.
106. Robert Whitman*?	Trinity, Holy Minories, London	Banks, *Planters of the Commonwealth*, 164; Pope, *Pioneers of Mass.*, 495.
107. Mr. [John] Whittingham	Boston, Lincolnshire	Pope, *Pioneers of Mass.*, 496; Waters, "Genealogical Gleanings," XXXIX, 170–173.
108. Theophilus Wilson		
109. Mr. [Robert] Woodmansey*	A.B., 1613, A.M., 1616, Magdalene College, Cambridge	Morison, *Founding of Harvard*, 410.
110. John Wyatt	Assington, Suffolk	Banks, *Top. Dict.*, 149 (Banks MSS).

Name	Place of Origin	Reference
111. Samuel [Simon?] Younglove	sailed on *Hopewell*, from London, Sept. 1635	Banks, *Planters of the Commonwealth*, 176.

The names of the 1642 Commoners were compiled from Town Grants, Town Meeting, 1634, p. 84, Town Clerk's Office, Ipswich, Mass.

In addition to the Ipswich "Commoners" of 1642, many other individuals who settled temporarily or permanently in Ipswich during the first two decades of settlement came from either the Suffolk-Essex region or from Hertfordshire. Still others came from other parts of East Anglia, the nearby Home Counties, or London. *Some* from the Suffolk-Essex and Hertfordshire areas who came prior to 1640 and presumably remained in the town who were not 1642 Commoners included: Jathnell and Thomas Bird (Hatfield Broad Oak, Essex?); Nathaniel Bixby (Little Waldingfield, Suffolk?); Arthur [Anthony?] Colebeye (Fressingfield, Suffolk); John Cross (Wolpitt, Suffolk); Daniel Denison (Bishop Stortford, Hertfordshire); Thomas French, Jr. (Assington, Suffolk); John Fuller (Lavenham, Suffolk); Richard Haffield (Sudbury, Suffolk); John Hanchet (Braughing, Hertfordshire?); Thomas Howlett, Jr. (South Elmham?, Suffolk); Henry Kimball (Rattlesden, Suffolk); Robert Lord (Sudbury, Suffolk); William Norton (Bishop Stortford, Hertfordshire); Robert Paine (Sudbury, Suffolk); Robert Scott (Glemsford, Suffolk); Samuel Sherman (Dedham, Essex); Thomas Sherman (Dedham, Essex); Samuel Symonds, Jr., and William Symonds (Great Yeldham, Essex); William Warner (Boxted and Great Horkesley, Essex?); John Webster (Ipswich, Suffolk?); William Whitred [Whittridge?] (Lilley, Hertfordshire); and Paul Williamson (Hertfordshire?).

Among those who came to live in Ipswich from Suffolk-Essex or Hertfordshire and subsequently left the town were the following settlers: Edward Allen (Wrentham, Suffolk); Richard Betts (Hemel Hempstead, Hertfordshire); Joseph Bixby (Little Waldingfield, Suffolk); Richard Brabrook (Groton, Suffolk?); George Bunker (Bengoe, Hertfordshire); Thomas Carter (Hinderclay, Suffolk); William Chandler (Bishop Stortford, Hertfordshire); James Chute [Choate] (Dedham, Essex); William Clark (Semer, Suffolk?); Robert Cole (Navestock, Essex); Robert Crane (Coggeshall, Essex); John French (Assington, Suffolk); William Fuller (Lavenham?, Suffolk); George Hadley (Reydon, Suffolk); Samuel Hall (Essex?); Job Hawkins (Sudbury, Suffolk); Luke Heard (Assington, Suffolk); Richard Jennings (Ipswich and Combs, Suffolk); Augustine Kilham (Dennington, Suffolk); Richard Kimball, Jr. (Rattlesden, Suffolk); John and Nathaniel Merrill (Wherstead, Suffolk); Francis Peabody (St. Albans, Hertfordshire); John? Robinson (Little Waldingfield, Suffolk); Theophilus Salter (Dedham, Essex); Thomas Stacy (Bocking, Essex); Thomas Waite (Wethersfield, Essex); John Ward (Haverhill and Stratford St. Mary, Suffolk, and Hadleigh and East Mersea, Essex); Nathaniel Ward (Haverhill, Suffolk, and Stondon Massey, Essex); John Warner (Boxted, Essex); and John Winthrop, Jr. (Groton, Suffolk).

PRINTED SOURCES FOR APPENDIX 4

Oscar Fay Adams *et al.*, "Our English Parent Towns—Sudbury," *New England Historical and Genealogical Register*, LVI (1902), 179–185; Adams, with notes by Walter Kendall Watkins, "Our English Parent Towns—Braintree (with Bocking)," *NEHGR*, LVI (1902), 271–276; Adams, with notes by Watkins, "Our English Parent Towns—Chelmsford," *NEHGR*, LVI (1902), 375–379; Adams, with notes by Watkins, "Our English Parent Towns—Reading," *NEHGR*, LX (1906), 57–61; William Aspinwall, *A Volume Relating to the Early History of Boston, Containing the Aspinwall Notarial Records from 1644 to 1651* (Boston Record Commission, *Report*, XXXII [Boston, 1903]); Charles Edward Banks, *The Planters of the Commonwealth: A Study of the Emigrants and Emigration in Colonial Times: To Which Are Added Lists of Passengers to Boston and to the Bay Colony; the Ships Which Brought Them; Their English Homes, and the Places of Their Settlement in Massachusetts, 1620–1640* (Boston, 1930); Banks, *Topographical Dictionary of 2885 English Emigrants to New England, 1620–1650*, ed. Elijah Ellsworth Brownell (Philadelphia, 1937), cited as Banks, *Top. Dict.*; Banks, *The Winthrop Fleet of 1630: An Account of the Vessels, the Voyage, the Passengers and Their English Homes from Original Authorities* (Boston, 1930); J. G. Bartlett, "Genealogical Research in England," *NEHGR*, LXIII (1909), 356–358; Bartlett, "Genealogical Research in England—

Bradstreet of Capel, etc., Co. Suffolk," *NEHGR*, LXV (1911), 72–74; Bartlett, "Genealogical Research in England—Parmenter," *NEHGR*, LXVI (1912), 167–176; Bartlett, "Historical Intelligence—Whipple Pedigree," *NEHGR*, LXXVIII (1924), 449; Bartlett, "Notes and Queries—New England Colonists from Rattlesden, Co. Suffolk, England," *NEHGR*, LVII (1903), 331–332; "Bradstreet Genealogy," *Essex Antiquarian*, XI (1907), 52–57; Joseph Lemuel Chester, "The Rogers Genealogy and the Candler MS.," Massachusetts Historical Society, *Proceedings*, V (1860–1862), 486–499; John Ward Dean, communicator, "Rev. Giles Firman: Additional Facts," *NEHGR*, XXV (1866), 47–58; John Dean and Dean Dudley, "Descendants of Gov. Bradstreet," *NEHGR*, VIII (1854), 312–325; "Descendants of Humphrey Bradstreet," *Essex Antiquarian*, XI (1907), 57–60; George Francis Dow, "William Averill of Ipswich and Some of His Descendants," Essex Institute, *Historical Collections*, XLVIII (1912), 133–148; Samuel G. Drake, "The Founders of New England," *NEHGR*, XIV (1860), 297–359; Drake, "Notes on the Perkins Pedigree," *NEHGR*, XI (1857), 315; Osgood Field, "A Contribution to the History of the Family of Osgood," *NEHGR*, XX (1866), 22–28; Edward Jacob Forster, "Genealogy of the Fo(r)ster Family, Descendants of Reginald Fo(r)ster, of Ipswich, Mass.," *NEHGR*, XXX (1876), 83–102; Elizabeth French, transcriber, "Genealogical Research in England," *NEHGR*, LXIV (1910), 135–140; French, "Genealogical Research in England—Payne," *NEHGR*, LXIX (1915), 251–252; French, "Genealogical Research in England—Quilter," *NEHGR*, LXVIII (1914), 181–190; Arthur E. Gage, "Some Descendants of John Gage of Ipswich, Mass.," *NEHGR*, LXII (1908), 254–263; Isaac J. Greenwood, "Gov. Simon Bradstreet's Ancestry," *NEHGR*, XLVIII (1894), 168–171; Abraham Hammatt, *The Early Inhabitants of Ipswich, Massachusetts, 1633–1700* (Ipswich, Mass., 1880–1899); Hammatt, "Physicians at Ipswich," *NEHGR*, IV (1850), 11–16; John Camden Hotten, ed., *The Original Lists of Persons of Quality, Emigrants, Religious Exiles, Political Rebels, Serving Men Sold for a Term of Years, Apprentices, Children Stolen, Maidens Pressed, and Others, Who Went from Great Britain to the American Plantations, 1600–1700 . . .* , 2d ed. (New York, 1880); Joseph Hunter, "Suffolk Emigrants: Genealogical Notices of Various Persons and Families Who in the Reign of King Charles the First Emigrated to New England from the County of Suffolk," Mass. Hist. Soc., *Collections*, 3d Ser., X (1849), 147–172; Isaac Appleton Jewett, comp., *Memorial of Samuel Appleton, of Ipswich, Massachusetts; with Genealogical Notices of Some of His Descendants* (Boston, 1850); "John Dane's Narrative, 1682: A Declaration of Remarkabell Prouedenses in the Corse of My Lyfe," *NEHGR*, VIII (1854), 147–156; Albert Matthews, "University Alumni Founders of New England," Colonial Society of Massachusetts, *Transactions*, XXV (1922–1924), 14–23; Orra Eugene Monnette, "Notes—Jackson," *NEHGR*, LXVI (1912), 84; G. Andrews Moriarty, Jr., "Genealogical Gleanings in England—Payne," *NEHGR*, LXXIX (1925), 82–84; Moriarty, "Genealogical Research in England—Clarke-Cooke (alias Carewe)-Kerrich," *NEHGR*, LXXV (1921), 273–301; Moriarty, "Genealogical Research in England—Morse," *NEHGR*, LXXXIII (1929), 70–84, 278–293; Moriarty, "Gleanings from English Records—Richard Payne of Lavenham, Co. Suffolk," *NEHGR*, CIII (1949), 183–184; Samuel Eliot Morison, *The Founding of Harvard College* (Cambridge, Mass., 1936); Ira J. Patch, copier, "Abstracts from Wills, Inventories, etc., on File in the Office of Clerk of Courts, Salem, Mass.," Essex Inst., *Hist. Colls.*, IV (1862), 20–28; "Some Notices of the Family of Perkins in America," *NEHGR*, X (1856), 211–216; Charles Henry Pope, *The Pioneers of Massachusetts, A Descriptive List, Drawn from Records of the Colonies, Towns and Churches, and Other Contemporaneous Documents* (Boston, 1900); Lilian J. Redstone, transcriber, "Genealogical Research in England—The Hammond Family," *NEHGR*, CVI (1952), 83–87; James Savage, *A Genealogical Dictionary of the First Settlers of New England, Showing Three Generations of Those Who Came before May, 1692, on the Basis of Farmer's Register*, 4 vols. (Boston, 1860–1862), cited as Savage, *Gen. Dict.*; Robert M. Search and Helen C. Search, "Garrett Church of Watertown, Mass.," *NEHGR*, CXXIII (1969), 182–190; Myles Standish, "Helen Francis Kimball, A.M.," *NEHGR*, LXXIX (1925), 115–119; Norman C. P. Tyack, "Migration from East Anglia to New England before 1660" (Ph.D. diss., University of London, 1951); Peter Walne, "Emigrants from Hertfordshire, 1630–1640: Some Corrections and Additions," *NEHGR*, CXXXII (1978), 18–24; Henry F. Waters, *Genealogical Gleanings in England*, 2 vols. (Boston, 1901); Waters, "Genealogical Gleanings in England," *NEHGR*,

XXXVIII (1884), 60–74, XXXIX (1885), 61–73, 160–175, XL (1886), 300–307, XLI (1887), 158–188, XLVI (1892), 299–338, L (1896), 105–141, LII (1898), 234–268; W[illiam] H. W[hitmore], "Gleanings," *NEHGR*, XII (1858), 294–295; *Winthrop Papers* (Mass. Hist. Soc., *Colls.*, 4th Ser., VI–VII, 5th Ser., I [Boston, 1863–1871]), I–III; P. Vincent, "A True Relation of the Late Battell Fought in *New England*, between the English and the Pequet Salvages . . . ," Mass. Hist. Soc., *Colls.*, 3d Ser., VI (1837), 29–43.

Appendix 5

English Origins of the Grantees of the First Division of Land, Watertown, Massachusetts, July 25, 1636

Name	Place of Origin	Reference
1. Robert Abbot*		
2. Thomas Arnold*	Kelshale, Suffolk	Jones, "Parentage of Arnold," 68; Waters, "Genealogical Gleanings," XLVIII, 374–375.
3. William Baker*		
4. Thomas Bartlet[t]		Banks, *Planters of the Commonwealth*, 66.
5. John Batchelor* [Bachelor]	Canterbury, Kent	*Ibid.*, 189; Pope, *Pioneers of Mass.*, 25–26.
6. Richard Beers		
7. John Bernard [Barnard]	Dedham, Essex	Banks, *Planters of the Commonwealth*, 119; Pope, *Pioneers of Mass.*, 33.
8. Robert Betts*		
9. Nathaniel Bowman*		Banks, *Planters of the Commonwealth*, 67.
10. William Bridges*	London? (sailed on *Little James*, to Plymouth, Mass., 1623?)	*Ibid.*, 55.
11. Henry Bright, [Jr.]	born Bury St. Edmunds, Suffolk	Bond, *Watertown Genealogies*, 97–99; Whitmore, "Henry Bright," 98; Savage, *Gen. Dict.*, I, 253; cf. D6/4/1, D11/3/2, West Suffolk R.O.
12. Thomas Brookes* [Brooks]	St. Gregory, London?	Banks, *Top. Dict.*, 100 (Banks MSS).
13. Abraham Browne (younger brother or nephew of Richard, below; probably uncle of John, below)	Hawkedon, Suffolk	Banks, *Planters of the Commonwealth*, 67; Bond, *Watertown Genealogies*, 124; Waters, "Genealogical Gleanings," XXXIX, 71.
14. John Browne (probably nephew of Abraham, above, and Richard, below)	Hawkedon, Suffolk	Bond, *Watertown Genealogies*, 118, 124.
15. Richard Browne* (probably brother of Abraham, above;	London; born Hawkedon, Suffolk	*Ibid.*, 122; Banks, *Planters of the Commonwealth*, 68; Savage, *Gen. Dict.*, I, 274.

Name	Place of Origin	Reference
probably uncle of John, above)		
16. William Bussum [Barsham]		Banks, *Planters of the Commonwealth*, 66.
17. Thomas Cakebread*	Hatfield Broad Oak, Essex	*Ibid.*, 68.
18. Charles Chadwick	Woodham Ferres, Essex?	Banks, *Top. Dict.*, 53 (Banks MSS); Savage, *Gen. Dict.*, I, 301.
19. Leonard Chester*	Blaby, Leicester	Bond, *Watertown Genealogies*, 735; Savage, *Gen. Dict.*, I, 375; Strong, "Chester Family," 338.
20. Ephraim Child	Bury St. Edmunds, Suffolk; married Nayland, Suffolk, 1625	Banks, *Planters of the Commonwealth*, 69; Bond, *Watertown Genealogies*, 152; Savage, *Gen. Dict.*, I, 377.
21. Garrett [Jared?] Church (related to Richard Church of Polstead, Suffolk?)		Banks, *Winthrop Fleet*, 64; Search and Search, "Garrett Church," 182.
22. John Coolege [Coolidge]	Cottenham, Cambridgeshire	Bond, *Watertown Genealogies*, 165, 186; "Coolidges of Cambridgeshire," 402.
23. Benjamin Crispe (servant of Major Edward Gibbons, who emigrated ca. 1629)	Plymouth, Devon?	Bond, *Watertown Genealogies*, 188; Pope, *Pioneers of Mass.*, 185.
24. Isaac Cummins*		Savage, *Gen. Dict.*, I, 483.
25. Henry Cuttris [Curtis]*	Southwark, Surrey?; London	Pope, *Pioneers of Mass.*, 126; Woods, "Henry Curtis," 258; cf. Appleton, "Parkers of America," 337, and Fothergill, "Notes and Queries," 393.
26. James Cutler*		
27. John Cutting*	Suffolk-Essex? (related to Richard and William Cutting, who sailed on *Elizabeth*, from Ipswich, Suffolk, Apr. 1634?)	Banks, *Planters of the Commonwealth*, 121.
28. Robert Daniel*		
29. Henry Dengaine* [Dengayne]		
30. Edward Dikes [Dix]	Rattlesden, Suffolk	*Ibid.*, 71; Bond, *Watertown Genealogies*, 198; Bartlett, "New England Colonists," 332; Savage, *Gen. Dict.*, II, 53.

Name	Place of Origin	Reference
31. John Doggett [Daggett]*	Groton, Suffolk	Banks, *Planters of the Commonwealth*, 72; Banks, *Winthrop Fleet*, 68.
32. John Dwight*		
33. John Eaton*	Staple, Kent	Banks, *Planters of the Commonwealth*, 189.
34. John Eddy	Boxted, Suffolk	Eddy, "Joshua Eddy," 201; Savage, *Gen. Dict.*, II, 98–99.
35. Simon Eire*	Lavenham, Suffolk; Bury St. Edmunds, Suffolk	Banks, *Planters of the Commonwealth*, 150; French, "Genealogical Research," LXIX, 250; Moriarty, "Payne," 82–84.
36. John Ellett [Elliot]		
37. Robert Feake	London; St. Nicholas Acon, London	Banks, *Planters of the Commonwealth*, 72; Banks, *Top. Dict.*, 103; Pope, *Pioneers of Mass.*, 163.
38. John Finch*		Banks, *Planters of the Commonwealth*, 73.
39. John Firman	Nayland, Suffolk	*Ibid.*, 73, 121; Adams *et al.*, "Sudbury," 182.
40. Edward Garfield	Kilsby, Northampton	Phillimore, "Garfield Family," 255.
41. John Gay*		
42. Edward Goffe*	Great Ellingham, Norfolk?; sailed on *Great Hope*, from Ipswich, Suffolk, late 1634 or early 1635	Banks, *Top. Dict.*, 116 (Banks MSS); Savage, *Gen. Dict.*, II, 267.
43. Henry Goldstone (son of Rev. William, vicar, Bedingfield, Suffolk)	Bedingfield, Suffolk; baptized Wickham Skeith, Suffolk	Bond, *Watertown Genealogies*, 774; Whitmore, "Henry Bright," 98–99; Savage, *Gen. Dict.*, II, 269–270.
44. John Gosse [Goss]	Little Waldingfield, Suffolk?	Banks, *Top. Dict.*, 116 (Banks MSS); *Winthrop Papers*, III, 198, 199n.
45. Christopher Grant		
46. John Grigs [Griggs]*		
47. John Gutterige [Goodrich]*? (brother of William)	Rattlesden, Suffolk; Hassett, Suffolk?; Bury St. Edmunds, Suffolk?	Bartlett, "New England Colonists," 332; Bond, *Watertown Genealogies*, 777; Savage, *Gen. Dict.*, II, 274–276; Tyack, "Migration from East Anglia," App. 1, cxiii; cf. John Goodrich, Bury Wills, 1632, Colman 127, West Suffolk R.O.

Name	Place of Origin	Reference
48. William Hammond	Lavenham, Suffolk	Adams *et al.*, "Sudbury," 184; Battell, "Benjamin Hammond," 28; Hammond, "John Hammond," 288–289; Moriarty, "Payne," LXXIX, 82–84; Pope, *Pioneers of Mass.*, 210; Redstone, "Genealogical Research," 83–87; Watkins, "Notes and Queries," 108; *Winthrop Papers*, I, 394–396.
49. Thomas Hastings	Suffolk? (sailed on *Elizabeth*, from Ipswich, Suffolk, Apr. 1634)	Banks, *Planters of the Commonwealth*, 120; Savage, *Gen. Dict.*, II, 374.
50. John Hayward*		Savage, *Gen. Dict.*, III, 410.
51. Matthew Hitchcock*	sailed on *Susan and Ellen*, from London, May 1635	Banks, *Planters of the Commonwealth*, 133.
52. Samuel Hosier	Colchester, Essex	*Ibid.*, 74; cf. Pope, *Pioneers of Mass.*, 240.
53. Edward How	Boxted, Essex; Bocking, Essex (1604?)	French, "Genealogical Research," LXIII, 285; Bond, *Watertown Genealogies*, 303, 795; Savage, *Gen. Dict.*, II, 474; Q/SR 169/29–36, Essex R.O.?
54. Edmund James	Earl's Barton, Northampton	Banks, *Planters of the Commonwealth*, 74; French, "Genealogical Research," LXIII, 164; Savage, *Gen. Dict.*, II, 534.
55. Robert Jennison (brother of William, below)	Colchester, Essex?; Holborn, Middlesex?	Banks, *Top. Dict.*, 111 (Banks MSS); Bond, *Watertown Genealogies*, 307; Pope, *Pioneers of Mass.*, 258.
56. William Jennison[*] (brother of Robert, above)	Colchester, Essex?; Holborn, Middlesex?	Banks, *Planters of the Commonwealth*, 63; Banks, *Top. Dict.*, 111 (Banks MSS); Pope, *Pioneers of Mass.*, 258.
57. Henry Kimball (probably brother of Richard, below)	Rattlesden, Suffolk	Banks, *Planters of the Commonwealth*, 118; Bond, *Watertown Genealogies*, 323; Bartlett, "New England Colonists," 331.
58. Richard Kimball* (probably brother of Henry, above)	Rattlesden, Suffolk	Banks, *Planters of the Commonwealth*, 118; Bartlett, "New England Colonists," 331–332; Cummings, "Moses Kimball," 335; Pope, *Pioneers of Mass.*, 269; Standish, "Helen Kimball," 115; Waters, "Genealogical Gleanings," LII, 247–248.

Name	Place of Origin	Reference
59. John Kingsbury*		
60. Nicholas Knap [Knapp]*	Bures St. Mary, Suffolk	Banks, *Planters of the Commonwealth*, 75; Pope, *Pioneers of Mass.*, 273; EL/37, West Suffolk R.O.?
61. William Knop [Knapp]	Bures St. Mary, Suffolk	Banks, *Planters of the Commonwealth*, 75; Pope, *Pioneers of Mass.*, 273.
62. Edward Lamb* (related to Thomas Lamb, of Stowe Langtoft, Suffolk?)		Banks, *Planters of the Commonwealth*, 76; Banks, *Winthrop Fleet*, 79.
63. John Lawrence*?	St. Albans, Hertfordshire?; married at Fokenham Magna, Suffolk, Oct. 12, 1630?; sailed on *Planter*, from London, Apr. 1635	Banks, *Planters of the Commonwealth*, 141; Bond, *Watertown Genealogies*, 819n; Moriarty, "Lawrence," 150; Gordon, "Notes and Queries," 85.
64. Edmund Lewis*	Suffolk? (sailed on *Elizabeth*, from Ipswich, Suffolk, Apr. 1634)	Banks, *Planters of the Commonwealth*, 117; Banks, *Top. Dict.*, 166.
65. John Livermore	Little Thurloe, Suffolk	Banks, *Planters of the Commonwealth*, 124; Bond, *Watertown Genealogies*, 338, 338n, 852; Mills, "Early Kilhams," 345–346; Savage, *Gen. Dict.*, III, 101; cf. E3/10/5, 8, West Suffolk R.O.
66. Robert Lockwood* (brother of Edmond)	Coombs, Suffolk	Banks, *Planters of the Commonwealth*, 76; Banks, *Winthrop Fleet*, 74.
67. John Loveran	Ardleigh, Essex; Dedham, Essex	Adams *et al.*, "Sudbury," 184; Savage, *Gen. Dict.*, III, 124; Q/SR 265/83, Essex R.O.
68. Hugh Mason	Maldon, Essex	Banks, *Planters of the Commonwealth*, 123; Byington, ed., "Necrology," 91–92; Lea, "Genealogical Gleanings," 189; Mason, *Descendants of Capt. Hugh Mason*, 2–4, 17; Mason, "Hugh Mason," 256–258.
69. Thomas Mason*		
70. Thomas Maihew [Mayhew]*	Tisbury, Wiltshire; Southampton, Hampshire	Banks, *Planters of the Commonwealth*, 77; Savage, *Gen. Dict.*, III, 185.
71. Isaac Mixer	Capel St. Mary, Suffolk	Banks, *Planters of the Commonwealth*, 119; French, "Genealogical Research,"

Name	Place of Origin	Reference
		LXIII, 277, LXVI, 178; Homan, "Mixer," 380.
72. Daniel Mosse [Morse]* (son of Samuel; second cousin of Joseph, below)	Burgate, Suffolk; Redgrave, Suffolk	Moriarty, "Morse," 70, 290–291.
73. Joseph Mosse [Morse] (son of Joseph of Ipswich, Mass.; second cousin of Daniel, above)	probably born Dedham, Essex; sailed on *Elizabeth*, from Ipswich, Suffolk, Apr. 1634	*Ibid.*, 70, 290–291, 292–293; Banks, *Planters of the Commonwealth*, 121; Bond, *Watertown Genealogies*, 371.
74. George Munnings*	Rattlesden, Suffolk	Banks, *Planters of the Commonwealth*, 119; Bartlett, "New England Colonists," 331.
75. Miles Nutt*		
76. Widow Frances Onge	Lavenham, Suffolk	Banks, *Planters of the Commonwealth*, 93; Pope, *Pioneers of Mass.*, 335–336.
77. John Page	Dedham, Essex; Boxted, Essex	Banks, *Planters of the Commonwealth*, 78; Bond, *Watertown Genealogies*, 383; Moriarty, "Page," 242–245; Pope, *Pioneers of Mass.*, 339; Prescott, "Page Family," 75.
78. William Paine*	Lavenham, Suffolk	Adams *et al.*, "Sudbury," 184; Banks, *Planters of the Commonwealth*, 150; French, "Genealogical Research," LXIX, 251–252; Moriarty, "Richard Payne," 183–184; Moriarty, "Payne," 82; Pope, *Pioneers of Mass.*, 340; Waters, "Genealogical Gleanings," L, 127.
79. William Palmer*	Great Ormsby, Norfolk?; Ormsby St. Margaret, Norfolk	Bartlett, "Manor of Ormesby," 342, 344; Bartlett, "Palmer," 79–80; Bond, *Watertown Genealogies*, 384, 865; Chamberlain, "Palmer," 158; Palmer, "William Palmer," 259; Pope, *Pioneers of Mass.*, 343; Savage, *Gen. Dict.*, III, 343.
80. Thomas Parish [*]	Nayland, Suffolk	Banks, *Planters of the Commonwealth*, 151; Pope, *Pioneers of Mass.*, 343; Savage, *Gen. Dict.*, III, 346.
81. Daniel Perse [Peirce]*	Norwich, Norfolk?; sailed on *Francis*, from Ipswich, Suffolk, Apr. 1634	Banks, *Planters of the Commonwealth*, 121.

Name	Place of Origin	Reference
82. Brian Pembleton [Pendleton]*	born Eccles, Lancaster?; married at St. Martins, Birmingham, 1619; resided at St. Sepulcher's, without Newgate, London	Pendleton, *Early New England Pendletons*, 6; Powell, *Puritan Village*, 169.
83. Thomas Philbrick* [Felbrigge]	Bures St. Mary, Suffolk	Moriarty, "Thomas Felbrigge," 257–258.
84. Rev. George Phillips	Boxted, Essex; baptized Raynham, Norfolk; A.B., 1613, A.M., 1617, Caius College, Cambridge	Bond, *Watertown Genealogies*, 872; Morison, *Founding of Harvard*, 395–396; Pope, *Pioneers of Mass.*, 357; *Winthrop Papers*, III, 123n.
85. Esther Pickeran [Pickering]*? (wife of John)	Sudbury, Suffolk	Banks, *Winthrop Fleet*, 86.
86. George Richardson	sailed on *Susan and Ellen*, from London, May 1635	Banks, *Planters of the Commonwealth*, 133.
87. Thomas Rogers	Dedham, Essex; St. Bartholomew Great, London?	Banks, *Planters of the Commonwealth*, 49; Banks, *Top. Dict.*, 99 (Banks MSS); T. Sherman, "English Shermans," 324–325.
88. John Rose*	Elmswell, Suffolk	Banks, *Planters of the Commonwealth*, 121.
89. Sir Richard Saltonstall [*]	Halifax, Yorkshire; Huntwicke, Yorkshire	Bond, *Watertown Genealogies*, 415, 915.
90. Richard Sawtel*?	Somerset?	Banks, *Top. Dict.*, 147 (Banks MSS).
91. Abraham Shaw*	Halifax, Yorkshire	Pope, *Pioneers of Mass.*, 410.
92. Edmund Sherman [*] (brother of Rev. John? cousin of Capt. John?)	Dedham, Essex	*Ibid.*, 412; Bond, *Watertown Genealogies*, 430, 432; D. Sherman, "Sherman Family," 64–65; T. Sherman, "English Shermans," 324–325; Waters, "Genealogical Gleanings," L, 414–417; Q/SR 129/12?, 244/73, Essex R.O.
93. John Simson [Simpson]	London? (sailed on *Truelove*, from London, Sept. 1635)	Banks, *Planters of the Commonwealth*, 173; Pope, *Pioneers of Mass.*, 416.
94. John Smith [Sr.] (father of John, Jr., below)	Sudbury, Suffolk	Adams et al., "Sudbury," 181–182.
95. John Smith [Jr.]* (son of John, Sr., above; father of Thomas, below)	Sudbury, Suffolk	*Ibid.*
96. Thomas Smith (son of John, Jr., above)	Sudbury, Suffolk?	Bond, *Watertown Genealogies*, 433; Savage, *Gen.*

Name	Place of Origin	Reference
		Dict., IV, 118; but see Locke, "Emigrants," 248.
97. John Spring	Suffolk? (sailed on *Elizabeth*, from Ipswich, Suffolk, Apr. 1634)	Banks, *Planters of the Commonwealth*, 118.
98. Isaac Sterne [Stearns]	Nayland, Suffolk; Stoke Nayland, Suffolk	*Ibid.*, 82; Adams *et al.*, "Sudbury," 183; French, "Genealogical Research," LXIV, 354; Bond, *Watertown Genealogies*, 451; Hammond, "Ezra Stearns," 195.
99. Gregory Stone* (brother of Simon, below)	Great Bromley, Essex	French, "Genealogical Research," LXIII, 285; Bartlett, *Stone Genealogy*, 10, 65–67; Bond, *Watertown Genealogies*, 548; Townshend, "Parish Registers," 42–44; Q/SR 134/11?, Queen's Bench Indictments Ancient, 698, Pt. i, 23, and T/A 428, Essex R.O.
100. Simon Stone (brother of Gregory, above)	Great Bromley, Essex; Boxted, Essex?	Banks, *Planters of the Commonwealth*, 150; French, "Genealogical Research," LXIII, 285; Bartlett, *Stone Genealogy*, 10, 65–67; Bond, *Watertown Genealogies*, 584; Savage, *Gen. Dict.*, IV, 209; D/DU 40/3, 172, Essex R.O.
101. John Stowers*	Parham, Suffolk	Adams, "Framingham," 197; Banks, *Top. Dict.*, 158; Bond, *Watertown Genealogies*, 592.
102. Samuel Swaine* (son of William)	father sailed on *Elizabeth and Ann*, from London, May 1635	Banks, *Planters of the Commonwealth*, 155; Savage, *Gen. Dict.*, IV, 236.
103. William Swift*	London?; Bermondsey, Surrey?; Bocking, Suffolk	Banks, *Top. Dict.*, 104, 167; Savage, *Gen. Dict.*, IV, 241.
104. Philip Tabor*	Kilmington, Somerset?; Essex?	Banks, *Top. Dict.*, 143 (Banks MSS); "Memoirs—Taber," 173.
105. Gregory Taylor*		Banks, *Planters of the Commonwealth*, 83.
106. John Tomson [Thompson]	sailed on *Elizabeth and Ann*, from London, May 1635?	*Ibid.*, 156.
107. Robert Tucke*	Gorleston, Suffolk	Bond, *Watertown Genealogies*, 609; Pope, *Pioneers of Mass.*, 463; Savage, *Gen. Dict.*, IV, 337.
108. John Tucker*		Savage, *Gen. Dict.*, IV, 338.

Name	Place of Origin	Reference
109. Martin Underwood	Elmham, Suffolk	Banks, *Planters of the Commonwealth*, 120; Hunter, "Suffolk Emigrants," 158; cf. Pope, *Pioneers of Mass.*, 468.
110. John Vahan [Vaughan]*		
111. Robert Veazy		
112. John Warren	Nayland, Suffolk	Banks, *Planters of the Commonwealth*, 84; French, "Genealogical Research," LXIV, 348–355; Bartlett, *Stone Genealogy*, 43.
113. Lawrence Waters* (related to John Waters of Nayland, Suffolk?)		Banks, *Winthrop Fleet*, 95; Savage, *Gen. Dict.*, IV, 434.
114. Roger Willington [Wellington]		
115. Emanuel White*		
116. John Whitney	St. Margaret, Westminster, London	Banks, *Planters of the Commonwealth*, 154; Banks, *Top. Dict.*, 101.
117. John Wincoll*	Waldingfield, Suffolk	Savage, *Gen. Dict.*, IV, 592; Sier, "Wincoll Family," 236–245; Waters, *Genealogical Gleanings*, 77; Exy 4/W.4/114, W.2/153, West Suffolk R.O.?
118. Barnabas Windes*	Ipswich, Suffolk?	Banks, *Top. Dict.*, 156 (Banks MSS).
119. John Winter	London?	*Ibid.*, 104; Savage, *Gen. Dict.*, IV, 605–606; Bond, *Watertown Genealogies*, 656.
120. Richard Woodward	Suffolk? (sailed on *Elizabeth*, from Ipswich, Suffolk, Apr. 1634)	Banks, *Planters of the Commonwealth*, 117; Banks, *Top. Dict.*, 166.

The names of the grantees were compiled from *Watertown Records . . .* [title varies], 6 vols. in 5 (Watertown, Mass., 1894–1928), I, "Lands Grants Divisions Allotments Possessions and Proprietors' Book," 3–5.

Besides the grantees of the "First Division," many other individuals from the Suffolk-Essex region settled temporarily or permanently in Watertown, or were found in the town records prior to 1644. Still others came from other parts of East Anglia, the nearby Home Counties, or London. Among those from the Suffolk-Essex region were: Edmund Angier (Dedham, Essex); John Bigelow (Wrentham, Suffolk); Edmund Blois (Brandestone, Suffolk); William Bond (Bury St. Edmunds, Suffolk); John Braybrook (Groton, Suffolk?); Henry Bright, "Sr." (Halstead, Essex?); Malachi Browning (Maldon, Essex); Benjamin, Robert, George, Anne, and Maudlin Bullard (Barham, Suffolk); Thomas Carter (Hinderclay, Suffolk); Lambert Chinery (Suffolk?); John Clark (Westhorpe, Suffolk); William Clark (Semer, Suffolk?); John Clough (Suffolk?); John Cloyes (Colchester, Essex); Robert

Coe (Boxford, Suffolk); John Cross (Wolpitt, Suffolk); Richard Cutting (Rattlesden?, Suffolk); Thomas and Simon Eire, Jr. (Lavenham, Suffolk); David and John Fiske (South Elmham, Suffolk); Nathan Fiske (Weybread?, Suffolk); Nathaniel Foote (Shalford, Essex?); Richard Gale (Groton, Suffolk); Henry Greene, Sr. (Great Bromley, Essex?); William Goodrich (Rattlesden or Hessett, Suffolk?); Justinian and Richard Holden (Lindsey, Suffolk); Miles Ives (Nayland, Suffolk); Henry Kimball, Jr. (Rattlesden, Suffolk); Thomas King (Dedham or Cold Norton, Essex); William Knapp, Jr. (Bures St. Mary, Suffolk); John Knowles (Colchester, Essex); Edmund Lockwood (Combs, Suffolk); John Marion (Stebbing, Essex); John Marrett (Woodbridge, Suffolk); John Masters (Hatfield Broad Oak, Essex); Simon Ong (Lavenham, Suffolk); George Parkhurst (Ipswich, Suffolk); Herbert Pelham (Bures, Essex); John and George Pickering (Sudbury, Suffolk); Thurston Rainer (Elmsett, Suffolk); Robert Reynolds (Nayland or Boxford, Suffolk); John Rogers (Moulsham or Chelmsford, Essex?); Thomas Ruck (Maldon, Essex); Capt. John Sherman (Great Horkesley or Dedham, Essex); Rev. John Sherman (Dedham, Essex); Francis Smith (Dunmow, Essex); John Warner (Boxted, Essex); John White (Messing, Essex); and John Wincoll (Little Waldingfield, Suffolk).

PRINTED SOURCES FOR APPENDIX 5

Oscar Fay Adams, "Our English Parent Towns—Framingham," *New England Historical and Genealogical Register*, LVII (1903), 193–198; Adams *et al.*, "Our English Parent Towns—Sudbury," *NEHGR*, LVI (1902), 179–185; William S. Appleton, "Parkers of America," *NEHGR*, XXXII (1878), 337; Charles Edward Banks, *The Planters of the Commonwealth: A Study of the Emigrants and Emigration in Colonial Times: To Which Are Added Lists of Passengers to Boston and to the Bay Colony; the Ships Which Brought Them; Their English Homes, and the Places of Their Settlement in Massachusetts, 1620–1640* (Boston, 1930); Banks, *Topographical Dictionary of 2885 English Emigrants to New England, 1620–1650*, ed. Elijah Ellsworth Brownell (Philadelphia, 1937), cited as Banks, *Top. Dict.*; Banks, *The Winthrop Fleet of 1630: An Account of the Vessels, the Voyage, the Passengers and Their English Homes from Original Authorities* (Boston, 1930); J. Gardner Bartlett, "Extracts from a Rental of the Manor of Ormesby, Co. Norfolk, England, 1610," *NEHGR*, LXIX (1915), 342–345; Bartlett, *Gregory Stone Genealogy: Ancestry and Descendants of Dea. Gregory Stone of Cambridge, Mass., 1320–1917* (Boston, 1918); Bartlett, ed., "Notes—Palmer," *NEHGR*, LXXV (1921), 77–81; Bartlett, "Notes and Queries—New England Colonists from Rattlesden, Co. Suffolk, England," *NEHGR*, LVII (1903), 331–332; Philip Battell, "Descendants of Benjamin Hammond," *NEHGR*, XXX (1876), 28–32; "Bradford's Letter to Winthrop, 1631," *NEHGR*, II (1848), 240–244; [Lydia Nelson (Hastings) Buckminster], *The Hastings Memorial: A Genealogical Account of the Descendants of Thomas Hastings of Watertown, Mass., from 1634 to 1864. With an Appendix and Index* (Boston, 1866); Ezra Hoyt Byington, ed., "Necrology of the New-England Historic Genealogical Society," *NEHGR*, L (1896), 77–104; George Walter Chamberlain, "Notes—Palmer, William of Watertown, Mass.," *NEHGR*, LXXV (1921), 158; Elias Child, *Genealogy of the Child, Childs and Childe Families, of the Past and Present in the United States and the Canadas, from 1630 to 1881* (Utica, N.Y., 1881); "Records of the Coolidges of Cambridgeshire, England," *NEHGR*, LXXX (1926), 401–415. Charles A. Cummings, "Moses Kimball," *NEHGR*, LVI (1902), 335–340; Zacheriah Eddy, "Capt. Joshua Eddy," *NEHGR*, VIII (1854), 201–206; Gerald Fothergill, "Notes and Queries—Notes from English Records," *NEHGR*, LXI (1907), 393–394; Elizabeth French, "Genealogical Research in England," *NEHGR*, LXIX (1915), 248–255; French, transcriber, "Genealogical Research in England," *NEHGR*, LXIII (1909), 159–166, 277–287, LXIV (1910), 346–355, LXVI (1912), 164–180; George A. Gordon, "Notes and Queries—Lawrence," *NEHGR*, XLV (1891), 85; F. S. Hammond, contributor, "John Hammond of Lavenham, Suffolk, England," *NEHGR*, LIV (1900), 288–289; Mary Lovering Homan, "Notes—Mixer," *NEHGR*, LXV (1911), 380; Joseph Hunter, "Suffolk Emigrants: Genealogical Notices of Various Persons and Families Who in the Reign of King Charles the First Emigrated to New England from the County of Suffolk," Massachusetts Historical Society, *Collections*, 3d Ser., X (1849), 147–172; Edson Salisbury Jones, "The Parentage of William Arnold and Thomas Arnold of Providence, R.I.," *NEHGR*, LXIX (1915), 64–69; J. Henry

Lea, communicator, "Genealogical Gleanings among the English Archives," *NEHGR*, LIV (1900), 188–197; John G. Locke, "Emigrants in Vessels, 'Bound to Virginia,' and Memorial of William Clarke, of Watertown and Woburn," *NEHGR*, V (1851), 248–249; Charles Francis Mason, communicator, "The English Home of Capt. Hugh Mason of Watertown, Mass.," *NEHGR*, LXXVIII (1924), 256–258; Mason, *Hugh Mason* . . . (Watertown, Mass., 1890); Edna Warren Mason, *Descendants of Capt. Hugh Mason in America* (New Haven, Conn., 1937); William Stowell Mills, "The Early Kilhams," *NEHGR*, LVI (1902), 344–346; G. Andrews Moriarty, "The English Connections of Thomas Felbrigge or Philbrick of Hampton, N.H.," *NEHGR*, CVIII (1954), 252–258; Moriarty, "Genealogical Gleanings in England—Payne," *NEHGR*, LXXIX (1925), 82–84; Moriarty, "Genealogical Research in England—Morse," *NEHGR*, LXXXIII (1929), 70–84, 278–293; Moriarty, "Genealogical Research in England—Page," *NEHGR*, CI (1947), 242–245; Moriarty, "Gleanings from English Records—Richard Payne of Lavenham, Co. Suffolk," *NEHGR*, CIII (1949), 183–184; Moriarty, "Notes—Lawrence," *NEHGR*, CXIV (1960), 150; William Lincoln Palmer, "Some Descendants of William Palmer of Watertown, Mass., and Hampton, N.H.," *NEHGR*, LXVIII (1914), 259–262; Everett Hall Pendleton, *Early New England Pendletons; With Some Account of the Three Groups Who Took the Name Pembleton, and Notices of Other Pendletons of Later Origin in the United States* (South Orange, N.J., 1956); William P. W. Phillimore, "The Garfield Family in England," *NEHGR*, XXXVII (1883), 253–263; Charles Henry Pope, *The Pioneers of Massachusetts, A Descriptive List, Drawn from Records of the Colonies, Towns and Churches, and Other Contemporaneous Documents* (Boston, 1900); William Prescott, communicator, "The Page Family," *NEHGR*, XXVI (1872), 75–78; Lilian J. Redstone, transcriber, "Genealogical Research in England—The Hammond Family," *NEHGR*, CVI (1952), 83–87; James Savage, *A Genealogical Dictionary of the First Settlers of New England, Showing Three Generations of Those Who Came before May, 1692, on the Basis of Farmer's Register*, 4 vols. (Boston, 1860–1862), cited as Savage, *Gen. Dict.*; Robert M. Search and Helen C. Search, "Garrett Church of Watertown, Mass.," *NEHGR*, CXXIII (1969), 182–190; Rev. David Sherman, "The Sherman Family," *NEHGR*, XXIV (1870), 63–72; Thomas Townsend Sherman, "The Early English Shermans," *NEHGR*, LXVI (1912), 322–326; T. Sherman, *Sherman Genealogy, including Families of Essex, Suffolk and Norfolk, England, Some Descendants of the Immigrants, Captain John Sherman, Reverend John Sherman, Edmund Sherman and Samuel Sherman, and the Descendants of Honorable Roger Sherman and Honorable Charles R. Sherman* (New York, 1920); L. C. Sier, "The Wyncoll Family," Essex Archaeological Society, *Transactions*, N.S., XI (1911), 236–245; Myles Standish, "Helen Francis Kimball, A.M.," *NEHGR*, LXXIX (1925), 115–119; Edward Strong, communicator, "Genealogy of the Chester Family," *NEHGR*, XXII (1868), 338–342; "Memoirs—George Hathaway Taber," *NEHGR*, XCV (1941), 173–174; Charles Hervey Townshend, "Gleanings from Parish Registers of Hessett, England, and Vicinity," *NEHGR*, LII (1898), 42–44; Henry F. Waters, "Genealogical Gleanings in England," *NEHGR*, XXXIX (1885), 61–73, XLVIII (1894), 373–408, L (1896), 105–141, 385–424, LII (1898), 234–268; Waters, *Genealogical Gleanings in England*, 2 vols. (Boston, 1901); Walter K. Watkins, "Notes and Queries," *NEHGR*, LV (1901), 108; William H. Whitmore, "Henry Bright, Jr.," *NEHGR*, XIII (1859), 97–98; *Winthrop Papers* (Mass. Hist. Soc., *Colls.*, 4th Ser., VI–VII, 5th Ser., I [Boston, 1863–1871]), I–III; Henry Ernest Woods, "The Family of Henry Curtis of Sudbury, Mass.," *NEHGR*, LXI (1907), 258–265.

Select Bibliography

No attempt is made here to present a thorough listing of sources used. In fact, most of the material cited in footnotes is not included here. Being of a local and singularly useful nature, each source was often used only once. Consequently, any additional explanation or elaboration of the material was discussed at that time in the notes. However elementary to some readers, this bibliography has been prepared to guide anyone interested in further research along these or similar lines. As all local history is particular, I have tried to include sources of a more general nature that are usually not referred to in the notes at all. Useful and specific material from the five Massachusetts towns or seven English counties that is illustrative or suggestive of the kinds of materials found elsewhere has also been added. Finally, particular emphasis has been placed on English materials, in manuscript and printed form, as I think that this knowledge may be especially useful.

The New England town has been the subject of much debate and interest for over a century. The early debate centered largely on the origin and early development of New England communities in terms of the "universality" of the "Teutonic experience." Much of this earlier scholarly activity, which involved such figures as Edward A. Freeman, Herbert Baxter Adams, Edward Channing, and Charles M. Andrews, among others, is summarized in A. S. Eisenstadt, *Charles McLean Andrews: A Study in American Historical Writing* (New York, 1956), especially 14–29. In the past two decades there has been renewed interest in the New England town, though it is based on a different perspective and uses different assumptions and sources. Drawn from English and Massachusetts materials, Sumner Chilton Powell's *Puritan Village:*

The Formation of a New England Town (Middletown, Conn., 1963) documents the story of the English experience, the migration and subsequent settlement of several early immigrants to Sudbury, Massachusetts. Other important recent studies of the colonial New England town include: Kenneth A. Lockridge, *A New England Town, the First Hundred Years: Dedham, Massachusetts, 1636–1736* (New York, 1970); Philip J. Greven, Jr., *Four Generations: Population, Land, and Family in Colonial Andover, Massachusetts* (Ithaca, N.Y., 1970); John Demos, *A Little Commonwealth: Family Life in Plymouth Colony* (New York, 1970); and Michael Zuckerman, *Peaceable Kingdoms: New England Towns in the Eighteenth Century* (New York, 1970). Many articles on town developments in the pre-Revolutionary period are referred to in the notes.

A useful chronology, listing the dates of each town's settlement, incorporation, and boundary changes, is found in the Commonwealth of Massachusetts, *Historical Data Relating to Counties, Cities and Towns in Massachusetts* ([Boston], 1966). General town histories, like all local records, vary widely in extent and quality. A general listing of histories in the twenty-nine communities settled in the Bay Colony prior to 1650 has been made in Appendix I of David Grayson Allen, "In English Ways: The Movement of Societies and the Transferal of English Local Law and Custom to Massachusetts Bay, 1600–1690" (Ph.D. diss., University of Wisconsin, 1974), 418–425. I found only three specific histories particularly helpful for three of the towns I studied: Amos Everett Jewett and Emily Mabel Adams Jewett, *Rowley, Massachusetts: "Mr. Ezechi Rogers Plantation," 1639–1850* (Rowley, Mass., 1946); Joshua Coffin, *A Sketch of the History of Newbury, Newburyport, and West Newbury, from 1635 to 1845* (Boston,

1845); and "Appendix I: The Early History of Watertown, Massachusetts; Including Waltham and Weston," in Henry Bond, *Family Memorials: Genealogies of the Families and Descendants of the Early Settlers of Watertown, Massachusetts, Including Waltham and Weston; to Which is Appended the Early History of the Town* (Boston, 1855), 977–1076. More recent treatments of some of these five towns include: Edward S. Perzel, "The First Generation of Settlement in Colonial Ipswich, Massachusetts: 1633–1660" (Ph.D. diss., Rutgers–The State University, 1967), and his "Landholding in Ipswich," Essex Institute, *Historical Collections*, CIV (1968), 303–328; John J. Waters, Jr., "Hingham, Massachusetts, 1631–1661: An East Anglian Oligarchy in the New World," *Journal of Social History*, I (1967–1968), 351–370; and Kenneth A. Lockridge and Alan Kreider, "The Evolution of Massachusetts Town Government, 1640 to 1740," *William and Mary Quarterly*, 3d Ser., XXIII (1966), 549–574, which discusses developments in Dedham and Watertown, Massachusetts.

The manuscript records of town and selectmen's meetings, proprietors' and charity minutes, and other local business also vary in extent, quality, and completeness. Carroll D. Wright, *Report on the Custody and Condition of Public Records of Parishes, Towns, and Counties* (Boston, 1889) surveys the records of each Massachusetts community and should be consulted before any research on a particular town is begun. An excellent example of a recent descriptive and analytical survey of a single town's records is Thomas C. Barrow, "The Town Records of Ipswich," Essex Inst., *Hist. Colls.*, XCVII (1961), 294–302. Town clerks can often be more helpful by specifically identifying the documents they have as well as informing the student of additional materials that might be available. Often, however, town historians or librarians have a better knowledge of the early records than the clerks do themselves. A number of towns in the nineteenth century voted to publish their early records, though some publications are better than others. Two of my towns had published records: Benjamin P. Mighill and

George B. Blodgette, eds., *The Early Records of the Town of Rowley, Massachusetts*, I, *1639–1672* (Rowley, Mass., 1894), and *Watertown Records . . .* [title varies], 6 vols. in 5 (Watertown, Mass., 1894–1928), which are as thorough, complete, and well-edited a set of records as those for any town in Massachusetts. The names of other towns with printed records are listed in Appendix I, Allen, "In English Ways," 425–426.

Charles A. Flagg, comp., *A Guide to Massachusetts Local History: Being a Bibliographic Index to the Literature of the Towns, Cities and Counties of the State . . .* (Salem, Mass., 1907) is particularly helpful in locating published seventeenth-century documents from or concerning the towns I studied. This source is supplemented by John D. Haskell, Jr., ed., *Massachusetts: A Bibliography of Its History* (Boston, 1976), the first in a new series of bibliographies of New England history.

Contemporary accounts of towns are particularly important since most official town business records often lack some of the dimensions of social, economic, and institutional life in the communities. For this purpose the early volumes of the Massachusetts Historical Society, *Collections*, I to date (Boston, 1792–) are useful. There are also reports of eyewitnesses, such as Samuel Maverick's "A Briefe Discription of New England and the Severall Townes Therein, Together with the Present Government Thereof," Mass. Hist. Soc., *Proceedings*, 2d Ser., I (1884–1885), 231–249; James Kendall Hosmer, ed., *Winthrop's Journal: "History of New England," 1630–1649*, 2 vols., Original Narratives of Early American History (New York, 1908); J. Franklin Jameson, ed., [Edward] *Johnson's Wonder-Working Providence, 1628–1651*, Original Narratives of Early American History (New York, 1910); the more specialized George Francis Dow, collector and annotator, *Two Centuries of Travel in Essex County, Massachusetts: A Collection of Narratives and Observations Made by Travelers, 1605–1799* (Topsfield, Mass., 1921); and the late seventeenth-century account of Ipswich minister William Hubbard, *A General History of New England from the Discovery to MDCLXXX*,

Mass. Hist. Soc., *Colls.*, 2d Ser., V–VI (Boston, 1815).

The diverse English origins of the various New England towns were first and most concretely discussed by George A. Moriarty, "Social and Geographic Origins of the Founders of Massachusetts," in Albert Bushnell Hart, ed., *Commonwealth History of Massachusetts: Colony, Province and State*, 5 vols. (New York, 1927–1930), I, *Colony of Massachusetts Bay, 1605–1689* (1927), 49–65. Many of his conclusions were partially wrong or simply incorrect, and I have reexamined the origins of settlers in those communities of Massachusetts settled before 1650 in Appendix I of "In English Ways," 415–425. The best single and continuing source for the verification of English origins is the published research in the *New England Historical and Genealogical Register*, I to date (1847–). The Society's library in Boston contains much unpublished material, including manuscript genealogies and research carried on by some of the pioneers of modern genealogical investigation in England such as John Gardner Bartlett. The standard genealogical works are James Savage, *A Genealogical Dictionary of the First Settlers of New England, Showing Three Generations of Those Who Came before May, 1692, on the Basis of Farmer's Register*, 4 vols. (Boston, 1860–1862), and Charles Henry Pope, *The Pioneers of Massachusetts: A Descriptive List, Drawn from Records of the Colonies, Towns and Churches, and Other Contemporaneous Documents* (Boston, 1900). Except for the detailed work in the *NEHGR*, the most impressive genealogical volumes are the well-documented *Genealogical Gleanings in England*, 2 vols. (Boston, 1901) of Henry F. Waters. Useful, too, are the passenger lists of Bay Colony settlers that were often, though not always, made out for ships leaving English ports during the Great Migration. Charles Edward Banks, *The Planters of the Commonwealth: A Study of the Emigrants and Emigration in Colonial Times . . .* (Boston, 1930) is one of the few compilations and deals strictly with the migration to Massachusetts from the 1620s through the 1640s. Less reliable is his *Topographical Dictionary of 2885 English Emigrants to New En-*

gland, 1620–1650, which was posthumously edited by Elijah Ellsworth Brownell (Philadelphia, 1937). Great care ought to be taken in using this latter volume, since other sources, published before and after, often conflict with and even contradict its findings. Drawing on all of this published material, Norman C. P. Tyack, in appendixes to his Ph.D. thesis "Migration from East Anglia to New England before 1660" (University of London, 1951), has compiled much useful information about the origins and occupations of many Massachusetts settlers who came from that English region.

Besides these general genealogical sources, some specific studies have been especially useful for the five towns studied here. Three very helpful town genealogies were: George Brainard Blodgette, comp., and Amos Everett Jewett, ed., *Early Settlers of Rowley, Massachusetts: A Genealogical Record of the Families Who Settled in Rowley before 1700 with Several Generations of Their Descendants* (Rowley, Mass., 1933); Bond, *Watertown Genealogies*; and George Lincoln, ed., *History of the Town of Hingham, Massachusetts*, 3 vols. in 4 (Hingham, Mass., 1893), II–III, *Genealogical*. Some printed documents, books, and articles have been very helpful in pinpointing the origins of groups of settlers in these Massachusetts towns. Especially useful were: "Daniel Cushing's Record," *NEHGR*, XV (1861), 25–27; Eleanor Davis Crosby, *Simon Crosby the Emigrant: His English Ancestry, and Some of His American Descendants* (Boston, 1914); and Tracy Elliot Hazen, "New Light on the Yorkshire Origins of Rowley Founders," in *1639[–]1939: The Tercentenary Celebration of the Town of Rowley* (Rowley, Mass., 1942), 131–139.

Unlike some of the seventeenth-century Massachusetts materials, nearly all of the contemporary local English sources still remain unpublished. My experience has been that while exploring local sources in the early stages, it is most profitable to contact the appropriate county record offices, rather than to start out at the British Library, the Public Record Office, or some other centralized repository. A letter to the county archivist inquiring about the availability of specific types of documents from specific towns, parishes, or manors is quite promptly answered and is often accompanied with further suggestions or additional and related information. A trip to the county office might also uncover other aids, ranging from unpublished histories to useful indexes or bibliographies. Another important resource for finding collections of local English documents is the National Register of Archives and its hundreds of volumes of inventories of local manuscript records held in private and public hands. The National Register of Archives is part of the Royal Commission on Historical Manuscripts and is located at Quality Court, Chancery Lane, London. Addresses of the county record offices as well as specialized libraries and national institutions housing historical documents are listed in a useful guide prepared by a joint committee of the Historical Manuscripts Commission and the British Records Association entitled *Record Repositories in Great Britain*, 3d ed. (London, 1968).

National repositories have published thorough guides to their manuscript collections to aid the local historian. For the British Library there is the *Catalogue of Manuscripts in the British Museum*, 1 vol. in 3 parts (London, 1834–[1841]) and eleven volumes of additional manuscripts, *Catalogue of Additions to the Manuscripts* (London, 1836–1930). Catalogs for special collections that I found helpful include those for the Harleian manuscripts, 4 vols. (London, 1808–1812), Lansdowne manuscripts (London, 1819), and Henry J. Ellis and Francis B. Bickley, eds., *Index to the Charters and Rolls in the Department of Manuscripts, British Museum*, 2 vols. (London, 1900–1912).

The other important national repository is the Public Record Office. This institution has published a *Guide to the Contents of the Public Record Office*, 3 vols. (London, 1963–1968), which is a revision of the M. S. Giuseppi guide published in the 1920s. The *Calendar of State Papers, Domestic Series 1547–1704 Preserved in the Public Record Office* (London, 1856–1872), published in ninety

volumes, has been used here for the years from 1619 to 1640 and is almost as valuable in its outline or calendared form as the manuscripts themselves. The P.R.O. has also published some fifty-five volumes of "lists and indexes" for various record groupings (London, 1892–1936), and these have all been reproduced by the Kraus Reprinting Company of New York during the last decade. I found several of them particularly useful, and they included: *List and Index of Court Rolls Preserved in the Public Record Office* (New York, 1963); *List of Rentals and Surveys and Other Analogous Documents, Preserved in the Public Record Office* (New York, 1963); *List of Rentals and Surveys; Addenda to Lists and Indexes No. 25* (New York, 1968); and *List of the Records of the Duchy of Lancaster Preserved in the Public Record Office* (New York, 1963).

The *Report* and appendixes in forty-eight volumes published by the Historical Manuscripts Commission (London, 1870–1967) is also a valuable published bibliography of English manuscript material. Helpful, too, are the *Guide to the Reports of the Royal Commission on Historical Manuscripts 1911–57* (London, 1966), and the earlier *Guide to the Reports on Collections of Manuscripts of Private Families, Corporations and Institutions in Great Britain and Ireland Issued by the Royal Commissioners for Historical Manuscripts*, 3 vols. (London, 1914–1938). Finally, there is for Oxford manuscripts *A Summary Catalogue of Western Manuscripts in the Bodleian Library at Oxford, Which Have Not Hitherto Been Catalogued in the Quarto Series, with References to the Oriental and Other Manuscripts*, 7 vols. in 8 (Oxford, 1895–1953). The Bodleian also has some specialized published calendars of manuscripts for the Tanner and Rawlinson collections, of which I have made some use.

Few published manuscript bibliographies exist for other, more localized institutions. One wide-ranging exception is Marjorie Alice Fletcher's pair of listings, "Guide to the Accessibility of Local Records of England and Wales: Part I, Records of Counties, Boroughs, Dioceses, Cathedrals, Archdeaconries, and in Probate Offices" and "Part II, Records of the Inns of Court, Collegiate Churches, Older Educational Foundations, Repositories Approved by the Master of the Rolls, and Local Societies, in England and Wales." Both appeared in the *Bulletin* of the Institute of Historical Research, *Special Supplement*, nos. 1–2 (1932). Unfortunately they are rather dated and sketchy, but still should provide some clues and suggestions for the location and availability of certain types of documents. Bibliographies for manuscripts in county record offices are rare but are growing in number, and students should consult the bibliographies of published sources, listed below, for the few that exist. One that does is for the county of Essex, whose record office is an excellent research facility and whose publications are far-ranging and informative. F. G. Emmison's *Catalogue of Essex Parish Records, 1240–1894, with Supplement on Nonconformist, Charities, Societies and Schools Records, 1341–1903*, 2d rev. ed. Essex Record Office, *Publications*, no. 7 (Chelmsford, Essex, 1966), for instance, is a model bibliography of important local records, which includes listings of extant parish registers, churchwardens' accounts, vestry minutes, accounts of overseers of the poor, constables' accounts, and records of the surveyors of the highways and of local charities in the county. An informative source on the usual contents of county record offices is contained in a pamphlet by Emmison and Irvine Gray, *County Records (Quarter Sessions, Petty Sessions, Clerk of the Peace and Lieutenancy)*, rev. ed. (London, 1973), the sixty-second pamphlet in a series sponsored by the Historical Association. Students may also benefit by consulting G. Kitson Clark and G. R. Elton, *Guide to Research Facilities in History in the Universities of Great Britain and Ireland*, 2d ed. (Cambridge, 1965).

There are several helpful sources that describe the social, economic, legal, and institutional uses of these documentary sources. Beginning students of English local history should be aware of the *Amateur Historian*, now renamed the *Local Historian*, I to date (1952–), which is singularly valuable for its discussion of various problems with and uses of local sources, ranging from reading medieval handwriting, to the location of documents, maps, and other historical material, to analyses of local institutions or the use of various data for local history. *Sources for English Local History* (Totowa, N.J., 1973) by W. B. Stephens offers a more thorough and up-to-date bibliography in this rapidly changing field of interest. John West's *Village Records* (London, 1962) illustrates and discusses manor rolls, books on paleography, lay subsidy rolls, county maps, parish records, quarter sessions papers, enclosure awards, and a host of other valuable local sources in one volume. W. E. Tate's *The Parish Chest: A Study of the Records of Parochial Administration in England* (Cambridge, 1946) is an almost indispensable tool for an understanding of both the civil and ecclesiastical roles of the local parish. The volume contains examples of parish registers, churchwardens' accounts, charity records, and glebe terriers, as well as vestry minutes, petty constables' accounts, records of poor law administration, highway maintenance, and so forth. Latin was still the primary recording language of many local records until the eighteenth century, with only a brief interlude of English during the Interregnum, so books such as Eileen A. Gooder's *Latin for Local History: An Introduction* (London, 1961) may be a necessity in the initial stages of working with documents. The University of York's Borthwick Institute of Historical Research, Peaseholme Green, York, has several series on "Sixteenth and Seventeenth Century Handwriting," compiled by Ann Rycraft (York, 1968–1969), containing facsimiles of documents with accompanying transcriptions and useful tips on transcribing or deciphering hard-to-read English, or English-Latin, documents of the period.

There are several good bibliographies of English printed or secondary sources. The British Library's *General Catalogue of Printed Books, Photolithographic Edition to 1955*, 263 vols. and 24 vols. in the 10-Year Supplement (London, 1959–1966) is readily available at most research libraries in the United States. In addition, there are special period bibliographies, such as Conyers Read, ed., *Bibliography of British History: Tudor Period, 1485–1603*, 2d ed. (Oxford, 1959); Godfrey

Davies, ed., *Bibliography of British History: Stuart Period, 1603–1714*, 2d ed., ed. Mary Frear Keeler (Oxford, 1970); as well as the good, shorter bibliographies such as Davies's *The Early Stuarts, 1603–1660*, 2d ed., in Sir George Clark, ed., *The Oxford History of England*, IX (Oxford, 1959). Some counties have excellent bibliographies, such as Edward H. Goddard's *Wiltshire Bibliography: A Catalogue of Printed Books, Pamphlets and Articles Bearing on the History, Topography and Natural History of the County* (Frome, Wiltshire, and London, 1929), and Walter A. Copinger, ed. and collector, *County of Suffolk: Its History as Disclosed by Existing Records and Other Documents, Being Materials for the History of Suffolk . . .* , 5 vols. (London, 1904), which is superb and thorough for manuscripts as well as printed sources. Essex has a bibliography and supplement, published in 1959 and 1962, respectively, which are part of *The Victoria History of the Counties of England*.

Seventeenth-century English history has been the focus of much interest by noted historians in the past several decades. For an important general treatment, see Christopher Hill, *The Century of Revolution, 1603–1714*, in Christopher Brooke and Denis Mack Smith, gen. eds., *A History of England*, V (New York, 1961). Peter Laslett, in *The World We Have Lost* (New York, 1965), has opened up whole new fields of inquiry with his discussions of various facets of local life in early modern England. Joan Thirsk's *English Peasant Farming: The Agrarian History of Lincolnshire from Tudor to Recent Times* (London, 1957) draws important implications for local history in sixteenth- and seventeenth-century England beyond that county's borders. There are also important older studies, such as Mildred Campbell's *The English Yeoman under Elizabeth and the Early Stuarts* (New Haven, Conn., 1942). At the county level, there are two important monographs: William Bradford Willcox, *Gloucestershire: A Study in Local Government, 1590–1640* (New Haven, Conn., 1940), and Thomas Garden Barnes, *Somerset, 1625–1640: A County's Government during the "Personal Rule"* (Cambridge, Mass., 1961). More recent studies

are too numerous to mention, although Anthony Fletcher's *A Country Community in Peace and War: Sussex, 1600–60* (London, 1975), Peter Clark's *English Provincial Society from the Reformation to the Revolution: Religion, Politics, and Society in Kent, 1500–1640* (Hassocks, Sussex, 1977), Alan Mcfarlane's *Witchcraft in Tudor and Stuart England: A Regional and Comparative Study* (London, 1970), Margaret Spufford's *Contrasting Communities: English Villagers in the Sixteenth and Seventeenth Centuries* (Cambridge, 1974), and Victor Skipp's *Crisis and Development: An Ecological Case Study of the Forest of Arden, 1570–1670* (Cambridge, 1978) are important examples of the ways in which historians are currently analyzing local English society. Unfortunately, all of these works focus on counties outside the geographical interest of this study.

In the past twenty years, English local history has become an absorbing area of interest to historians. A good part of this attention has been generated by W. G. Hoskins, whose books, *The Midland Peasant: The Economic and Social History of a Leicestershire Village* (London, 1957), *Local History in England* (London, 1959), and *Provincial England: Essays in Social and Economic History* (London, 1963), have discussed the scope and range of the subject in a creative, stimulating manner. Two articles that have particularly shaped some of my ideas about English local history in the period are Alan Everitt, *Change in the Provinces: The Seventeenth Century*, Department of English Local History, *Occasional Papers*, 2d Ser., no. 1 (Leicester, 1969), and Joan Thirsk, "Industries in the Countryside," in F. J. Fisher, ed., *Essays in the Economic and Social History of Tudor and Stuart England in Honour of R. H. Tawney* (Cambridge, 1961), 70–88. The fragility of life for many in the age is well presented in W. G. Hoskins, "Harvest Fluctuations and English Economic History, 1620–1759," *Agricultural History Review*, XVI (1968), 15–31.

The quality and quantity of English local history periodicals vary from county to county as much as local records do. By far the best for this study were those of Wiltshire, the *Wiltshire Archaeological and Natural*

History Magazine, I to date (1854–), and *Wiltshire Notes and Queries*, I–VIII (1893–1916). Similarly, volumes in the *Victoria History of the Counties* series range from excellent for Wiltshire and Essex to poor for Norfolk. Local antiquarians often provide important detail. In Norfolk, Walter Rye wrote many monographs about the county, and Francis Blomefield compiled eleven volumes for *An Essay towards a Topographical History of the County of Norfolk, Containing a Description of the Towns, Villages, and Hamlets, with the Foundations of Monasteries, Churches, Chapels, Chantries, and Other Religious Buildings . . .* (London, 1805–1810). A century later Walter A. Copinger performed a comparable service in neighboring Suffolk with his *The Manors of Suffolk: Notes on Their History and Devolution*, 7 vols. (London, 1905–1911). Somewhere between the contemporary and the antiquary stands Philip Morant, whose *History and Antiquities of the County of Essex, Compiled from the Best and Most Ancient Historians; From Domesday Book, Inquisitiones Post Mortem, and Other the Most Valuable Records and MSS, etc.*, 2 vols. (London, 1768) contains rare and often lost documents of the period.

Local agriculture was the very core of life in most seventeenth-century English communities and was reflected in and interdependent upon various social, economic, legal, and institutional relationships. *Agricultural History Review*, I to date (1953–) is the primary journal for this specialized and prolific area of historical writing. Since volume XIV (1966), H. A. Beecham, John Sheail, and David Hey have compiled annual bibliographies of books and articles on the subject issued during the previous year. For an earlier listing, see Joan Thirsk's "Bibliography, 1954–1965," in her edition of C. S. and C. S. Orwin, *The Open Fields*, 3d ed. (Oxford, 1967), 183–187. For a discussion of the different types of documents that can be used in agrarian history, see W. B. Stephens, "Sources for the History of Agriculture in the English Village and Their Treatment," *Agricultural History*, XLIII (1969), 225–238, and his *Sources for English Local History*, 105–130. English agricultural practices have regional terms and

specialized meanings, so articles such as R. A. Butlin's "Some Terms Used in Agrarian History: A Glossary," *Ag. Hist. Rev.*, IX (1961), 98–104, are often helpful.

The regional and subregional character of English agricultural and social life is discussed in Joan Thirsk, "The Farming Regions of England," in Thirsk, ed., *The Agrarian History of England and Wales*, IV, *1500–1640* (Cambridge, 1967), 1–112, and another application of this theme is carried out in Alan Everitt's article, "The Marketing of Agricultural Produce," 466–592, in the same volume. Eric Kerridge, *The Agricultural Revolution* (London, 1967) adds further agricultural detail to Mrs. Thirsk's work but without the valuable social, institutional, and economic implications she has included. A pioneering study that describes an important aspect of local and national English agriculture is Howard Levi Gray's *English Field Systems* (Cambridge, Mass., 1915). Historians have since become doubtful of the racial origins Gray gave as reasons for differing farming systems. They have also begun to study regions more systematically and now realize that many local factors altered the clear-cut lines and distinctions Gray discussed. An example of the detail and sophistication of recent works is found in Alan R. H. Baker and Robin A. Butlin, eds., *Studies of Field Systems in the British Isles* (Cambridge, 1973), which includes a thorough bibliography. Among the most useful articles on farming in the English regions that I have studied are Eric Kerridge's "Agriculture c.1500–c.1793," *Victoria Hist. of Counties, Wiltshire*, IV (1959), 43–64; W. Harwood Long, "Regional Farming in Seventeenth-Century Yorkshire," *Ag. Hist. Rev.*, VIII (1960), 103–114; and several by Alan Harris, including "The Agriculture of the East Riding of Yorkshire before the Parliamentary Enclosures," *Yorkshire Archaeological Journal*, XL (1959), 119–128.

The common-field system, one of the two predominant land systems in seventeenth-century England, has received wide and detailed attention from historians. Useful general accounts include the Orwin volume mentioned above, as well as F. G.

Emmison's *Some Types of Common-Field Parish* [with maps] (London, 1965), and Joan Thirsk's "The Common Fields," *Past and Present*, no. 29 (1964), 3–25. Some additional information about the physical and economic character of the system can be obtained from M. W. Beresford's "Glebe Terriers and Open Field, Yorkshire," *Yorkshire Arch. Jour.*, XXVII (1950), 325–368, and "Glebe Terriers in Open Field Leicestershire," Leicestershire Archaeological Society, *Transactions*, XXIV (1948), 77–127. Common-field bylaws or regulations are covered by M. W. Barley, "East Yorkshire Manorial By-Laws," *Yorkshire Arch. Jour.*, XXV (1943), 35–60, and, more generally, by Warren O. Ault for such studies: "Some Early Village By-Laws," *English Historical Review*, XLV (1930), 208–231; *The Self-Directing Activities of Village Communities in Medieval England* (Boston, 1952); "Village By-Laws by Common Consent," *Speculum*, XXIX (1954), 378–394; and "Open-Field Husbandry and the Village Community: A Study of Agrarian By-Laws in Medieval England," American Philosophical Society, *Transactions*, N.S., LV (1965), pt. vii.

Contemporary comment on local conditions is vital to any study like this. For some of Henry Spelman's remarks on regionalism in Norfolk in the early seventeenth century, see T. S. Cogswell, communicator, "Reasons agst a General Sending of Corne to the Marketts in the Champion Parte of Norfolke," *Norfolk Archaeology: or Miscellaneous Tracts Relating to the Antiquities of the County of Norfolk*, XX (1921), 10–21. The comments of Wiltshire's John Aubrey are contained in John Edward Jackson, ed., *Wiltshire. The Topographical Collections of John Aubrey, F.R.S., A.D. 1659–70, with Illustrations* (Devizes, England, 1862), while the insights of Suffolk's Robert Reyce are recorded in *Suffolk in the XVIIth Century: The Breviary of Suffolk, by Robert Reyce, 1618; Now Published for the First Time from the MS. in the British Museum, with Notes by Lord Francis Hervey* (London, 1902).

To date, the institutional history of local English communities is probably the least studied aspect of local life. Since the web of community living brought most factors of

life into close and intimate contact, many histories dealing with agriculture or economic and social life have discussed only to a very limited extent the manor, the parish, local courts, and other institutions as well. The history of most of these bodies, particularly in the various localities, is still to be written in detail, since the manuscript records—for example, the Braintree vestry minutes in the Essex Record Office or the Holme bylaws in the British Library—remain lodged and virtually untapped in local record offices or national repositories. The Webbs' multivolume *English Local Government from the Revolution to the Municipal Corporations Act*, 9 vols. (London, 1906–1929), still remains the single first-rate account. The one-volume *The Parish and the County* (1906), especially 3–276, and the two-volume *The Manor and the Borough* (1908), especially I, 9–211, offer our only generalized view of these important institutions. Ault's articles, cited above, reemphasize the lawmaking role of manors, while the printed English county court, or quarter sessions, records referred to in Appendix I of Allen, "In English Ways," 488–489, provide a wealth of information on manors and parishes and their officers, as well as for the county itself. Some more recent views of borough government during this period are offered in Peter Clark and Paul Slack, eds., *Crisis and Order in English Towns, 1500–1700: Essays in Urban History* (Toronto and Buffalo, 1972), but as W. G. Hoskins remarks in his introduction to the volume, this is still an "almost untilled field" of study.

Regrettably, there are few contemporary accounts of the actual transplantation of colonists to the New World that describe their thoughts, fears, anticipations, and expectations upon leaving and their settlement after arrival in the Bay Colony. As suggested in chapter 5, John Dane's "A Declaration of Remarkabell Prouedenses in the Corse of My Lyfe," *NEHGR*, VIII (1854), 149–156, is the "remarkabell" exception, although it was not written by Dane until he reached old age. Some account of life in England, removal and resettlement, and continuing contact with the homeland is found throughout the papers of

Adam and John Winthrop and those of later generations in *The Winthrop Papers*, 5 vols. (Boston, 1929–1947). In addition, there are some scattered examples throughout the early volumes of the Mass. Hist. Soc., *Colls.*, but other than these few sources, most evidence of the lives of the common, ordinary people who departed from England for this colony is found only in scattered manuscripts on both sides of the Atlantic.

By the last third of the seventeenth century the ability of Massachusetts towns to continue to maintain these disparate English regional and cultural heritages within their communities began to decline. I have commented on some of the elements in this changing universe in my review, "The Zuckerman Thesis and the Process of Legal Rationalization in Provincial Massachusetts," *WMQ*, 3d Ser., XXIX (1972), 443–460. Other important differences have been noted by Kenneth Lockridge in "Land, Population and the Evolution of New England Society, 1630–1790," *Past and Present*, no. 39 (1968), 62–80; John M. Murrin, "The Legal Transformation: The Bench and Bar of Eighteenth-Century Massachusetts," in Stanley N. Katz, ed., *Colonial America: Essays in Politics and Social Development* (Boston, 1971); 415–449; and James A. Henretta, "The Morphology of New England Society in the Colonial Period," *Journal of Interdisciplinary History*, II (Autumn, 1971), 379–398. Increasingly, other institutions, ranging from the county courts to the colony government, began to affect the lives of townsmen more directly by the eve of the eighteenth century.

The shifting locus of authority placed greater emphasis on extracommunal institutions. Documentation concerning the General Court of the colony is in Nathaniel B. Shurtleff, ed., *Records of the Governor and Company of the Massachusetts Bay in New England*, 6 vols. in 5 (Boston, 1853–1854), while editions of the colony's laws have been republished by William H. Whitmore, *The Colonial Laws of Massachusetts, Reprinted from the Edition of 1672, with the Supplements through 1686* (Boston, 1887). Legislation during the provincial period appears in *The Acts and Resolves, Public and Private, of the Province of the Massachusetts Bay . . .*, 21 vols. (Boston, 1869–1922). A unique group of records, the petitions from towns to the General Court on various matters, appears in the "Town Series," XLVIII–L and CXIII–CXVIII in the Massachusetts Archives, State House, Boston. The collection comprises a total of 327 volumes of papers for the colonial and provincial periods.

Power during this transition did not simply shift from the towns to the General Court, but appears to have gravitated to the county and into its courts and personnel. A helpful list of manuscript and printed court records for early Massachusetts has been compiled by David H. Flaherty, "A Select Guide to the Manuscript Court Records of Colonial New England," *American Journal of Legal History*, XI (1967), 107–126, and an excellent summary of the judicial system in the colonial and provincial periods is found in chapter 5 of Joseph H. Smith, ed., *Colonial Justice in Western Massachusetts, 1639–1702: The Pynchon Court Record, an Original Judge's Diary of the Administration of Justice in the Springfield Courts in the Massachusetts Bay Colony* (Cambridge, Mass., 1961), 65–88. In addition to the manuscript court material, some seventeenth-century records for eastern Massachusetts counties have been published. The most thorough is George Francis Dow, ed., *Records and Files of the Quarterly Courts of Essex County, Massachusetts*, 8 vols. (Salem, Mass., 1911–1921), which covers the period to 1683. See also Samuel Eliot Morison, ed., *Records of the Suffolk County Court, 1671–1680*, with an introduction by Zechariah Chaffee, Jr., 2 vols., Colonial Society of Massachusetts, *Publications*, XXIX–XXX (Boston, 1933). County courts also dealt with socially significant probate matters and deeding of land. I have used the published *Probate Records of Essex County, Massachusetts, 1635–1681*, 3 vols., ed. George Francis Dow (Salem, Mass., 1916–1920), in addition to unpublished inventories from Essex, Middlesex, and Suffolk counties. Essex contains three sets of deed records for the seventeenth century, all of which are now housed in the Registry of Deeds, Essex County, Salem, Massachusetts.

The justices of the peace increasingly performed a significant share of the local legal work throughout the provincial period and began to acquire the social significance their counterparts in England had assumed several centuries earlier. Few records of their activities remain, but there are some notable exceptions, such as Smith's *Pynchon Court Record*, referred to above. At the top of the provincial court structure was the Superior Court of Judicature. Historians are only now beginning to use the Superior Court records, though some background on them has been supplied by John Noble in two articles in the Col. Soc. Mass., *Pubs.*, one entitled "The Early Court Files of Suffolk County," III (1895–1897), 317–326, and the other, "The Records and Files of the Superior Court of Judicature, and of the Supreme Judicial Court,—Their History and Places of Deposit," V (1897–1898), 5–26.

Index